Birmingham Central Tramways Company Ltd

Bristol Tramways Co.

Southampton Tramways Company

The Edinburgh & District Tramways Co. Ltd

Morecombe Corporation Tramways

Sheffield Tramways Company

The Age of the Horse Tram

A History of Horse-Drawn Passenger Tramways in the British Isles

by David Voice

Published by Adam Gordon

ALSO BY DAVID VOICE
How to Go Tram and Tramway Modelling
London's Tramways and How to Model Them
What Colour was that Tram?
Tramway Modelling in 'OO' Gauge
More Tramway Modelling in 'OO' Gauge
The Illustrated History of Kidderminster and Stourport Electric Tramway Company
(with Melvyn Thompson)
How to Go Tram and Tramway Modelling, 2nd edition
The Millennium Guide to Trams in the British Isles
The Definitive Guide to Trams in the British Isles, 2nd edition
The Definitive Guide to Trams in the British Isles, 3rd edition
Toy and Model Trams of the World, Volume 1: Toys, Die-casts and Souvenirs (with Gottfried Kuře)
Toy and Model Trams of the World, Volume 2: Plastic, White Metal and Brass (with Gottfried Kuře)
Next Stop Seaton! (with David Jay)
How to Go Tram and Tramway Modelling, 3rd edition
Hospital Tramways and Railways 1st edition
Hospital Tramways and Railways 2nd edition
Freight on Street Tramways in the British Isles
Hospital Tramways and Railways 3rd edition
British Tramcar Manufacturers, British Westinghouse and Metropolitan-Vickers
Next Stop Seaton! 2nd Edition
Works Tramcars of the British Isles

First Edition
© David Voice 2009
All rights reserved. No part of this publication may be reproduced, stored in a retrieval system or transmitted in any form or by any means electronic, mechanical, photocopying, recording or otherwise, without prior permission in writing from the author David Voice.
British Library Cataloguing in Publication Data
Voice, David
The Age of the Horse Tram

ISBN 978-1-874422-75-4
Publication no. 79
Published in 2009 by Adam Gordon, Kintradwell Farm, Brora, Sutherland KW9 6LU
Tel: 01408 622660
E-mail: adam@ahg-books.com
Website: www.ahg-books.com

First printing limited to 400 copies

Printed by: Ashford Colour Press, Gosport, Hampshire
Production by: Trevor Preece, 2 Sella Bank, The Banks, Seascale, Cumbria CA20 1QU
E-mail: trevor@epic-gb.com

Contents

Glossary

COLLAR
Large padded part of the harness of a horse. It fits over the horse's head and distributes the load on to the horse's shoulders. The traces of the harness are attached to the collar allowing the horse to pull the tramcar

CROSSBENCH TRAMCAR
Similar to a toastrack tramcar but having a roof and possibly bulkheads, but no side panels.

FLANGE
The extended portion of a rail wheel that provides it with directional guidance.

GARDEN SEATING
Upper deck seating that was transverse in either 2-1 or 2-2 across the tramcar. The back of the seat was hinged to allow passengers always to travel facing the direction of the tramcar.

GAUGE
The distance apart of rails on tramway track measured between the inside edges of the running surfaces of the rails.

GIRDER RAIL
Rail where the cross section is in the form of an 'I', giving strength to carry heavy loads while flexible enough to be curved.

GROOVED RAIL
Rail where a narrow and shallow groove allows a flanged wheel to run on it without interfering with other road traffic.

KNIFEBOARD SEATING
Upper deck seating that was longitudinal with the passengers sitting back to back.

LINE OF SIGHT CONTROL
A method of operation that requires a tram to travel at a speed low enough to allow it to stop before an obstruction.

LOOP (1)
At the terminus of a route a length of track circular in shape allowing a single ended tram to turn around ready to commence its return journey.

LOOP (2)
On a single track route a passing place for trams where the single track is doubled for a short distance.

NORMAL STAIRS
Spiral stairs where the passengers move anti-clockwise when ascending.

PLATEWAY
An early type of railway using cast or wrought iron angle as the running surface. The wheels do not have flanges, but are guided by the upright angle of the track.

POLE
On some two horse tramcars there is a pole. This is a shaft connected by shackles to the tram that passes between the horses and which carries some of the harnesses.

RAILROAD
American term for railway.

REVERSED STAIRS
Spiral stairs where the passengers move clockwise when ascending.

SAND BOX
A small box attached to the dash of a tramcar at the driver's end. The box contained sand and when braking the driver would throw a handful of sand on to the rails to shorten the stopping distance as the sand increased the friction between the wheel and the rail.

STREET RAILWAY
This is the term used in America for what in Britain is called a tramway. In America there was a far more relaxed attitude to mixing roads and railways, with main line railways laid along town streets. So when the first passenger services were started there was no clear distinction between early railways and the street railways. Later, after electrification, the term trolley became more common for tramways, including those not using electric power. It was used by George Francis Train in all his tramways, but was overtaken in Britain by the term tramway.

SWINGLE TREE
A wooden or metal bar connected between the horses' harness and the tramcar. The middle of the swingle tree is attached to the tramcar allowing it to hinge and it has the harness straps at either end. Its purpose is to allow the pull from each side of the collar to be balanced, reducing the risk of rubbing the shoulders of the horse.

TOASTRACK TRAMCAR
A single deck tramcar with seats set transversely across the whole width of the car and which had no roof. When fitted with a roof the tram should strictly speaking be a crossbench car, but was more usually known by the public as a toastrack car.

TRACES
Leather straps attaching the horse's collar to the tramcar.

TRAMROAD
This word goes back to 1798 when it was used to describe a railway using wrought iron angle as the rails. In this book the word is used to mean that part of a tramway that is laid either on a private way or along the side of the road rather than in the road.

TRAMWAY
The term tramway goes back to the mid 1700s and it has been used to mean a wide variety of mining and mineral railways. In this book the term is used to mean a passenger transport using rails laid in the street.

Section 1

HORSE TRAMWAYS HISTORY AND OPERATION

Tramway Pioneers

The history of rail transport goes back many thousands of years and at this distance it is not clear exactly when the starting point can be defined. As far back as Neolithic times (3000 BC) man had laid planks of wood as pathways over wet and boggy ground. These were made of transverse planks of wood with longitudinal beams along the edge, holding the planks in place. At this time man had sledges for carrying goods around and the wooden pathways would provide an easier way of hauling the sledges, the edge beams guiding the sledges on the pathway. Later, around 2,000 BC, ruts were made in natural rock or paved surfaces to guide wheeled carts. While often these ruts were naturally formed by wear, some are believed to have been deliberately carved by man. This practice was continued by the Romans and the distance apart of the ruts is remarkably similar, averaging around 4 feet 8 inches, which became the railway standard gauge of 4 feet 8½ inches.

Hero of Alexandria (around 200 AD) was the first to record the use of wooden planks with edge strips forming artificial ruts that guided the wheels. However, it was not until the Middle Ages, around the 16th century, that railed transport was really developed. Mining became a large-scale operation requiring the movement of massive quantities of materials. It was found that the wooden trays on sledges used to haul ore out of the mines were easier to pull if they had wooden planks to run on rather than the bare floor. Wheels were added to the trays and even greater loads could be moved. At first these were simple wheel barrows. Later four-wheel trucks were used, again on wooden planks to make movement easier. At first the men hauling the trucks had to guide the trucks, doing their best to keep them on the planks. Later edge strips were fixed to the planks that kept the trucks from wandering off the wooden surface. Another method of keeping the trucks on the wooden planks was to have a gap longitudinally along the centre of the planks and a projection from the truck that fitted into the gap, thus guiding it. In the 17th century there was a development where the wheels were given a groove, rather like a pulley wheel, and the wooden planks made narrow so that the wheels ran along the top edge of the wooden planks. The flanged wheel system was developed in the 18th century, still using wooden wheels and planks.

The wooden planks, now more like rails, tended to wear and needed frequent replacement. To get more usage from them, metal strips of wrought iron were fixed to the surface of the wooden planks. Wooden wheels were difficult to make and easily damaged. So as metal work skills improved in the 18th century, metal was used to cast the wheels. The flange was cast on the wheel and these were used on wooden rails. In the last quarter of

Mine trucks using round wooden rails and a very crude flange on the wheels.

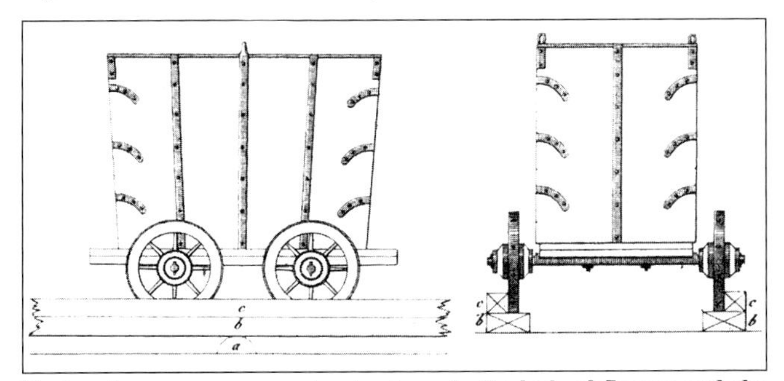

Early mine wagon on wooden track; note the lack of flanges and the guide strips of wood to keep the wheels on the track.

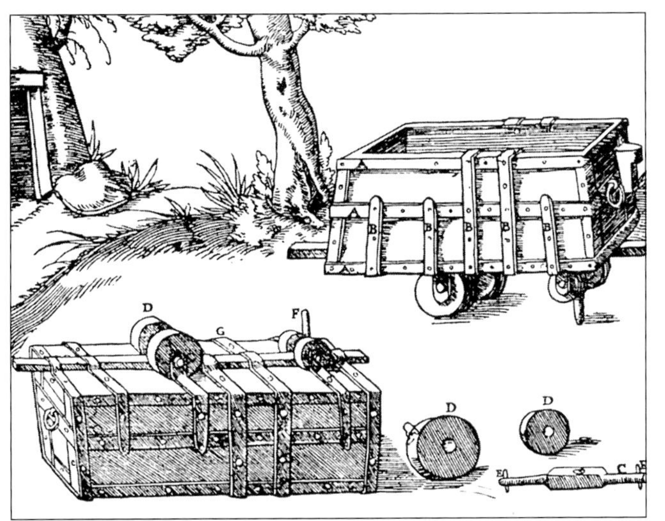

Mine trucks that used a central spigot to guide the truck and keep the wheels on the track.

Another early solution to making flanges; note also the very simple and crude point.

the 18th century plateways were developed. Here cast iron was used to make plate rails, looking very much like angle iron. There was a flat surface carrying the wheels and a vertical side flange. The side flange acted as a guide to keep the wheels on the rails and also stiffened the rail so it could carry the weight of the trucks without needing a full support. The rails were held by transverse wooden planks, now known as sleepers. As the trucks did not need to have flanged wheels they could be run off the track and used on normal road surfaces when required. Today the name for a railway worker who looks after the track is a 'platelayer'. Around the same time an edge rail was developed using cast iron that was 3 feet long. This was also supported on an early form of sleeper. For strength the rail was deeper in the centre than the ends, thus gaining the name 'fish belly' rails (hence the name 'fishplate' for the rail joiner). The trucks needed flanged wheels to ensure that they stayed on rails. This led to the railways that we know today. In the 19th century many industrial railways were built using plate rails while others used edge rails.

The move to metal wheels with flanges and metal rails.

The first railed passenger service came into being in South Wales. A plateway, using angle iron on granite blocks and wagons without flanges, the Oystermouth Tramroad, was built in 1806 to link Oystermouth with Swansea as an industrial mineral line. However, in 1807 an entrepreneur, Benjamin French, paid a rent to allow him to use the line to carry a horse-drawn passenger carriage, becoming the world's first passenger service by rail. At this stage the service was far more like a tramway than a main line railway. A rough sketch by an American visitor shows a carriage that could have been a converted mineral truck. This was replaced with a more coach-like vehicle; this was seen by a young girl, J. Ashford, in 1819 who made a drawing of it. The service ran until around 1826 when a good road was constructed between the two towns. Competition from horse buses proved terminal and the tramway service ceased until the line was rebuilt in the 1850s.

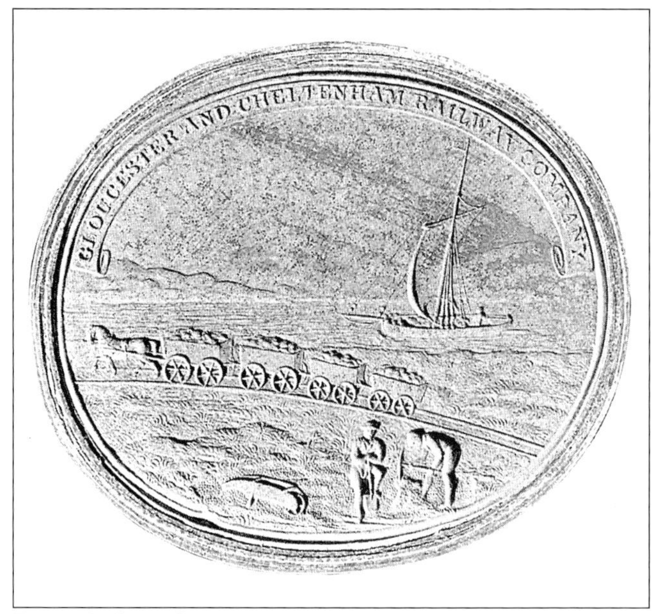

The seal of the Gloucester and Cheltenham Railway, a very early tramway that probably was the second to provide a passenger service.

A more sophisticated form of wooden track, with a double thickness 'rail' using short batons overlapped for strength.

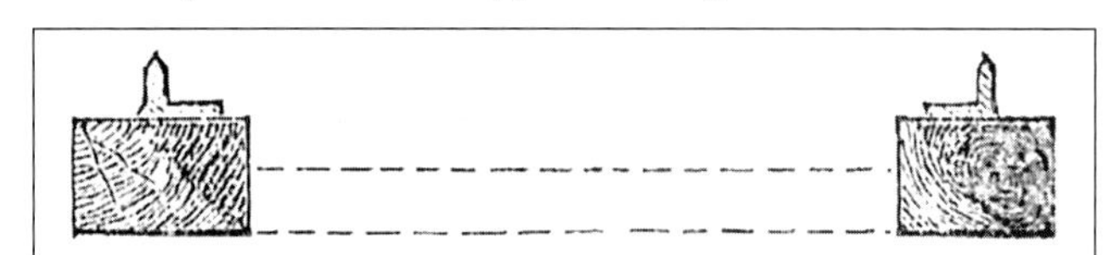

To increase the life of the track, cast iron plates were fixed to longitudinal wooden sleepers.

Another tramway was approved by Parliament to link Gloucester with Cheltenham and it opened in 1810. Though primarily constructed for the carriage of freight, it carried passengers on the opening journey and Henry Gore, in his paper to the Society of Engineers in 1873, implies that carrying passengers was a regular part of the operation of the line. We know that passengers were carried in 1831, when a steam locomotive was tried on the line, as metal tickets made for the service show the locomotive hauling trucks with passengers.

The next major event was the opening of the Stockton and Darlington Railway in 1825. The railway was worked by both steam locomotive and by horse-drawn vehicles. This was

The Stratford and Moreton Tramway provided another very early passenger service. One of the trucks, much restored, has survived. Note the early wrought iron rails.

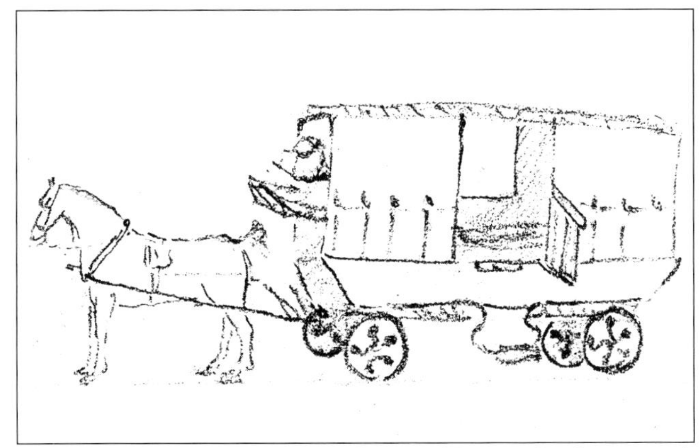

A sketch drawn in 1809 by an unknown visitor to the Oystermouth Tramway of what is regarded as the world's first passenger tramcar.

Drawing by Miss J. Ashford of the second passenger tramcar used by the Oystermouth Tramway during her holiday in 1819.

followed in 1830 by the Liverpool and Manchester Railway, built with passengers in mind and hauled by the winner of the Rainhill trials. These demonstrations that railways could carry people and goods over long distances quickly led to the proliferation of new railways all over the world.

At the same time the demand for road public transport was increasing. Workers lived in slums close to the industries where they were employed. There was a wish to have better housing and that meant being further away from their work. So transport was needed and horse buses initially provided the means. But the streets were far from the smooth asphalt that we know today. So horse buses had to be small and light with a restricted carrying capacity to allow the horses to haul them. America was the first country to build a railway in the street to provide a public service better than the buses. Some sources identify the first passenger street tramway as that built in Baltimore in 1828. However, this was built as part of the Baltimore and Ohio Railroad. The rails were described as being wooden with metal straps and laid on stones. It is probable that the line did not run in the street, but alongside it, rather like the Oystermouth Tramroad. The first street railway in the world is generally acknowledged as that between New York and Harlem opened in 1832 (though there are some that consider the New Orleans and Carrollton Railroad, first section opened in 1834, as the first, because it did run entirely in the street sharing it with carts, drays, carriages and other street traffic). It was thought that the first street tramcar was built by John Stephenson, mainly because he claimed the honour. However, research by J.W. McCloy in America has uncovered a report in the *"Morning Courier and Enquirer"* on the opening of the line in 1832 stating that the two tramcars were built by Milne Parker, quite possibly in England. The design is similar to the coaches used on the Stockton and Darlington Railway. Such detail did not stop John Stephenson from patenting a very similar tramcar in 1833 and then claiming that his tramcar named "John Mason" after the president of the railroad was the world's first tramcar, though indications are that it was not built until 1836. Even then the design owed much to railway carriages (the first low floor tramcars appeared in 1852 on the Sixth Avenue line in New York). The particular features that make a tramcar are examined in the section on the evolution of the tramcar. John Stephenson has made much in his advertising throughout the years that he was the first to build tramcars. This focussing on his products and entirely ignoring any others has created a myth and it is difficult to determine the sequence of events at the beginnings of street tramway history. It seems that as well as making good quality tramcars John Stephenson was a master publicist and business-

Another contemporary sketch of the Oystermouth tramcar.

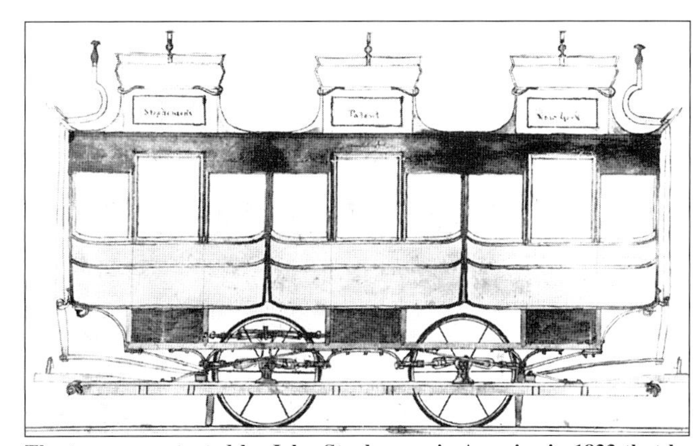

The tramcar patented by John Stephenson in America in 1833 that he claimed was the first in the world; however it is likely that a British company, Milne Parker, supplied the first tramcars for the New York and Harlem line in 1832.

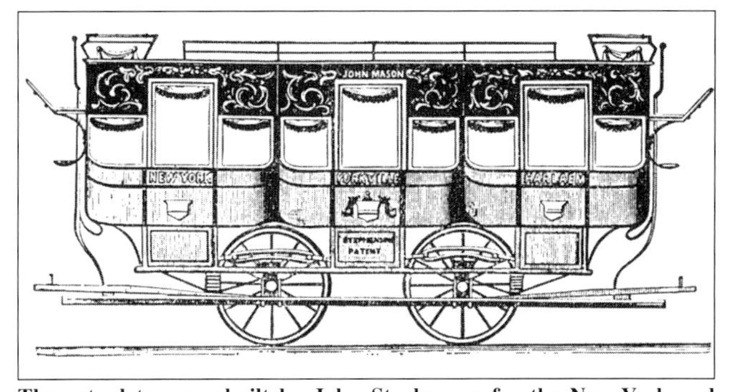

The actual tramcar built by John Stephenson for the New York and Harlem line. The purpose of the tramcar was a 'Director's Saloon' and was named by Stephenson after the tramway company's Chairman John Mason.

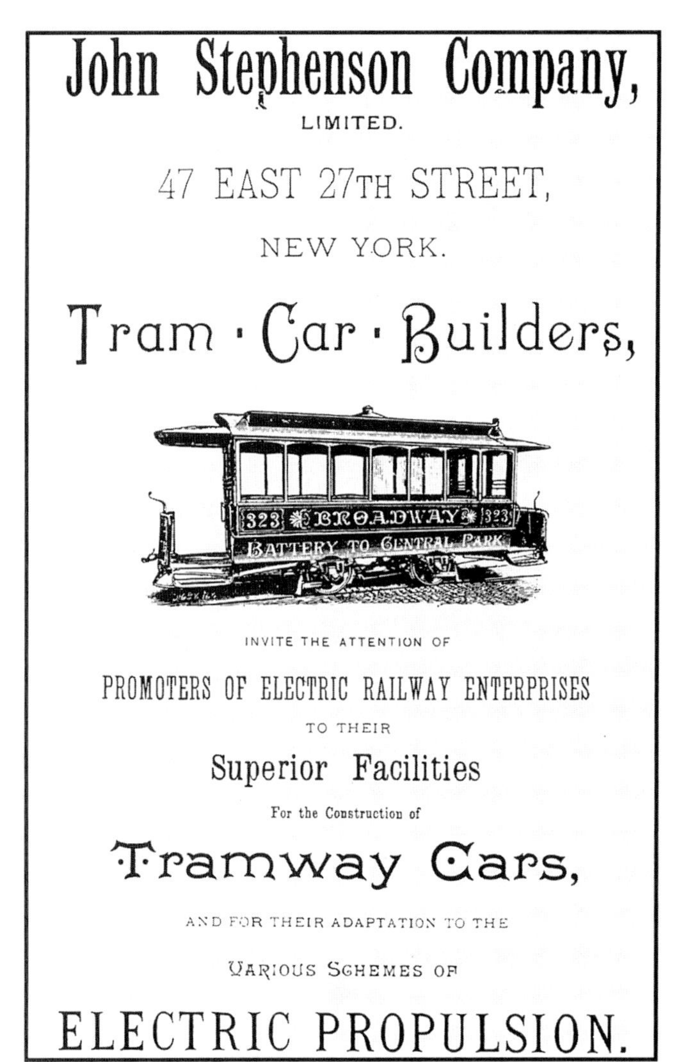

A later advertisement for the tramcars of John Stephenson.

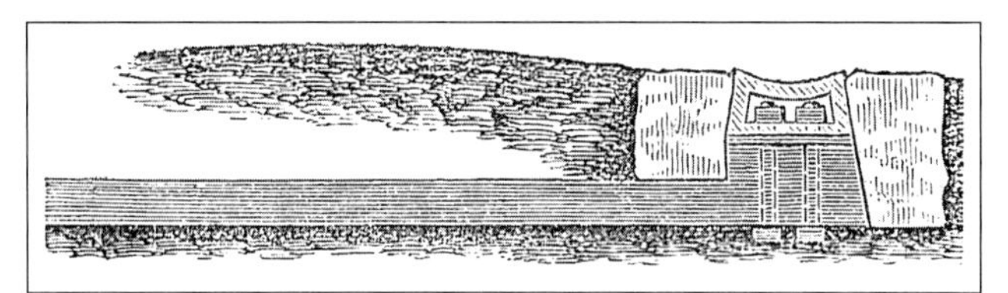

The early tramways used this 'Gutter' rail that was despised by other road users.

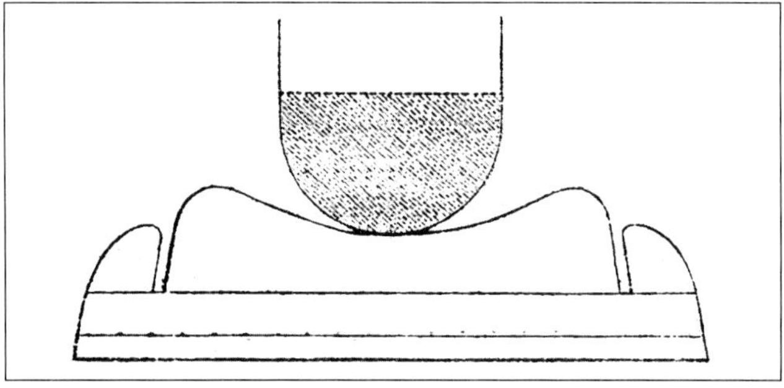

How the plain (without flange) wheel ran on the 'Gutter' rail.

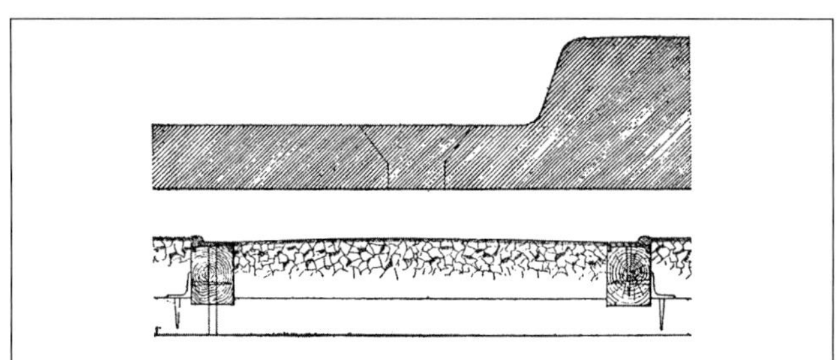

The step rail used by George Train, that was equally reviled by the other road users as the gutter rail.

man. His astute management created the largest tramcar manufacturing organisation in the world.

This was a time of experimentation, particularly for the tram rails. It was impossible to use normal railway rails in the street because they would interfere with other street traffic, so new ideas had to be used. In New York a particular type of rail was used. This was about 6 inches wide with a 1.5 inches deep groove that was 2.5 inches wide (15cm x 3.75cm x 6cm) in which the tram wheel ran (it had no flange). This was considered to be a nuisance by other road users and was known as the 'gutter' rail, such was its size. It was replaced with a 'step' rail. Here the tram wheels ran on a flat plate with the tread running on the upper part and were kept on the rail by a flange on the wheel. The top of the step was level with the road surface. This was better than the 'gutter' rail but still interfered with other road users. When street tramways were built in Philadelphia in 1855 the 'step' rail was used. It was an unusual decision because an alternative rail had been developed in 1852 by a Frenchman, Alphonse Loubat, and used on a new tramway in New York. This had a small groove and was very much like the profile of the grooved rail adopted throughout the world for street tramways, with the rail head laid flush with the road surface. The rail was 3 inches wide with a groove ¾-inch deep and 1-inch wide. This meant that the wheels of the tramcars had a small flange, far less than those used on railways. Alphonse Loubat returned to his native land in 1853 and built a street tramway, using his grooved rail, in Paris. This was the first street tramway in Europe.

In Britain the first street tramway is often quoted as that opened in 1860 by George Francis Train. As with all these facts things are not quite so clear cut. Mention has already been made of the passenger service operated on the Oystermouth Tramroad near Swansea in 1807. This had many of the characteristics of a street tramway and could be considered as the first. If the Oystermouth Tramroad is not a contender to be the first tramway in Britain, then the Birkenhead tramway was preceded by another passenger service. Across the Mersey River in Liverpool, the dock railways ran through many streets. A local entrepreneur, William Curtis, in 1856 had patented a 'railway omnibus' a horse bus with facility to move a flange to enable the wheels to run on rails. He gained agreement in 1859 to allow a local omnibus operator to run his vehicles to provide a passenger service on the Docks railways. Beyond the railways the vehicles operated as normal omnibuses. After arguments about payments for the use of the railway lines the service ceased early in 1860. William Curtis had plans to run a tramway in London and he gained agreement to lay track in Liverpool Road, Islington. However, the line was not built, which meant that the honour of opening the first street tramway in London went to Train.

In 1860 another type of tramway was proposed in Salford. Two owners of a horse bus enterprise, John Greenwood and John Haworth, sought permission to lay flat rails in the street. They wanted to use the patent developed by John Haworth, where a horse omnibus could run on the flat rails using a central guide rail and a wheel on the omnibus that ensured the carriage wheels ran on the flat rails. They laid one hundred yards of demonstration track and after showing the system to the authorities they gained agreement and opened the full route in 1861. While the system was not an outstanding success it did continue to operate until 1872.

The groove rail developed by Alphonse Loubat, first used in New York and later in Paris, resolved the problems of the other types of rail.

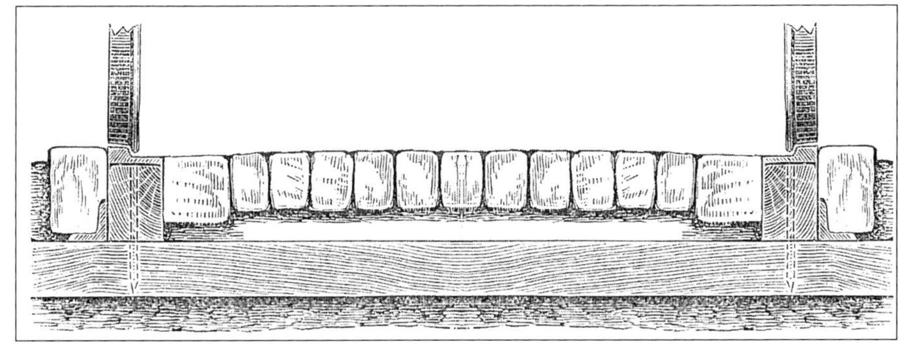

Relationship between the flanged wheels of the tramcar and the step rail.

While these were all part of the historical development of street tramways it was Train who in 1860 made the greatest impact and set the scene for more tramways in Britain. Train was a larger than life individual and he was a PR man never happier than when promoting himself. His own records are economical with the truth and need to be treated with care. In his autobiography he claims to have travelled around the world four times, the second time achieved in 80 days, and he claims that he was the inspiration for Jules Verne's "Around the World in 80 Days". His accounts also need to be seen in the light of the day, when brash American entrepreneurs were not in favour with influential people in Britain.

In 1858 Train's work took him to Philadelphia where he saw the street tramway system in the town. He realised that a tramway system could be a success in London, then the largest city in the world, however, he realised that he had little influence in the city, so he decided to introduce tramways to Britain by building one in Liverpool, as he had worked in the city for two years from 1850. He was an Agent for his uncle's shipping company and his role was to tranship goods from the ships to land transport. He annoyed the port managers by insisting on lighting bonfires on the docks so as to enable the ships to be unloaded during the night. It is likely that these clashes came back to haunt him in 1858 as his applications to build a tramway met with great resistance.

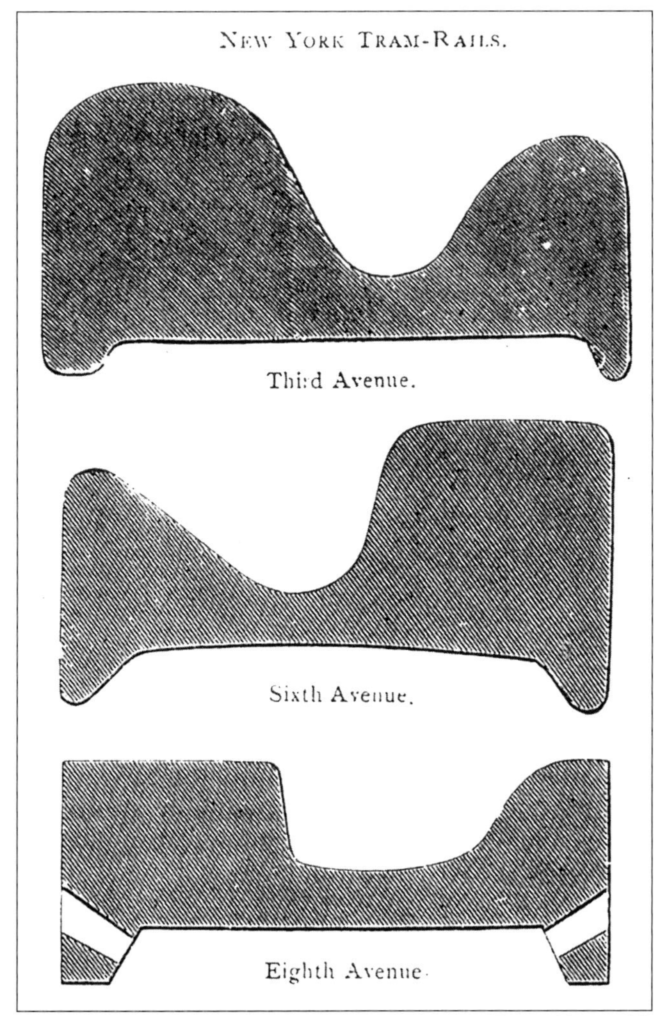

Different types of rail used in New York to overcome the problems with the step and gutter rails.

Train had connections with John Laird, Chairman of the Commissioners of Birkenhead. The Commissioners agreed that Train could lay at his own expense tramway lines in the street; if the Authorities were not satisfied, then he would remove the rails and reinstate the road, again at his own expense. The line was laid and the tramway formally opened on 30th August 1860. The PR in Train came to the fore and he invited to a large banquet the good and the influential businessmen, politicians and journalists in Birkenhead, Liverpool, Manchester and London. He also invited the crowned heads of Europe. After the banquet he published a booklet describing the event, who was invited, the letters of apology of most of those invited, and extracts from articles in newspapers covering the opening of the tramway. This he sent to politicians and other influential people in London.

Having seen the tramway in Philadelphia, he chose the 'step rail' design and took out a patent in Britain for a 'step rail' very similar to that used in Philadelphia; in those days patents were restricted to individual countries and it was possible for someone other than the inventor to take out a patent in another country. The gauge has been the subject of debate. Train defined it in the booklet describing the banquet as being 5 feet 2 inches. However, he did not indicate how he measured it. The guide 'step' was on the outside of the rail and inside this was a flat plate 4 inches wide. If the gauge was measured from the outside of the rails, then the wheels of the tramcars would have been about the right place for a 4 feet 8½ inches grooved track. The tramcars were described by Train in his booklet as being built by Robert Main (a Birkenhead coachbuilder). However, it is more likely that the tramcars were made in New York, by John Stephenson, and shipped by Prentiss & Co (Train's father-in-law) in parts to Birkenhead. Robert Main, being a local coachbuilder, probably assembled and

Very early tramcars in Philadelphia.

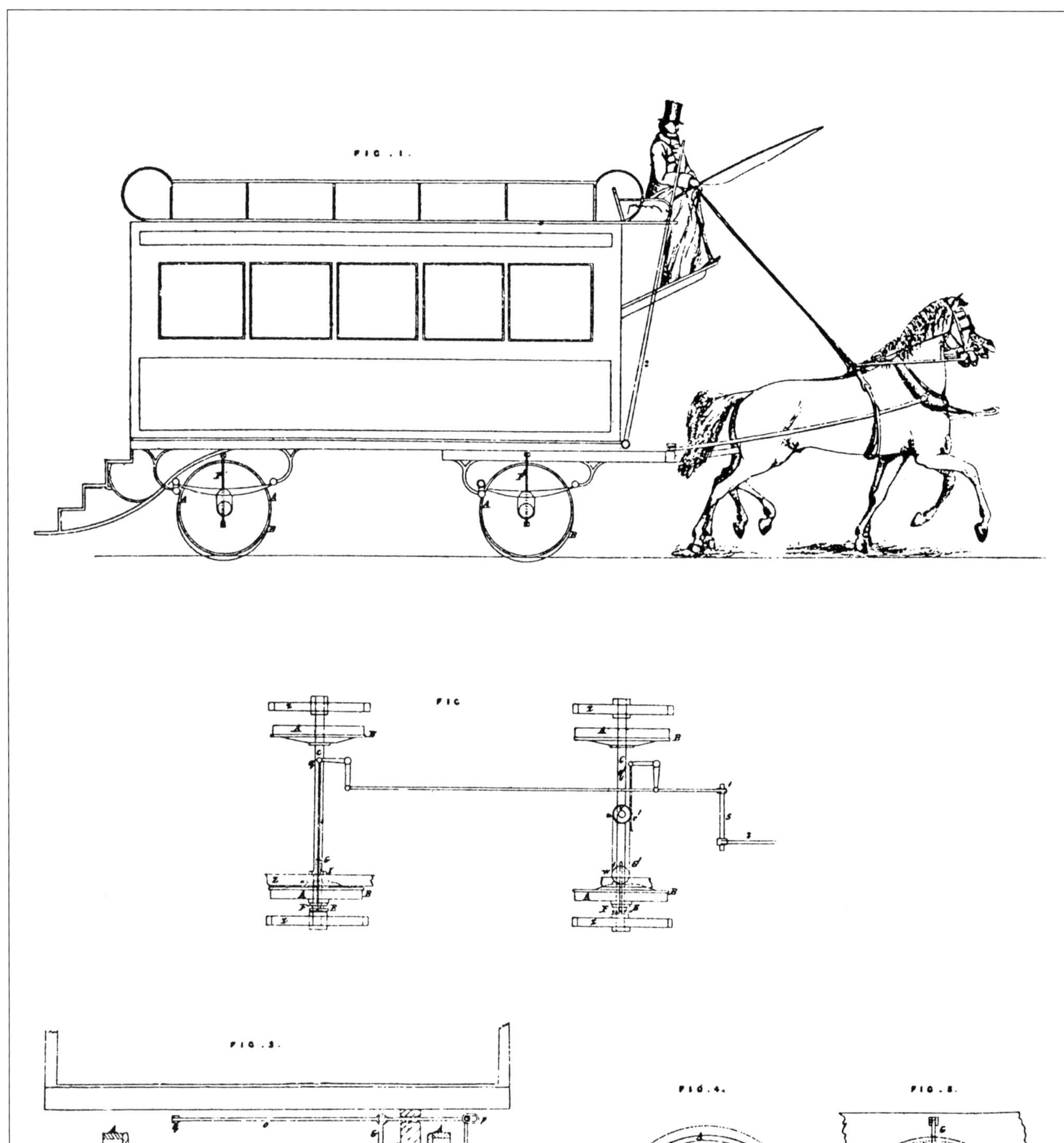

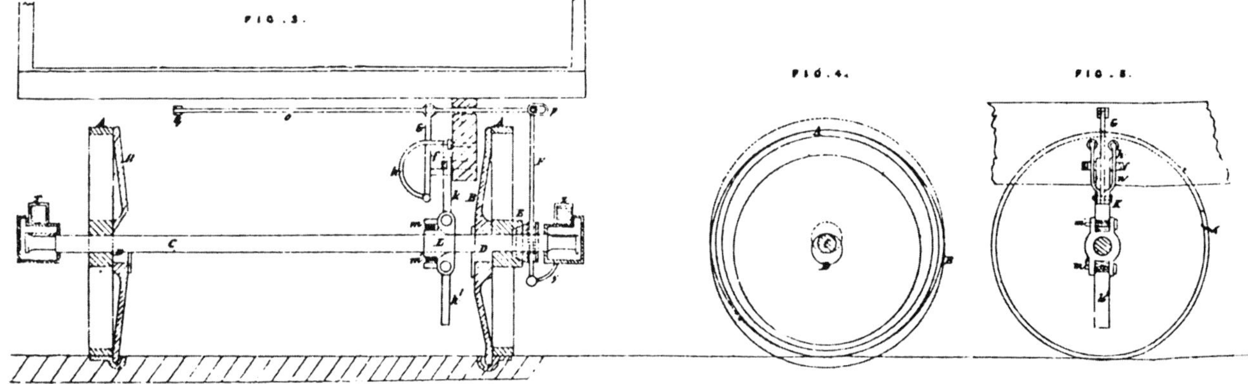

An extract from the specification of British Patent No. 1071 of 1856, granted to William Joseph Curtis for a road-rail omnibus. Vehicles constructed on this principle ran on the Line of Docks railway at Liverpool from March 1859 until at least 1872. To allow the car to get off the rails, the wheels and the flanges were separate discs carried on 'dead' axles; a half-rotation of the flange discs, applied by the driver through a friction-clutch, lifted the flanges clear of the track.

(Patent Office

William Curtis developed a road/rail carriage that ran on the Liverpool Dock railways.

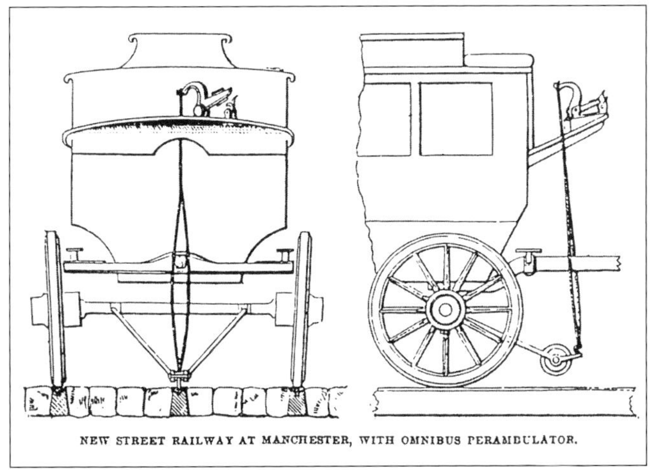

The system patented by John Haworth used a central groove that guided the omnibus so that the wheels stayed on the flat metal plates.

painted the tramcars, but aware of anti American feeling Train would have emphasised the Britishness of the tramcars. To assist his businesses Train had appointed George Starbuck, a young carriage builder from Boston, as his clerk (and no doubt general factotum) who accompanied him to Britain.

The tramway was a great success with many people patronising it, no doubt the novelty factor helped a great deal. The drivers and conductors were dressed in a smart green uniform with their names and numbers emblazoned on their caps. All who rode the tramway on the first day were given a small oval medal with "Birkenhead Street Railway Co. Limited" on one side and a picture of a horse tram beside Marble Arch with "Train's Patent" on the other. This was repeated for each of the later tramways that he opened. Train was pleased with the reception by the public of his tramway and set his sights on introducing street tramways to other parts of Britain. In 1860 he had approached Birmingham Corporation proposing to build a tramway (to be

Portrait of George Francis Train.

This engraving is often described as being of the Marble Arch Street Tramway, in fact it was used on a promotional booklet Train wrote to aid his application for permission to build tramways in London. It was drawn a couple of years before any tram lines were laid in London. The canopy on the double deck tram is pure fiction as are the destinations on the single deck car.

A contemporary drawing of the Birkenhead tramway showing a tramcar very similar in design to the photograph of the tramcar on the Westminster Street Rail Company Limited line shown on the next page.

called the Warwickshire Street Railway Company, Birmingham being in Warwickshire at that time) between New Street and Five Ways. The Corporation agreed to his project provided he extended the line to Monument Street and they expected Train to seek finance for the line. However, Train seemed to have lost interest as nothing further was heard. No doubt Train had his sights set on London. (Birmingham Corporation was obviously keen on the idea of having a tramway as it was authorised to lay tram track under the 1861 Birmingham Improvements Act. Unfortunately the Corporation forgot to request authority to lease the tramways or to run them and so the line was never built.) So at the end of 1860 he sold his interest in the Birkenhead tramway and headed for London.

Train was not the first to propose a tramway in London. In 1857 the French-owned London General Omnibus Company (LGOC) published a prospectus for the London Omnibus Tramways Company Limited for a tramway from Notting Hill to the Bank, but the necessary Bill was defeated in Parliament. As mentioned previously William Curtis had also made approaches to build a tramway, but nothing came of it. In 1860 Train started promoting his tramways. After opposition he did get agreement to build a tramway along the Bayswater Road, with the name the

A few railway companies used short tramways to link towns with their railways and some of these were very early. This shows the Inchture tramway with a dedicated tramcar; it had earlier used a railway coach hauled by a horse.

Marble Arch Street Railway Company Limited. One of his strategies was to hold 11.00am Sunday breakfasts in his residence at Covent Garden, inviting MPs, peers, novelists (including Dickens and Trollope), Punch illustrator George Cruikshank, assorted Mayors, barristers and journalists. All were entertained by tales from his travels and shown two models of tramcars, one from Philadelphia and the other New York – all part of his PR campaign to get agreement to his proposals. Indeed George Cruikshank became the first paying customer on a London tramcar.

The second London line was laid in Victoria Street and called the Westminster Street Rail Company Limited, while the third, the Surrey Side Street Railway Company Limited, was built along Westminster Bridge Road and Borough Road, on the south side of the Thames. George Starbuck was appointed as manager for all three London tramways. The tramcars were probably imported from New York and assembled in Britain. The trams have been described as of Starbuck design, however, Starbuck did not start manufacturing horse tramcars until 1862, but no doubt he used his role as manager as an opportunity to examine the tramcars very closely. In constructing these lines Train had gained agreement from the local authorities; he had not gone to Parliament to get a proper Act of Parliament. With other road users objecting to the step rail, Train found himself in trouble and he was hauled before the Surrey Assizes and was instructed to remove the rails and reinstate the road surface. London was not to see another tramway for eight years.

Still wishing to continue promoting tramways Train moved to the Potteries and in 1861 built the Potteries Street Railway Company's tramway from Longton to Goldenhill. For once he found that the local authorities supported him. It is not clear, but some of the London tramways equipment may well have been used on the Potteries line. Again the 'step' rail was used and the complaints from other road users continued and within a few years it was replaced by the more usual 'grooved' rail.

Following the success in the Potteries, Train then went on to Darlington where he promoted the Darlington Street Railroad Company Limited to build a tramway from the Shambles to the station. The tramway opened in 1862, apparently without any permission from Parliament or the local authorities. In addition to the usual problem with the 'step' rail, was the issue of the track being laid to the side of the road, rather than the middle. This meant that when wagons were being loaded or unloaded they blocked the tramcars causing delays to the passengers. However, the tramway continued to operate until a prize greyhound was run over. The subsequent court action bankrupted the tramway company and the system closed in 1865.

The souvenir token produced by Train and given to passengers on the first day of operation of the Birkenhead tramway.

George Train's tramcar on the Westminster Street Rail Company Limited line; it is not possible to identify Train on the photograph.

This was Train's last tramway proposal. There were two major flaws in his tramway ventures. The first was the use of the step rail that caused difficulties for the other road users and the second was his view that tramcars would be the chosen method of travel for the rich. The lines were laid in the affluent areas of the towns and cities and the fares were high. However, most of the rich people had their own carriages and had no need to ride in a public transport vehicle. Indeed the tramway was an inconvenience built on the roads outside their houses. So when they complained they had great influence, as he found in London. He returned to America where he became involved in the development of the Union Pacific Railroad, among many other projects.

During this experimental period there were two other horse-drawn tramways/railways. In 1847 the Dundee and Perth Railway opened with a station at Inchture that was two miles

The Ryde Pier tramway that was later extended to the railway station at St John's Road.

The National Rifle Association used a temporary tramway each year for their annual shooting competition on Wimbledon Common.

from the village. A rail link was laid to the village and worked by a horse-drawn carriage. To begin with an ordinary railway carriage of the time was used, but a dedicated tramcar was purchased in 1895 and the line was worked as a horse-drawn tramway. In a similar manner a short branch was built to connect Fintona Junction Station with Fintona village in Ireland. The line opened in 1853 and was worked by a horse-drawn railway carriage that was replaced by a tramcar built by the Metropolitan Railway Carriage and Wagon Company Ltd. in 1883. While these lines are both earlier than Train's tramways, they were both built on private rights of way, using normal railway track and so did not influence street tramways in any way.

In Liverpool, while Train was trying to persuade the city authorities to agree to allow him to lay a street tramway two entrepreneur brothers, horse bus operators William and Daniel Busby, were also making applications to the City Council, meeting with the same lack of enthusiasm that Train encountered. The brothers wanted to build a tramway on the Liverpool to Prescot road linking the city with the 'Old Swan' and they set up the 'Liverpool Road and Rail Company'. Not having any success in the city they approached the turnpike trust and obtained agreement to lay a tramway on the turnpike outside the city boundary to the 'Old Swan'. This was opened in 1861 and used a rail with a 'step' on each side, leaving a trough for the wheels to run on, presumably similar to that originally used in New York. This allowed the vehicles not to have flanges and so they could leave the tramway and run as buses on the ordinary road.

The turnpike line ran well and the Busby brothers applied again to the City Council. After lengthy discussions the Council decided against the line. By this time things were not going well on the turnpike, the rails were interfering with other road traffic and there were complaints about the state of the track; presumably the road sank in places allowing the rails to protrude and damage the carts and carriages travelling on the road. So the track was removed in 1862.

In 1863 a short horse-drawn tramway was opened on Ryde Pier, this was lengthened over the streets in 1871 to St John's Road and the railway station. However this was not a standard street tramway because the rails were of the flat bottom railway design and more like a docks railway. Another minor horse tramway was opened in London in 1864 when the National Rifle Association held its annual competition on the Woolwich Trial Ranges at Erith Marshes. In 1886 the competition was held on Wimbledon Common and a temporary tramway was laid then and each subsequent year until the National Rifle Association moved to Bisley Camp in 1883. The tramway was horse worked until 1877 when a steam tram locomotive was used. Again being entirely off road the tramway had no influence on the development of street tramways of the time.

Like many major developments, the introduction of street tramways to Britain was neither smooth nor universally successful. The Oystermouth Tramroad passenger service continued for 19 years before ceasing, though it was resurrected after a 25-year gap. The William Curtis experiment in Liverpool ceased within the year, while the Salford road/rail system of John Haworth lasted 11 years. Of the six tramways opened by Train, three closed within a year, one lasted a short three years and only two continued to develop and then only because the 'step' rail was replaced with grooved rail.

Expansion and Decline

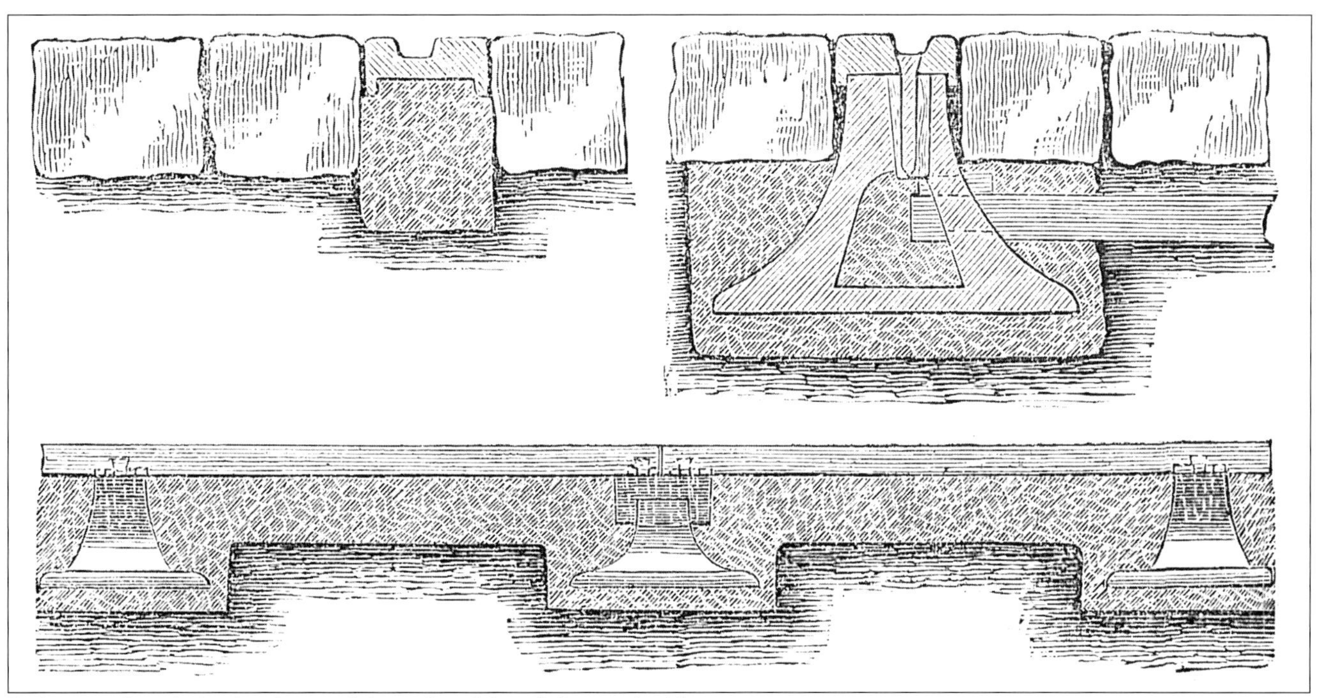

Early grooved track showing the very light section of the rail that required frequent supports.

It is considered that the problems with George Francis Train's tramways delayed the introduction of street tramways in Britain by ten years. This may not be quite right as the next successful proposal for a street tramway came in 1863, The Landport and Southsea Tramways Act, to build a tramway in Portsmouth. The line opened in 1865 and was the country's first street tramway to be built with the authorisation of an Act of Parliament. However, this was a one off. Although applications were made to construct tramways in several towns, Parliament rejected all the requests until the pressure became great and they authorised a tramway in Liverpool in 1868 and three tramways in London in 1869. The latter were the Metropolitan Street Tramways Company; Pimlico, Peckham and Greenwich Street Tramways Company; and North Metropolitan Tramways Company. By now Parliament had realised a different approach was needed and so the 1870 Tramways Act was enacted and this is discussed in greater depth in the "Political Affairs" section. In 1870 there were several schemes waiting for the law to be brought in and applications were then made for authority to build tramways. The first tramways to be authorised under the new Act were for the construction of tramways by the Birmingham and District Tramways Company Limited; Edinburgh Street Tramways Company; Glasgow Tramways and Omnibus Company Limited; Leeds Tramways Company; London Street Tramways Company; and Plymouth, Stonehouse & Devonport Tramways Company. These tramways opened either the same year or one or two years later.

One continuing problem was the track and particularly rails. The step rail had been disgraced and replaced by the grooved rail. However, this was not the girder rail we are used to today. In the 1860s and 70s metal working had not developed enough to be able to roll steel rails. Rails at this time were either cast iron or wrought iron. This severely restricted the size that the rail could be. Rails were light in cross section and fairly short. At this time there was a profusion of different rail designs, each patented and claiming all kinds of benefits for those that bought their particular design. The earliest broadly had longitudinal wooden planks kept apart with wooden cross pieces and with metal grooved rails fixed to the top. To meet the 1870 Tramways Act requirements the road surface was built up so as to be level with the top of the rail. Others used cast iron fixings to hold the rails in place, the fixings being bolted to sleepers, like the construction of railway track. A few addressed the problem of rail wear by having a rail with a groove on the bottom as well as the top.

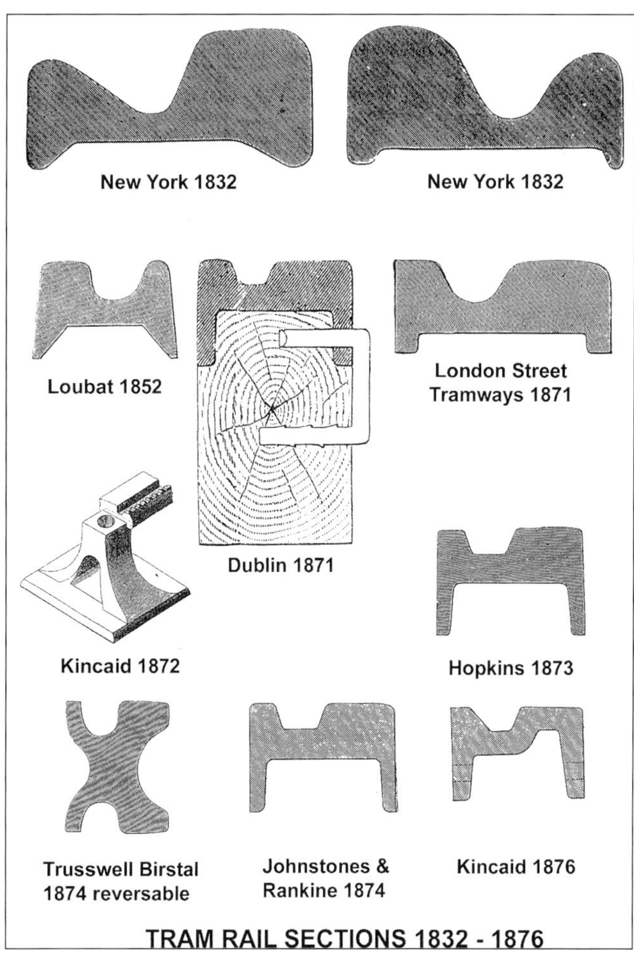

In the early days there were plenty of ideas and patents on solving the problem of tram track in the street.

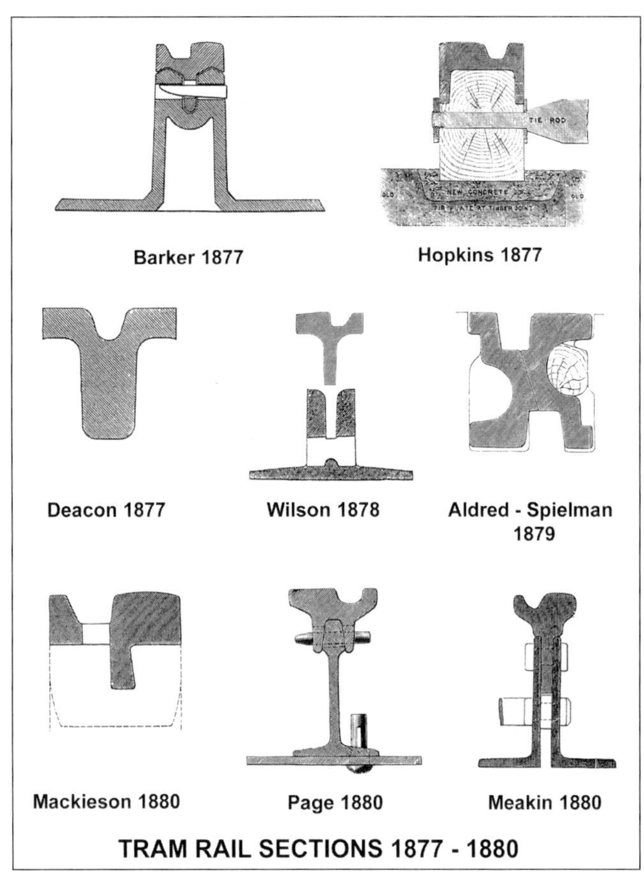

More patents including reversible rails that, when worn, could be removed and turned upside down to give a new surface. However the idea never caught on.

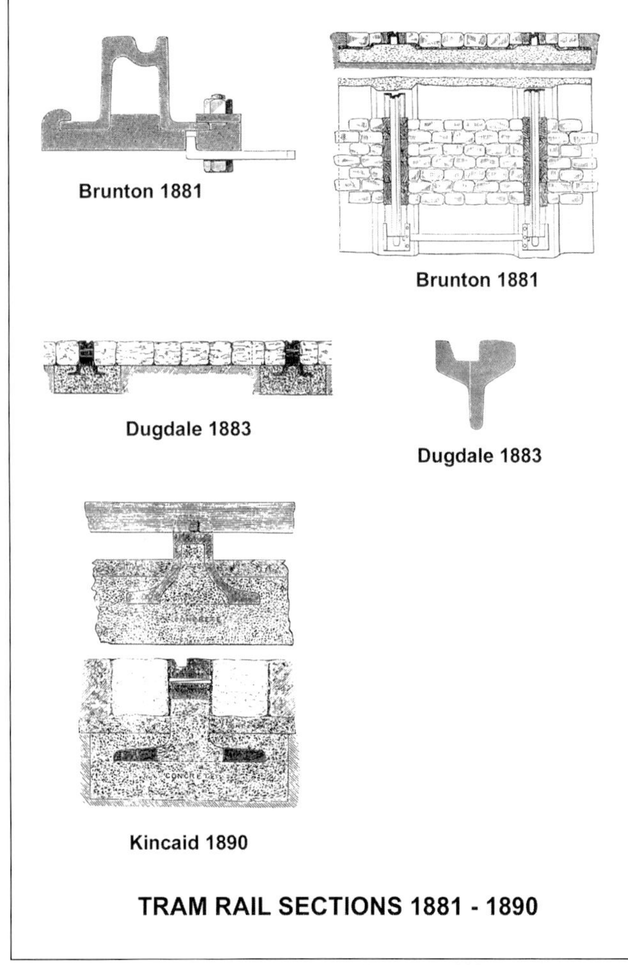

The situation had still not been resolved by the 1890s and it was only when the greater weight of electric trams needed a stronger track that the girder rail became almost universally used.

When the top was worn the rail could be removed and turned up-side-down to give a new running surface and groove. By the 1880s concrete was being used to form the foundation, though this was unyielding and would have given a hard and rough ride. Very often stone setts were used as the road surface as they were extremely hard wearing. The diagrams show the wide variety of rails that were used on the early horse tramways.

The expansion of tramways in Britain can be judged from the graph of tramway route mileage. Note that statistics are only available from 1878 and that the route mileage includes all types of street tramways including horse, steam and electric. The unusual shape of the graph is particularly informative. Broadly it falls into three periods: up to 1890; from 1890 to 1900 and after 1900. The first period shows the growth of the company horse tramways. To begin with many town authorities were reluctant to agree to this very new form of transport that needed to have the streets dug up and metal rails laid on the path of the other road traffic. As tramways were laid and the experience of those towns could be seen, the reluctant towns began to change their minds. Indeed the mood changed from opposition to encouragement as it became apparent that a town without a tramway was considered to be either too insignificant for the new mode of transport or just behind the times. By 1890 over 90 towns had acquired a tramway.

It has often been said that the growth of tramways led to a major change in the lot of the working man. Up until affordable transport was available working men's families had to live within walking distance of their place of work. In towns and cities this meant that housing and factories abounded in the same areas. Housing was expensive and while a family would rent a property, to be able afford to keep it usually meant having lodgers. Personal genealogical tracing found census returns for the time with a husband and wife, four children and three lodgers all living in the same house. Such high density housing close to

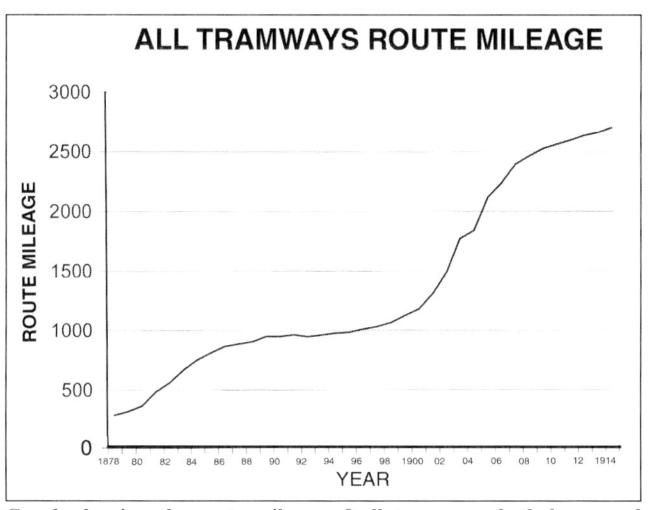

Graph showing the route mileage of all tramways, both horse and mechanical, showing the levelling out at the end of the horse tram era and the steep rise with the introduction of electric tramways.

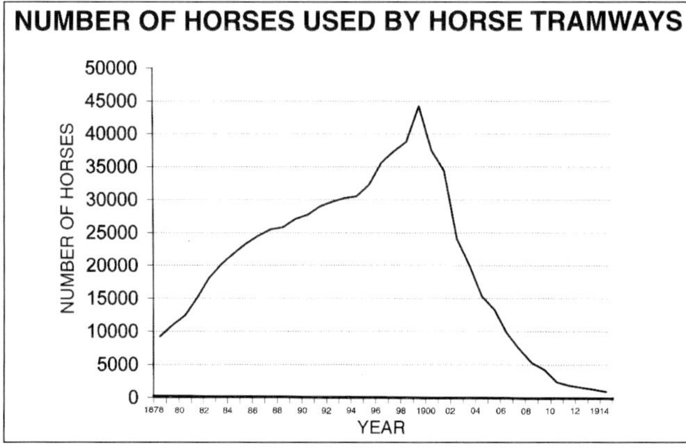

Graph showing the steady rise and sudden decline in the number of tramway horses in the country.

industry formed the slums of the day. The tramway has been said to be the catalyst that allowed workers to live further from their places of employment. John Pollard in his articles on the growth of tramways suggests that it may have been the other way; that tramways benefited from the mobility of the workers. The example he cites is Glasgow where tram routes were only placed where there were already potential passengers, ensuring good returns from the first day of operation. Like so much of human history the truth probably lies between the two, the desire and financial ability of the worker to have better living conditions coincided with the means of transport that allowed this to happen. Housing would be constructed on the outer edges of the then towns, some workers would move out, accepting a long walk to work. The tramway sees the opportunity and builds a route and this makes it easier for more workers and the speculators build more houses. The later census returns show the previous family were now living in a home without any lodgers. More housing and better wages meant that there was less overcrowding, although slums were not entirely eliminated. The growth of tramways may also have had some connection with the railway boom that had started in the 1840s, and by the time horse tramways were being built it was at its height. Fortunes were being made from building railways and no doubt investors thought that tramways would follow suit. In some cases they were right, but then, like the railways, not all prospered.

The growth of tramway systems slows considerably between 1890 and 1900. The reason is that around this time the 21 year compulsory purchase provisions of the 1870 Tramways Act started to be taken into account by the tramway companies. They were more concerned with seeking assurance about their future than investing in new routes or new tramways. By the early 1890s it was clear that the new electric traction was the future. It was cheaper to run, could carry more passengers at greater speeds and was not affected by animal illnesses. However, the new electric tramcars were far heavier than the horse tramcars and so considerable investment was required to convert existing tramways to suit the new form of traction. If a private company was to raise such capital it needed to know that it would have opportunity to run the tramway for sufficient time to recoup the investment. So approaches were made to local corporations for contracts giving guaranteed periods of operation. In a few instances agreement was reached. In the majority of cases the corporation would be debating whether they should take over the tramway and do the conversion themselves and so become tramway operators. So between 1890 and 1900 the future was uncertain for most tramway companies. Naturally they were extremely reluctant to commit any investment that might end up being purchased compulsorily at scrap price. By 1900 it was clear that most corporations had decided to take over the trams in their town or city. They purchased the company tramways (usually starting with compulsory purchase, but then by negotiation, when routes less than 21 years old were needed for conversion). At the same time the corporations took the opportunity to extend routes and introduce new routes to cater for town expansion. So from 1900 to 1910 the route mileage increased at its most rapid rate and this was almost exclusively for electric tramways. After 1910 the rate of increase slowed, but as this was in the electric tramway era it is outside the scope of this book.

Naturally the development of horse tramways follows the route mileage to begin with. The Board of Trade statistics for tramways makes it difficult to determine the expansion of the horse tramways precisely. The returns for the period are given as a whole. So the route mileage mixes horse, steam and later electric tramways. To extract the horse tramways a different statistic has to be used. The returns give the total numbers of horses owned by the tramway companies. However, even this is not as clear cut as it seems at first. This is because some tramway companies also ran horse omnibuses and the horses required for these may be included in the returns made to the Board of Trade. However these are the only statistics that are available and have been used for the graph to show the expansion and decline of horse tramways. For the period to 1890 the two graphs are similar, showing growth. From 1890 to 1900 the two graphs differ considerably. While the route mileage shows a levelling off the number of horses used continues to climb at much the same rate as pre 1890. The likely explanation is that the extra horses were needed to cater for an increase in demand for travel. The numbers of passengers would increase and to meet this demand service frequencies were increased. This also covers the period when companies were being taken over by corporations. It was very common that the first action of the corporations was to reduce fares and so make tram transport much more attractive. The lower income per passenger was more than compensated by the increased numbers of passengers. So the number of horses increases until 1890. Then the impact of the conversion of tramways to electrical traction is apparent. There is a dramatic reduction in numbers. Indeed over the next ten year period the numbers of horses had fallen by over 95% and by 1910 the only horse tramways left were those where conversion was not considered viable.

The Landport and Southsea Tramway was the first tramway to be built under an Act of Parliament. To be as convenient as possible for the Isle of Wight ferries, the tramway was built onto Clarence Pier.

The Metropolitan Street Tramways Company was one of the three London tramways authorised by an 1869 Act.

Another London tramway in the 1869 Act was the Pimlico, Peckham and Greenwich Street Tramways Company.

The final one included in the Act was the North Metropolitan Tramways Company.

Chronology of Passenger Horse Tramway Opening Dates

1807 Oystermouth Tramroad
1826 Stratford-on-Avon and Moreton-in-the-Marsh Tramway
1830 Herne Bay Pier Tramway
1849 Inchture Horse Tramway
1850 Southend Pier Tramway
1853 Fintona Tramway
1859 Liverpool Line of Docks Tramway
1860 Birkenhead Street Railway Company
1861 Liverpool Road & Railway Omnibus Company Limited (Old Swan Tramway); Marble Arch Street Rail Company Limited; Westminster Street Rail Company Limited, Surrey Side Street Rail Company Limited, Haworth Patent Perambulating System Salford
1862 Darlington Street Railroad; Staffordshire Potteries Street Railway Company Limited
1864 NRA Wimbledon Common Tramway; Ryde Pier Tramway
1865 Landport & Southsea Tramways Company
1869 Liverpool Tramways Company Limited
1870 Metropolitan Street Tramways Company; Pimlico, Peckham and Greenwich Street Tramways Company; North Metropolitan Tramways Company
1871 Edinburgh Street Tramways Company; Leeds Tramways Company; London Street Tramways Company
1872 Belfast Street Tramways Company; Birmingham and District Tramways Company Limited; Cardiff Tramways Company; Cork Tramways Company Limited; Dublin Tramways Company; Glasgow Tramways and Omnibus Company Limited; Plymouth, Stonehouse & Devonport Tramways Company
1873 Glyn Valley Tramway; Southport Tramways Company Limited
1874 Aberdeen District Tramways; Dewsbury & Batley

One of the first tramways to take advantage of the 1870 Tramways Act was the Birmingham and District Tramways Company Limited.

Another of the first tramways to use the 1870 Act was the Edinburgh Street Tramways Company.

Tramways Company; Leicester Tramways Company Limited; Southall, Ealing & Shepherds Bush Tram-Railway Company; Middlesbrough & Stockton Tramways Company; Stirling & Bridge of Allan Tramway Company Limited.

1875 Bristol Tramways Company Limited; East Suffolk Tramways Company; Continental & General Tramways Company; Neath & District Tramways Company; Newport (Mon) Tramways Company; Wantage Tramway Company Limited

1876 Douglas Bay Tramway; Wrexham District Tramways Company

1877 Wirral Tramway Company; Dundee & District Tramways Company Limited, Royal Navy Hospital Haslar; Manchester and Salford Tramways; Sheffield Tramways Company; Warrenpoint & Rostrevor Tramways Company

1878 Newcastle & Gosforth Tramways & Carriage Company Limited; Nottingham & District Tramways Company Limited; Wolverhampton Tramways Company

1879 Chester Tramways Company; Galway & Salthill Tramway Company; Gloucester Tramways Company Limited; Harlech Tramway; Croydon Tramways Company; Preston Tramways Company; Reading Tramways Company; Southampton Tramways Company; Sunderland Tramways Company; Wallasey Tramways Company

1880 Bath Tramways Company Limited; Bolton & Suburban Tramways; Cambridge Street Tramways Company; Derby Tramways Company; Ipswich Tramway Company; Skegness Tramway; Tynemouth & District Tramways Limited; Wigan Tramways Company Limited; York Tramways Company

1881 Aldershot & Farnborough Tramway Company; Burnley & District Tramways Company Limited; Cardiff Tramways Company; Great Grimsby Street Tramways Company; Leamington & Warwick Tramways & Omnibus Company Limited; Southwark & Deptford Tramway Company; Woolwich & South East London Tramways Company Limited; South London Tramways Company; North London Suburban Tramways Company; Northampton Street Tramways Company; Oxford Tramways Company Limited; and St Helens & District Tramways Company

1882 Cavehill & Whitewell Tramway Company; Bradford Tramways Company; Chesterfield & District Tramways Company Limited; Exeter Tramways Company; Gosport Street Tramways Company; Lincoln Tramways Company; Llanelly Tramways Company Limited; Rothesay Tramways Company Limited; and Shipley (Joseph Speight)

1883 Manchester, Bury, Rochdale & Oldham Steam Tramways Company Limited; Dudley, Sedgley & Wolverhampton Tramways Company Limited; Gravesend, Rosherville & Northfleet Tramways Company Limited; Huddersfield Corporation Tramways; London Southern Tramways Company; Lea Bridge, Leyton & Walthamstow Tramways Company; South Shields Tramways Company; and Birmingham & Midland Tramways Limited (West Bromwich)

Also taking advantage of the 1870 Act was the Glasgow Tramways and Omnibus Company Limited.

1884 Brighton District Tramways Company; and Tramway Trust Company (Worcester)
1885 Paisley Tramways Company Limited
1887 Blackburn Corporation Tramways Company Limited; Morecambe Tramways Company; and Pontypridd & Rhondda Valley Tramways Company
1888 Harrow Road & Paddington Tramways Company
1889 Greenock & Port Glasgow Tramways Company: and Keighley Tramways Company Limited
1890 Fairbourne Tramway; Lancaster & District Tramways Company Limited; South Eastern Metropolitan Tramways Company; Stockport & Hazel Grove Carriage & Tramways Company Limited
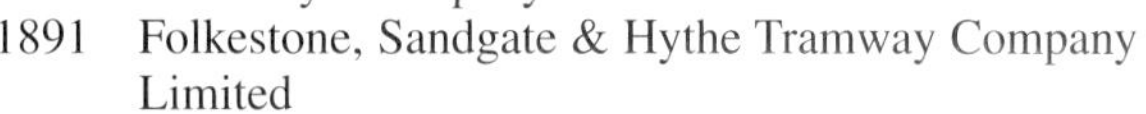
1891 Folkestone, Sandgate & Hythe Tramway Company Limited
1895 Perth & District Tramways Company Limited
1896 Peckham & East Dulwich Tramways Company; Blackpool, St Annes & Lytham Tramways Company Limited; and West End Tramway (Pwllheli)
1897 Glenanne and Loughgilly Horse Tramway (George Gray & Sons); Joyce Green Hospital Tramway; and City of Derry Tramways Company
1899 Barmouth Junction & Arthog Tramways; and Strabathie & Blackdog Light Railway
1901 Canvey Island Tramway
1904 Leith Corporation Tramways (formerly part of Edinburgh Street Tramways)

The Leeds Tramways Company was also included in the first Act under the 1870 legislation. (Trevor Hartley Collection)

Another 1870 approved tramway was London Street Tramways Company.

A photo of the Plymouth, Stonehouse & Devonport Tramways Company, another of the 1870 tramways.

Horse Power, Man Power and the Public

By 1880 the horse was still very much the dominant source of power. There were some steam and cable tramways operating, but the electrical revolution was still some distance away. The first British public electric railed transport, the Volks Electric railway did not start until 1883 and the first electric street tramway, the Giant's Causeway and Portrush Tramway later the same year. So from the 1870s the expansion of tramways used considerable numbers of horses. In the British Isles the number of tram horses rose from 9,222 in 1878 to 27,719 in 1890. By 1890 tramways companies were paying £827,584 a year just on buying horses and a further £854,226 a year on working costs.

The prominent ribs and gaunt flanks of this horse on the Pwllheli and Llanbedrog tramway are a frequent sight on tramway horses, but do not necessarily mean the animal is starved.

The tramway horse was a very particular animal. There is a tendency today to think that a tramcar full of passengers would need a heavy horse to pull it and the mind goes to the Shire, Clydesdale or Suffolk breeds. But this is not so, the ideal tramway horse was, and still is, a lighter more general type of animal and the most commonly found type was the Hackney (they were so often used to haul coaches and cabs that the name got transferred to the vehicle, hence Hackney Carriage, used today to mean a black cab). The name comes from the French "haquenee" (French was the Court language in Medieval times) meaning an ambling or walking horse. Originally it described a riding horse with a comfortable trot, but over the years the term was used to mean a general purpose ridden and driven animal with excellent stamina and then later it meant a horse for hire. Typically it would look slightly emaciated, with ribs often prominent. In fact this was not starvation, but the normal way a fit horse should look. Tramcar horses were always mares and they entered tramway service aged between five and seven years old (costing around £30-£40) and had a working life on the tramway of around four years (this is compared with around five years for an omnibus horse). A two horse double-deck tramcar operating around 70 miles a day required ten horses. That is five pairs, each pair working around 14 miles per day. In addition the system would often need additional 'trace' horses to assist tramcars going uphill. Indeed in Liverpool the hills meant that there was an average of 12 horses per tramcar (including the single-deck trams). A young lad would hook the harness of the trace horse to a metal loop on the body of the tramcar or to the collars of the regular horses. The lad would be required to walk alongside the horse up the hill while it helped tow the car. At the top he would unhook the harness and then jump on to it and ride bare back down the hill to the next tram, though some also rode the horse up the hill. On very steep hills two trace horses were used. As four horses abreast would occupy too much road width, the harnesses of the trace horses

This horse on the Birkdale and Southport tramway has a similar appearance.

On the other hand this horse on the Bradford tramway looks distinctly thin and malnourished.

A good meal would not go amiss also for this horse in Portsmouth.

The public were quite aware of the plight of some tramway horses, as this cartoon of the Cambridge tramway illustrates.

were attached to the collars of the regular horses and the trace horses would lead. Most tramways had a system where horses were only required to work on very steep routes for a few weeks and then would be placed on an easier route for a similar period to allow them to recover their health and strength.

It was a common scene to see the horses of carters being fed using a nose bag when they waited for goods to be loaded or unloaded. However there is no photograph of any tramcar horse being fed in this way. It is presumed that the less loading and distances that a carter's horse travelled would allow it to be out all day, while tram horses went back to the stables after three or four hours and so would not need to be fed while at work. Similarly carters' horses would drink from the horse troughs scattered around towns, usually provided by charitable animal organisations. However, this was not an option for tramway horses as the tramcar was restricted to the tram track, not allowing the horse to reach the water troughs. Although it is likely that had access been available the operators would not have allowed their horses to drink from the troughs, for fear of them contacting water borne diseases.

The tramway operator needed to have sufficient stabling for the horses and in the crowded city environment this often meant having a two storey stable building, with a ramp leading to the stables on the upper floor. The tramway had to have extra horses to cover those that were unfit for work. North Metropolitan Tramways Company reported a level of 4% for sick and lame horses (with nearly 2,500 horses it means that 100 were unable to work at any one time), while Liverpool Tramways Company reported 4.7% sick, meaning 160 of their 3,350 horses were off work.

The life of the tram horse was tough. A pair of horses was expected to haul a two ton tramcar which, with its full load of passengers, gave a total weight of around five tons. There were no predetermined stopping places, passengers would hail the tram at any place on its route and similarly would be put down wherever they wished. This could well mean the horses having to start a stationary tramcar several times along a single street. The stress placed on the horses had an unfortunate side effect as it prompted the horses to defecate more frequently, increasing the volume of manure in the streets. Indeed the strain was so great on the horse's hearts that the sight of a horse collapsing and dying in the street was not unusual (hence the term "dying in harness"). Indeed some 12% of the stable of horses would die while still with the tramway company and would be sold to the knacker's yard. To gain some idea of the size of the problem, in the year 1880 the New York authorities had to remove 15,000 dead horses from their streets, this of course included all types of horse including omnibuses, cabs and carts. The leg joints of horses also suffered from a condition similar to our osteoarthritis. This restricted the movement of the leg and meant the horse was no longer able to work. While each horse had its own specific harness collar, hung on the end wall of their stall when not working, it is unlikely that they were a perfect fit and if the collar was ill-fitting it could cause pressure sores that became worse each time the horse worked and might turn septic. Other troubles included injuries caused by accidents with other road traffic or by being run over by their own tramcars. There was a box of sand on the front dash of the tramcar that the driver could throw on the track to prevent skidding when braking, but this did not

The only photograph of a tramway horse being watered was this one of the tramway in New York.

always work, though tramway companies always insisted that their tramcars could stop within their own length. In London, of the horses no longer fit for tram work, 40% would be sold for around £5 – £10 and would usually be unfit for any further road work, but would be sold for agricultural use, where they were not required to haul such heavy loads. The remaining 60% were sold to the knacker's yard fetching 30/- sold as cat food (a euphemism for all animal food, but no doubt some went into pies, sausages and stews).

Some of the public were concerned about the work the tram horses were expected to do. In 1873 there was a letter in the Times entitled "Cruelty to Tramway Horses" that said:

> *"Will you, as you have so often done before, render a service to the cause of humanity by permitting me to call attention to the treatment of the unfortunate horses employed by the North Metropolitan Tramways Company in drawing their cars?*
>
> *Anyone who has watched a pair of these wretched animals hauling one of their huge cars with its full complement of 42 passengers up the steep incline of the City-road, near the Angel, will be able to testify that the demands made by the company on the strength and endurance of their horses are cruel and excessive. But if anyone should hesitate to accept such testimony, a sight such as I and many others witnessed today would alone be sufficient to convince them. About 2 o'clock this afternoon I observed two horses very slowly and with the most painful difficulty drawing a car along the Holloway-road a short distance above the archway and station of the Great Northern Railway. One of the poor brutes was evidently in the last stage of exhaustion nearly dropping from fatigue, and, indeed, had to be held up tight by the driver to prevent his doing so. He was, in fact, 'nursed' along as it were, his companion, almost as exhausted as himself, doing all the work, until he reached the Nag's Head Inn, when on being taken out of the traces he immediately dropped. It was clear to anyone who looked at him that he would never go on his painful journey again; he had simply been worked to death.*
>
> *This, Sir, is only one of many such instances which have come to my knowledge, and I trust that you, by giving publicity to it, may induce the tramway company to make some alteration in their present system."*

The Victorian street often had horse troughs, but as can be seen in this view from Bolton – the tram horse is trapped by the tracks and cannot reach the water.

Inside the stables of the London General Omnibus Company (they supplied the horses for the North Metropolitan Tramways Company); note the horse collars hanging on the end wall of each stall, as they were individually fitted to each horse.

The horses also suffered from ruptured stomachs and intestines, twisted bowels and burst blood vessels from the strain of pulling the tramcar. The drivers were required to report any problems with the health of the horses. They also had to be alert for those lazy but clever horses that would appear to be working, but actually left most of the work for their partner. As well as the desire to keep the horses fit to work the operators were very aware that they could at any time be reported to the RSPCA for working the horses too hard. The Swansea tramway company was successfully prosecuted by the RSPCA for cruelty in expecting the horses to pull their tramcar up Union Street unaided. This forced the operator to arrange for a trace horse to be available to assist the tramcar up the hill. In Hull the Rev C.H. Booker would step in front of a tramcar he thought was overloaded, forcing the driver to stop the car and he would tell the conductor to remove some of the passengers. The company soon became fed up with

The purpose of including this photograph of a Sheffield tramcar is not the smartly turned out crew, but the small box with the number 55 on it fitted to the dash. This contained sand and the driver would grab a handful and throw it on to the rails to provide extra grip for the wheels when braking.

An Ashbury built tramcar on the Leeds tramway with a trace horse attached to the pole of the tramcar so it can pull ahead of the regular horses.

these antics and took the Reverend to court. The court let him off with a warning and a caution. Nothing further was heard, so presumably he would direct his objections to the local RSPCA. Obviously horses are unable to tell us what it is like hauling a tramcar. However, there is an account by the entertainer Jimmy Savile. He volunteered to haul a horse tramcar along the front in Douglas to raise money for charity. He practised one night and pulled the tramcar along, using a horse collar. The day came for him to carry out his project. Being famous meant that a large crowd assembled, including many Isle of Man dignitaries. The dignitaries then climbed aboard the tramcar to be hauled by Jimmy along the promenade. Jimmy found that hauling a full tramcar was very much more difficult than an empty car. In addition he suffered when the driver applied the brakes, stating that it nearly pulled his shoulders off. The project ceased when the horse of an on-coming tramcar took exception and reared up risking the safety of others on the road. Jimmy stopped and abandoned the stunt. But the experience does give us a clear idea of the effect of hauling tramcars has on a horse. There was one other occasion when a Douglas tramcar was taken down the promenade by hand power. Late one night a group of young men who had been sampling the local brew to excess thought it would be fun to take a horse tram from outside the depot and push it along the front. All went well for a short while, with revellers alternately riding and pushing the tramcar. The adventure came to an end when a police car told them to stop the tram. The police then instructed the group to push the tram back to the depot before taking them to the police station.

In this view of a Leicester tramcar the trace horse (the one furthest from the camera) has had its harness hooked on to a bracket on the side of the tramcar.

The horses were also reliant on the tramway staff. As most of the tramway operators had a policy of sacking staff for what today would be considered minor misdemeanours (at that time there were always plenty of men seeking work), the men were

In this view of a Worcester Tramways car the trace boy is not the lad running alongside the horse, rather he is hidden behind the horse, holding the harness ready to hook it on to the tramcar.

often very disgruntled and might well take out their grievance against their employers by mistreating the horses. This could range from rough treatment to actually poisoning them. Then the operators also ran the risks of epidemics that could run rife through the crowded stables. The most feared diseases were "Glanders" and "Farcy". In fact these were two forms of the same disease. It is a serious bacterial disease of the respiratory tract and skin, called "Glanders" when the principal lesions are seen in the nostrils, submaxillary glands and lungs, and "Farcy" when located on the surface of limbs or body. It can also be contracted by people and if untreated has a mortality rate of up to 95% (it has been eradicated in Britain, but is still found in other parts of the world). Probably the worst epidemic was in 1872 when the eastern United States was struck by the Great Epizootic (an equine influenza) that had such an effect on horses that transport all but disappeared from the streets. In Britain the Keighley tramway system had a severe problem soon after it opened in 1888 when the stable had a contagion of 'pinkeye'. This shut the service for two months while the illness was being treated.

As if this was not enough risk there was the ever-present fear of having a fire in the stables. To reduce the risk and impact of such fires the systems often would have several smaller stables, rather than one large one. The stable buildings could well be made of wood, but even with a brick built building the inside was full of combustible materials. The stalls and rafters were wooden, there was straw laid all over the floor and the lofts filled with hay. Once a fire started it was difficult to extinguish, not helped by panicking horses. The Glasgow Tramway and Omnibus Company had tram depot fires in 1883, 1884 and 1885. In the 1884 fire of the 251 horses in the stable 174 died. In the three fires no fewer than 42 cars from a fleet of 240 were destroyed as well as the buildings of the three depots.

The horses were the most expensive element of a horse tramway operation. It cost around £26 a year just to feed one horse and £7 per year per horse on replacements, so to run a tramcar cost nearly £363 on average a year, though this varied considerably according to the price of feed, which depending on the harvest could double or halve in price. So each day a tramcar had to sell 280 1d tickets just to feed and replace the horses. The shareholders were usually less than sympathetic, accusing the horses of eating away their dividends. The operators were able to get some money back by selling the horse manure (a horse produces about 10

Plymouth Corporation had to use two trace horses on this route. One is hauling ahead of the regular horses, the other is alongside them. Note the trace boy riding on the leading horse.

On another Plymouth route the tram needs the assistance of three trace horses. Two have been attached in front of the regular horses and the third in front of those two. The leading horse has the trace boy riding on it, who is looking after all three trace horses. The single horse to the side of the tramcar is probably a relief horse waiting to take over from one of the trace horses.

The Manchester reversible tramcar has a trace horse attached in front of the regular horses. There is no sign of the trace boy, presumably he is just out of the photograph.

The size can be understood from this view of a London General Omnibus Company stable. The noise and smell of the stables when in full operation can only be surmised.

The operation needs almost one man for each horse. The fire risk of the stables can be assessed from the amount of wood and straw as well as the crowded conditions.

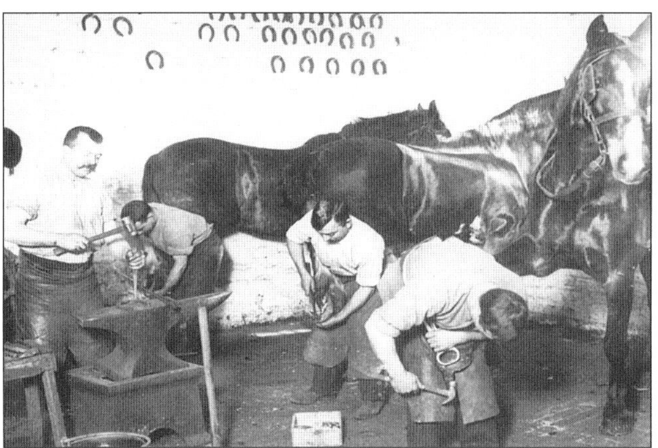

A team of blacksmiths were kept fully occupied shoeing the horses.

The quantity of fodder necessary was immense, as this view of a dedicated Dublin United Tramways cart delivery of feed to the company's stables shows.

pounds of manure a day that was sold for 5 shillings per ton) and the company would employ men to sweep up the manure from the tramway routes, no doubt collecting all that lay on the road, irrespective of the donor. The manure from the stables would be added and it would be stored (much to the complaint of neighbours, who had good cause as the piles of manure were described as having an intolerable stench) while it 'rotted down' and when sufficient volume was collected it was carted out to farms. Indeed in 1872 Dr Pearce took the London Tramways Company to court complaining that the new depot built next door to his house caused a smell from the stables and manure heaps and noise from the workshops causing a serious nuisance to himself and his household. The tramway company agreed to remove the manure every twelve hours and the complaint was withdrawn. Two years later Mr Orton took the North Metropolitan Tramways Company to court over a similar issue. Mr Orton argued that he could not sleep at night because of the noise or walk in his garden because of the stench. The court determined that there was a nuisance and issued an injunction to prevent the tramway from keeping horses on the site.

Those horses no longer suitable for tram work would be sold. In an attempt to reduce costs some operators tried using mules rather than horses. Mules were more resilient and sturdier than horses. It was said by tramway operators that two mules could be fed for the same price as one horse and would do one-third more work. However, they had no re-sale value when they were no longer fit for tramway work and they were far harder to control than horses, as they had a strong will of their own and were prone to refusing to do what the driver wanted, though at times the same could be said about horses. There was an occasion when two carts collided and bags of salt and flour fell on to the road, splitting and spilling the contents across the road. Tram drivers suddenly found that their horse flatly refused to tread on to the powders and the tramway ground to a halt. The tramway operators had to employ men to sweep the road and clear away all the salt and flour before the horses would continue their journeys. The use of mules in the British Isles was rare, but in other countries, such as America, mules were frequently used.

As if this was not more than enough to worry the tramway operator there was yet another problem for them. The government had the power to commandeer horses if they were needed in the case of war. Over the main period of horse trams in the British Isles there were two wars involving the British and one that did not involve Britain but that did affect the country. These were 1861-1865, the American Civil War; 1877-1879, the Zulu War; 1899-1902, the Boer War. The Government would have a retainer of ten shillings per year on horses to make them available for the war effort when needed.

If life was hard for the horses it was not much better for the tramcar crew. For each tramcar there would be just one driver and conductor. They would work up to 16 hours a day, six days a week where the horse tramway did not run on Sundays or seven days a week without any relief, other than a day off in every fourteen. The only breaks were the turn round time at the end of each run. These few minutes had to be used to eat their meals and have a hot drink, usually brought to them by their wives or children. In addition to their duties as drivers and conductors they were also expected to wash the outside of the car and clean the inside at least once a week. To become a tramcar conductor an applicant had to be accepted and they were then told to attend the depot for the first tramcar that went into service for the day. Here all the aspirant individuals formed a pool of spare drivers/conductors. If a regular driver or conductor failed to turn up for his shift then the replacement would come from the pool, the most recent applicant being the last to be used. Most days the pool would spend the day sitting in the depot and not be required to go out with a tram. As they had not worked they did not get paid. This continued with the longest serving people in the pool being offered regular work as it became available. They were required to learn on the job or in their own time and had to lodge a deposit of between £2.00 and £5.00 with the operator which

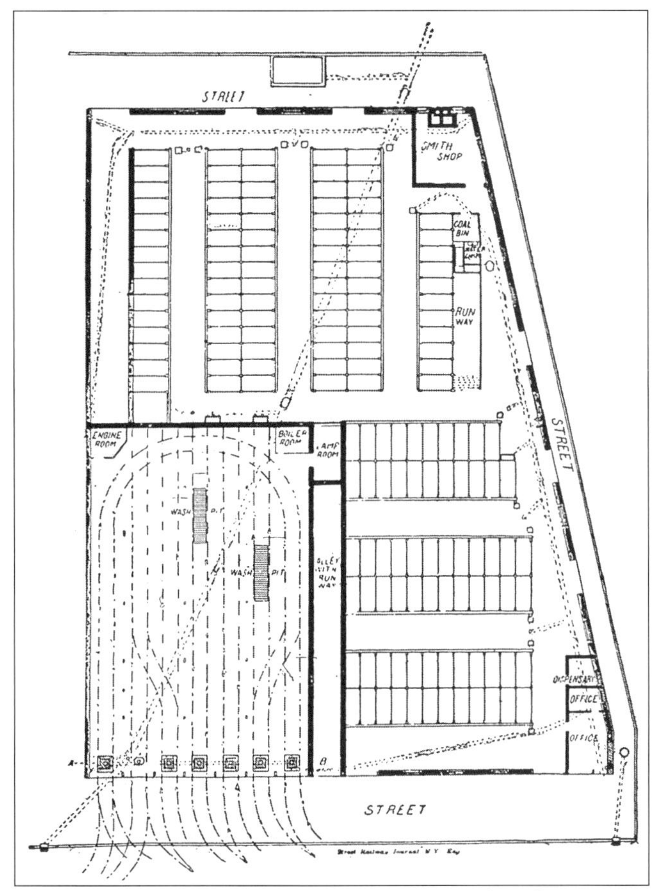

This plan of a London tram depot shows the proportion of space taken up by the horses compared to the tramcars.

Where ground space was at a premium, for example in London, the stables were built with two storeys. This is the access ramp for the horses to get to the upper floor.

was forfeited if the man was dismissed. Once they had a regular job then they were expected to turn up in all weathers. Ernest Acheson records in his memoirs that when working for Glasgow tramways he reported for work at 7.00am, but there were no cars so he was instructed to carry sacks of feed into the stores. At 5.30pm, as he was preparing to go home he was told to conduct on a car just going out. He continued working on the car until 10.00pm when he was allowed home. This was equivalent to working two days on just one. So he expected extra pay for the very long day. But when pay day arrived there was no extra money, despite the long hours. No wonder staff turnover was high. Mr Acheson also recalled that when he wanted to visit his home in Ireland he had to resign from his job in order to get time off.

Any sickness or other absence was not paid and too much absence led to immediate dismissal. Frequently operators would engage young boys, as they did not expect as high a wage as men. It was common for boys to be responsible for the trace horses, often riding bareback on them. In Worcester a trace lad, who was 14 years old, was expected to work from 7.00am to 11.00pm a day for a wage of three shillings and sixpence a week. Quite often lads were employed as conductors and many of the photographs of horse trams show remarkably young boys with a cash satchel over their shoulders. However, being young also had its problems and Paisley tramways found itself often being criticised for the inattentiveness of the boy conductors. In reply the company stated that the boys only worked a 14-hour day, with 1 hour 10 minutes breaks for meals, which they said were the shortest working hours in the Kingdom. For this the boys were paid 8 shillings a week (an adult conductor was paid 20 shillings a week). In Portsmouth, staff were given one Sunday off duty each twelve months. The staff were also at risk of having their wages cut. In 1879 Sheffield Tramways Company cut the wages of drivers by 7s from 31s 6d to 24s 6d, some 22%. In 1887 the Liverpool tramways reduced pay by 9%, while working hours were increased to reduce the number of men needed. In both cases the excuse given was falling receipts.

Naturally enough the staff were unhappy with the long working hours and low wages. Indeed, although the job was seen as respected by society, the pay was no better than labourers, but

During the working day a large number of horses were out hauling tramcars, so the conditions were a little easier and not so many men were needed.

This photograph was probably taken at the end of the day with all the horses back in the stables and it shows much of the equipment, harnesses, collars and blankets for the horses.

The tramway required a vast amount of harnesses that had to be repaired and kept in good condition. This is the harness room of the stable.

the tramway expected far longer hours of duty. The only pressure staff could place on the company was to strike, but usually there was a long queue of men wanting jobs on the tramway. In the years 1871-1873 there was a boom in employment and the availability of men was diminished. This gave an opportunity for them to press for better wages and working conditions. However, the working man was not organised and relied on the generosity of managers and shareholders. In most tramways the latter were experiencing a very profitable period, but often wanted to keep the prosperity to themselves. A workers union was formed in Liverpool in 1875 to support the claims of the tramway and omnibus drivers and conductors. Wages did increase, but the union found this to be a double-edged sword, as when a strike was started to reduce working hours, the company found it easy to recruit new men as the pay was attractive. The Union had hoped that the Corporation would refuse to issue licences to the new men, but all requests were granted and not only did the strike fail, but many of the men on strike lost their jobs. In Hull there was a strike in 1881, but the company told the men that if they did not get back to work they would be sacked and replaced by unskilled and uneducated men from the countryside. The strike was over by lunchtime. A second strike in 1882 lasted two days. On another company tramway the staff on strike picketed the depot to prevent tramcars from leaving it with new drivers. The Manager went out to address the strikers saying that the police had instructions to arrest any man standing in front of a moving tramcar and charge them with attempted suicide. In the late 1880s the tramways suffered a fall in revenue and there were cut-backs in staffing numbers and pay was decreased.

Grooming the horses ready for work. No doubt the dry weather allowing the grooming to be done in the relatively more spacious outside was most welcome to both men and horses.

Conductors had an additional burden, as they were the only staff handling money without immediate supervision. Tramway companies worked on the basis that all conductors were stealing money from the company and so sent checkers to spy on them. For each passenger that paid a bell punch had to be operated. This rang a bell for each penny paid and a counter on the machine would increase. However, the counters were inside the machine and not able to be read by the conductor. Only clerks in the tramway offices were able to open the machines. The problem for the conductor was that when the machines were collected and sent to the office they could be jolted and register additional numbers. The conductor was held liable and any shortages in the takings were made up from his wages. If the conductor allowed too many passengers on his tram, overloading it, he could be taken to court and would have to pay his own fine, but if a spotter saw him refuse to take on passengers he was reported to the company and fined for failing to take as much revenue as possible. In Liverpool a new union was formed in 1889 and knowing the limited effectiveness of strike action tried

The smaller towns had smaller stables, as seen by this one for the Ipswich tramways.

a new tactic. They made it very publicly known the hardships the tramway workers were under and invited the public to boycott the tramways. They also ran their own omnibuses in competition with the trams. This had some effect on the company and concessions were made in raising wages and replacing the bell punches with a new design where the number could be recorded by the conductor.

By 1899 even more of the public became concerned with the long hours and letters were written to *The Times* newspaper. This was prompted by the creation of the London and Counties Tramways and Omnibus Employees Union that started to negotiate with tramway companies over hours of work and wages. The employers argued that the hours were reasonable, being 13 hours per day spread over 16 hours, the breaks being too short to allow staff to get back home. The Union sought shorter hours, their aim being a 12-hour day. This generated letters from the public, generally sympathetic to the tramway workers. The North Metropolitan Tramways Company agreed to reduce the working day to 12 hours, others followed, but not immediately. The Union had better results when they negotiated with the London County Council when it took over the old horse tramways.

The Times records a strike in 1889 in Cardiff. The tramway company decided unilaterally to change the pay scale from a progressive scale (23s to 28s) to a single amount of 25s per week. This meant that many staff would have a pay cut and so they went on strike. This included the drivers, conductors and all the stablemen. A protest rally was held in the streets blocking all the traffic, as they petitioned the company for arbitration. All the Cardiff police were mobilised and they guarded a few tramcars that were put into service. The police could not stop the crowd and tramcars were lifted off the rails and placed across the tracks. Stones were thrown and all the tramcar windows were smashed. The police advised the company to take all the tramcars into the depot for safety. Arrests were made and 16 people appeared in court the next day. The next morning the crowds gathered again and the company ran a few cars with policemen on each to protect them. But stones were thrown, windows smashed and passengers hurt. Pebbles were jammed in the groove of the rail to de-rail the tramcars, as well as large slabs of stone being placed across the tracks. Even Solomon Andrews, a director of the tramway, was mobbed and in danger of harm until he was surrounded by the police and taken away for safety. By the end of the morning all the tramcars were back

Looking after the health of the horses was a major task and a special area in the stables was set aside as a horse hospital.

Probably not the most sought-after job was that of cleaning the horse muck off the streets. Here two men sweep up the mess from the streets in Bristol.

At the terminus the horses were taken from one end of the tramcar to the other. First the driver would unhook the harnesses from the tramcar, as seen on this Leyton tramcar.

Then the horses are walked around the tramcar, while the harnesses are held by the driver, as seen in Aberdeen.

This driver in Dublin has the help of his conductor in moving the horses to the other end of the tramcar at the Nelson's Pillar terminus.

A very rural terminus on the Wolverhampton tramway with the horses being taken to the other end of the tramcar.

In Gloucester the horse is moving back to the track to be attached to the tramcar.

in the depots. In the evening the directors met a deputation from the staff and a settlement was arranged so that no-one had their wages cut.

Another British horse tramway strike reported in the *The Times* was on the North Metropolitan Tramways Company in 1898. Two horsekeepers at the Stamford Hill depot reported in late and were sacked. The other horsekeepers were fed up with an autocratic management style and went on strike, preventing the trams from running. Quick negotiations came to an agreement and the two men were re-instated and the strike ended. But it was found that one of the strikers had not been re-instated and the Stamford Hill horsekeepers went on strike again. No trams left that depot and the company threatened them all with dismissal if they did not report for work the next day. But the strike held and no trams left the depot for a second day. While they were on strike the men also asked for a pay rise. Of the other depots, only Wood Green had joined the strike so the tramway service continued, but in a much reduced state. The next day the men at Wood Green went back to work, but Stamford Hill remained on strike. The company then sought new staff and recruited many ex-cavalry and artillery men. They were taken to the depot under police protection and were able to get two-thirds of the tramcars out. The company informed the men on strike that they were dismissed, having been replaced by new men. Over the next few days a nearly normal service was provided, though the new men were slower than the experienced ones on strike. The strike had been on for six days and many of the strikers approached the company to ask for their old jobs back. Some said that they had been prevented from working by the other men. The company agreed with them and re-instated 18. Then 150 also came forward but were told there were no vacancies. It was then found that some of the horses were getting sores on their shoulders. The cause was found to be that when the men went on strike someone had moved many of the horses' collars to different pegs, so that the new men sent horses out with the wrong collars, causing injury to many of them. The company

The horses are almost ready to be attached to the tramcar at this Edinburgh terminus.

The double loop on the North Metropolitan Tramways suggests that this was a regular place to change horses.

said that due to the strike over 330 men had lost their jobs. The Directors gave a vote of confidence to the General Manager. The company had paid all the men who remained loyal to them full wages, even if they had been prevented from working and the company also gave them all an extra 10s as compensation for their loyalty.

Britain was not the only country where there were tramway strikes. In 1899 there was a major strike in New York, requiring over 600 police to try to keep order, with over 100 arrests. Things were even more fraught in Berlin in 1900 when 486 arrests were made over one weekend, with the authorities threatening to call the armed forces if necessary. So the British experience was perhaps not so bad.

The terminus was a useful place to change horses. The North Metropolitan Tramways had a spare pair of horses ready to take on their work.

Although George Francis Train had given his tramcar crews a uniform (based on army designs) later tramway companies did not issue a uniform; the staff had to provide their own clothes, though tramcar staff would often wear bowler hats as a mark of authority. At the terminus there was usually an opportunity to have a short rest, possible a bite to eat or a mouthful of hot tea. The driver had one more responsibility at the terminus and that was to turn the horses. The driver would detach the swingle tree from the tram drawbar and holding the swingle tree would walk the horse(s) around the tram to the other end and re-attach to the car. If the tramcar was an Eades reversible then the driver would unhook the handbrake chain, release the locking bar and the horses would walk sideways turning the body of the tramcar on its chassis. When in the new position the locking bar would be re-engaged and the handbrake chain reattached.

A fresh pair of horses for this Leicester tramcar.

The age of the horse tram coincided with the Victorian era in Britain and with strong views on the observance of the Sabbath. The middle class considered Sunday to be a day of rest and wanted their views to be followed by the rest of the population (other than their own servants and cooks of course). So public travel was discouraged and omnibuses were usually required not to operate on Sundays. This requirement was continued when the horse trams arrived. In some rare instances trams were allowed to run on Sundays but on the whole Sunday was a day without public transport. So, tramway operators were prevented from earning revenue one day a week. When the Southampton Tramway Company opened in 1879 it found itself at the receiving end of vociferous criticism for running trams on a Sunday. A petition was raised with 3,500 signatures objecting to the Sunday service. The Manager of the Company, W.G. Lankester, responded by saying that the Sunday service gave a profit and this showed that plenty of citizens valued the provision and so the Sunday trams would continue as long as they showed a profit. However, the anti attitude began to change with the conversion of tramways to electric operation and often the new trams operated seven days a week. However, this was not always accepted quietly. In Ayr when the Council took over running the trams in 1901 and converted the system to electric power the Councillors voted to allow Sunday running. This became the subject of pulpit sermons and letters were written to the newspapers complaining of the change and signatures were collected on petitions. The pro-Sunday Councillors pointed out that private and hired carriages were often seen outside churches and that church ministers had been seen travelling in them. The Councillors asked why should the poorer inhabitants be denied their own form of transport? Much to the annoyance of church elders the Council agreed to allow Sunday trams for six months and then to hold a referendum. The six months proved that Sunday trams were popular and the referendum result was 1252 votes for Sunday transport and 433 against.

Although most of those on the tramcar are children it is hoped they were only on this Lincoln tramcar for the photograph and the horse was not expected to haul them all.

This driver in Leicester has covered his horse with a blanket to stop it getting chilled.

There were also some less obvious problems. A Pimlico,

A typical tramcar driver with his whip and seated on a stool.

A young lad as conductor completing his waybill.

Peckham & Greenwich Street Tramways Co. conductor was taken to court for allowing his tramcar to park on the roadway for longer than was considered necessary and thus obstructing the highway. The conductor argued that it was at the terminus and he was entitled to a break of eight minutes. The magistrates disagreed and he was fined three shillings. It appeared that discussions between the tramway company and the authorities reached an unwritten agreement and no other conductors were so charged. However, there was a degree of public support for the tramway staff. In 1871 "Fair Play" (many correspondents to *The Times* newspaper wrote under a nom-de-plum) wrote to say:

> *"In the Times of Saturday there appeared an account of a case, heard before Mr Bushby at Worship-street Police Court, in which the police charged the servants of the Tramway Company with obstructing the traffic and carrying more passengers than their licences allowed. This last charge was briefly dismissed.*
>
> *With respect to the charge of obstruction, it appears that they were actually more than one half minute in changing their horses. Compare this frightful delay to the time occupied by that immaculate body, the omnibus servants.*
>
> *I am frequently obliged to travel by omnibus, and the time they take to change horses is never less than four minutes, and in many instances nearer ten minutes, and during this time most of the drivers and ostlers amuse themselves by shouting the most indescribable filth, and insulting every woman who passes them.*
>
> *Without considering the superior comfort of one vehicle to another, I should like to know which of the two companies the police, in justice, should prosecute, or persecute."*

In addition to these prosecutions for obstruction there were many for overloading tramcars. These were always taken against the individual conductor and never against the tramway management. The defence by many conductors that they were unable to

A young Chesterfield conductor, used because he was cheaper than an adult.

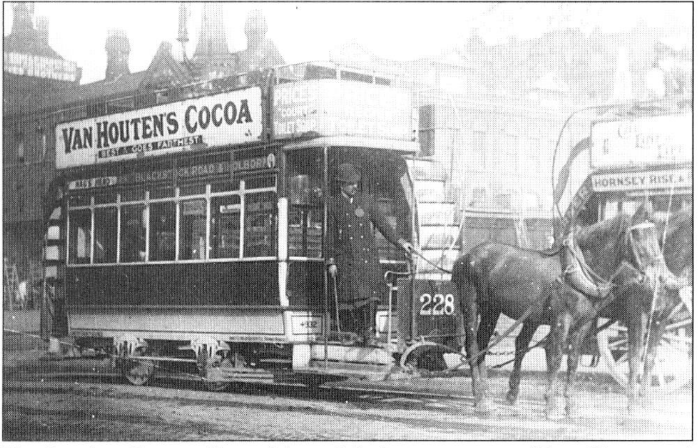

The London County Council issued their tram crews with uniforms and this driver cuts quite a dash.

control the crowds, particularly on Bank Holidays was listened to sympathetically by the judges. Indeed one remarked that he could understand that the only recourse open to the conductor in such situations would be to stop the tramcar and refuse to proceed until sufficient passengers alighted to keep within the loading limit. But then he said this would no doubt result in the conductor then being prosecuted for obstructing the highway! Despite this sympathy the judge went on to fine the conductor 3s with 2s costs (more than a day's pay).

There were no press button bells on the tramcars so the means of communication between conductor and driver was difficult, though most used a whistle. This led to one tram in Stirling starting off from one stop while its conductor was delivering a parcel. After a while the driver noticed his conductor was missing and stopped the car. The conductor came into view breathlessly running along the road. It transpired that a parrot in a house near the stop had imitated the whistle fooling the driver into thinking it was the conductor giving him the signal to start.

Preston seems to have favoured an older conductor.

Winter time was particularly difficult for the tram crew. The conductor did have the opportunity to enter the lower saloon and escape the worst of the cold. But the driver had no choice and was obliged to stay on the front platform. Though he would have an overcoat and gloves these would be covered in ice and his only crumb of comfort was a box of straw for his feet.

The tramways relied entirely on the fare receipts to keep their operation going. So it was very important that the operators did receive the appropriate payment from each passenger. The theory of fare collection states that there are three requirements for effective fare collection:

The conductor on this Brighton and Shoreham tramcar looks hardly old enough to be working.

1 Ensure that each passenger does not evade paying their fare to the conductor.
2 Ensure that the conductor does not embezzle any of the fares and returns to the operator the full moneys collected.
3 Ensure that the passenger does not travel further than the distance he has paid for.

In the early days of tramways passengers dropped their fare into a box. The role of the conductor was to ensure that the passenger did pay, though it was not possible for him to ensure that the correct sum was paid and that a washer was not dropped into the box. Indeed the tramway in Newport Monmouthshire had to change the box system because they found far too many penny sized washers being dropped in. The conductor rang a bell that also advanced a counter. It was also possible for the conductor to take some of the money by taking fares from passengers as they entered the car and then putting most into the box, but holding one or two coins for themselves. The very unofficial practices in many tramways meant that the conductor was expected to 'tip' his driver and tips were also expected by the inspector, the timekeeper and regulator, all paid daily. So it is not

If anything, this conductor in Chesterfield looks even younger.

surprising that conductors did not pass all the takings to the company. The fare collection issue had been addressed earlier by the railways and some of the issues were resolved by the use of tickets, though the early ones were hand written. The ticket system was developed by Thomas Edmondson and an adaptation of the principles was applied to tramways. On the larger systems the conductors were issued with a set quantity of tickets of various fares. All the tickets were individually numbered to allow a quick calculation to determine the number sold. The conductors also had way bills that had to be filled in on every journey. After two round trips the conductor would hand his takings and the way bills to cash officers. These would be checked by female clerks. On the last journey the conductor would complete a summary way bill and hand this with his bag, remaining tickets and money received. The clerks checked that the money tallied with the tickets used, worked out the highest and lowest amounts taken as well as the average amount for each car.

To ensure that the passenger does not travel beyond the distance paid for, the ticket is punched indicating the location where the passenger boarded. The price marked on the ticket indicating the distance that the passenger paid for. The conductor had a punch machine that made a clean hole in the ticket, the conductor locating the hole in the area of the ticket indicating the place the passenger boarded. This allowed an inspector to check the tickets of passengers and determine if it was valid for the place where the inspection took place. The punch machine had other functions as well. It had a bell when operated, so the passenger knew that the hole in the ticket had just been made, preventing the conductor from picking used tickets from the floor and selling them to passengers, pretending to punch the hole. In fact it was known that fraudulent conductors would have a bell concealed up their sleeve that they could operate by a piece of string, thus fooling the passenger into thinking that

The crew on this Harrow Road and Paddington tramways car show many of their items of equipment. The driver has his licence badge and whistle, while the conductor has a ticket punch, money bag and his licence badge hooked on his belt.

The very young conductor in Chesterfield looking very fed up with his job and being photographed.

Looking like a couple of young blades, the Derby crew strike a pose for the camera – note they are not issued with a uniform.

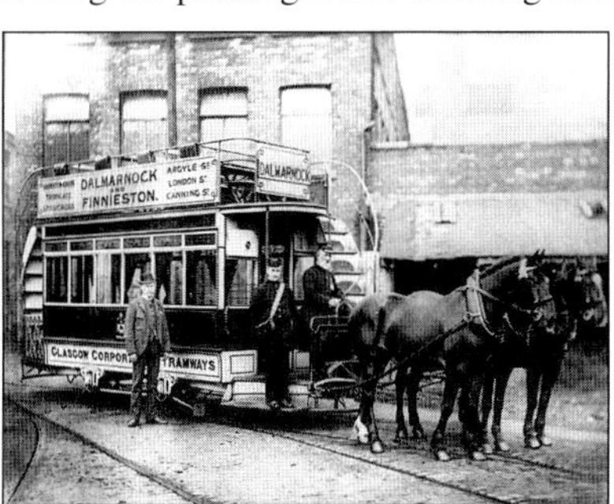

One of the first things that corporations did when they took over horse tramways was to fit the crews out with uniforms, as these two Glasgow employees demonstrate.

they had just punched the ticket. Needless to say being caught with such a machine meant immediate dismissal and possible prosecution. The official punch machine would not operate unless a ticket had been placed in its slot (only one ticket could be inserted at a time) and it had a counter for the number of times it had been operated. The latter allowed a check that the number of punches is equal to the number of tickets sold. The final check was that the little circle of card removed by punching fell into a container in the machine. This could be unlocked by the ticket department and the number of tickets punched could be counted. The value of the punched circle was identified as each value of ticket was a different colour.

Though the drivers and conductors were the most obvious of the tramways employees the systems needed many more people to ensure that it ran smoothly. The North Metropolitan Tramways Company employed Inspectors, Washers, Timekeepers, Stable Foremen, Housekeepers, Regulators, Trace Boys, Pointsmen, Pole Shifters, Lampmen, Track Cleaners, Shoeing Smiths, Mechanics, Harness Department Staff (the system made its own harnesses), Permanent Way Staff, Granary Staff, Cashiers, Clerks and Youths, Punch Clerks, Inquiry Staff and Messengers.

Attitudes to the safety of the horses and the employees were far more cavalier in those days. There was no health and safety legislation and this approach by the tramway owners extended to the passengers and the public. On many systems the tramway horses had bells attached to their harness to warn people of their approach, however, elderly pedestrians were probably deaf, as this was before the days of hearing aids. On some systems even the use of this primitive warning was banned. For example the South London Tramways Company was unfortunate when a tramcar ran over an elderly lady who had stepped out in front of the tramcar. The driver shouted a warning, but the lady appeared not to hear and was run over by the tram. At the inquest the Coroner recommended that the tram should carry warning bells. However, the requirements of the 1870 Act meant that this was only possible if every local authority through which the tramway ran, all agreed and there were many, some of whom complained that the noise would be a nuisance. The tramways' legal representatives wrote to the major local authorities asking if they could convene a conference of the interested parties and come to a decision about the use of bells. What the response was is unknown.

The only record available for the

In Bradford the conductor tips his hat to the photographer.

Looking rather grumpy the conductor poses with the driver, passengers and horses for the camera on the Brighton tramway.

The Belfast tramcar demonstrates the crew, trace boy and trace horses.

Another pair of trace horses in Belfast.

Not all trace boys were young as this elderly gentleman in York shows.

Trace horses on a Derby tramcar purchased second-hand from Glasgow.

This Newcastle trace boy leads his horse up the hill.

number of accidents is the reports in *The Times* newspaper. A compilation has been made of all the horse tramway accidents between 1870 and 1900. There are 38 recorded, most being in the form of court claims for damages. It is clear this is only the tip of the iceberg, as two letters demonstrate. One was published in 1879 and was titled Accidents by Tramcars and said:

> *"These accidents are now happening too frequently and I notice the shocking deaths of two children on Sunday. There are many accidents that could be prevented by ordinary care without great expense to the company. In the present instance, had the tramcar been provided with guards to the wheels similar to those used on our locomotive engines neither of these children need have been killed."*

Some tramway companies did fit crude metal guards around the wheels, but it seems that things got no better because in 1890 a surgeon from St Bartholomews Hospital wrote:

> *"I was called to the hospital this morning to see a small child of four years old, both of whose lower limbs were nearly completely severed from the body by a tramcar. The little creature was quite sensible, and asked to be taken home. Its terrible injuries placed it beyond all hope of surgical aid, and within a couple of hours it died quietly in one of the hospital wards. I regret to say that the number of these tram accidents brought to the hospitals is appalling, and out of all proportion to the comparatively small number of cars running.*
>
> *The explanation of this is probably simple. When a child runs in front of an ordinary vehicle the driver in nine cases out of ten, though unable to stop, can rapidly swerve a little to one side or the other, thus by a shave avoiding an accident. With a tramcar this is impossible, and unless the driver can stop dead the wheels must inevitably pass over the victim.*
>
> *I venture, Sir, to hope that you may use your powerful influence to induce the tramcar companies to fix in front of the fore wheels of their cars a simple projecting guard, which would push any obstacle aside or in front of it till the car could be stopped. This, I am confident, could be done with ease, and would be the means of averting many horrible accidents of which my experience this morning is only a pathetic example."*

This can be compared to the attitude of the tramways companies when the Secretary of the Edinburgh tramways, Mr W. Paterson, actually boasted that of the 34 million passengers carried by the trams the tramways had killed only 7.

These letters raise an issue regarding road safety. In these days we are used to seeing traffic on our roads running at 30mph in towns and far faster on other roads. Our perception is that in the 1800s horse traffic moved at around walking pace and there should have been no conflict between road traffic and pedestrians. Yet the facts show that there were indeed many such accidents and that trams seem to have been more dangerous than other traffic. As well as the excellent reasons given in the above letter (and it is surprising that lifeguards and lifetrays were not required to be fitted to tramcars until the electric era) there may be other factors. The reason for having tramways was that a steel wheel on a steel rail had much less rolling resistance allowing greater weights to be hauled at a faster pace. It is probable that both these advantages contributed to the number of accidents. The first is that a tramcar was a larger and heavier vehicle than other horse-drawn traffic. So once moving it had a far greater momentum than other vehicles. This meant that stopping the tramcar required more effort and more distance. This is illustrated today by the difference between a car and a train. At 30mph a car can stop in a few feet while a train, with its vastly greater momentum, takes many hundreds of yards. In the case of the tramcar the driver is able to apply its brake and throw sand onto the rails to improve the grip and prevent skidding, but the tram will still need a far greater distance to stop than other road users. With the additional problem of not being able to swerve out of the way, as identified above, the tram will inevitably hit a pedestrian. The pedestrian is probably far more used to other traffic and will not be expecting the tram to move as fast as it does; observations on the Douglas horse tramway show that the trams move faster than human walking pace, nearer to a jogging speed. So the pedestrian is likely to misjudge the time the tram will take to reach him. In the case of children, many would both be unpractised at judging the speed of a tramcar and may well be easily distracted by other things and not notice the tram. The lack of effective guards in front of the wheels meant that the likelihood of being run over was great.

A Leicester trace boy riding his horse.

Examination of legal actions against horse tramways reported in *The Times*, show that the majority were not taken by passengers, but members of the public affected by the tramway. Of the 38 claims recorded in *The Times* 14 were by passengers and 24 by members of the public. There was no record of any actions taken by the parents of children who had been run over by a tramcar, presumably they were too poor to go to law and the likelihood would be that the cause of the accident would be found to be that the child ran out in front of the car. The most dangerous activity was getting on or off the tramcar with 12 claims being made. Next was being run over by a tram, closely followed by collision with another vehicle (respectively 8 and 7 cases). The inevitable defence by the company was that the injured individual was either tipsy or downright drunk at the time and so acted irresponsibly. It is interesting to wonder how the directors of the North Metropolitan Tramways Company felt about these accidents. In 1870 they announced that they carried 1,053,181 passengers without accident attributable to the fault of the company or its servants, when over the next thirty years the tramway had to pay compensation for injuries amounting to £2,990. This is equivalent to £1.7 million at today's values. The North Metropolitan Tramways Company was by far the most dangerous of all the tramway companies, even allowing for its size. The total sum paid in damages by horse tramway companies, as recorded in *The Times,* during that period was £5,922 (£3 million at today's values). No doubt the Derby Tramways Company were relieved when they were found not to be negligent when they were taken to court by a gentleman claiming £1,200 in damages for the death of a race horse. The gentleman was riding the horse in the street when it was in collision with a tramcar. Had the tramway company been found negligent the

A poor photograph, but used because it shows two trace boys riding their horses; usually just one boy would be able to look after two horses.

The Glasgow trace boy rides his horse down the hill to be ready to help take the next tramcar up the hill.

This Nottingham tramcar has a trace horse in front ridden by the trace boy and a second trace horse alongside the regular horses.

A London Street Tramways depot with all the workers having their photograph taken. Tram crews can be identified by the licence badges they wear, and included in the photo is the depot dog.

Bath employees pose by their tramcar outside one of the depots.

sum claimed, equal to £620,000 in today's values might well have made the company bankrupt. This is not as speculative as it may seem. The Darlington Street Railway Company was made bankrupt when in 1864 it was determined that they were responsible for the death of a prize greyhound run over in the street and had to pay substantial damages. The comment of a judge in one case is interesting when he said that when a case went before a jury they inevitably found for the injured party, indicating that juries were more sympathetic to the individual than the tramway company. The highest amount of compensation awarded was £1,000 against the North Metropolitan Tramways Company in 1883, to the children of a man who died after being thrown from his cart when driving over the tram track. The track was in such bad condition it caused the axle of the cart to be broken. Even for such a large company the amount, equivalent today to around £500,000, would be difficult to find and would dramatically reduce the profits.

Keeping the tramcars clean was one of the depot jobs, particularly in London's County Council fleet.

Passengers were also at risk of theft from their own fellows. On open cars, particularly the open upper decks, there was a particular danger in wet weather on garden seat type upper decks. The tramway operators supplied oilskins that could be unrolled from the seat in front and wrapped over the passenger's legs, covering them from the rain, but also concealing the activities of pickpockets. Early double-deck tramcars had primitive safety railing around the upper deck, however the legs of the passengers could be seen from the road and this deterred ladies from travelling on the upper deck. Later, decency boards were fitted to prevent pedestrians being able to see the legs of upper deck passengers and this allowed ladies to travel upstairs, though care was needed in ascending and descending stairs.

Another important aspect of the tramway was the maintenance and repair of the tramcars themselves. The London County Council had a great pride in the appearance of trams, crews and horses.

The condition of the roads also created a nuisance to the public. The problems caused by the vast quantity of horse manure were not confined to the smell. In summer the material would dry out and be churned to a fine powder by road traffic. This powder would be blown by the wind and stick to peoples clothes and be breathed in taking all kinds of ailments with it. In wet weather the situation was different, but no better. The manure would be mixed with mud, dirt and horse urine, often forming ankle deep pools of stinking filth. The fashions of the day meant that clothing went to the ground, particularly for women, and it would drag in the muck. Men would make a living by offering to sweep a clean path across the road for people in return for a tip. As the trams ran in the centre of the road (to prevent delivery vans blocking their way) passengers had to walk from the pavement to the tram. It was not unusual for passengers leaving a tramcar to find that they had stepped into a pile of fresh manure deposited by the very horses pulling their tramcar. The unfortunate person would then traipse the muck on their shoes to wherever their destination was.

Sometimes the trams were called on to perform unusual duties. A young lad had been playing on a building site and had fallen from a partly completed house, breaking his leg. Passers-by put him into a wheel barrow and wheeled him to the tramway where he was taken into the tramcar and laid on the longitudinal seat. The tram carried on to the town centre. Someone had run ahead and when the tramcar arrived a policeman was waiting with a cart that the lad was transferred to and then carried to the hospital for treatment.

Staff stand outside a Lincoln depot. The man in front is probably the manager and he is holding a tramcar cash box.

This Liverpool tramcar shows the crude guards in front of the wheels. While they did make some concession to pedestrian safety they were not very effective as accidents and injuries continued.

Not all comments about tramway practices were sensible. In November 1881 the following letter appeared in *The Times* newspaper referring to the practice of advertising on the back of the tickets issued by conductors. The reader is left to decide if it was written tongue in cheek or not.

"As this is about the time of the year when companies, seeking fresh powers from parliament, may naturally be supposed to be on their best behaviour, let me ask your attention to a feature of tramway travelling which seems a little out of the ordinary groove. Looking also to the thousands of all classes – young persons, tradesmen, shop assistants, servants, and others, who use these carriages daily, perhaps you will think that a word in season may not be amiss. This is what happens on one of the principal metropolitan tramways lines. As soon as you are seated and have paid your fare, the conductor, in his official capacity, hands you the following printed notice:-
MONEY
Three pounds to 500 pounds on Easy Terms without Enquiry Fees. The Old Established Confidential Loan and Discount Office -----
Advances, with or without securities, on Freehold and Leasehold Deeds, without expense of Mortgage, Furniture without removal, or on any other security.
Forms of Applications with full Particulars Gratis.
I have suppressed the address, not desiring further to advertise the establishment; but the capital letters, &c., are exactly as printed. It is impossible to refuse this precious document, or to tear it up, or throw it with indignation into the street, for it is issued with the company's authority, and a printed notice on the other side warns you that 'it must be produced for inspection on demand of the conductor or other official of the company, and given up on leaving the car.'
So you have to keep it, with the conductor's eye full upon you, either in your hand or in your glove or waistcoat pocket, taking every care what becomes of it, for you are further warned that if you attempt 'to use this ticket for a second journey, or otherwise defraud the company, you will be liable to prosecution and a fine of 40s.'
Now what does this all mean? Can the directors of the tramway company or some of them have an interest in the Old Established Confidential Loan and Discount Office? Or is it a private venture of the conductors, or what? The question is one that deserves an answer; if not now, when the company in question comes before parliament."

As far as can be ascertained the question was never answered!

A Croydon tramcar approaches a point and the horses have already moved towards the pavement. The points had no moving blades and the driver relied on the horses pulling the car in the correct direction to take the right track.

The horse as passenger! Not found on street tramways in this country (though some narrow gauge mineral lines did use this practice), the horse could have a break on routes that were all uphill, by climbing on the platform and riding the tram back down. This is a scene on the Cherrelyn, Denver tramway.

Evolution of the Horse Tramcar

Until the coming of the passenger railways, the only conveyances for paying passengers were road vehicles and particularly stage coaches, carriages, carts, and from 1820s, omnibuses. With the opening of the Stockton & Darlington Railway in 1825 it was natural that the operators turned to the stage coach manufacturers for their first carriages. Hence the strong stage coach influence on the earliest railway carriages, which at the time were described as several stage coach bodies fixed to a wagon chassis. With steam locomotives as the motive power, carriages could be larger and more could be hauled in a train. However, street tramcars were hauled by horses and were limited in weight. As has been mentioned earlier this was recognised by John Stephenson (himself a stage coach manufacturer) and the design of his tramcars was heavily influenced by coach design.

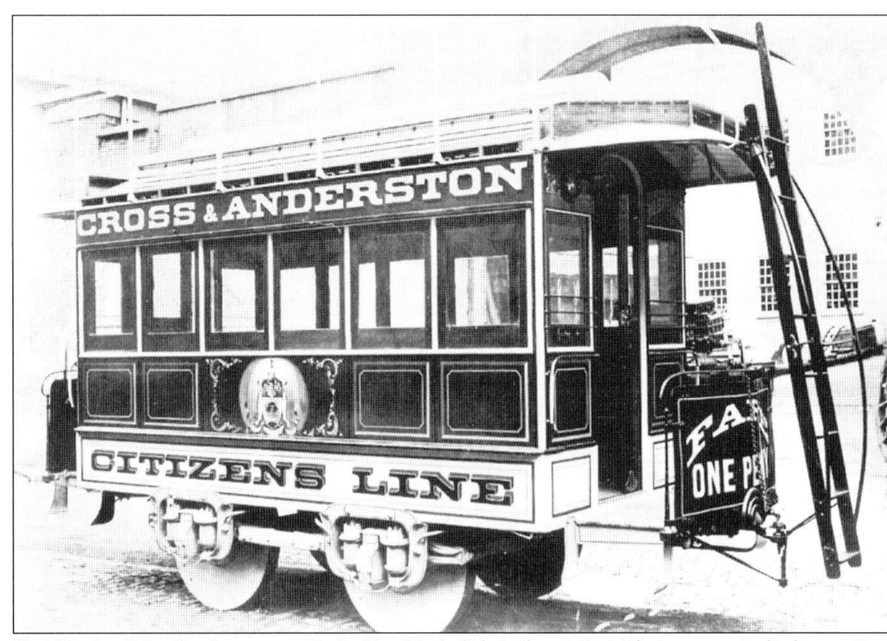

Outside the John Stephenson works in New York, it is believed that this tram was built for another customer, but painted in a livery suitable for Glasgow as an example of what Stephenson cars would look like if Glasgow ordered some. In the event the Glasgow Company purchased their tramcars from the Tramway Car and Works Company, a company that the directors of the Glasgow tramway had an interest in.

The cost of the horses and the length of their working life were discussed earlier. One major factor on the expenses was the effort needed by the horses, so any reduction in weight was a bonus to the operator. At the same time the tramcars had to be strong and resilient enough to withstand the rigours and abuses of operation day after day carrying the public and needed to be able to carry sufficient paying passengers to make it profitable for the operator. The materials used in the construction were of the best quality, with a wide range of wood being used, including white oak, white ash, beech, pine and poplar. The American manufacturers had an advantage over the British builders, as wood was more plentiful and cheaper in the USA. That is why the John Stephenson Company was able to undercut the prices of British manufacturers, even though the trams had to be shipped across the Atlantic. In those days wood was not used until it had been properly seasoned, meaning storing the planks of wood, spaced apart, for about three years. The wood would slowly dry out until its internal humidity equalled that of the atmosphere; during this process the wood shrinks and warps. The danger of using wood that was not seasoned is that it shrinks and warps after being made into a tramcar, weakening the vehicle. The most evident examples of this process are those churches with twisted steeples, most famously Chesterfield. The framework of the steeple might be made from long timbers not seasoned properly, with the present day result. All tramcar builders used a combination of storing their own green timber (freshly felled) and having reliable wood merchants who sold well seasoned timber. These days the process is shortened by kiln and oven seasoning.

Many early tramcars were built as lightly as possible, as this Rothesay tramcar shows.

The Douglas tramway had, and still has, light open toastrack tramcars.

The traditional horse tramcar became a four-wheel vehicle (there was only ever one bogie horse tram, a light narrow gauge car used on the Fairbourne Tramway; normally they

Generally used only in the summer, the Fairbourne tramway had light open tramcars. Note that this narrow gauge tramcar has bogies and is probably the only bogie horse tramcar to run in the British Isles.

On the South coast, with probably better weather than other tramways, the open toastrack tramcars were very popular.

Stirling in Scotland is not the first place that comes to mind as suitable for toastrack tramcars.

Another very lightly constructed toastrack, this time on the Warrenpoint and Rostrevor tramway.

South Shields is another place that does not seem suitable for toastrack tramcars.

A light toastrack car made by Solomon Andrews for the Pwllheli tramway.

Bradford also had toastrack tramcars.

This Dublin toastrack tramcar is extremely popular with no spare seats for any more passengers.

A Gloucester toastrack tramcar with curtains that appear more an essential requirement than an ornament.

One wonders if the gentleman in the top hat is a director of the South Shields tramway.

The Lancaster tramway had unusual toastrack trams with the seats being raised higher than normal, giving the appearance of an observation tramcar.

This Northampton tramcar has longitudinal seats but is still of a very light construction with no windows and a light roof.

The Cambridge tramcar has more comfort in the cold weather with a fully enclosed saloon.

A Chesterfield inside (single deck) tramcar, a very similar tramcar has been restored and can be seen at Crich Tramway Village.

Very typical of the light construction used on the early horse trams. This was the first tramcar to run in Leicester.

The Wirral tramways had very similar inside tramcars.

A small one horse tramcar used on the West Metropolitan Tramways in London.

Despite being a lightweight single deck tramcar this Darlington car still needs two horses to haul it.

Paisley tramways obviously wanted to maximise the advertising potential of their trams.

Inside passenger cars on the City of Oxford & District Tramways Company made by Starbuck.

A very early double deck tramcar of the Metropolitan Street Tramways – note the simple spiral stairs.

In 1927 the Birkenhead tramway celebrated the 50th anniversary of the Act formally approving the town's tramway. A replica of an original tramcar was made, complete with simple ladder stairs. While the passengers are in period costume, in reality ladies would not have travelled on the upper deck until decency panels were fitted to trams.

This Dublin tramcar has been fitted with decency panels, but still retains the simple stairs. The knifeboard seating on the upper deck is clearly shown.

would have been far too heavy for the horses) with either a single-deck or open-top double-deck body. The wheelbase of the tramcar was around a quarter of its whole length. This was to reduce the friction on the tight curves that were necessary to follow the twists and turns of town and city streets. While this did reduce the effort needed by the horses there was an unfortunate side effect. The tramcar tended to pitch considerably on uneven track and many systems had poorly maintained trackwork, particularly towards the end of their life. The life of a tramcar was expected to be at least 25 years and some lasted for far longer than this.

The recognised expert in horse tramways, Rob Jones, has defined the seminal points of a street tramcar to be:

- A low floor with wheels that protruded through the floor, usually disguised under a seat.
- No separate chassis, the axle-guards are bolted directly to the car body.
- A short wheelbase for tight cornering.
- A platform for the driver with a sight line just above the horse(s) (as opposed to the elevated position on coaches and omnibuses).
- A step up to platform.
- Driveable from both ends (excluding reversible or single ended cars).
- Have multiple access points at platforms i.e. both sides.
- A vehicle that is lightweight compared to other vehicles on the road.
- Generally of elegant design.

Inside Passenger Car

This is the terminology of the time for what today is called a single-deck tramcar; the earliest tramcars were mainly single-deck. The very first (the Oystermouth Tramroad and the New York and Harlem Railroad) show the influence of the stage coach and horse omnibus, including placing the driver on a seat on the roof copying stage coaches and omnibuses. By the time the first lines opened in Britain the single-deck tramcar had

Another early tramcar, this time from Bristol, showing the simple spiral stairs and no decency boards. It is obviously some occasion, with the gentleman with a top hat on the step next to the driver.

The opening of the Cardiff Tramways Company line in 1872, with early design tramcars, note the spiral stairs are of the reversed design.

Liverpool also had reverse stairs tramcars.

developed into a recognisably different vehicle. One major difference between tramcars and coaches and omnibuses is that the latter two had shafts or central poles that the horses were attached to. This meant that the horses could slow the vehicles as well as pull them along. On most tramcars the horse(s) were attached to the tramcar by a harness that was unclipped at the terminus and the horse led around to the other end. This did not allow the horse to slow the tram down, so the driver had to apply a brake to prevent the tramcar running into the back of the horses harming them. By placing the driver on the platform the handbrake could be made more efficient. The handbrake on the tramcar acted on the outer edges of the wheels, so applying the brake put pressure on the wheel bearings and forced them towards each other, tending to shorten the wheelbase. The leverage on the braking system was such that a firm application of the handbrake could put as much as one ton pressure on the wheels. There was also a small box clipped onto the dash panel that held sand, so the driver could throw a handful onto the rails when they were wet or greasy to prevent skidding. In most instances the driver stood on the platform or if he was really lucky he could sit on a stool.

To counter the pressure of the brakes the bodies of the trams had tension struts on each side going from the inside of the bulkhead going up at an angle then supported above the floor of the car to the other bulkhead. Where the braking effect tried to bend the platforms down, the tension struts held them up to prevent a 'banana' effect happening to the bodywork. These struts were not seen by the public because they were mounted under the saloon seats.

For the first tramway line opened in Birkenhead Train had purchased two double-deck and two single-deck cars. The single-deck tramcars had seating for 22 passengers and he claimed room for a similar number standing. They were hauled by two horses. George Shillibeer's early horse omnibus was single-deck, had a capacity of 22 passengers (none standing) and was hauled by three horses. Later the single-deck tramcar settled to a vehicle seating between 14 and 16 passengers and was hauled by one horse. Early single-deck cars had roofs whose section was double curved in a design called "Turtle Back", where the centre line of the roof was raised above the sides giving more headroom for passengers walking down the central isle. The seating was longitudinal with two lines of passengers sitting opposite each other.

Later the roof design changed to a "Monitor Roof" with a clerestory and vertical windows to give additional light into the tramcar. The manufacturers were constantly seeking ways of reducing the weight of the tramcar. As materials and techniques developed the windows became larger and so there were less of them on each tram. Train's original trams had nine windows on each side and by the time electric tramcars replaced them, the number of windows on some horse trams had reduced to three. The standard single-deck tramcar weighed around 1¼ tons unloaded and 2½ tons fully loaded and was usually hauled by a single horse.

Some systems, usually the smaller companies, made major changes to reduce the weight of their trams by going to the minimum of tramcar, the "Toastrack" type, that was merely rows of seats on a chassis, with a slight deference to the British weather in some instances by having a roof making the tramcar into a "Crossbench" type. These were particularly popular on seaside systems, though some unlikely systems had toastrack trams including Aberdeen, Belfast, Bradford, Leeds, Nottingham, Sheffield and Stirling. To be fair they were usually used on the very lightly patronised routes where a light tramcar with a single horse would be used as a one man operated car to minimise costs.

Inside and Outside Passenger Car

This is the terminology of the time for what is now called a double-deck open top tramcar. All double-deck horse tramcars were open top as adding a closed top would increase the weight so much that the strain on the lower deck saloon would be too excessive, and also the effort required to haul the vehicle would mean needing far more horses at considerable extra cost. This was accepted by the travelling public because the alternative, the double-deck horse bus, was also open topped. Like so many things the result was both welcomed and abhorred. On a hot summer's day travelling on the open top meant a cooling breeze and a view of the town, but on a rainy day without an umbrella the passengers crowded inside the saloon, cursing the open top.

The early double-deck tramcars had very crude stairs, really just iron ladders, to give access to the upper deck. The seating on the open top was 'knifeboard', that is longitudinal back to back seats with the passengers looking out sideways. These seats were fitted on top of the monitor roof. The passengers on the upper deck had a simple railing to prevent them from falling off the tramcar. So the whole of their legs were visible from the street. This prevented the prudish Victorian ladies from using the upper deck, the climb up the ladder and the risk of exposing an ankle to view when seated on the upper deck meant they were confined to the saloon. The simple stairs, seating and railing were all designed to keep the weight to a minimum.

The first two changes were to provide spiral stairs, but still simple iron ladders, making access to the upper deck simpler and speeding up passenger flow; and the provision of "decency panels", planks of wood along the outer sides of the upper deck, that were fitted to hide passenger's legs. These were found to have a beneficial side effect, they could be used as advertising hoardings and thus gain more revenue for the operator.

The next change was to provide a proper staircase, a set of spiral stairs with a flat step, solid riser, stringers and a handrail. This was far easier to use and again sped up the movement of passengers at stops and made it more acceptable for ladies to use the upper deck. This was heavier than the previous types of stairs, but the ease to the passenger more than made up for this. Around the 1880s the type of seating on the upper deck underwent a major change. It was found that by placing a more level upper deck floor "garden seating" could be fitted. In this design a number of double seats were fitted across the tramcar with a narrow passageway between them. The seating was relatively lightweight and had a back that was hinged so the seat could be set the other way at the terminus, so passengers always faced the direction of travel.

The standard double-deck open top tramcar weighed around 2½ tons unloaded and 6 tons with a full passenger complement and was usually hauled by two horses though on hilly routes "trace" horses were used to help the regular horses haul the tramcar up the hills. The principle that the tramway aspired to was to have sufficient tramcars in service to ensure that a tramcar was always in sight. Trams were required to stop on average four times per mile. This stopping and starting placed the most stress on the car body, particularly on double-deck tramcars where the weight of the upper deck passengers placed a great strain on the woodwork, particularly when braking. There was a similar strain when the tramcar started off with the horses dragging the car along. Such was the effect of the weight of the upper deck passengers that the single-deck tramcar always lasted longer than the double-deck car.

In the late 1870s some tramway companies looked at the possibility of putting light canvass covers on the top deck of the tramcar in wet weather. The cover was made very light and it was thought that the extra weight would not affect the horses. However, it was soon found that the covers acted like the sails of a ship. When the wind was either at the side or directly into the tram the force was sufficient to impede the horses and exhaust them. One tramcar was fitted with such a cover and was tried by the North Metropolitan Tramways Company. They found that the teams of horses were so exhausted that after ten days they were no longer able to work and had to be rested.

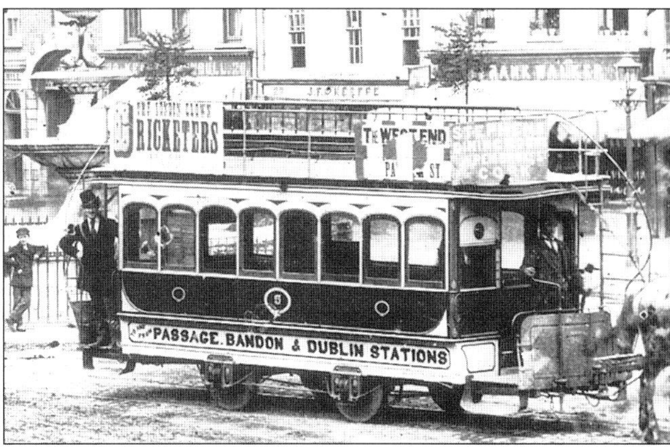

Cork Tramways Company had reverse spiral stairs and this photograph shows the construction, with a centre pole and metal rod steps like the spokes of a wheel.

This Birkenhead tramcar now has a more conventional set of stairs. In future this design was used almost exclusively on tramcars.

In Sheffield the old style stairs were retained, but the trams were fitted with decency panels (while taking the opportunity to earn more revenue by selling advertising).

This Southampton tramcar shows a later form of the double deck tramcar, with decency panels and substantial stairs, but retaining the upper deck knifeboard seating. Note also the sand box on the dash panel.

The lack of decency panels on this Falcon built Derby tramcar allows full view of the new garden type seating on the upper deck.

Similarly this Great Grimsby car has the new style garden seats and staircase but has yet to be fitted with decency panels.

Once decency boards were fitted the upper deck became suitable for ladies, as this group show in Aberdeen.

Views of horse tramcars from above are scarce; this shows the tops of two Belfast tramcars with the garden seats.

The restored Eades reversible tramcar at Heaton Park Heritage Tramway. (Alan Kirkman)

This North Metropolitan Tramways car has access from both sides of the platform. This was dangerous as passengers could alight towards the centre of the road and were liable to be knocked down by other traffic. After a series of such accidents tramcars were modified so that passengers could only access and alight on the pavement side.

There was a type of tramcar in New York that used similar principles to the Eades cars that gained the name 'Balloon' car owing to its shape.

There were other single ended tramcars in America such as this New York tramcar, but they had to be turned at the terminus using turning circles, triangles or turntables.

Reversible Tramcar

The standard double-deck horse tramcar is a double-ended vehicle, with two platforms and two stairs. However, for any one journey the staircase at the driver's end is surplus to requirements and is carried just to be ready for use on the return journey. In 1877 the manager of the Manchester Carriage & Tramway Company workshop, Mr John Eades, designed a tramcar to obviate this disadvantage. His idea was to have a single ended body mounted on a special chassis, so that at the terminus the body of the tramcar could be swivelled around on the chassis so it faced the other way. A prototype was built and tried by the Manchester operator and proved a great success and more were built. Other operators expressed an interest in buying this design of tramcar, so the design was licensed to the Ashbury Railway Carriage & Iron Company Limited. However, Eades' design was not the first to use this idea. John Stephenson in 1859 in New York built a reversible tramcar, patenting aspects of the design. Also in the 1860s in San Francisco the Sutter Street Railway Company used reversible "balloon cars" on their line. These tramcars were designed by Henry Casebolt. Similar types of tramcars were also used in Paris. It is not possible to say at this distance whether Eades was influenced by these developments or if he came to a similar idea independently.

The reversible design was not quite as simple as it may seem. The first problem was to ensure that the body could rotate on the chassis. The chassis had a central king pin with a circular support strip. The weight distribution of the body had to be calculated with care to keep everything level and stable while the body was turned. The body had to be locked in position after turning (to make sure it did not try to turn around during normal use). This was achieved by using a locking lever located by the driver's position. The final problem was the brakes. There was only one brake handle and this was on the driver's platform. So the chain attachment to the underfloor braking levers was on a hook. The chain would be unhooked from under the tramcar before turning the body and then hooked back on to the brake gear on the other end of the tram (during this manoeuvre the brakes were locked in place). In fact there was a second, emergency, brake on the bulkhead on the passengers' platform that would be used by the conductor if the driver became unable to operate his brake (because there was no access to the driver's platform from the rest of the tramcar). The actual turning of the body was done by the horse(s) pulling the front around while still attached to the harness. The tramcar incorporated one further refinement as the wheels on one side were free to revolve on the axle. This reduced the effect of friction on curves as the wheels could rotate at the most effective speed for them on the curve, hence reducing the effort required from the horses.

To save further weight the Eades' design shortened the standard tramcar, though it was still able to seat 16 passengers inside and 18 outside (on a knifeboard seat), giving a total of 34 passengers. The total weight of the tramcar was under 1¾ tons, or equivalent to one cwt per passenger, the lowest ratio by far of any British double-deck tramcar. Eades claimed that his design gave a saving of 30% over a standard double-deck tramcar and it could be operated by just 8 horses, compared to the 12 needed by a standard car. These claims must have been justified as many other systems used the design.

Tramcar Liveries

It has been often said that horse tramcars were painted different colours, depending on which route they were operating on, because the population of the time was largely illiterate and could only recognise the tram they needed by its colour. This is a simplistic way of seeing the situation. There are two reasons for believing that the literacy of the population was much better, first the custom of tramcar (and omnibus) operators to write the termini and intermediate places on the vehicle and secondly many tramcars were covered in advertising posters, which needed to be read to make sense. Indeed the very large Manchester horse tramway system painted all their cars red and white, irrespective of the route. It is more likely that public service operators wanted their vehicles to stand out. So they were painted in bright primary colours, so they were easily seen. The practice of assigning a particular colour to a route was probably done so that intending passengers could recognise the tramcar they wanted from a much further distance than trying to read route boards. This is a practice that some of today's bus operators have experimented with. The main disadvantage is that once painted a vehicle is committed to just one route and the operator loses the flexibility of being able to use any of the fleet on any route.

Many early tramcars followed the stage coach and omnibus practice of naming vehicles, for example the tramcar used by Train on his Westminster route was named "The People", although he did not name the first tramcars he used in Birkenhead. However, one thing they did have in common was an elaborate and ornate finish. All of Train's tramcars had large coats of arms, the Birkenhead cars also had their number on the side enclosed in a large painted floral wreath. This was all to promote the tramcar as a refined mode of transport. As tramways expanded the operators favoured either displaying the company name on the side of the tramcar or the major place(s) visited on the route. Quite early on the trams acquired numbers and started a new hobby among young boys, spotting tram numbers. This had started earlier in the century with stage coaches, but in the larger towns and cities the larger fleets would definitely occupy boys.

Where route colours were used they were bright primary colours, to be highly visible. Generally the trams were painted a light colour around the windows, usually white or pale cream and then on the panel below the windows the darker colour for the top half of the panel and the white or cream on the bottom half. The dividing line being the horizontal waist rail, a piece of wood designed to prevent the panel from being damaged if the tram rubbed against another vehicle. Possibly the most unusual route colour was "Tartan". The latter is a difficult livery to paint, so what the operators did was to paste tartan printed paper over the tram's panels and varnish over to make it waterproof. However it was more usual for solid colours to be used.

As tramways sought every possibility for income they would sell advertising space on their cars. The favourite place was the side of the decency boards of double-deck cars. This was a large flat area that was easily seen by the public and so attractive to advertisers. Some single-deck cars would have advertising boards fitted to their roofs, making them look at first glance like a double-deck car. Sometimes the advertising became so extensive that, with destination indicators, the actual colour of the tramcar was almost completely hidden.

Paris also had reversible tramcars, shown clearly in this photograph.

In Sheffield an Eades reversible tramcar made by the Ashbury company is being turned around.

On the driver's bulkhead is the handle that unlocks the body from the chassis, allowing it to be turned around.

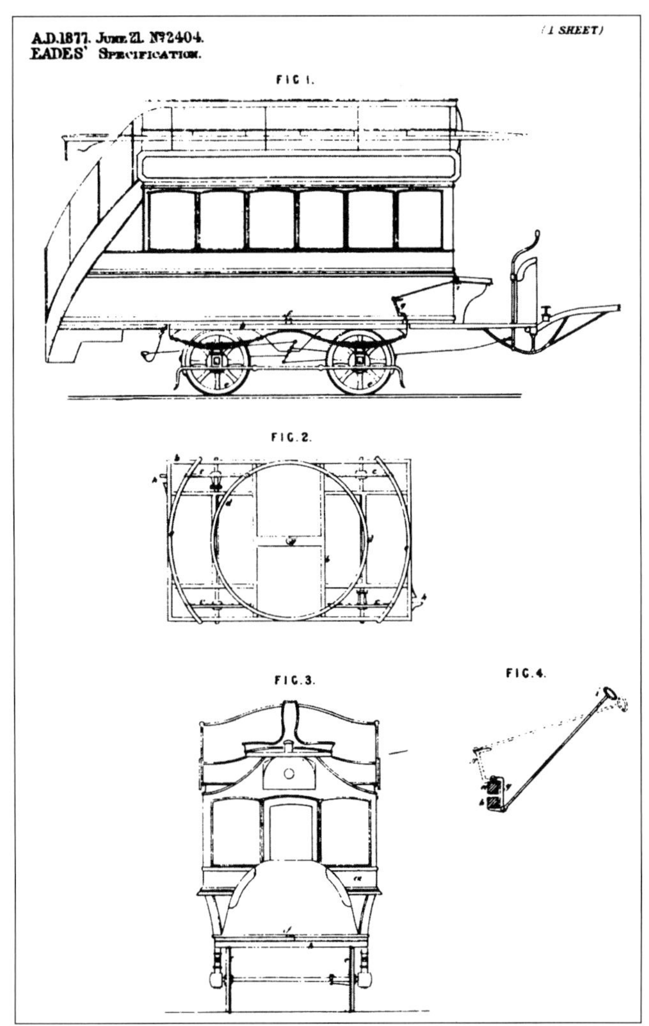

The Eades design as detailed in his patent.

On the passenger platform is another lever, this is a handbrake for the conductor to use in emergency.

Single deck reversible tramcars were also made to the Eades patent.

Liverpool had some single-ended tramcars with double staircases at the passenger end. Built by the tramway itself after failing to get a licence to build to the Eades design, the track layouts at the termini had to be altered with triangles or loops allowing the whole tram to be turned.

Political Affairs

The history of the development and subsequent decline of horse tramways is intertwined with national and local politics. From the very beginning laying tramway track in public streets has caused disagreements between tramway promoters and those in public office. The first to suffer from the views of politicians was George Francis Train. When he laid tracks in Birkenhead he had the agreement of the local Councillors and no major objections were raised, so the matter did not come to a head. However, things were far more complex when he moved to London. He did obtain the agreement of the local Councillors for each of his three lines. However, the step rail he used did cause inconvenience and damage to the vehicles of other road users. Some of these were very powerful and influential people including omnibus operators who resented the competition. The local authorities had to take notice and the matter came to a head on the Surrey Side Street Railway Company tramway. He was charged with making the roads dangerous for the public and appeared before the Kingston Assizes. The magistrates determined that it was illegal to lay track in the street without parliamentary authority, because it interfered with the rights of the public to use the road. Therefore they found him guilty and he was ordered to remove the track. Being Train he did not remove the track, but carried on running his trams. This forced the Sheriff of Surrey to order a gang of workmen to remove the track, thus closing the tramway operation. Faced with the likelihood of this situation being repeated for the other two London lines, Train ceased operating and removed the rails. He then headed for the quieter surroundings of the Potteries. Given that Train had not obtained any Acts for any of his tramways he was perhaps lucky to have been prosecuted only once. However, it must be realised that this was all very new to the British legal system and tramway entrepreneurs and legal experts alike were very unsure of what laws applied. Train had gained approval of the local authorities and until the Surrey Side Street Railway Company no one had complained about this aspect of the tramway.

This now meant that future tramways needed to obtain a Private Act of Parliament to legally build tramways in the street. Of all the countries in the world only Britain and France put the authorisation and control of tramways in the hands of central government. All other countries, including America, allowed the local authorities to authorise and control tramways in their districts. Private Acts of Parliament were costly and lengthy processes, subject to the whims of politicians, most of whom were resistant to this new form of transport. Despite this a number of smaller tramway Bills were presented to Parliament. The Landport and Southsea Bill was presented in 1863 and became an Act the same year and, soon after, Bills were brought in for much larger systems, three for London and another for Liverpool. These all failed, being thrown out by Standing Orders. In 1869 the Liverpool Tramways Bill entered Parliament and succeeded, though not without some opposition in the House of Commons. The following year Bills for tramways in London were passed and became Acts. In 1870 the then President of the Board of Trade proposed an Act that would authorise the Board of Trade to issue certificates allowing tramways to be built without the need for Parliament to agree through an Act. The proposal was considerably changed and emerged as the 1870 Tramways Act, in which the basic requirements were set out. The Act required

[33 & 34 VICT.] *Tramways.* [CH. **78.**]

CHAP. 78.

An Act to facilitate the construction and to regulate the working of Tramways. [9th August 1870.]

A.D. 1870.

BE it enacted by the Queen's most Excellent Majesty, by and with the advice and consent of the Lords Spiritual and Temporal, and Commons, in this present Parliament assembled, and by the authority of the same, as follows:

Preliminary.

1. This Act may be cited for all purposes as "The Tramways Act, 1870." — Short title.

2. This Act shall not extend to Ireland. — Limitation of Act.

3. For the purposes of this Act the terms herein-after mentioned shall have the meanings herein-after assigned to them; that is to say, — Interpretation of terms.

The terms "local authority" and "local rate" shall mean respectively the bodies of persons and rate named in the table in Part One of the schedule (A.) to this Act annexed:

The term "road" shall mean any carriageway being a public highway, and the carriageway of any bridge forming part of or leading to the same:

The term "road authority" shall mean, in the districts specified in the table in Part Two of the schedule (A.) to this Act annexed, the bodies of persons named in the same table, and elsewhere any local authority, board, town council, body corporate, commissioners, trustees, vestry, or other body or persons in whom a road as defined by this Act is vested, or who have the power to maintain or repair such road:

The term "district," in relation to a local authority or road authority, shall mean the area within the jurisdiction of such local authority or road authority:

The term "prescribed" shall mean prescribed by any rules made in pursuance of this Act:

[*Public.-78.*] A 1

The first page of the Tramways Act 1870 that had an enormous effect on the development of tramways.

This photograph of the Folkestone, Sandgate & Hythe tramway clearly shows the part of the roadway under the responsibility of the tramway and the remainder maintained by the local authority.

promoters to make application to the Board of Trade for a Provisional Order. Where there were any issues then the Board of Trade could institute an enquiry. Once the Board of Trade were satisfied that the requirements of the 1870 Act were met they could issue a Provisional Order to the promoters. The Board of Trade would then have to put the Provisional Order before Parliament to confirm it. This confirmation was achieved by Parliament agreeing to the Provisional Order and making it an Act of Parliament (which may amend the original Provisional Order). Anyone objecting to the tramway could appear before a Select Committee to put their case. This procedure did not prohibit a tramway being sought under the old system of applying for a Private Act through a Private Bill and many tramways and extensions were authorised through that route as well.

The smooth surface of the rails were not just enjoyed by the tramcars. Solomon Andrews, an omnibus builder, patented this bus where the wheels were made to run on the tops of the rails.

The hands of politicians can be seen throughout the 1870 Act, with many obligations being placed on the tramway companies and few on the local Councils. Not least was the requirement prohibiting the local authority from operating tramways, though they could build and own the track and lease it to a commercial company. There was a strict time limit for each Act by which the tramway had to be laid, or the authority lapsed. In addition local concessions were often required to get agreement from local interests in order to obtain the removal of objections. Such requirements might well include free travel for firemen, postmen or telegraph messengers (the usual requirement was that they would have to be both in uniform and on duty). The local authority may well require the tramway to operate early morning tramcars at reduced fares for workmen. This was often resented by the tramway companies and there were instances of passengers on the workmen's cars being charged full fare because they wore clothes too good for workmen. The local authorities may also require the use of the tramway at night to move road material, sewage matter or refuse using tramcars owned by the local authority, though no record of this happening has been seen by the author, however it is quite likely that where the local authority was responsible for the up keep of the tram tracks, they may well have had their own tramcars and wagons to carry road material and rails. This can be seen today in the arrangements for the Blackpool Tramways where the Corporation is responsible for maintaining and replacing track and have their own works tramcar and trailers.

The Act placed the onus for the repair of the road surface of the tram tracks on the tramway operators. It was felt that the horses drawing tramcars would not only walk between the rails, but would wander either side of the track and so wear away the road surface. So the tramway operator was responsible for the maintenance and repairs of the road surface between the rails and for 18 inches either side of the track, or in the case of double track, for all the road surface between the tracks if the distance between the inner rails was not more than four feet. In the early days it was not unusual for the part of the road maintained by the tramway to have a surface of granite or wooden setts, while the part maintained by the Council was mud and stones. So it was not surprising that other road users travelled on the good surface with double problems for the tramway, the carts and omnibuses wore out the surface and at the same time they interfered with the running of the trams. This provision was particularly onerous on later electric tramways when their trams only wore away the tops of the rails, while the tramway had to pay for the maintenance of most of the road that was worn by other road traffic, particularly their opponents the bus services. In addition, and just as acrimonious, the tramway was required to pay rates on the track (in addition normal rates were also payable on buildings and land) on the basis of the gross income of the tramway. So the tramway paid rates on the road that they maintained! This was equally true for municipal tramways as well as privately owned tramways. Much later, when tramways were being closed, the local Councils kept very quiet about the loss to the public purse of the rates paid by the tramways.

For many systems the track was owned, built and maintained by the local authority and then leased to a private company to run the tram service. Frequently the contracts that were entered into meant that the local authority could build routes where they chose and the company had to pay rent on those routes, whether they were profitable or not. In some cases the geography of the new routes was unsuitable for horse tramways due to steep hills, but the company still had to pay rent even thought the tracks were never used. It can be understood that this would lead to considerable acrimony between the Corporation and the company. The second major difficulty with this arrangement was that the Corporation would make savings by failing to repair or maintain the track to the proper standards. The resulting poor track would make travel uncomfortable for passengers and damage the tramcars, all seen by the public as the fault of the tramway company.

Other systems were built by the promoters who then owned the track, but had to pay the local authority rates for the privilege of having rails in the streets. In these circumstances promoters would need to obtain the agreement of the local authority. Unless they agreed, any approaches by the company to government would be immediately rejected because the 1870 Act stated:

'Provisional Orders authorizing the construction of Tramways in any district may be obtained by-
(1) The local authority of such district; or by-
(2) Any person, persons, corporation; or company, with the consent of the local authority of such district; or of the road authority of such district where such district is or forms part of a highway district formed under the provision of "The Highway Acts".'

Even this was not as straightforward as it seems. In many of the proposed tramway systems the routes that appeared to offer the best prospects of revenue might well cross boundaries into different districts, particularly in large conurbations where the city Corporations had smaller geographic areas than today, where boundaries have been expanded on many occasions. So the promoters of the new tramway would need to get the consent of two, possibly more, local authorities. Sometimes a small local authority, that needed to give consent for a small length of tramway that was essential for a route that was likely to be well patronised, found themselves in a powerful position and may well make costly demands. They may insist that where a proposed route went through a narrow road the tramway company would have to pay for the road widening. Other contentious areas were bridges, where the bridge was sufficient for a horse and cart, but not for a tramcar. Of course the local authority could take a pessimistic view of what needed improv-

This end view of the Solomon Andrews car shows the relationship of the wheels and rails. Ironically Solomon Andrews was also a director of several tramways.

A contemporary sketch of the Westminster Street Rail Company tramway, one of Train's first tramways in London.

ing, since the tramway company would be paying for the improvements. There were further complications if the proposed tramway was to pass over a railway on a level crossing. (This got even more difficult when electric traction was being introduced, as the railways were concerned that stray currents would interfere with the railway signalling systems.) Local Authorities would also demand a deposit to be paid by the promoters which was sufficient to reinstate the roads should the tramway go into liquidation before the tramway was completed. This was because of the experiences of the authorities when water and gas companies dug up roads to lay their pipes and then failed to reinstate the road properly. The result was that the local authority got the blame for bad roads then had to pay for repairs to damage caused by the companies. There were some rather unusual conditions, such as some London Councils insisting on the tramway agreeing to the Council using Council trams to remove sewage waste during the night. It is likely that the local inhabitants were grateful that this provision was never used.

Another disadvantage to the companies was the contentious clauses allowing local authorities to compulsory purchase tramways (21 years after the authority to build). As they started to become effective, so the Corporations wanted to operate the tramways themselves. This was prohibited in the 1870 Act and Corporations wanting to operate tramways had to get a private Act passed. The situation changed slightly with the passing of the 1896 Light Railways Act, which allowed local authorities to run their own light railways. As there was no definition of 'tramway' or 'light

Like many Councils the London County Council found itself the operator of all the horse tramways in their area as it purchased tramways compulsorily prior to electrification.

railway' and the provisions of the 1896 Act were better than the 1870 Act many systems were built under the light railway provisions, though to the layman they looked just like tramways. [As mentioned later the term 'tramway' was not defined until The Transport and Works Act 1992 and this was refined by the Railways and Other Guided Transport Systems (Safety) Regulations 2006. There is still no legal definition of a 'light railway']. This change in attitude meant that where local authorities wanted to operate their own tramways Parliament was more amenable and was passing private Acts to allow various Corporations to become tramway operators.

However, the compulsory purchase of existing tramways was probably the most contentious issue between tramway companies and public bodies. An independent observer must have sympathy for the owners of a successful tramway operation when they are told that the Corporation had the power to buy the system at scrap metal value. All the potential profits and the goodwill built up by the operators were disregarded. Obviously the owners wanted the very best price for their operation, while the Corporation wanted to pay the absolute minimum. Negotiations were often very contentious, not made any easier where the Corporation wanted to change from horse operation, but did not know what was the best alternative for their town. The Corporation knew that they would have to relay the rails, as all the alternatives meant much heavier tramcars. So conversion was going to be expensive and no matter how good the tracks were, they would have to be replaced. In most instances the discussion over the price to be paid went to arbitration and like many arbitration situations the recommendation was somewhere between the two prices. Sometimes the Corporation did not wish to be involved with horse tramway operation and would arrange for the company to continue to run the horse side of the service until they were all replaced by the electric trams (inevitably the system of choice). Other Corporations took a different view and took over the horse car operation while their system was being converted. Possibly the most acrimonious takeover was that of Glasgow, where it appears that the councillors deliberately made difficulties for the company and although the company had offered to sell their tramcars to the Corporation they refused and then told the public that new tramcars would have to be purchased because the company refused to sell their trams to the Corporation. This appears to have been done to ensure that the Corporation started with a new fleet of tramcars without the voters feeling that the Corporation was wastefully spending their rates. In 1870 these disadvantages were not seen as overwhelming. The tramways were horse-drawn so the road repair provisions were accepted and 21 years was a long time when a tramway was just starting off. So the 1870 Act was used by most if not all new tramways in the following few years, until some tramways were able to use more favourable provisions under the Light Railways Act 1896.

The precise wording of the 1870 Act was:

> *"Where the promoters of a tramway in any district are not the local authority, the local authority, if, by resolution passed at a special meeting of the members constituting such a local authority, they so decide, may, within six months after the expiration of a period of twenty-one years from the time when such promoters were empowered to construct such tramway, and within six months after the expiration of every subsequent period of seven years, or within three months after any order made by the Board of Trade under either of the two next preceding sections, with the approval of the Board of Trade by notice in writing, require such promoters to sell, and thereupon such promoters shall sell to them their undertaking, or so much of the same as is within such district, upon terms of paying the then value (exclusive of any allowance for past or future profits of the undertaking, or any compensation for compulsory sale, or other consideration whatsoever) of the tramway, and all lands, buildings, works, materials, and plant of the promoters suitable to and used by them for the purposes of their undertaking within such district, such value to be in the case of difference determined by an engineer or other fit person nominated as referee by the Board of Trade on the application of either party, and the expenses of the reference to be borne and paid as the referee directs."*

Note that the language is typical of Acts of Parliament and all the complexities referred to are contained in one sentence. What it does mean is that the local authority had a six-month slot after twenty-one years and similar slots every seven years in which to write to the promoters if they wished to purchase the tramway

Glasgow Corporation was in a similar situation.

compulsorily. Some Corporations missed this critical fact and wrote outside that period and the promoters were able to reject the approach. This meant that if the local authority wanted to buy the tramway they had to negotiate a commercial price. There was an added complexity as most tramways did not obtain authority for a complete tramway from the outset. It would often evolve, with different routes being approved at different times. So when the local authority wanted to buy the tramway they would have to buy it in parts, often spread over many years. This was a particular problem for the London County Council where there were not only different dates, but also many different operators. Also the powers only extended to the lines laid within the local authority district. So a route that crossed the district boundary to finish a few hundred yards inside an adjoining district meant that the local authority had to negotiate with their neighbour that the neighbour would give notice of compulsory purchase at the same time and then once having purchased that part of the line they would allow the first local authority to run the tramway. At times this became very complex and if there were extensive cross-boundary routes, such as Manchester and Salford, each may well wish to run their own systems and complex through-running agreements had to be made. Manchester had similar through running agreements with Ashton-Under-Lyne but had a confrontation with them when the Manchester parcels cars made deliveries using Ashton tram lines. Ashton Corporation objected arguing that the agreement did not cover the running of the parcels cars and Manchester were effectively stealing Ashton's electricity. The city of Glasgow had particular problems, some of which were resolved as the city boundary grew and absorbed other local authority land. In Morecambe the Corporation purchased three-quarters of the Morecambe Tramways Co. system, leaving the company with just 1¼ miles of tramway. It is not surprising that in such complex situations the legal profession found much work.

There was another, more hidden, control that the local authorities had over tramways. This was to do with the fares charged, the local rates and where the local authority owned the track, leasing charges. The 1870 Act required the definition of the fares to be charged, generally set at 1d per mile with a minimum charge of 2d. Later the Board of Trade required that any application for a new tramway needed to have a requirement that passenger fares could be revised by the Board of Trade three years from the opening of the tramway, or after three years from a previous similar revision. The revision could be requested by the local authority, or a body of twenty ratepayers, or the promoters. Before any changes were made there was to be an enquiry conducted by a referee appointed by the Board of Trade. In effect the request from the promoter would be to increase the fares while those from the local authority or the rate payers would seek to reduce the fares. No doubt the referee would seek to discover the profits made by the tramway and where these were considered excessive there could be an order for a reduction in fares. The tramway promoters were also required to pay rates where they owned the track or leasing charges where the local authority owned it. This was in addition to the usual rates payable on all the business buildings and premises they had. The rates charged for the track was directly related to the receipts on the tramway for the previous year. The higher the income of the tramway then the greater the amount was taken by the local authority. Similar situations existed for the leasing costs. The result for the tramway was the threat of financial penalties for being successful and a reduction in the dividends payable to the shareholders.

Strangely the vital thing missing from the 1870 Act was a definition of a tramway and from the 1896 Act a definition of a Light Railway. Subsequently a judge stated that such a definition was not needed because it was self evident when an operation was a tramway. However, in later days such a definition was felt necessary and a legal definition of a tramway was included in "The Transport and Works Act 1992", while Light Railway, strangely, is still in a legal limbo. The new definition was:

> *"tramway" means a system of transport used wholly or mainly for the carriage of passengers and employing parallel rails which—*
> *(a) provide support and guidance for vehicles carried on flanged wheels, and*
> *(b) are laid wholly or mainly along a street or in any other place to which the public has access (including a place to which the public has access only on making a payment);*

This definition was found not to cover the new tramways as they are wholly or mainly laid on a private right of way. Therefore a new definition was given in "The Railways and Other Guided Transport Systems (Safety) Regulations 2006" thus:

> *"tramway" means a system of transport used wholly or mainly for the carriage of passengers—*
>
> *(a) which employs parallel rails which—*
>
> *(i) provide support and guidance for vehicles carried on flanged wheels;*
>
> *(ii) are laid wholly or partly along a road or in any other place to which the public has access (including a place to which the public has access only on making a payment);*
>
> *and*
>
> *(b) on any part of which the permitted maximum speed is such as to enable the driver to stop a vehicle in the distance he can see to be clear ahead;*

The Tramways Act 1870 had defined the "the uppermost surface of the rail shall be on a level with the surface of the road". This allowed the use of the 'step' rail where the road surface was built level with the top of the step, but then there was a ¾ inch drop to the lower part of the rail. Other road users complained and with court actions for damaging other carriages and carts the tramways had no alternative but to use the grooved rail. In the earliest days it was thought that tramcars would not stay on the rails unless the flange of the tram wheels was at least 1¼ inches deep. But by the time British street tramways were being constructed it had been found that just ½ inch was sufficient.

Then it was discovered that the brakes acting on the tread of the wheels wore it away, without affecting the flange. So the flange became deeper, while the groove remained the same. After a while the flange started to roll on the base of the groove. This did two things; firstly it increased the friction considerably because of the contact by two different radii on the same rail; secondly the flange wore away the bottom of the groove, where the rail was inherently weaker, eventually splitting away the thinner groove edge from the rail. The solution was remarkably simple and is still used today. The brake block was shaped to cover the whole of the tread and the flange. So when the brake was applied the flange was worn away at the same rate as the tread. This gave the operator a fortuitous advantage; the life of the wheel was prolonged.

At this early date there were enormous differences about what sort of grooved rail should be used. There were many different types of rail being patented, all claiming to be better than the others. The main differences were not in the design of the groove, but in the support and method of fixing. The technology of the time did not allow a 'girder' type of rail to be rolled. The section of the rail had to be much smaller and consequently it was far lighter than later rail. On many designs the top of the rail was a separate piece fixed either on wooden supports or on further metal components. But by the time tramways were being converted to electrical traction the girder rail was universally accepted.

Section 2

THE TRAMCAR MANUFACTURERS

The earliest tramcars to run in the British Isles were either American imports from a variety of manufacturers in the New York area or were produced locally by carriage manufacturers. The American John Stephenson set up his company in 1830 and made his first tramcar in 1832. However his first recorded export of trams to Britain was not until 1869 – an order for 24 cars for the Liverpool system (though it is likely that some of the trams used by George Francis Train came from Stephenson). George Starbuck set up his tramcar business in 1868 and sold his first trams to a British operator in 1871 (to the Leeds Tramways Co.). As the tramway boom accelerated more manufacturers turned their hands to making tramcars. Some came from the railway background such as The Metropolitan Railway Carriage and Wagon Co.; Ashbury Railway Carriage and Iron Co.; Brown Marshalls Ltd; Gloucester Railway Carriage and Wagon Co.; Lancaster Railway Carriage and Wagon Co.; and Oldbury Railway Carriage and Wagon Co.

As the larger tramway operators gained experience in repairing their tramcars they moved into modifying them, such as making single-deck cars into double-deck and replacing knifeboard seating with garden seats. From there it was a logical step to make the whole tramcar themselves. Some even manufactured tramcars for other operators. Smaller tramway systems often turned to local coach builders to supply tramcars, with very variable results. The manufacturers are examined in more detail below.

NOTE

The lists of customers and numbers of trams produced by each manufacturer have been compiled from such information as is available, mainly from the researches that have established the suppliers to the various tramway systems. They include only horse trams for systems in the British Isles, they do not include any exported or any steam or electric tramcars also built by the manufacturer.

The tramcar manufacturers are listed in alphabetical order. The numbers of tramcars in the listings does not indicate the size of the manufacturer as some also made considerable numbers of railway carriages and wagons, others made road coaches, omnibuses and carts and wagons, while some made considerable contributions to steam, cable and electric tramways, as well as having significant export sales.

KEY

D/D	Double-deck tramcar
S/D	Single-deck tramcar
T/R	Toastrack tramcar

The tables for each manufacturer show in the first column the year of manufacture; the second column the tramway system the tram(s) were sold to; and in the third column the number and type of tramcar.

ABERDEEN DISTRICT TRAMWAYS COMPANY

The beginnings of the Aberdeen and District Tramways Company are described in Section 3. The tramway company wanted a toastrack tramcar in 1889 and presumably being the simplest design the company asked their repair workshops to build the tramcar. This is the only tramcar that the company manufactured.

1889	Aberdeen District Tramways Co.	1 T/R

SOLOMON ANDREWS & SON

Solomon Andrews was a transport entrepreneur from Cardiff. He started in 1863 running a cab business with five hansom cabs and landaus. The business thrived and by 1873 he had 35 vehicles.

Solomon Andrews tramcar as supplied to Pontypridd.

Another Solomon Andrews tramcar, this on the Pwllheli and Llanbedrog tramway.

Around 1866 he expanded into omnibuses. The maintenance side of his empire had developed and around the 1870s he started manufacturing cabs and omnibuses. He patented a new design of omnibus with springs outside the wheels so that they could be set at the same distance as 3 feet 6 inches gauge tram track, thus allowing the driver to run on the rails, making life easier for the horses. He moved his workshops to the Atlas Coach Works and produced omnibuses for other operators. When the Cardiff District and Penarth Harbour Tramway was promoted he saw an opportunity and won the contract to build the tramcars. Owing to the conflict between his bus business and the Cardiff Tramways Company he was prevented from supplying them with tramcars. In 1887 he took on the running of the Pontypridd and Rhondda Valley Tramways Company and supplied the tramcars for the system. In 1893 he purchased land on the Welsh coast at Pwllheli to build a holiday resort called West End Estate. As part of the construction of houses and hotels he laid a tramway from a nearby quarry to the estate to carry building stone. Once the West End Hotel and the first houses were built he opened the tramway for passengers, using simple toastrack tramcars. He carried out a similar venture near Fairbourne, buying several farms and building a holiday resort by Arthog. Again a tramway was built to take stone from a local quarry to the building site. This line was laid to pass by Barmouth Junction Station so that it could be used by passengers going to the housing estate. A single toastrack tramcar was made by the Cardiff workshops and sent to the Barmouth Junction & Arthog Tramway in 1899. After completing nine houses as Mawddach Crescent it became evident that people were not attracted to the new holiday resort and the tramway was closed in 1903. The toastrack car was the last tram to be built by Solomon Andrews, though his omnibus business flourished.

1881	Cardiff District and Penarth Harbour Tramways Co.	5 D/D
1884	Cardiff District and Penarth Harbour Tramways Co.	2 D/D
1886	Cardiff District and Penarth Harbour Tramways Co.	4 D/D
1887	Pontypridd and Rhondda Valley Tramways Co.	6 D/D, 2 S/D
1894	Pwllheli and Llanbedrog Tramway	4 S/D, 8 T/R
1897	Pwllheli and Llanbedrog Tramway	2 T/R
1899	Pwllheli and Llanbedrog Tramway	1 S/D, 1 T/R
1899	Barmouth Junction & Arthog Tramways	1 T/R

ASHBURY RAILWAY CARRIAGE & IRON COMPANY LIMITED

John Ashbury established the Ashbury Carriage Company in 1837 in Manchester, the factory being in Commercial Street, Knott Mill, to build road carriages, carts and wagons. Soon a larger factory was required and the firm moved to Oxford Road, Ardwick. As the demand for railway rolling stock increased Ashbury started manufacturing railway rolling stock and larger premises were needed, so a new factory was built in 1846 on a site next to the Ashton-Under-Lyne & Manchester Railway in Ashton Old Road, Openshaw. The Ardwick workshop continued to be active until 1866. In 1862 it was registered as a limited company under the name Ashbury Railway Carriage & Iron Company Limited. In 1874 they had an order from the Glyn Valley Tramway for three tram-like carriages. However, tramcar production did not really get going until they reached an agreement with John Eades and the Manchester Carriage and Tramways Company to build the single ended reversible tramcars under licence. This tramcar had been very successfully used in Manchester and there was interest from other tramway systems, but the Manchester workshops were unable to manufacture them for other systems. So this licensing arrangement was agreed, with John Eades as Chief Designer. Some histories state that tramcars to the Eades patent were made by other manufacturers, under licence. Examination of photographs of the trams show that they are all built to a very standard design with all details the same. So it is more likely that the Ashbury factory built all the Eades type tramcars and for more distant clients shipped them out in parts for local assembly and painting, probably under the supervision of an Ashbury foreman. This hypothesis is supported by the failure of the Liverpool United Tramway to obtain a licence from Eades to build trams to his patent. The Ashbury factory had a steady flow of orders, interspersed with occasional double ended tramcars. Production of tramcars continued until the mid 1880s when demand started to tail off. Like most of the railway rolling stock manufacturers the company did not enter the electric tramcar field, although they built a sample electric tramcar for Manchester Corporation, but the Corporation were unhappy at the quality and placed their substantial order elsewhere. So in 1890 they built their last tramcar and the company continued making railway rolling stock. In 1902 the company was merged into the Metropolitan Amalgamated Railway Carriage & Wagon Co Ltd. (later to become Metropolitan-Cammell Carriage and Wagon Co. Ltd).

1874	Glyn Valley Tramway	2 S/D, 1 T/R
1878	North London Suburban Tramways Co.	12 S/D
1878	Newcastle & Gosforth Tramways & Carriage Co. Ltd	?
1879	Chester Tramways Co.	8 D/D
1879	Glasgow & Ibrox Tramway Co.	2 D/D
1880	Bolton & Suburban Tramways	30 D/D

An Ashbury made tramcar to the Eades reversible patent for the Liverpool tramways.

1880	Glasgow & Ibrox Tramway Co.	1 D/D
1880	Wigan Tramways Co. Ltd	8 D/D
1880	Glasgow & Ibrox Tramway Co.	1 S/D
1880	Wallasey United Tramways and Omnibus Co. Ltd	5 D/D
1881	St Helens and District Tramways Co.	6 D/D
1881	North London Suburban Tramways Co.	8 S/D
1882	Bradford City Tramways	13 D/D
1882	Chesterfield & District Tramways Co. Ltd	2 D/D, 1 S/D
1882	Lincoln Tramways Co.	2 S/D
1882	Bolton & Suburban Tramways	18 D/D
1883	Dudley, Sedgley & Wolverhampton Tramways Co. Ltd	7 D/D
1883	Huddersfield Corporation Tramways	2 D/D
1883	Leeds Tramways Co.	3 D/D
1883	Lincoln Tramways Co.	2 S/D
1883	Liverpool United Tramways & Omnibus Co.	55 D/D
1884	Lincoln Tramways Co.	1 S/D
1884	Sheffield Tramways Co.	4 S/D
1885	Bradford City Tramways	4 D/D
1885	Lincoln Tramways Co.	1 S/D
1886	Sheffield Tramways Co.	2 D/D
1887	Sheffield Tramways Co.	2 D/D
1887	Stirling and Bridge of Allan Tramways Co. Ltd	1 D/D
1890	South Shields Tramways & Carriage Co. Ltd	6 S/D

THOMAS B. AYSHFORD

In 1864, when the Ryde Pier Company sought a tramcar for the pier tramway there were no established tramcars. Indeed the tramcars in the country had been imported from America. So a representative was sent to London who found an omnibus and agricultural wagon manufacturer Thomas B. Ayshford, of Britannia Works, Walham Green. An order was placed for a vehicle that was similar to the horse omnibuses of the time, but with a platform each end. A second was ordered in 1865. These were the only tramcars made by Thomas Ayshford.

1864	Ryde Pier Tramways	1 S/D
1865	Ryde Pier Tramways	1 S/D

BELFAST STREET TRAMWAYS COMPANY LIMITED

The Belfast horse tramway company began operations in 1872 using German-built tramcars. As the system expanded they purchased Starbuck cars, but found that their own repair workshops were able to build tramcars for themselves. The first such trams were rolled out in 1888 and from that point the new tramcars were all built in the company facilities. The Belfast Street Tramways only built trams for their own system and not for any other tramway.

Home made by Belfast Street Tramways in their own workshops.

1888	Belfast Street Tramways Company Ltd	2 D/D
1889	Belfast Street Tramways Company Ltd	7 D/D
1890	Belfast Street Tramways Company Ltd	11 D/D
1891	Belfast Street Tramways Company Ltd	8 D/D
1893	Belfast Street Tramways Company Ltd	10 D/D
1894	Belfast Street Tramways Company Ltd	2 D/D
1895	Belfast Street Tramways Company Ltd	2 D/D
1897	Belfast Street Tramways Company Ltd	21 D/D
1898	Belfast Street Tramways Company Ltd	7 D/D
1899	Belfast Street Tramways Company Ltd	12 D/D
1900	Belfast Street Tramways Company Ltd	16 D/D
1901	Belfast Street Tramways Company Ltd	10 D/D
1902	Belfast Street Tramways Company Ltd	13 D/D

The Birmingham Railway Carriage & Wagon Company made this tramcar for Croydon tramways.

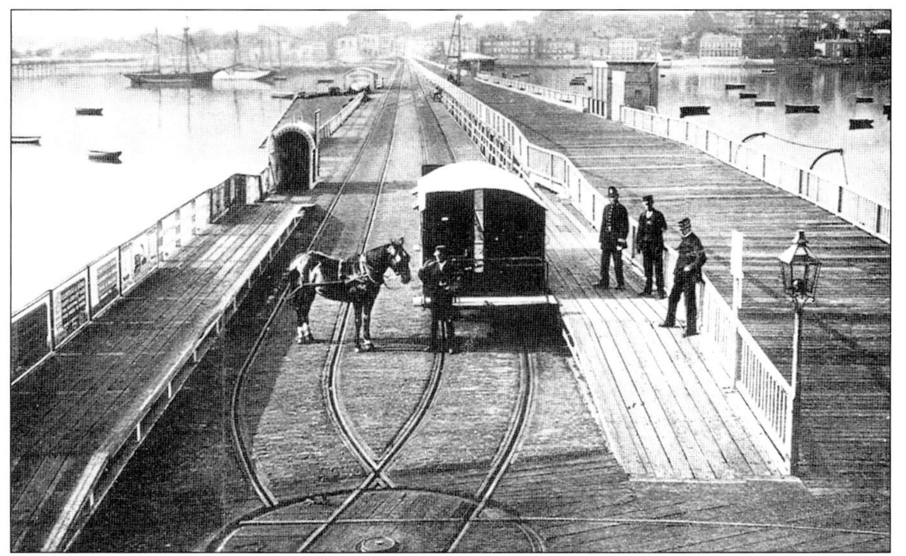
Thomas Ayshford built two of these types of tramcars for the Ryde Pier tramway.

BIRMINGHAM RAILWAY CARRIAGE & WAGON COMPANY LIMITED

The Birmingham Wagon Company was founded in 1854 as a company based in New Street, Birmingham that leased or sold under hire purchase railway wagons. At this stage they purchased their wagons from Brown, Marshalls and Co. The company became concerned that Brown, Marshalls would be unable to supply sufficient wagons, so they decided to manufacture their own and opened a factory in Smethwick in 1864. Business thrived and the range of rolling stock was increased to include carriages. In 1878 the name was changed to the Birmingham Railway Carriage & Wagon Company to recognise this expansion. Like many railway rolling stock manufacturers they diversified into horse tramcar production. In the event tramcars were a very small element of the total production and the only recorded sales were to Northampton and Croydon.

1881	Northampton Street Tramways Co	8 D/D
1883	Northampton Street Tramways Co	2 D/D
1883	Croydon Tramways Co	3 D/D
1890	Croydon Tramways Co	1 D/D
1893	Northampton Street Tramways Co	4 S/D

RICHARD J. BOYALL

It is mentioned under the Edinburgh Street Tramways Co entry (Section 3) that the tramway company had in 1872 ordered tramcars from several manufacturers. One of these is recorded as being Richard. J. Boyall coachbuilder of Grantham. Photographic evidence shows that the Edinburgh system had some single ended tramcars and it is quite possible that the Boyall tramcars were these single ended cars. This means that some of the routes would have required turning loops or reversing triangles at the termini, but this would have been offset by the saving in weight of the single ended design.

Richard Boyall is credited with manufacturing tramcars for the Edinburgh tramways that may have included this single ended tramcar. It is unlikely to have been a reversible car as the Eades Patent covered all such tramcars and no Eades-manufactured cars ran in Edinburgh.

1872	Edinburgh Street Tramways Co	6 D/D
1876	Edinburgh Street Tramways Co	? D/D, ?T/R

BRADFORD TRAMWAYS & OMNIBUS COMPANY

The Bradford horse tramway opened in 1882 with tramcars from Ashbury. These were added to by other tramcars that were built locally. Then in 1894 the company decided it required two toastrack type tramcars. These are the simplest of all the designs and the company chose to manufacture the tramcars themselves. The following year the two cars were renumbered and later fitted with roofs to give an element of protection to the passengers from the Bradford weather.

1894	Bradford Tramways & Omnibus Company	2 T/R

BRISTOL WAGON & CARRIAGE WORKS COMPANY LIMITED

Note: This company has no connection with the Bristol Tramways and Carriage Company other than a similarity of name.

Albert Fry, a Bristol coachmaker set up a workshop in 1851 somewhere around the Temple Gate area to make carts and mainly agricultural vehicles. After changes of management the then company of Albert and Theodore Fry (of the Fry Chocolate family) was acquired in 1866 by the newly formed Bristol Wagon Works, to supply the expanding railway industry. The company carried on making agricultural vehicles as well as railway rolling stock. The name was changed in 1889 to reflect the expanded range to the Bristol Wagon & Carriage Works Company Limited. Amongst the vast numbers of vehicles they also produced a small number of horse tramcars for a couple of

Two Exeter tramcars built by the Bristol Wagon & Carriage Works Company Limited.

Wolverhampton tramcar extensively rebuilt and restored by the British Horse Tram Enthusiasts group.

British systems. The Bristol company merged with the Leeds Forge Company Limited in 1918 that led to a complete takeover in 1920 and the factory in Bristol was closed in 1923. Ironically the factory site was sold in 1924 to the Bristol Tramways and Carriage Company.

1879	City of Gloucester Tramways Co. Ltd	6 S/D
1882	Exeter Corporation Tramways	3 D/D
1883	Exeter Corporation Tramways	3 D/D
1884	Exeter Corporation Tramways	2 D/D
1885	Plymouth Tramways Co.	12 D/D
1894	Plymouth Corporation Tramways	6 D/D
1896	Exeter Corporation Tramways	2 D/D

BRITISH & FOREIGN TRAMWAYS COMPANY LIMITED, GREENWICH

See TRAMWAY CAR & WORKS COMPANY LIMITED

BRITISH HORSE TRAM ENTHUSIASTS

The British Horse Tram Enthusiasts is an organisation devoted to giving advice on the restoration of horse trams; help research the history of all tramcar design up to 1900; and suggesting fund raising ideas for those interested in horse trams preservation. They have also actively restored preserved horse tramcars that are now displayed in museums around the country.

1988	Birkenhead Street Railway	1 D/D
1993	Pwllheli & Llanbedrog Tramway	1 S/D
1998	Wolverhampton Tramways Company No. 23	1 D/D

BROWN, MARSHALLS & COMPANY LIMITED

Brown and Marshall were established stage coach manufacturers in Birmingham. Like Joseph Wright they saw the rise of the railways and moved production to railway carriages and wagons, so they opened a new factory near Adderley Park station, on the London and Birmingham Railway. The factory, opened in 1853, was named the Britannia Railway and Wagon Works. Initially most of the production of the new factory was for railway rolling stock. The surviving partner, George Marshall, decided to sell the business in 1870 and it was purchased by Francis Bolton of Birmingham who immediately registered it as a limited company under the name Brown, Marshalls & Company Limited. Much of the production was being exported. The manufacture of horse tramcars did not start until 1876 when the Birmingham Tramways and Omnibus Co Ltd ordered six single-deck tramcars. From then tramcar orders were sporadic until 1894 when Glasgow Corporation needed lots of tramcars very quickly. That year Glasgow ordered 90 tramcars and a further 45 the following year. Apart from 5 trams for Perth Tramways in 1895 that was the end of horse tramcar production by Brown, Marshalls & Company Limited.

The company was voluntarily wound up in 1897 and reorganised as a new company with the same name.

1876	Birmingham Tramways and Omnibus Co. Ltd	5 S/D
1878	Birmingham Tramways and Omnibus Co. Ltd	1 S/D
1880	Edinburgh Street Tramways Co.	5 D/D
1881	Leamington & Warwick Tramways and Omnibus Co.	2 D/D
1894	Glasgow Corporation Tramways	90 D/D
1895	Perth and District Tramways Co. Ltd	4 D/D, 1 T/R
1895	Glasgow Corporation Tramways	45 D/D

Brown, Marshalls & Co Ltd made tramcars for the Perth tramways.

BRUSH ELECTRICAL ENGINEERING COMPANY LIMITED

See FALCON ENGINE & CAR WORKS LIMITED

CAILLET MONORAIL PORTABLE RAILWAY

The unique Caillet Monorail Portable Railway used for a couple of years on the Canvey Island tramway.

The Caillet monorail is a fascinating byway of tramway history. Frederick Hester, a local builder, started to develop a large area of Canvey Island in 1900 as a housing and holiday resort. To convey prospective purchasers to the building site he had the Caillet monorail tramway laid across the island from the ferry terminus to the south beach. The Caillet system used just one rail, which took the weight of the tramcar, with a horse attached to a rigid frame at the side of the car, both providing the motive power and keeping the balance. It was the intention that this would be a temporary measure and an electric tramway was laid, but before it could open the island suffered severe flooding and would-be house purchasers lost interest. The tramway closed in 1904 and the project abandoned. Interestingly a copy of the Caillet monorail catalogue was found in the papers from the Bryn Y Pys estate, Overton, six miles southeast of Wrexham. So there might well have been a second example of this unique design of tramway, but the estate owners did not follow up the catalogue with an order.

1901	Canvey Island Tramway (Monorail)	? T/R

CALEDONIAN RAILWAY COMPANY

The Caledonian Railway built their line from Perth to Dundee that passed approximately 2 miles from Inchture village. It was suggested that the Caledonian Railway should build a branch from Inchture Station to the village itself. This it did and the line opened in 1849. It was originally worked by a railway carriage drawn by a horse. In 1895 it was decided to replace the original coach and the Caledonian Railway built a horse tramcar for use on the line. The tramcar served until 1916 when the line was closed and the rails lifted for use in armaments for the First World War.

1849	Inchture Tramway	1 S/D
1895	Inchture Tramway	1 S/D

CHESTER TRAMWAYS COMPANY

Details of the Chester Tramways and the tramcars built by Mr Kerneen in 1880 are given below. In 1886 the General Manager, John Gardner, designed a double-deck tramcar and had it made in the company's workshops. It had garden seats on the upper deck and these proved popular with passengers and over time the other tramcars were converted from knifeboard seating to garden seats.

1886	Chester Tramways Co.	1 D/D

JOHN CROALL & SONS

Around 1810 William Croall and Henry Kinross set up a coachbuilding company called Croall and Kinross Carriageworks. This may have been connected with an earlier coachbuilder John Croall. It appeared that John Croall moved back to Edinburgh and started running stagecoaches and probably also making them, using the name John Croall and Company. In the 1830s the sons of William Croall, having served an apprenticeship with their father's business, moved to Edinburgh. It is unsure whether they set up their own business or linked with John Croall and Company. Their business was situated in Castle Street and was called John Croall Coachworks. They only made a few tramcars for their local Edinburgh system and mainly concentrated on stage coaches and omnibuses. Moving with the times they transferred into the internal combustion motor car business at an early stage and had connections with the Rolls Royce Company.

John Croall and Company made ten tramcars for the Edinburgh tramway, including this one.

1872	Edinburgh Street Tramways Co.	10 D/D

B. CROWTHER

In 1893 the Birmingham and Midlands Tramways Company decided to cease running steam trams on two of their short routes, called the "Lanes" routes. Rather than cease the tramway service they agreed with a Mr B. Crowther that he would run the two lines as a horse tramway. Mr Crowther was a Funeral Director and he also hired out horse vehicles and horses from premises in Paradise Street, West Bromwich. The tramway company had ordered two tramcars from the Metropolitan Railway Carriage and Wagon Company Limited but these had not yet been delivered. So Mr Crowther built two single-deck tramcars, though it is possible that he had a local coachbuilder actually make them. He did not make any more horse tramcars, paying a rent for the use of the two Metropolitan built cars owned by Birmingham and Midlands Tramways Company.

1893	B. Crowther/Birmingham and Midlands Tramways Co.	2 S/D

Mr B. Crowther built and operated two single-deck cars on the Birmingham and Midlands Tramways Company.

DICK, KERR & COMPANY LIMITED, (later ELECTRIC RAILWAY & TRAMWAY CARRIAGE WORKS LIMITED, and UNITED ELECTRIC CAR COMPANY LIMITED)

Despite its name the Electric Railway & Tramway Carriage Works Limited did build some horse tramcars including five for the Joyce Green Hospital.

The Electric Railway & Tramway Carriage Works Limited (ERTCW) was a development by the tramway entrepreneurs William Bruce Dick and John Kerr, who founded Dick, Kerr & Company in 1883. They decided to enter the electric tramcar business by purchasing a carriage factory in Preston in 1898 that had been empty for some years and formed the Electric Railway & Tramway Carriage Works Limited to manufacture all types of rolling stock (though the firm's name indicates their focus). This was at the time that horse tramways were being converted to electric operation and new electric tramways were being opened all over the country. The Great Grimsby Street Tramways Company found it needed some extra horse trams, but was in the process of changing to electric power. So they ordered horse trams from ERTCW that would also be suitable as trailers for electric tramcars. Later specialist ambulance horse tramcars were built by ERTCW for use in the Joyce Green Hospitals. In 1905 the ERTCW purchased the Hadley works of G.F. Milnes and the Trafford Park works of the British Electric Tramway Co. To reflect the changes a new name was taken so the company became the United Electric Car Company Limited to reflect the expansion. Surprisingly the new company obtained orders for horse tramcars for systems in the British Isles. This was for the long lived Douglas horse tramway and a repeat order for Joyce Green Hospital.

1899	Great Grimsby Street Tramways Co.	4 D/D
1905	Joyce Green Hospitals	1 S/D
1907	Douglas Bay Tramway	2 T/R
1908	Joyce Green Hospitals	4 S/D
1909	Galway & Salthill Tramway Co.	5 D/D

DREW & BURNETT

Drew and Burnett were established coachbuilders in Fountainbridge, Edinburgh. They probably thought that with the passing of the 1870 Tramways Act there would be opportunities for them to expand their business into tramcar building. They won a contract to supply nine double-deck tramcars to the Pimlico, Peckham & Greenwich Tramways Co. in 1870. Soon after this the Pimlico company merged with the Metropolitan Street Tramways Company to become the London Tramways Company Limited, who purchased most of their cars from Stephenson and Starbuck. So the only other order that Drew & Burnett won was for two tramcars for their local system the Edinburgh Street Tramways Company.

1870	Pimlico, Peckham & Greenwich Street Tramways Co.	9 D/D
1872	Edinburgh Street Tramways Co.	2 D/D

DUBLIN UNITED TRAMWAYS COMPANY LIMITED

When the Dublin United Tramways Co. Ltd. was formed in 1881 by amalgamating the Dublin Tramways Co., the North Dublin Street Tramways Co. and the Dublin Central Tramways Co. it allowed the system to be expanded and the new company realised that additional tramcars were required. The directors of the company wanted to encourage Irish manufacturing and support local employment. So it was determined that they would build their own tramcars. A new workshop had been built in 1882 and it was used to make all its tramcars. Indeed one of the first tramcars to be built was an exhibition piece for the Irish Exhibition in Dublin. Subsequently another 180 horse tramcars were built in the workshops. The construction work continued when the tramways were electrified and many electric tramcars were also built for the Dublin system. The workshops did not make any tramcars for any other system.

1882-6	Dublin United Tramways Co. Ltd.	181 D/D

EDINBURGH STREET TRAMWAYS COMPANY & EDINBURGH & DISTRICT TRAMWAYS COMPANY LIMITED

The Edinburgh Street Tramways Company started operating in 1871 and in their early years they purchased tramcars from British & Foreign Tramways Co. Ltd; John Croall &. Sons; Drew & Burnett; R.J. Boyall; John Stephenson Co. Ltd; and Starbuck Car and Wagon Company Ltd, but they were never really satisfied with the cars. In 1879 they appointed a new rolling-stock

Drew and Burnett built the tramcars for the opening of the Pimlico, Peckham & Greenwich Street Tramways Company lines.

When Dublin United Tramways needed to expand its fleet they decided to build their own tramcars that included number 33.

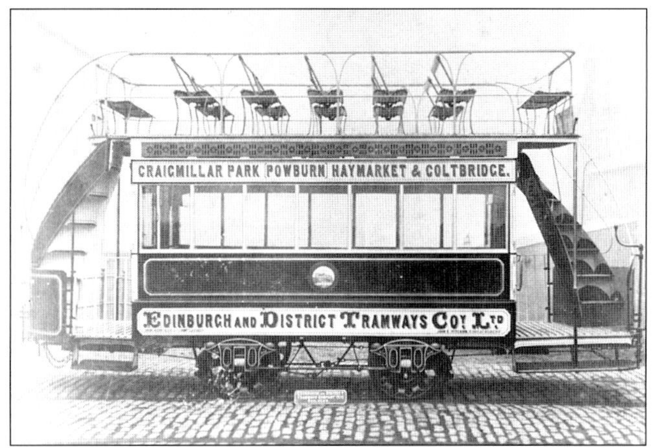

Edinburgh and District Tramways Co. Ltd was another company that decided to build its own tramcars.

superintendent and he began manufacturing tramcars for the system. However the company workshop was not able to meet the demands of the system and further tramcars were purchased from outside. Around 24 tramcars were built by the workshop by the time the Edinburgh & District Tramways Co. Ltd took over the system in 1893. This company continued to use the workshop to manufacture tramcars for themselves and added a further 15 to the fleet. The system was taken over and electrified by Edinburgh Corporation in 1919, though the Corporation also built tramcars in their own workshops.

1880	Edinburgh Street Tramways Co.	14 D/D
1885	Edinburgh Street Tramways Co.	96 D/D
1895	Edinburgh & District Tramways Co. Ltd	7 D/D,
1896	Edinburgh & District Tramways Co. Ltd	6 D/D, 1 T/R
1897	Edinburgh & District Tramways Co. Ltd	1 D/D

ELECTRIC RAILWAY & TRAMWAY CARRIAGE WORKS LIMITED

See DICK, KERR & COMPANY LIMITED

ENGLISH ELECTRIC COMPANY LIMITED

The English Electric Company Limited was established in 1918 with an amalgamation of Dick, Kerr & Company Limited (who had taken over Siemens Brothers of Stafford in 1917 from the custodian of enemy property) with William & Robinson of Rugby, the Phoenix Dynamo Manufacturing Company of Bradford and the Coventry Ordnance Works. The larger part of the group was Dick, Kerr & Company Limited. Despite its name its first tramcar order was for horse tramcars for Morecambe Corporation Tramways. These were the only horse trams built for the British market and probably the only horse cars built by the company.

1919	Morecambe Corporation Tramways	1 D/D, 1 T/R
1922	Morecambe Corporation Tramways	1 D/D, 1 T/R

REES EVANS, HARLECH

Rees Evans was a local coachbuilder in Harlech and he was asked to build a simple toastrack tramcar for the 2ft gauge Harlech Tramway. He did not build any other tramcars.

1878	Harlech Tramway	1 T/R

FALCON ENGINE & CAR WORKS LIMITED, (Formerly HUGHES' LOCOMOTIVE & TRAMWAY ENGINE WORKS, later BRUSH ELECTRICAL ENGINEERING COMPANY LIMITED)

In Loughborough in 1865 an engineer and timber merchant, Henry Hughes, set up the Falcon Engine & Car Works in Derby Road. He acquired about seven acres and built a factory for the manufacture of railway carriages, wagons and horse-drawn tramcars. Henry Hughes designed and manufactured a steam tramway locomotive and this was successful. He set up Hughes' Locomotive & Tramway Engine Works Ltd and this took over the business of the Falcon works. To help with the design and manufacture of tramcars, in 1877 he purchased a Stephenson tramcar from the North Metropolitan Tramway Co and this was sold back to them in 1878. He then started making horse tramcars to a similar design, but they were lighter. The company did not prosper and went into liquidation in 1881. The bankrupt company was purchased by Norman Scott Russell and registered as the Falcon Engine and Car Works Limited. He improved the Hughes design of steam tram locomotive and was more successful. In 1889 the Falcon Company was taken over by the Brush Electrical Engineering Company and the focus of production turned to electrical transport, though they still made horse trams when orders came through.

1876	Sheffield Tramways Co.	1 D/D
1878	Wolverhampton Tramways Co. Ltd	4 D/D
1879	City of Gloucester Tramways Co. Ltd	6 S/D
1879	North Metropolitan Tramways Co.	9 D/D
1879	Reading Tramways Co.	1 S/D
1880	Birmingham Tramways and Omnibus Co. Ltd	4 D/D
c1880	Wolverhampton Tramways Co. Ltd	12 D/D
1881	North Metropolitan Tramways Co.	5 D/D

English Electric Company Limited (a combination of companies including Dick, Kerr & Company Limited) built four tramcars for the Morecambe Corporation Tramways.

The Falcon Engine & Car Works (later to become the Brush Electrical Engineering Company) built this light car for the West Metropolitan tramways.

The Falcon Engine & Car Works also built many double-deck tramcars including this car for Glasgow.

1882	West Metropolitan Tramways Co. Ltd	9 S/D
1882	North Metropolitan Tramways Co.	14 D/D
1883	West Metropolitan Tramways Co. Ltd	4 S/D
1883	London Southern Tramways Co.	?
1884	Birmingham Central Tramways Co. Ltd	10 D/D
1884	Worcester Tramways Ltd	6 D/D
1886	West Metropolitan Tramways Co. Ltd	4 D/D
1887	West Metropolitan Tramways Co. Ltd	1 S/D
1888	Blackburn Corporation Tramways Co.	5 D/D
1890	Croydon Tramways Co.	4 D/D
1890	Harrow Road and Paddington Tramway Co.	9 D/D
1892	Wolverhampton Tramways Co. Ltd	4 D/D
1893	Glasgow Corporation Tramways	2 D/D
1893	Northampton Street Tramways Co.	2 D/D
1894	Derby Tramways Co.	2 D/D
1895	Leamington &. Warwick Tramways and Omnibus Co.	3 D/D
1897	Croydon Tramways Co.	8 D/D
1899	Northampton Street Tramways Co.	14 D/D
1900	Lincoln Tramways Co.	2 S/D
1900	Worcester Tramways Ltd	1 D/D, 2 S/D

BENJAMIN FRENCH

The story of the Oystermouth tramway has been detailed in Section 1. When Benjamin French obtained a lease to use the Oystermouth Tramroad he constructed a passenger carriage for the line, probably using a mineral truck. Later he replaced this with a tramcar that resembled a road carriage.

1807	Swansea & Oystermouth Tramroad	1 S/D
c1815	Swansea & Oystermouth Tramroad	1 S/D

Benjamin French built the world's first railed passenger tramcar for the Oystermouth Tramroad. This is a reproduction of the second tramcar he built for the same line.

GLASGOW TRAMWAY & OMNIBUS COMPANY

The Glasgow Tramway and Omnibus Company opened its first routes in Glasgow in 1872 with tramcars built by the Tramway Car and Works Company, a firm set up by directors of the Glasgow company. The system expanded rapidly and within 16 years had over 30 miles of routes with over 200 tramcars. In the early days of the tramway the maintenance and repair of the trams was carried out in a small workshop and at the back of depots. In 1877 this changed and a new larger works was built alongside Crownpoint Depot. With the purpose-built workshops they now had the capacity to build their own trams. The company used a technicality by calling these new cars replacements and giving the numbers of scrapped cars, so eliminating the need and cost of obtaining a new magistrate's licence. Apart from two other Scottish tramways the company only ever built tramcars for its own use. When the Corporation bought the system in 1896 they also purchased 21 tramcars from the company. However, they needed around 160 tramcars to run the tramway. Arguments between the company and the Corporation meant that the latter refused to buy the now redundant tramcars from the former. So the Corporation had to find a large number of tramcars in a short time. This was an unexpected boost to the tramcar construction industry and significant orders were placed with many firms, including 29 built by the Corporation in the ex-company workshop.

The Glasgow Tramway and Omnibus Company built many tramcars for itself and the adjoining Paisley system. Here is one of them.

1877	Dundee & District Tramway Co.	2 D/D, 3 S/D
1880	Glasgow Tramway and Omnibus Co. Ltd	47 D/D, 2 S/D
1887	Paisley Tramways Co. Ltd	2 S/D
1890	Paisley Tramways Co. Ltd	2 S/D
1895	Glasgow Corporation Tramways	29 D/D
1901	Paisley Tramways Co. Ltd	2 D/D

GLOUCESTER RAILWAY CARRIAGE & WAGON COMPANY

The Gloucester Railway Carriage and Wagon Company Limited was established for the same reasons as many wagon builders. A group of businessmen were finding themselves frustrated by the lack of railway wagons on the expanding railways. To enable themselves to make best use of the railway system they combined to set up their own wagon factory. A new factory was built in 1860 in Gloucester and started production. It was immediately apparent that the company filled a much needed gap in the market and the firm thrived, even through the difficulties of the American Civil War from 1861 to 1865 (the Chairman of the company reported that the war had caused "a violent and deep disturbance of trade").The company built railway carriages, omnibuses and vans. When the City of Gloucester Tramways Co. Ltd opened they purchased tramcars from the Bristol Railway Carriage and Wagon Company Limited and the Falcon Engine &

The City of Gloucester Tramways Co. naturally turned to the Gloucester Railway Carriage and Wagon Company Limited to make their tramcars.

Car Works. Later they purchased cars from Starbuck, but in 1886 they placed an order for four tramcars with their local factory. When the Corporation took over the tramway they placed a similar order with the Gloucester company. The Gloucester company did not make any other horse tramcars for British tramways, though they did supply tramcars for foreign systems.

1886	City of Gloucester Tramways Co. Ltd	4 S/D
1902	Gloucester Corporation Tramways	4 S/D

MR HARVEY

In 1867 the Ryde Pier managers asked Mr Harvey, Clerk of Works, to construct a first class tramcar for the pier. The tramcar was designed by Mr Harvey, but actually made by a local coachbuilder, John Knapp (see below).

1867	Ryde Pier Tramways	1 S/D

HUGHES' LOCOMOTIVE & TRAMWAY ENGINE WORKS

See FALCON ENGINE & CAR WORKS LIMITED

HYSLOP & COMPANY

The Edinburgh Street Tramways Co decided to build their own tramcars from 1880. However, the system grew in route miles faster than the workshop could produce tramcars. So they turned to a local coachbuilder, Hyslop & Co, to assist in building additional tramcars. These are the only tramcars built by Hyslop & Co.

1883	Edinburgh Street Tramways Co.	1 D/D, 4 S/D

FREDERICK JONES

The Wrexham District Tramways Company started service in 1876 with two tramcars from Starbuck. The system was not entirely successful, but kept operating until 1884 when Frederick Jones took over running the line. He was the proprietor of an inn and also kept livery stables. He felt that an extra tramcar was necessary and proceeded to build a double-deck tramcar in his workshop. Unfortunately he failed to measure the doorway and once the tramcar was complete it could not be taken through the door. So the upper deck fittings had to be removed in order to get the car out of the workshop. This was the only tramcar he built.

1884	Wrexham District Tramways Co.	1 D/D

KERNEEN

Mr Kerneen was an American who had a small carriage workshop in Chester, close to the Chester Tramways Company offices. When the system opened in 1879 the company purchased eight Eades Patent reversible tramcars. These were small tramcars hauled by two horses that proved unsuitable for the lightly used system in Chester. So the company turned to Mr Kerneen to manufacture seven lightweight single-deck tramcars to be hauled by single horses. These were delivered probably in 1880. In his enthusiasm to reduce weight Mr Kerneen had omitted the proper support below the platforms and in use they gradually parted company with the rest of the tramcar and the cars had to be rebuilt. Not surprisingly these were the only tramcars made by Mr Kerneen.

c1880	Chester Tramways Co.	7 D/D

Frederick Jones was the operator of the Wrexham Tramways and built one tramcar for the tramway. In order to get it out of the workshops the upper deck fittings had to be removed. The crude windshield around the stairs must have given the driver an enormous blind spot.

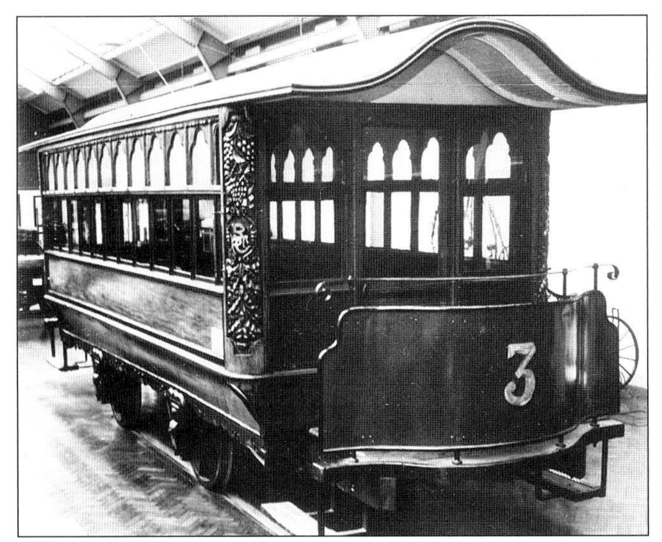

John Knapp, a Ryde coachbuilder, was commissioned to build this one tramcar, that has been preserved and can be seen in the Streetlife Transport Museum, Hull.

JOHN KNAPP

In 1871 the Ryde Pier management decided they needed a high quality tramcar and a design was produced by the Clerk of Works, Mr Harvey, with the construction being given to John Knapp, a local coachbuilder. The outside of the car carried ornate decoration and the corner pillars were elaborately carved with grapes, foliage and the Ryde Pier Company monogram. It was this feature of the car that gave it the name the "Grapes" tramcar.

Not surprisingly the Morecambe Tramways Company turned to the local builder, Lancaster Railway Carriage & Wagon Company Limited.

The tramcar was usually reserved for visiting VIPs. It has survived and can be seen today in the Streetlife Museum of Transport, Hull.

1871	Ryde Pier Tramways	1 S/D

LANCASTER RAILWAY CARRIAGE & WAGON COMPANY LIMITED

In the early days the railway companies were unwilling to provide goods wagons for conveying coal. In order to get the coal moving colliery owners and industrialists set up their own wagon factories, making and maintaining wagons with the names of the owners displayed on the sides. One such company was the Lancaster Wagon Company. The new factory was opened in 1865 in Caton Road, Lancaster. The name was changed to the Lancaster Railway Carriage & Wagon Company Limited in 1892. Like many railway carriage makers the company expanded their range to include tramcars. Production of horse trams was limited and mainly confined to local tramways, though the first order was from the South London Tramways Company. The main production of the company was railway rolling stock. With the decline in horse tram orders the company made a few electric tramcars, but it always was a side-line to the predominant production. The company was merged with others to become part of the Metropolitan Amalgamated Railway Carriage & Wagon Company Limited. The Lancaster factory closed in 1908.

1881	South London Tramways Co.	14 D/D, 14 S/D
1885	Blackpool Corporation Tramways	4 D/D, 2 T/R
1887	Morecambe Tramways Co.	2 D/D, 2 T/R
1888	Morecambe Tramways Co.	2 D/D
1889	Morecambe Tramways Co.	1 D/D
1890	Lancaster and District Tramways Co.	14 D/D
1897	Morecambe Tramways Co.	4 D/D
1901	Morecambe Tramways Co.	2 D/D

WILLIAM LAUDER

In the 1890s the Rothesay system required new tramcars and probably based on their earlier experiences they ordered them from a local coachbuilder. Two were ordered in 1891 and these were successful because another two were ordered in 1894 and a final tramcar in 1897. William Lauder did not make any further tramcars.

1891	Rothesay Tramways Co. Ltd	2 T/R
1894	Rothesay Tramways Co. Ltd	2 T/R
1897	Rothesay Tramways Co. Ltd	1 T/R

William Lauder was a Rothesay coachbuilder who built tramcars for the town's tramway.

The Liverpool United Tramways & Omnibus Company was another operator that decided to build its own tramcars when it needed to expand its fleet – it eventually built nearly 200 cars.

LEEDS TRAMWAY COMPANY

The Leeds Tramway Company opened in 1871, purchasing tramcars from the major manufacturers. During 1880 the company had been undertaking major refurbishment to their tramcars in the Headingley depot and workshop. This encouraged them to develop into making their own tramcars. Three toastrack tramcars were made for the system, but these were not considered a success. There was another try in 1885 with one double-deck tramcar. The result of this trial was that the company reverted to buying its trams from established manufacturers.

1879	Leeds Tramways Co.	3 T/R
1885	Leeds Tramways Co.	1 D/D

LIVERPOOL UNITED TRAMWAYS & OMNIBUS COMPANY

The Liverpool Tramways Company opened its first line in Liverpool in 1869 and became a competitor to the buses of the Liverpool Road and Railway Omnibus Company. After a year of litigation the companies decided to amalgamate into the Liverpool Tramways & Omnibus Company but this was not achieved until 1876. Then in 1884 more omnibus companies were taken over and the title changed to Liverpool United Tramways & Omnibus Company. The tramway part of the business purchased its trams from Stephenson, but under the new management the decision was taken for the company to build its own trams at the Tramway Road carriage works, Aigburth (that moved in 1893 to a new workshop in Lambeth Road). Roughly 200 tramcars were built by the company for its own use. Previously they had purchased Eades reversible cars from Ashbury and they wanted to add similar cars built by themselves. However, they had difficulty getting a licence and so they built single-ended cars that were not reversible. So track layouts were modified with reversing circles or triangles. The company did not make any tramcars for any other operators.

The London Tramways Company built around 300 tramcars for their own use.

1884	Liverpool United Tramways & Omnibus Co.	24 D/D
1885-7	Liverpool United Tramways & Omnibus Co.	175 D/D

LONDON SOUTHERN TRAMWAYS COMPANY

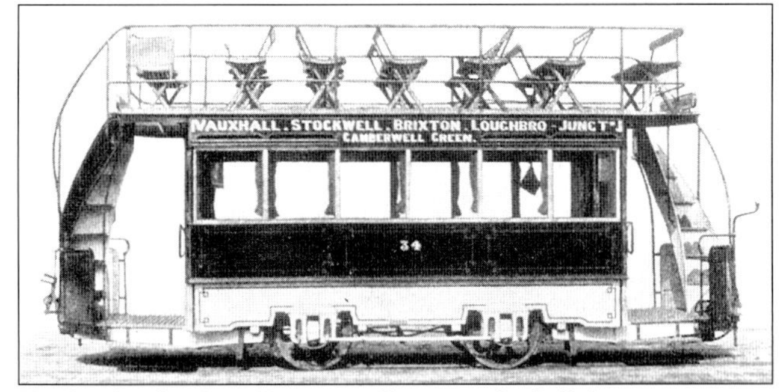

The London Southern Tramways Company also built its own tramcars.

Like many of the larger tramway systems the London Southern Tramways Company started to use their repair workshops to manufacture new tramcars for the company's use. No records have survived but it is likely that around 33 tramcars were built "in house" from 1890.

1890	London Southern Tramways Co.	33

LONDON TRAMWAYS COMPANY

The London Tramways Company was formed by the merger of the Metropolitan Street Tramways Company and the Pimlico, Peckham & Greenwich Street Tramways Company, with all the associated tramcars. The company was large enough to have its own workshops for the repair of tramcars. Like many large

Needing replacement cars quickly the London United Tramways Limited built 10 in its own workshops.

systems the London Tramways Co. decided to build their own tramcars. The precise number has not been determined but it is likely to have been around 300.

From 1878	London Tramways Co.	Approx 300

LONDON UNITED TRAMWAYS LIMITED

In 1893 the West Metropolitan Tramways Company Limited had severe financial problems leading to it being declared bankrupt. The Receiver tried to auction the operation, without any bidders. So it was sold privately to August Krauss an agent for the Imperial Tramways Company Limited (a company where the Receiver was managing director). Within a couple of months the undertaking had transferred to the newly created London United Tramways Limited. It had taken over the existing tramcars, but realised that additional trams were needed and hired some from other London horse tramways. Then they ordered fifteen from Milnes. The LUT had a workshop at Chiswick and when there was sufficient capacity the workshops built ten tramcars for themselves. It is likely that these were extensive rebuilds of older tramcars rather than completely new. By this time conversion to electric operation had begun and there was no further call for horse trams.

1897	London United Tramways Ltd	10 D/D

LONDONDERRY & ENNISKILLIN RAILWAY

This is another example of a main line railway going near, but not that near, to a town. In this case it was the Northern Irish line from Londonderry to Enniskillen, opened in 1854, that missed the town of Fintona. So a branch was built from Fintona Junction to Fintona Town. In early days the passenger service was served with a railway coach with seats fitted to the roof and built by the railway. This was removed in 1883 and replaced with a purpose built double-deck tramcar, built by the Metropolitan Railway Carriage and Wagon Company Limited and hauled by a horse (always called Dick).

1854	Fintona Tramway	1 D/D

MANCHESTER CARRIAGE & TRAMWAYS COMPANY

The Manchester Carriage Company was established in 1865 as an amalgamation of local horse omnibus operators in the Manchester area (including the John Greenwood and John Haworth guided bus system mentioned in Section 1). The company sought powers to operate a tramway in Manchester and Salford but the Government had told them to wait until they had details of the new Tramways Act. After the passing of the 1870 Tramways Act the company made application to the Corporations to lay tramways. However, many other entrepreneurs had the same idea and there was a plethora of applications. So the Corporations of Salford and Manchester each made application in 1875 to lay tram lines. However, they were not allowed to operate the systems themselves but had to lease them to private companies and in 1876 both Corporations agreed to lease the lines to Daniel Busby and William Turton to run "The Manchester and Salford Tramways". They promoted more routes under the title "Manchester Suburban Tramways". The first route was due to open in May 1877, however, a short time before the opening Busby and Turton had reached an agreement with the Manchester Carriage Company's directors where the latter took on the lease and operation of the tramway. So the system opened, using Starbuck tramcars, under the management of the Carriage Company, indeed the directors of the Carriage Company and the Manchester Suburban Tramways were the same. The position was regularised in 1880 by an Act of Parliament where the two companies were combined under the title "The Manchester Carriage and Tramways Company".

The Manchester Carriage Company had a workshop in Church Street, Pendleton where their omnibuses were manufactured and repaired. The manager of the workshop since 1867 was John Eades. As part of the conditions of the lease the company had to run early morning "Workmen's Cars" with cheaper fares. As the clothing of such people was often dirty special, probably more basic, tramcars were to be used. Two tramcars were designed and manufactured in 1877 by Eades in

The Manchester Carriage Company built tramcars for itself using the Eades patent. It was one of the largest manufacturers, making in excess of 1,000 tramcars.

the workshop and proved a success. Eades then designed a special single ended tramcar where, at the terminus, the body could be rotated on the chassis so it faced the correct direction for the return journey. By doing this the tramcar only needed one staircase giving a significant weight (and cost) saving. These were tried by the company and proved a great success and so Eades took out a patent and carried on constructing many more for use on the tramway. John Eades built over 400 of his design of tramcar for the Carriage Company between 1877 and 1888 and was the workshop manager until 1903.

It was clear that this design of tramcar could be used on other systems. Not having the capacity to make tramcars for others the design was licensed to a Manchester based carriage builder, the Ashbury Railway Carriage & Iron Company Limited (see above). Indeed William Busby, the brother of Daniel Busby, was a director of Ashbury.

1878	Manchester and Salford Tramways Co.	2 D/D
1880	Manchester and Salford Tramways Co.	24 S/D
1884	Manchester and Salford Tramways Co.	326 D/D
1888	Manchester and Salford Tramways Co.	56 S/D
1895	Manchester Carriage & Tramways Co.	515 D/D 84 S/D

JAMES MCBRIDE

Following the problems with the canvass awnings on the tramcars built by Savile Street Foundry & Engineering Co. Ltd (see later entry) the Rothesay Tramways Company in 1882 ordered two toastrack tramcars from James McBride, a joiner from the town. These cars were actually crossbench cars as they had substantial sheet iron roofs with strong iron supports.

1882	Rothesay Tramways Co. Ltd	2 T/R

MERRYWEATHER & SONS LIMITED

Merryweather and Sons Limited of Greenwich are most famous for their expertise in firefighting and manufacturing fire engines. They can trace their origins back to 1690 and so by the time street tramways were developing they had been established a very long time. In the 1860s they were making horse-drawn fire engines and developing steam driven engines in their Greenwich Road factory. They diversified into steam tram locomotives and this aspect of their involvement in tramways is covered in detail in David Gladwin's "A History of the British Steam Tram, Volume 1". They appear in this book by virtue of a single order in 1883 for ten horse tramcars for the Lea Bridge, Leyton and Walthamstow Tramway Company. By this time Merryweather were well established as steam tram locomotive manufacturers and this may have been the reason for this order being placed with them, other factors may include the use by London local authorities of Merryweather fire engines and that Merryweather was a local (albeit across the River Thames) company.

The Lea Bridge, Leyton and Walthamstow Tramways Company turned to Merryweather and Sons Limited of Greenwich for its tramcars.

1883	Lea Bridge, Leyton and Walthamstow Tramways Co.	10 S/D

METROPOLITAN RAILWAY CARRIAGE AND WAGON CO LTD

The Metropolitan Railway Carriage and Wagon Company Limited of Birmingham built tramcars for many systems including this car for the Dublin Tramways Company.

Joseph Wright was an established stage coach builder in Birmingham in the early 1800s. He saw the London and Birmingham Railway being built and fully opened in 1838 and realised that demand for stage coaches would decline and the new railways would need specialised carriages. So he started manufacturing railway carriages, including the first coaches for the London and Birmingham Railway. He realised that it would be better to have a factory close to a railway link. He chose a site in Saltley, Birmingham, next to the Birmingham and Derby Railway and the new factory was opened in 1845. Joseph Wright died in 1859 and his sons, Henry and Joseph, took over management of the business. Demand for railway rolling stock was high and competitors sought some of the business and having newer factories and up to date machinery were able to undercut the Saltley factory. The Wright brothers decided in 1862 to expand by creating new capital through making the factory a limited company. The name was changed to the Metropolitan Railway Carriage and Wagon Company Limited. The company took on the new idea of selling rolling stock (particularly wagons) on hire purchase, or even leasing them. This was very popular and the Metropolitan Railway Carriage and Wagon Company Limited became one of the largest manufacturers, supplying rolling stock to railways not only in Britain, but all over the world.

The company started making its first horse trams in the early 1870s, probably the first order being from Birmingham & District Tramways Company Limited in 1872. From then on there was a steady flow of tramcar orders. In 1884 and 1886 Glasgow Tramways & Omnibus Co. Ltd put in orders for a total of 48 tramcars, then in 1894 Glasgow Corporation took over the tramways in the city and in the negotiations the Corporation did not purchase the tramcars from the Glasgow tramways. Therefore the Corporation had to start operations with no vehicles. They quickly placed orders with several tramcar builders and Metropolitan had orders for 90 cars in 1894 and a further 45 in 1895. A real boost to the company as by then horse trams orders had tailed off. The last horse tramcars to be built were two double-deck cars for the Woolwich & South East London Tramways Co. Ltd in 1902. This was the year that five railway rolling stock manufacturers; Ashbury Railway Carriage and Iron Co. Ltd; Lancaster Railway Carriage & Wagon Co. Ltd; Metropolitan Railway Carriage and Wagon Co Ltd.; Oldbury Railway Carriage and Wagon Co. Ltd.; and Brown Marshalls Ltd were brought together under the title Metropolitan Amalgamated

Railway Carriage & Wagon Co. Ltd. At the time of the merger and subsequently horse tramcar production had ceased completely.

1870	Metropolitan Street Tramways Co.	?
1872	Birmingham & District Tramways Co. Ltd	12 D/D
1872	Dublin Tramways Co.	70 D/D
1873	Birmingham & District Tramways Co. Ltd	? D/D
1876	Birmingham Tramways and Omnibus Co. Ltd	17 D/D
1876	North Dublin Street Tramways Co.	8 D/D
1877	North Dublin Street Tramways Co.	6 S/D
1877	Haslar Royal Naval Hospital	1 S/D
1878	North Dublin Street Tramways Co.	6 S/D
1880	Southwark and Deptford Tramways Co.	26 D/D, 6 S/D,
1881	Leamington &. Warwick Tramways and Omnibus Co.	2 D/D
1881	Woolwich & South East London Tramways Co. Ltd	6 D/D
1882	Cavehill &. Whitewell Tramway Co.	1 D/D, 1 T/R
1882	Leamington &. Warwick Tramways and Omnibus Co.	2 D/D
1882	Woolwich & South East London Tramways Co. Ltd	6 D/D
1882	St Helens and District Tramways Co.	3 D/D
1883	Bristol Tramways and Carriage Co. Ltd	7 D/D
1883	Fintona Tramway	1 D/D
1883	South Shields Tramways Co.	5 D/D
1884	Cavehill &. Whitewell Tramway Co.	1 D/D
1884	Woolwich & South East London Tramways Co. Ltd	10 D/D
1884	Glasgow Tramway and Omnibus Co. Ltd	24 D/D
1884	Ramsgate and Margate Tramways Company	1 D/D
1885	Paisley Tramways Co. Ltd	5 D/D
1886	Glasgow Tramway and Omnibus Co. Ltd	24 D/D
1887	Douglas Bay Tramway	6 D/D
1894	Glasgow Corporation Tramways	90 D/D
1895	Glasgow Corporation Tramways	65 D/D
1895	Edinburgh & District Tramways Co. Ltd	4 D/D
1895	Woolwich & South East London Tramways Co. Ltd	5 D/D
1899	Leamington &. Warwick Tramways and Omnibus Co.	3 D/D
1900	Woolwich & South East London Tramways Co. Ltd	6 D/D
1902	Woolwich & South East London Tramways Co. Ltd	2 D/D

MIDLAND RAILWAY CARRIAGE & WAGON COMPANY LIMITED

The Midland Railway Carriage and Wagon Company Limited built this tramcar for the Pwllheli Corporation tramway among several systems.

The company probably started in 1844 and was incorporated as a limited company in 1853. It seems that the factory was originally sited in Rotherham, but by 1861 the head office and factory were in Birmingham. In 1877 they purchased the company of Richard France that had a factory at Abbey Works in Shrewsbury. This became the principle factory for the company and from then on the Birmingham factory made parts rather than complete rolling stock. When orders for horse tramcars ceased the company made some electric trams, but their main production was for railway rolling stock. The company was taken over by Cammell Laird & Co. Ltd in 1919, though continued under its own name until 1928 when it became part of Metropolitan-Cammell Carriage, Wagon and Finance Co. Ltd.

1875	Yarmouth and Gorleston Tramways Co. Ltd	10 D/D
1887	Derby Tramways Co.	2 D/D
1894	Glasgow Corporation Tramways	20 D/D
1895	Glasgow Corporation Tramways	60 D/D
1896	Peckham & East Dulwich Tramways Co.	4 T/R
1899	Pwllheli Corporation Tramways	1 S/D, 1 T/R
1901	Pwllheli Corporation Tramways	1 T/R
1921	Pwllheli and Llanbedrog Tramway	1 S/D, 1 T/R

G.F. MILNES & COMPANY

As is described below, George Frederick Milnes of Fallowfield, Manchester, in 1878 became the Company Secretary of the Starbuck Car and Wagon Company Ltd. When the company was wound up in 1886 he purchased the factory, plant and goodwill at scrap value. Renaming the business George F. Milnes and Co. the company carried on making tramcars, carriages and wagons. Around this time the upper deck seating was changing from the longitudinal 'knife board' to the 'garden seat' with a tip over back so the passenger always faced the direction of travel. Orders and production progressed steadily with construction including steam trailers, cable cars and electric tramcars, with a very strong order book from abroad. The electric tramway construction expanded and overtook the horse tram business. The railway wagon and carriage companies were less keen to enter the electric tramcar business and soon there were just two suppliers, Milnes and Brush (in Loughborough). The opportunity for a newcomer was seen by Dick, Kerr & Co who set up the Electric Railway and Tramway Carriage Works Ltd in Preston. This was a large factory making a standard design tramcar at very competitive prices that soon had an effect on the market. At this time German tramcars were being supplied to Liverpool and the company Busch of Bautzen approached Milnes with a proposal. This resulted in the Milnes company being turned into a public limited company and called G.F. Milnes & Co Ltd. The German Company purchased shares, raising capital for a new and larger factory. After searching around it was decided to build the new factory at the derelict Castle Ironworks, Hadley, Shropshire. The iron works and land were purchased in 1899 at a knock down price owing to the movement of industry away from the area. The old ironworks were demolished and a new factory built that opened in 1900 and by 1901 had a workforce of over 750. Owing to the heavy demands trams were still being built in Birkenhead and the old factory did not close until 1902 when trade had started to diminish. The last tramcars built in the Birkenhead factory may well have been three toastrack tramcars (numbers 38, 39 & 40) for the Douglas Bay horse tramway. The 1902 dip in demand for tramcars was the start of a long decline. It was a buyers' market with tramway systems beating down prices until it became unprofitable to make trams. Milnes made a loss in 1903 and the company went into voluntary liquidation in August 1903. Trams were being made to fulfil orders up to May 1904.

G.F. Milnes & Co. Ltd. took over the Starbuck factory and made tramcars for many systems. This is one of the cars they manufactured for the Bristol tramways.

Finding a buyer for the company was fruitless and it was decided to auction the business. At the auction the bids only reached £26,000 (the works had cost £100,000) and the auctioneer withdrew the property. The factory stayed open with a minimal number of staff and the very last tramcars were built in 1904. A syndicate of railway wagon and carriage manufacturers were keen to ensure that the Castle Car Works was not purchased and used for railway rolling stock manufacture. At the same time the British Electric Company of Trafford Park, Manchester also went bankrupt. So the syndicate purchased both for £65,000. It then entered discussions with the Electric Railway and Tramway Carriage Works Ltd, Preston and persuaded that company to purchase both factories in order to prevent anyone else entering into tramcar manufacturing there. It was agreed and the sale was made for £85,000 a profit of £20,000 for the syndicate! The Electric Railway and Tramway Carriage Works Ltd changed its name to The United Electric Car Company Ltd. While the names of the old companies were kept for a while, they did not do any trading and were wound up in 1917.

NOTE: G. C. Milnes, Voss & Company of Birkenhead was an entirely separate company and will be examined in more detail below.

1887	Leeds Tramways Co.	2 D/D, 4 S/D
1887	Birkdale & Southport Tramways Co.	7 D/D
1888	Harrow Road and Paddington Tramway Co.	12 D/D
1888	St Helens and District Tramways Co.	1 S/D
1889	Douglas Bay Tramway	2 T/R
1889	Greenock and Port Glasgow Tramways Co.	11 D/D
1890	Chesterfield & District Tramways Co. Ltd	2 S/D
1890	Douglas Bay Tramway	2 T/R
1890	South Shields Tramways & Carriage Co. Ltd	6 D/D
1891	Burnley and District Tramways Co. Ltd	4 D/D
1891	Douglas Bay Tramway	4 T/R
1891	Folkestone, Sandgate and Hythe Tramways Co.	2 S/D
1892	Bristol Tramways and Carriage Co. Ltd	8 D/D
1892	Douglas Bay Tramway	3 S/D
1892	Nottingham and District Tramways Co. Ltd	4 D/D
1893	Glasgow Corporation Tramways	1 D/D
1893	Wallasey United Tramways and Omnibus Co. Ltd	7 D/D
1894	Wirral Tramway Co. Ltd	2 D/D
1894	Douglas Bay Tramway	2 T/R
1894	West Metropolitan Tramways Co. Ltd	15 D/D
1894	Plymouth Corporation Tramways	3 D/D, 2 S/D
1895	Wirral Tramway Co. Ltd	1 D/D
1895	Bristol Tramways and Carriage Co. Ltd	18 D/D
1895	London United Tramways Ltd	10 D/D
1895	Nottingham and District Tramways Co. Ltd	3 D/D
1895	Plymouth Corporation Tramways	2 D/D
1895	Wolverhampton Tramways Co. Ltd	1 D/D
1896	Wirral Tramway Co. Ltd	2 D/D
1896	Bristol Tramways and Carriage Co. Ltd	6 D/D
1896	Douglas Bay Tramway	6 C/B
1896	Sheffield Corporation Tramways	12 D/D, 12 T/R
1897	Leeds Corporation Tramways	4 D/D
1898	Chesterfield Corporation Tramways	1 S/D
1898	Leeds Corporation Tramways	10 D/D, 10 S/D
1899	Chesterfield Corporation Tramways	2 S/D
1900	Greenock and Port Glasgow Tramways Co.	3 D/D
1900	City of Derry Tramways Co. Ltd	2 D/D
1902	Douglas Bay Tramway	3 T/R
1903	City of Derry Tramways Co. Ltd	2 D/D

Douglas tramway purchased a G.C. Milnes, Voss & Company tramcar for their long-lived system.

G.C. MILNES, VOSS & COMPANY

George Milnes must have been very unhappy with the German majority shareholders when they decided in 1902 to close the Birkenhead factory and concentrate all production at Hadley in Shropshire. He also had a contract with the company that he would work for them for seven years and during that time not be involved in any other tramcar building company. However, these restrictions did not apply to George Comer Milnes, his son and cashier in the company nor to Thomas Voss, chief draughtsman. The latter two formed a new company, G.C. Milnes, Voss & Company (actually a partnership) in 1902 to make and supply tramcar accessories. They took on premises also in Cleveland Street, but not those of G.F. Milnes, but near to Duke Street.

They identified a gap in the market, specialising in tramcar spares such as seats and of making specialised one-off tramcars, such as the funeral tramcar for the Durban tramway. Early on the firm specialised in making and fitting removable top covers for open top tramcars. At this stage in tramway history operators were finding that the open-top car was at a disadvantage in the rain, as everyone wanted to sit in the dry lower saloon. The early experimenters with top covers soon reported increased revenue and other operators wanted to follow suit. As Milnes, Voss had the patent they were able to claim royalties from any other tramcar manufacturer making similar covers. After a challenge from the London County Council the royalty claims faded away. So in 1905 the company looked to making complete tramcars. Without the experience of electrical equipment the company made unpowered trams, such as horse trams and trailers for motor trams.

The horse trams were purchased exclusively by the Douglas Bay tramway. Later they teamed with Mountain & Gibson who produced tram trucks. They were now able to produce electric tramcars.

The company became a limited company in 1906. Sales of the electric trams went well, with the company often under bidding more established companies like Brush and Dick, Kerr. In 1910 G.C. Milnes decided to emigrate to Canada and he sold his share of the business to Thomas Voss. The company continued until January 1912 when an exceptionally heavy snow fall caused the roof of the factory to collapse stopping all production for several weeks. But orders had already started to dry up.

One of the last orders was for a single horse tram for the Douglas Bay tramway. The company finally closed in 1914, with a life of just 12 years.

1905	Douglas Bay Tramway	2 T/R
1908	Douglas Bay Tramway	1 T/R
1909	Douglas Bay Tramway	1 T/R
1911	Douglas Bay Tramway	1 T/R
1913	Douglas Bay Tramway	1 S/D

NEWCASTLE & GOSFORTH TRAMWAYS & CARRIAGE COMPANY LIMITED

Tramways come to Newcastle in the form of the Newcastle & Gosforth Tramways & Carriage Co. Ltd, opened in 1878 with tramcars built by Ashbury. It seems that, like other tramway companies, the organisation started to build their own tramcars sometime in the 1880s. There is no record of the number or type of trams constructed.

c1880	Newcastle & Gosforth Tramways & Carriage Co. Ltd	?

NORTH METROPOLITAN TRAMWAYS COMPANY

The North Metropolitan Tramways Company was formed in 1869 to build tramways in the northern part of the Greater London area. Initially the company purchased tramcars from Stephenson in the USA and later it also purchased tramcars from Starbuck and Hughes. In 1877 a purpose-built repair works was opened in Union Road, Leytonstone. This was used to repair and reconstruct their tramcar fleet – many of the old trams were rebuilt and modified. Then under the North Metropolitan Tramways Act 1885 the company was authorised to build tramcars for itself and other undertakings. The Union Road Works was used as the factory to make the tramcars and they also manufactured a few omnibuses. As far as can be determined over 300 tramcars were built by the company, most for their own use but cars made by North Metropolitan Tramways Company were sold to Glasgow, Portsmouth, Southampton, South East Metropolitan and Plymouth. Tramcar construction continued from 1885 to 1906 when the company was acquired by the London County Council Tramways.

1885	North Metropolitan Tramways Co.	66 D/D
1887	North Metropolitan Tramways Co.	44 D/D
1888	North Metropolitan Tramways Co.	20 D/D
1889	North Metropolitan Tramways Co.	18 D/D
1890	North Metropolitan Tramways Co.	38 D/D
1890	South Eastern Metropolitan Tramways Co.	10 D/D
1891	North Metropolitan Tramways Co.	26 D/D
1892	North Metropolitan Tramways Co.	42 D/D
1893	Glasgow Corporation Tramways	3 D/D
1893	North Metropolitan Tramways Co.	32 D/D
1893	Southampton Tramways Co.	4 D/D
1893	Provincial Tramways Co.	10 D/D
1894	North Metropolitan Tramways Co.	36 D/D
1895	North Metropolitan Tramways Co.	48 D/D
1896	North Metropolitan Tramways Co.	50 D/D
1897	North Metropolitan Tramways Co.	22 D/D
1898	North Metropolitan Tramways Co.	40 D/D

The North Metropolitan Tramways Company made many tramcars for their own use and then sold their new trams to other systems. This is one they used on their own tramway.

The Oldbury Railway Carriage and Wagon Company Limited made a few tramcars. This Brighton & Shoreham tramcar was one of them.

1898	Gravesend, Rosherville and Northfleet Tramways Co. Ltd	4 D/D
1899	North Metropolitan Tramways Co.	40 D/D

OLDBURY RAILWAY CARRIAGE & WAGON COMPANY LIMITED (FORMERLY RAILWAY CARRIAGE COMPANY)

The Railway Carriage Company was founded around 1847 in premises alongside Bromsgrove Railway Station and moved in 1854 to a larger factory in Oldbury. A trade magazine of the time reported that the Railway Carriage Company built a double-deck tramcar for Train's London tramway. If this is correct it would be the first tramcar to be built in Britain. However, it is possible that this tram was completed after the London tramways closed and the vehicle was delivered to the Old Swan Tramway in Liverpool. Horse tramcar production was limited, making just 20 trams over a 26-year period. The name of the company was changed in 1886 to the Oldbury Railway Carriage and Wagon Company Limited.

1861	Old Swan Tramway	1 D/D
1882	Shipley Tramways	1 D/D, 1 S/D
1882	St Helens and District Tramways Co.	3 S/D
1885	Brighton & Shoreham Tramways Co. Ltd	3 S/D
1886	Brighton & Shoreham Tramways Co. Ltd	7 D/D
1887	Blackburn Corporation Tramways Co.	6 D/D

RAILWAY CARRIAGE COMPANY

See OLDBURY RAILWAY CARRIAGE & WAGON COMPANY LIMITED

RANDERS JERNBANEVOGN-FABRIK, LATER VOGNFABRIKKEN SCANDIA

In 1861 an English company opened a factory in Randers, Denmark and Frederick James Rowan, an English railway engineer, became the Managing Director. In 1869 the company decided to pull out of the country and the factory was sold to Frederick Rowan. He renamed it Randers Jernbanevogn-Fabrik, a railway carriage works, and started making rolling stock and other items for railways and tramways. The majority of his customers were in Sweden, where the tramcars gained a reputation for being of high quality and very comfortable to ride. The company did have one British order for horse tramcars from the Metropolitan Street Tramways Company in 1870. In 1872 Frederick Rowan retired from the job and passed the managing directorship to his son William R. Rowan. By this time the factory had a workforce of over 100. In 1876 the company was sold and the name changed to Vognfabrikken Scandia, though William Rowan stayed as a Board director. He ventured into steam tram locomotives and patented a system that was incorporated into a steam tramcar, similar in outward appearance to the Grantham steam tramcar. The patents were taken up by Kitson of Leeds, who manufactured a number of steam rail cars and tramcars using the patent. The company continued to supply the railway industry becoming ABB Scandia and that was later taken into the Adtranz Group.

1870	Metropolitan Street Tramways	? D/D

SAVILE STREET FOUNDRY & ENGINEERING COMPANY LIMITED

When the Rothesay Tramway was built the company advertised for tenders for 12 tramcars. The contract was placed with the Savile Street Foundry & Engineering Company of Savile Street East, Sheffield. This factory was mainly a foundry, making steel castings, stone crushers and similar heavy engineering machines. They also made bone mills, coprolite, phosphate and lime crushers and stationary engines, all of which had applications for agricultural use. The Rothesay order was an attempt to diversify. When delivered the toastrack trams appeared to give problems, associated with the canvass roof they had. The tramway company ordered two more tramcars from a local joiner that had more substantial roofs. These appeared to be more successful as they had the Savile Street cars re-roofed with sheet iron. They started action against the Savile Street builders but after a year it was dropped, possibly because the contract specified a canvass awning that could be removed. It is likely that such an arrangement could not withstand the Rothesay winds. Savile Street Foundry & Engineering Company did not make any further horse trams, possibly as a result of their experiences at Rothesay. They did patent a steam tramway locomotive around 1882 that was tried on the Sheffield and Burnley systems, but nothing came of it.

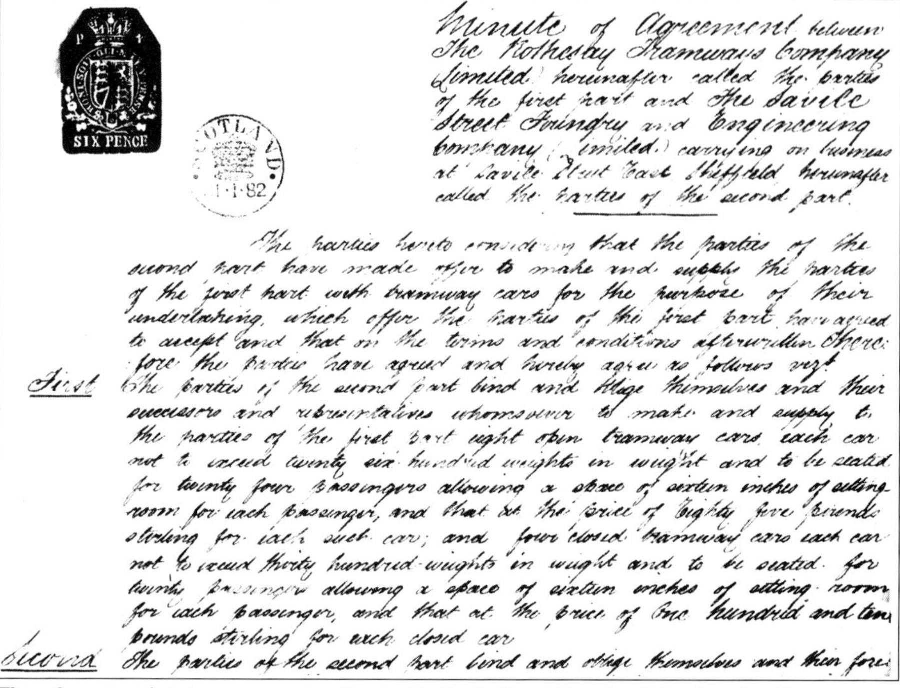
SIX PENCE

SCOTLAND 1·1·82

Minute of Agreement between The Rothesay Tramways Company Limited hereinafter called the parties of the first part and The Savile Street Foundry and Engineering Company Limited carrying on business at Savile Street East Sheffield hereinafter called the parties of the second part.

The parties hereto considering that the parties of the second part have made offer to make and supply the parties of the first part with tramway cars for the purpose of their undertaking, which offer the parties of the first part have agreed to accept and that on the terms and conditions afterwritten Therefore the parties have agreed and hereby agree as follows vizt

First The parties of the second part bind and oblige themselves and their successors and representatives whomsoever to make and supply to the parties of the first part eight open tramway cars each car not to exceed twenty six hundredweights in weight and to be seated for twenty four passengers allowing a space of sixteen inches of sitting room for each passenger, and that at the price of Eighty five pounds sterling for each such car; and four closed tramway cars each car not to exceed thirty hundredweights in weight and to be seated for twenty passengers allowing a space of sixteen inches of sitting room for each passenger, and that at the price of One hundred and ten pounds sterling for each closed car

Second The parties of the second part bind and oblige themselves and their fore[illegible]

The only venture into tramcar construction by the Savile Street Foundry & Engineering Company was for 12 trams for the Rothesay tramways that led to recriminations and threatened legal action.

1882	Rothesay Tramways Co Ltd	4 S/D, 8 T/R

R. & J. SHINNIE

Aberdeen District tramways commissioned R. and J. Shinnie, local coachbuilders to build trams for their system.

Aberdeen and District Tramways Company commenced operation in 1874 using tramcars probably purchased from Starbuck. More tramcars were needed in 1882 and the company turned to a local coachbuilder R. and J. Shinnie, with workshops in Union Row, and an example tramcar was ordered. The tramway company was satisfied and further tramcars were purchased. Indeed from 1882 the only tramcars purchased by the company came from the local coachbuilder, a director describing a tramcar as "one of the two beautiful new cars constructed by Messrs R. and J. Shinnie". The Aberdeen coachbuilder did not make any other tramcars.

1882	Aberdeen District Tramways Co.	1 D/D
1888	Aberdeen District Tramways Co.	4 D/D
1889	Aberdeen District Tramways Co.	3 D/D
1891	Aberdeen District Tramways Co.	5 D/D
1894	Aberdeen District Tramways Co.	9 D/D
1896	Aberdeen District Tramways Co.	3 D/D

SMITH & WILLEY, WINDSOR FOUNDRY, LIVERPOOL

The Smith & Willey Windsor Foundry was established in Edge Hill, Liverpool well before the coming of railways, so when the railways arrived in Liverpool the company could offer experience in casting to the railway industry. They specialised in railway wagon and carriage manufacturing, though the earliest known example of their work was for a tramway, the Stratford and Moreton Tramroad purchasing at least one wagon from them. Records of production ceased in 1849 and it is likely this was when the factory closed, as in 1850 there is a record of some of the equipment being sold.

c1830	Stratford & Moreton Tramway	1 truck

The Stratford and Moreton Tramroad purchased wagons from the Smith & Willey Windsor Foundry and these were used to carry passengers as well as goods.

SOUTH EASTERN RAILWAY COMPANY LIMITED

More used to building railway rolling stock the South Eastern Railway built tramcars for their tramway in Folkestone.

The South Eastern Railway (SER) has a long and complex history and as the tramway involvement of this main line railway company is such a minute part of their business the history of the company will not be explored. If the reader wishes to explore this more it is suggested they read one of the many railway histories. The tramway interest arises from the Folkestone, Sandgate and Hythe Tramways Company, a tramway that ran between Sandgate and Hythe (never reaching Folkestone), that was owned by the SER. Built partly on an existing contractor's light railway, the tramway opened in 1891. Two tramcars, one crossbench the other a toastrack, were ordered from Milnes, both with a surprising capacity of 40 seated passengers. All subsequent tramcars were built by the SER workshops in Ashford. The tramway closed during the First World War, but reopened with a summer service using mules rather than horse power.

1892	Folkestone, Sandgate and Hythe Tramways Co.	1 S/D 1 T/R
1897	Folkestone, Sandgate and Hythe Tramways Co.	1 T/R

STARBUCK CAR AND WAGON COMPANY

George Starbuck was born in 1834 in Massachusetts not far from G.F. Train's home and it is likely that the two families knew each other because he joined Train as his assistant during the development of the Birkenhead Street Railway in 1860. It was always Train's ambition to operate street railways in London, as London was the largest city in Europe and what happened there usually made its way to other cities. So Train sold his share of the Birkenhead tramway to his fellow directors later in 1860 and moved to London, with Starbuck. In 1861 the three short lived London tramways were built with Starbuck being Managing Director. When all three lines were closed in 1862 Starbuck was out of a job. Train moved to the Potteries where he opened the Staffordshire Potteries Street Railway in 1866.

It is not clear if Starbuck helped in this project as around 1862 he returned to Birkenhead and opened a carriage workshop possibly in the Mahogany Shed, Vittoria Wharf, which had been the premises of Prentis & Co., where the original Birkenhead tramcars had been assembled and finally finished. They had arrived in England in what would now be described as 'flat-packed' and required to be assembled ready for use. It is a matter of speculation as to the relationship between Starbuck and John Stephenson. Both were American and probably knew each other through Train's contacts. Starbuck had plans to be a

The Starbuck Car and Wagon Company Ltd. was Britain's largest horse tramcar manufacturer. One of the early orders was for the Liverpool Tramways Company.

tramcar builder and recognised the potential in the expanding number of tramways. He may well have been chosen by Stephenson to assemble the 'flat pack' tramcars shipped to Britain, in which case he would have gained plenty of knowledge on the design and construction of the trams. George Starbuck's first tramcars were eight double-deck cars for Copenhagen in 1863. But there was a lull in demand for tramcars in Britain and Starbuck must have turned to other vehicles such as omnibuses, carriages and carts to keep his business going (a clue is given by the name change in 1872 to the Starbuck Car and Wagon Company Ltd. from the 1871 name George Starbuck and Company Limited). With the passing of the Tramways Act in 1870 there was a rush of tramway proposals and the upsurge in business saw George Starbuck seeking larger premises in 227 Cleveland Street.

Business was very good and Starbuck needed to expand, so in 1873-74 he acquired the buildings along Cleveland Street up to and including number 241. Business was good up to 1880 with orders from Britain, Ireland and the continent. The demand for tramcars was high and other companies had joined the market and were competing heavily against Starbuck, forcing prices down and reducing profits. Shareholders were not happy about this and voted in 1886 to wind up the company. This was set in motion. However, the factory in Birkenhead was not closed. Instead the Company Secretary, George Federick Milnes, purchased the factory, machinery and goodwill and changed the name to G.F. Milnes & Co.

Some Starbuck horse tramcars continued in service when steam traction was introduced, as this photograph of the North Metropolitan tramways shows.

1862	Staffordshire Potteries Street Railway Co. Ltd	2? S/D
1869	Liverpool Tramways Co.	18 D/D
1870	Metropolitan Street Tramways Co.	?
1871	Leeds Tramways Co.	4 D/D
1871	Ryde Pier Tramways	5 D/D
1872	Cork Tramways Co. Ltd	6 D/D
1873	Belfast Street Tramways Co.	16 D/D
1873	Hoylake and Birkenhead Railway and Tramway Co.	8 D/D
1873	Birmingham & District Tramways Co. Ltd	? D/D
1873	Leeds Tramways Co.	8 D/D, 2 S/D
1873	Sheffield Tramways Co.	12 D/D
1873	Southport Tramways Co. Ltd	16 D/D
1873	Vale of Clyde Tramways Co.	12 D/D
1874	Aberdeen District Tramways Co.	4 D/D, 2 S/D,
1874	Dewsbury, Batley & Birstal Tramway Co.	5 D/D, 2 S/D
1874	Leeds Tramways Co.	9 D/D, 9 S/D
1874	Leicester Tramways Co. Ltd	30 S/D
1874	Sheffield Tramways Co.	18 D/D
1874	Southall, Ealing & Shepherds Bush Tram Railway Co.	2 D/D
1874	Middlesbrough and Stockton Tramways Co.	2 D/D, 2 S/D
1875	Belfast Street Tramways Co.	26 D/D
1875	Bristol Tramways and Carriage Co. Ltd	7 D/D
1875	Leeds Tramways Co.	13 S/D
1875	North Metropolitan Tramways Co.	5 D/D
1875	Newport Tramways Co.	2 S/D
1875	Sheffield Tramways Co.	8 S/D
1875	Wantage Tramways Co. Ltd	1 D/D, 1 S/D
1875	Aberdeen District Tramways Co.	2 D/D
1876	Birkenhead Street Railway	8 D/D
1876	Birmingham Tramways and Omnibus Co. Ltd	? D/D
1876	Bristol Tramways and Carriage Co. Ltd	5 D/D
1876	Douglas Bay Tramway	2 D/D, 1 S/D,
1876	Leeds Tramways Co.	6 S/D
1876	Wrexham District Tramways Co.	1 D/D, 1 S/D
1876	Edinburgh Street Tramways Co.	11 D/D, 10 T/R
1877	Bristol Tramways and Carriage Co. Ltd	33 D/D, 5 S/D
1877	Wirral Tramway Co. Ltd	7 S/D
1877	Southall, Ealing & Shepherds Bush Tram Railway Co.	1 D/D
1877	Manchester and Salford Tramways Co.	30 D/D
1877	Sheffield Tramways Co.	18 D/D, 5 S/D
1878	Birkenhead Street Railway	8 D/D
1878	Birmingham Tramways and Omnibus Co. Ltd	2 S/D
1878	Southall, Ealing & Shepherds Bush Tram Railway Co.	1 D/D
1878	Manchester and Salford Tramways Co.	4 S/D
1878	Nottingham and District Tramways Co. Ltd	8 S/D
1878	Southport Tramways Co. Ltd	16 D/D
1879	Wirral Tramway Co. Ltd	7 S/D
1879	Dublin Central Tramways Co.	22 D/D
1879	Galway & Salthill Tramway Co.	6 D/D
1879	Croydon Tramways Co.	5 S/D
1879	Wallasey United Tramways and Omnibus Co. Ltd	7 S/D
1879	Southampton Tramways Co.	9 D/D, 6 S/D
1879	Birkenhead Street Railway	8 D/D
1880	Bath Tramways Co.	6 S/D
1880	Wirral Tramway Co. Ltd	2 S/D
1880	Cambridge Street Tramways Co.	2 D/D, 2 S/D
1880	Derby Tramways Co.	16 S/D
1880	Dewsbury, Batley & Birstal Tramway Co.	6 D/D
1880	Galway & Salthill Tramway Co.	1 D/D
1880	Ipswich Tramways Co.	2 S/D
1880	Croydon Tramways Co.	2 S/D
1880	Nottingham and District Tramways Co. Ltd	5 S/D
1880	City of York Tramways Co.	3 S/D
1881	Bristol Tramways and Carriage Co. Ltd	21 D/D
1881	Burnley and District Tramways Co. Ltd	7 D/D
1881	City of Gloucester Tramways Co. Ltd	6 S/D
1881	North Metropolitan Tramways Co.	7 D/D
1881	North Staffordshire Tramways Co. Ltd	20 D/D
1881	Nottingham and District Tramways Co. Ltd	5 S/D
1881	Southampton Tramways Co.	4 D/D
1881	City of Oxford and District Tramways Co. Ltd	4 S/D
1881	City of York Tramways Co.	2 T/R, 2 S/D
1882	Douglas Bay Tramway	1 D/D
1882	Liverpool United Tramways & Omnibus Co.	10 D/D
1882	North Metropolitan Tramways Co.	5 D/D
1882	City of York Tramways Co.	2 S/D
1883	Bath Tramways Co.	1 S/D
1883	Douglas Bay Tramway	2 D/D
1883	Manchester, Bury, Rochdale & Oldham Steam Tramways Co. Ltd	3 D/D
1883	Middlesbrough & Stockton Tramways Co.	3 D/D
1883	Nottingham and District Tramways Co. Ltd	2 S/D
1883	Sheffield Tramways Co.	7 D/D
1884	Burnley and District Tramways Co. Ltd	5 D/D
1884	Douglas Bay Tramway	2 D/D, 2 T/R
1884	Nottingham and District Tramways Co. Ltd	2 T/R
1884	Burnley and District Tramways Co. Ltd	5 D/D
1885	Blackpool Corporation Tramways	2 D/D, 2 T/R
1885	Chester Tramways Co.	2 D/D
1885	Nottingham and District Tramways Co. Ltd	1 D/D, 2 S/D
1885	Cambridge Street Tramways Co.	2 S/D
1886	Douglas Bay Tramway	1 T/R
1888	Douglas Bay Tramway	1 T/R
1888	Galway & Salthill Tramway Co.	1 S/D
1889	Keighley Tramways Co. Ltd	7 D/D
1894	Cambridge Street Tramways Co.	1 D/D

1894	Greenock and Port Glasgow Tramways Co.	6 D/D
1897	City of Derry Tramways Co. Ltd	2 D/D
1905	City of Derry Tramways Co. Ltd	2 D/D
1909	Cambridge Street Tramways Co.	1 D/D

JOHN STEPHENSON COMPANY LIMITED

John Stephenson was born in 1809 in County Armagh having a Scottish mother and an English father. At the age of two his parents moved to New York and John Stephenson was brought up in America. After leaving school at the age of sixteen he started work as a clerk. However, he was not happy and persuaded his parents to support him in getting an apprenticeship with Andrew Wade, a coachmaker, as his interest lay in woodworking and mechanics. He made a favourable impression with Abram Brower, a stage coach operator and when John Stephenson finished his apprenticeship he was encouraged by Brower to set up his own workshop and in 1831 Brower gave him space at the rear of his stables. Brower had heard of a larger carriage used in Paris and called an omnibus. Brower asked Stephenson to build one. He soon had orders from other stage coach operators. But within a year, in 1832, his workshop and Brower's stables were burnt down. With no insurance it was difficult, but Stephenson built a new workshop in Elizabeth Street. The New York and Harlem Street Railroad needed passenger carriages and initially Milne Parker supplied the first two tramcars. John Stephenson was interested in this new opportunity and he patented a very similar tramcar in 1833, then built it for the New York and Harlem Street Railroad and called it the "John Mason" after the Railroad's President. This astute piece of business shows the commercial acumen of John Stephenson that was to lead to him becoming the head of the world's largest tramcar manufacturer.

The rise of public transport, particularly in New York, meant that there were heavy demands for Stephenson's tramcars, railway carriages and omnibuses. By the middle of the 1830s railway carriages had lengthened and were mounted on bogies. He now needed a new workshop as his Elizabeth Street premises were not large enough. These were completed in 1837 at 4th

Inside the Stephenson factory showing the extremely cramped conditions.

The Stephenson factory machine shop, no health and safety in those days!

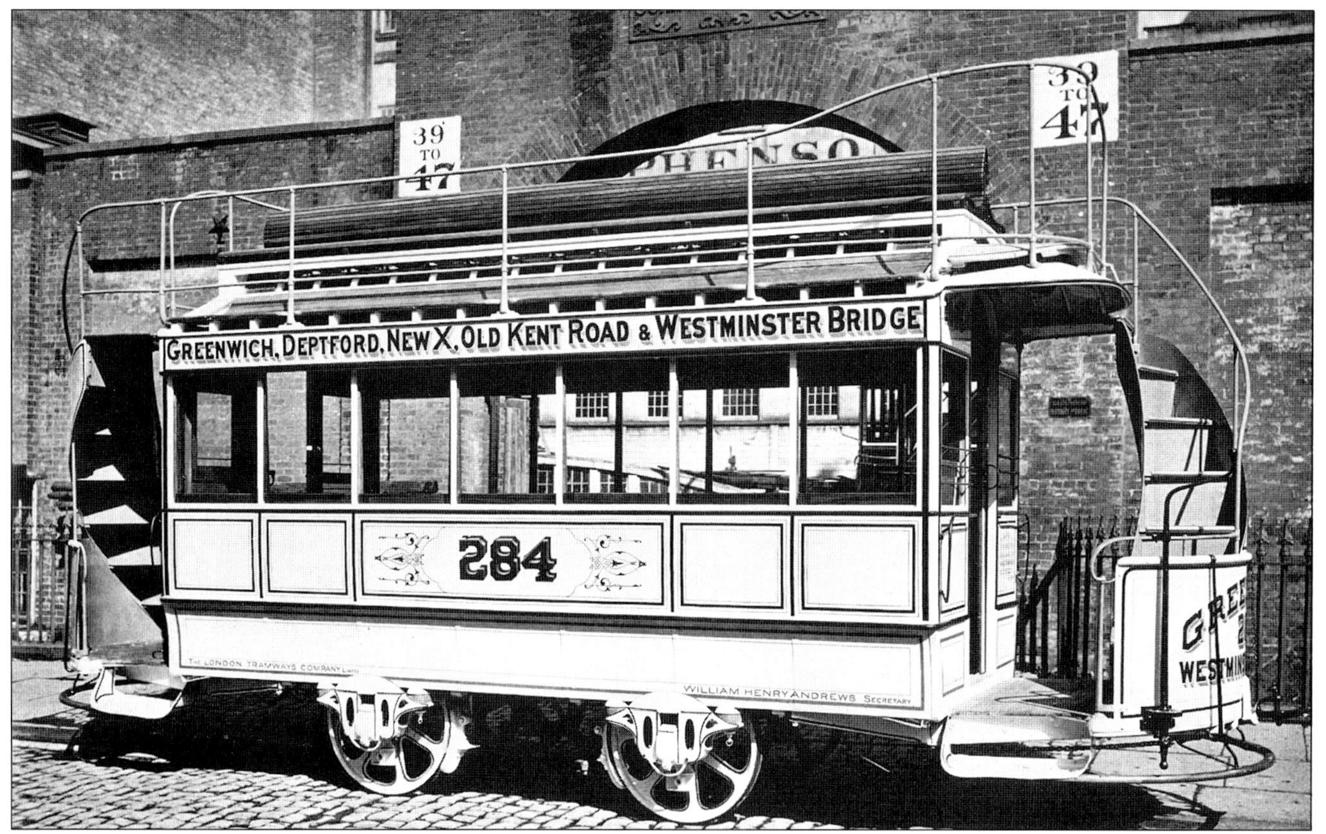

Seen outside the Stephenson factory in New York, this London Tramways Company car waits to be transported to England.

Avenue and 129th Street, further away from the city centre with more room and good access to the New York and Harlem Railroad. This opening coincided with a recession and orders started to dry up. To keep the business going he sold railway carriages against stock certificates of the railroad. However, as the recession continued these proved worthless and he could not pay his creditors. He carried on until 1842 when his workshop and assets were seized.

He reached an agreement with his creditors and they were paid 50 cents in every dollar. However he felt obliged to find a way of paying them their full amount. He managed to raise capital for a new workshop at Fourth Avenue and 27th Street that was opened in 1843. His experience with the railroad industry made him ignore that side of manufacture and instead concentrated on making trams, carriages, carts and omnibuses. The expansion of public transport meant his omnibuses were in demand and by 1856 he had 200 workers just making omnibuses. The use of the grooved rail in New York from 1852 meant that street tramways were more acceptable and with the profits being made by the New York and Harlem Railroad more attractive as a business and John Stephenson was at hand to provide the tramcars more attractive as businesses. From this time the manufacture of omnibuses declined as the tram production increased. His aim was always to make his tramcars strong, yet as light as possible to ease the burden on the horses. One idea to reduce weight was the reversible tramcar, where the body could be turned on the chassis at the terminus. John Slawson had developed this in 1855 and Stephenson used the design with Slawson becoming Treasurer of the company. The reversible tramcar was rather like that adopted by Eades some 22 years later. Another innovation, in 1860, was the bobtail car, a small single horse tramcar operated by one man. By 1883 no less than half the tramcars in America were of this type, despite the complaints by the passengers of the cramped conditions and slower journeys, as the driver had to collect the fares.

The 1860s saw the beginning of street tramways in Britain. With Train being the initial promoter it was not unusual that he went to the largest manufacturer of tramcars for his vehicles. So they were built by John Stephenson. He had plenty of experience of sending tramcars long distances and it is believed that the trams crossed the ocean in pieces for final assembly (or possibly re-assembly) in Britain. Other promoters recognised the quality of the Stephenson tramcars, partly promoted by the availability in America of inexpensive good timber. Many operators placed orders for their new tramways. So Stephenson had a thriving trade with Britain. In America there was another panic in 1873 leading to a four-year recession. To keep his creditors happy, in 1876 Stephenson made the workshop into a joint stock company, giving his creditors stock in payment for their bills. Its name became John Stephenson Company Limited. Bankruptcy was only narrowly avoided when the company was saved by the economy picking up in 1878. Orders increased and Stephenson was able to continue to supply quality tramcars at competitive prices. In 1878 the London tramway, North Metropolitan Tramways Co., advertised for 30 tramcars and received twenty bids. Despite coming from America the Stephenson tramcars were $165 cheaper than the next lowest bid, while being of a high quality. Not surprisingly they won many orders from all over the world.

Stephenson opened new workshops in Feigel (1873) and Lewis and Fowler (1883) and three factories opened in St Louis between 1875 and 1887. Stephenson himself died in 1893 at the age of 84, still working for his company. Another recession in 1893 highlighted the shortcomings of the old workshop in New York. A new factory was planned and land was purchased at Bay Way, New Jersey for the new workshops. The old 27th Street premises were sold when the new factory opened in 1898. But the optimism was dashed in 1898 when the company had to go into voluntary bankruptcy. This saw a decline in the company with the new workshop being sold in 1900. By 1905 the company was open to offers and it was sold to J. G. Brill and Company. By this time production of horse tramcars had virtually completely finished.

1860	Train's Tramway Birkenhead	2 S/D 2 D/D
1861	Train's Tramway Birkenhead	4 D/D
1861	London: Train's Tramways	5 S/D
1869	Liverpool United Tramways & Omnibus Co.	24 D/D
1870	North Metropolitan Tramways Co.	10 D/D
1870	Metropolitan Street Tramways Co.	?
1871	Leeds Tramways Co.	10 D/D
1871	Liverpool United Tramways & Omnibus Co.	6 D/D
1871	North Metropolitan Tramways Co.	20 D/D
1871	Pimlico, Peckham & Greenwich Street Tramways Co.	?
1873	North Metropolitan Tramways Co.	4 D/D
1875	North Metropolitan Tramways Co.	6 D/D
1875	Glasgow Tramway and Omnibus Co. Ltd	2 S/D 54 D/D
1876	Liverpool United Tramways & Omnibus Co.	6 D/D
1876	North Metropolitan Tramways Co.	4 D/D
1876	Edinburgh Street Tramways Co.	? D/D ? T/R
c1878	Liverpool United Tramways & Omnibus Co.	50 D/D
1878	North Metropolitan Tramways Co.	30 D/D
1878	Swansea Improvements and Tramways Co. Ltd	10 ?
1878	Wolverhampton Tramways Co. Ltd	4 S/D
1879	North Metropolitan Tramways Co.	19 D/D
1879	Nottingham and District Tramways Co. Ltd	3 D/D 1 S/D
1882	West Metropolitan Tramways Co. Ltd	10 D/D
c1890	Croydon Tramways Co.	2 D/D

SWANSEA IMPROVEMENTS AND TRAMWAYS COMPANY

When the tramways were built in Swansea the system opened in 1878 with 10 tramcars purchased from John Stephenson & Co. Over the next two years the workshop in the depot had experi-

Swansea Improvements and Tramways Company also built their own tramcars when the fleet needed additional cars.

ence in the maintenance and rebuilding of these tramcars and when the company wanted more trams they turned to their own craftsmen and all the subsequent tramcars were built 'in-house'. The company only built trams for themselves and did not sell any to other systems.

c1800	Swansea Improvements & Tramways Co.	57 D/D

THOMAS SWINTON & SONS

When Dundee & District Tramway Company Limited opened in 1877 it hired tramcars from the Glasgow Tramway and Omnibus Company. In 1879 they decided to purchase their own trams and chose the Eades reversible type. It is stated that these tramcars were built by a local coachbuilder, Thomas Swinton of Queen's Hotel Buildings, Dundee. This poses a problem as the photographs of the tramcars show clearly that they copied the Eades design, yet there are no such cars recorded as being sold in Scotland. It is more likely that the tramcars were built by Ashbury and possibly sent in parts for final assembly in the Thomas Swinton workshops.

1879	Dundee & District Tramway Co.	5 D/D
1880	Dundee & District Tramway Co.	2 D/D

It is likely that this Ashbury tramcar was assembled and painted by local coachbuilder Thomas Swinton.

TRAMWAY CAR & WORKS COMPANY LIMITED (BRITISH & FOREIGN TRAMWAYS COMPANY LIMITED, GREENWICH)

One of the major early tramway entrepreneurs was a London lawyer, John Morris, who joined with the legal firm Baxter, Rose, Norton & Co. and other businessmen to establish the British and Foreign Tramway Company with the aim to promote tramway systems in Britain and abroad. The company backed the development of the Glasgow Tramway and Omnibus Co. Ltd system, and the British and Foreign Tramway Company set up a subsidiary, the Tramway Car and Works Company, to construct tramcars among other activities. This subsidiary was based in Greenwich, including its workshop. Shipping complete tramcars to

The Tramway Car and Works Company made tramcars for the Glasgow system, looking suspiciously like the Stephenson tramcars used by Train.

Scotland proved uneconomic and later cars were sent "flat-packed" for final assembly in a workshop located in Glasgow. It seems to have sold tramcars only to tramway companies where the British and Foreign Tramway Company had an interest. The first customer was Edinburgh Street Tramways in 1871 with the Glasgow system following in 1872. However, the tramcars were found to be very heavy and overworked the horses. The Glasgow company cancelled the remainder of the order and purchased trams from Stephenson before making their own. The British and Foreign Tramway Company then had a downturn. It was wound up in 1874, becoming the Tramways Union Company, which gradually disappeared and by 1904 it was struck off the Register of Companies and dissolved.

1871	Edinburgh Street Tramways Co.	12 D/D
1872	Glasgow Tramway and Omnibus Co. Ltd	114 D/D
1873	Vale of Clyde Tramways Co.	12 D/D
1874	Stirling and Bridge of Allan Tramways Co. Ltd	2 D/D 1 S/D

UNITED ELECTRIC CAR COMPANY LIMITED

See DICK, KERR & COMPANY LIMITED

The Vulcan Motor & Engineering Company Limited was a very late comer into horse tramcar production making just three trams in 1935 for the Douglas tramway. Tramcars 48 and 50 are the Vulcan cars, stored in the Manx Electric Railway depot.

VULCAN MOTOR MANUFACTURING & ENGINEERING COMPANY LIMITED

The Vulcan Motor & Engineering Company Limited was founded in 1901 in Southport by brothers Thomas Hampson and Joseph Hampson and also E. Hope to manufacture internal combustion engine motor cars. The name was later changed to the Vulcan Motor Manufacturing & Engineering Company Limited. In 1906 a new factory was built in Crossens, three miles north of Southport. They continued to make private motor cars until the 1914-1918 War when much of the production moved to the war effort. At the same time the factory began making commercial vehicles and after the war the company further developed this side of their production and in 1927 the last cars were being built. The production continued with commercial vehicles, particularly those used by municipalities. In 1935 the Douglas Bay Horse Tramway required three new horse trams. The then Manager of the tramway, C.F. Wolsey, designed a novel all-weather tramcar. It was basically a crossbench tramcar with sides that could be fitted to turn it into a saloon car. Normally when the sides were fitted the seating would occupy the full width of the car. So he designed a neat arrangement on one side where the equivalent of a single seat would fold down leaving an access corridor between the seats and the side of the car.

In 1935 there were no horse tram manufacturers left and the contract was given to the Vulcan company, the only tramcars that they ever made. Unfortunately the commercial production side of the company was not a success and it went into receivership in 1931.

The company continued under the receiver until 1937 when it was purchased by Tilling-Stevens and production was moved to the Maidstone factory of the new owner. The Vulcan name continued to be used until 1950 when Tilling-Stevens was taken over by the Rootes Group, the Vulcan name disappearing in 1953.

1935	Douglas Bay Tramway	3 S/D

WGH TRANSPORTATION ENGINEERING

This company operated from the early 1990s and has the distinction of making the last completely new horse tramcar in the British Isles. In 1992 the Bradford Industrial Museum added the Horses at Work feature and as part of this development they commissioned a replica horse tramcar from WGH Transportation Engineering, a company based in Old Edlington, Doncaster that specialised in fairground rides. Unlike the other museum horse trams that are restored and renovated original cars, the Bradford tramcar is entirely new, being built to the original plans. The fate of WGH Transportation Engineering is not known.

1992	Bradford Industrial Museum	1 S/D

Britain's most recent tramcar is this replica tramcar made by WGH Transportation Engineering for the Bradford Industrial Museum. Author.

Section 3

THE TRAMWAY SYSTEMS

ABERDEEN

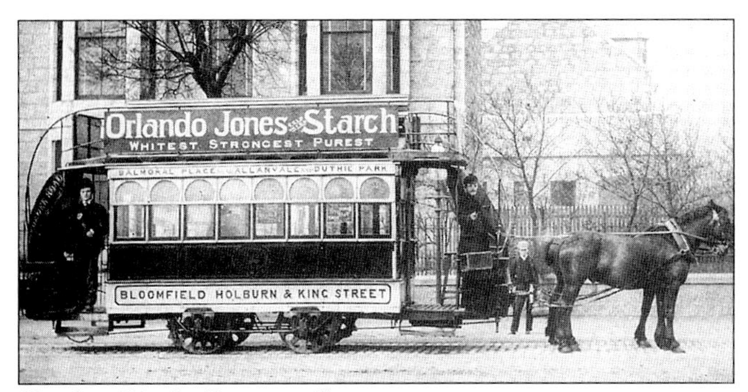

Aberdeen District Tramways Company.

ABERDEEN DISTRICT TRAMWAYS

4' 8½" gauge; 11 route miles; opened 1874; acquired by Aberdeen Corporation 1898.

Public transport began in Aberdeen with horse omnibus services starting around the 1860s. Thoughts turned to horse tramways in 1871 when a group of businessmen advertised shares in a horse tramway, making use of the 1870 Tramways Act. However, the offer was largely ignored and the scheme was saved by a London tramway agent offering to equal locally subscribed capital and nominate half the directors. The Aberdeen District Tramways Company was established in 1872 and the Aberdeen District Tramways Act was passed in 1872, but capital was still well below what was targeted, so building did not start until 1874 on a truncated system. The first public tramcar ran on 31 August. The start was financially disappointing and a fare increase was badly received by the public so the company had to sell horses to raise funds. The service frequency was re-arranged and the fares reduced, combined with some working savings the company made a profit. 1878 saw heavy snow falls and the company had a unique solution, they operated their services with horse-drawn sledges, until the snow could be cleared from the track. This continued each winter after each heavy snow fall.

Further business was generated by using feeder bus services extending public transport beyond the tramway termini. The tramway routes were extended in 1880 and again in 1883, 1888, and 1896. By then the company realised that horse power would need to be replaced by electric, but they did not have the money and the spectre of council compulsory purchase in 1908 loomed over them. So they made approaches to sell the system to the council in 1896. Negotiations were protracted as the council tried to reduce the price asked. The Great North of Scotland Railway put in an offer that was accepted by the tramway. All that was needed was the agreement of the council. This was the first instance of a main line railway wishing to buy a tramway and it created a lot of interest. The council refused to agree to the sale as they wished to run the tramway themselves, so they increased their offer and the tramway company agreed to the sale to the council. The council took over on 27 August 1898 after the Aberdeen Corporation Tramways Act, 1898 had been passed.

ABERDEEN CORPORATION TRAMWAYS

The council celebrated the purchase with all the tramcars being decorated. Six specially garlanded tramcars, each hauled by four horses, took dignitaries on a tour of the system, ending up in the Town Hall for a cake and wine banquet, while employees had a free supper that evening. The general public also benefited with a two day application of a flat rate one penny fare. While the Corporation continued to run the horse tramway, introducing official stopping places by marking lamp posts, they immediately started converting the system for electric operation and the first electric car ran in 1899 and the last horse tram ran in 1902.

Routes at largest extent

Bridge of Dee – Bridge of Don (Red/White route colour)
City – Bayview (Blue route colour)
City – Mannofield (Green route colour)
City – Woodside (Red route colour)
City – Queens Cross (Yellow route colour)
Rosemount Circle (White route colour)

Tramcars purchased

Year	Cars	Builder
1874	4 D/D 2 S/D	Starbuck Car & Wagon Co.
1875	2 D/D	Starbuck Car & Wagon Co.
1882	2 D/D	Unknown
1882	1 D/D	R. & J. Shinnie of Aberdeen
1888	4 D/D	R. & J. Shinnie of Aberdeen
1889	3 D/D	R. & J. Shinnie of Aberdeen
1889	1 T/R	Aberdeen District Tramways
1891	5 D/D	R. & J. Shinnie of Aberdeen
1894	9 D/D	R. & J. Shinnie of Aberdeen
1896	3 D/D	R. & J. Shinnie of Aberdeen
		Sledge service from 1878 during winter

Livery of Aberdeen District Tramways Co.

Years	Livery
1874-1888	Yellow / Cream (White)
1874-1898	Red (Vermilion) / Cream (White)
1880-1898	Green / Cream (White)
1888-1898	All White
1896-1898	Blue / Cream

Livery of Aberdeen Corporation Tramways

Years	Livery
1898-1899	As Aberdeen District Tramways (Horse trams)

Aberdeen Corporation Tramways.

ALDERSHOT

ALDERSHOT & FARNBOROUGH TRAMWAY CO.

4' 8½" gauge; 3 route miles; opened 1881 or 1882; closed c1906.

Proposals to build a tramway in Aldershot began very early in tramway history when G.F. Train and others founded the Aldershot Street Railway Company in 1861, but nothing came of this initiative. The next proposal came in 1871 (following the Tramways Act 1870), however this too came to nothing. The next attempt came in 1878 and tram lines were laid, though with much modification, including placing the track by the side of some roads rather than in the roadway, and at a leisurely pace. Records are scarce and the system may have opened in 1881 when the line was passed by the Board of Trade Inspector. If it did then it closed very soon afterwards and did not recommence operation until 1883 when two single-deck tramcars were in use, both with first and third class accommodation. It appears the tramway closed after a short time and did not operate from 1884 to about 1887. It is reported that the tramcars were sold to gypsies. The system opened again around 1887 with four tramcars, two single-deck enclosed cars and two toastrack cars. Once again this only lasted a short time and then the company settled down to just one journey each evening from the depot in Farnborough to near North Camp. It is thought that this meagre service ceased in 1906 when some lines were laid for an electric tramway. However, this was never completed and Aldershot and Farnborough lost their tram system.

Route at largest extent
Farnborough Station – North Camp Station

Tramcars purchased

1882	2 S/D	Unknown
1884	2 S/D, 2 T/R	Unknown

Livery of Aldershot & Farnborough Tramway Co.

1882-1883	Blue / White or Dark Brown / White or Dark Green / White
1887-1906	Red / White
1887-1906	All White

ANDREWS (SOLOMON)
See Barmouth, Cardiff, Newport & Pwllheli

BARMOUTH

BARMOUTH JUNCTION & ARTHOG TRAMWAYS

3' 0" gauge; 2 route miles; opened 1899; closed 1903.

Solomon Andrews was an entrepreneur with interests in tramways, omnibuses, coach building and property development. Based in Cardiff he was on a rare holiday in North Wales in 1893 when he saw land for sale in Pwllheli. He purchased it and the story continues under the Pwllheli & Llanbedrog Tramway. The next year he purchased more land for development near Arthog, the other side of the estuary from Barmouth. In 1899 a builder's tramway was constructed to move materials from a local quarry to the building site. Later that year a tramcar was delivered and a passenger service commenced to take prospective tenants to the site.

It took some time to find tenants for all the houses and Andrews decided that it would not be viable to further develop the site. So building ceased and the tramway closed in 1903.

Route at largest extent
Barmouth Junction Station – Mawddach Crescent – Barmouth Bridge

Barmouth Junction & Arthog Tramways.

Tramcar purchased

1899	1 T/R	Solomon Andrews & Son

Livery of Barmouth Junction & Arthog Tramways

1899-1903	Dark Red / White

BATH

BATH TRAMWAYS COMPANY LIMITED, LATER PATENT CABLE TRAMWAYS CORPORATION, LATER DICK, KERR & CO LIMITED, LATER BATH ROAD CAR & TRAMWAY COMPANY LIMITED

4' 0" gauge; 1 route mile; opened 1880; acquired by Bath Corporation 1902.

In 1879 some of the Directors of Bristol Tramways, with some others, set in motion the preliminaries to build a tramway in Bath and later formed the Bath Tramways Company. In 1880 track laying started and the first tram service began later that year. However the tramway did not produce the receipts expected. So the company sold the system to the Patent Cable Tramways Corporation in 1884. Despite the name the tramway continued to be operated by horses, though seven new tramcars were purchased. Fortunes were not turned and the new company limped on for four years before going bankrupt. The ailing business was bought by Dick, Kerr & Co Limited in 1888. As operating tramways was not part of their core activity they were happy to sell it on a year later to the local omnibus operator, the Bath Omnibus Road Car Company Limited, that immediately changed its name to Bath Road Car & Tramway Company Limited. Operating both the bus and tram services meant that economies could be made and the company turned the loss making tramway into part of a profit making group. In 1902, at the end of the 21-year period the Corporation exercised their

Bath Road Car & Tramway Company Limited.

Belfast Street Tramways Company.

right to purchase the tramway to allow the promoters of the Bath Electric Tramways to change the system to electric operation. Horse tram services ceased and were replaced by horse buses to allow the rebuilding of the lines to take the heavier electric trams. The last owners of the tramway changed their name to Bath Carriage & Omnibus Limited to reflect their omnibus services, but they ceased trading in 1904 due to the electric tramways attracting the passengers.

Route at largest extent

Bath Railway Station – Lambridge

Tramcars purchased

1880	6 S/D	Starbuck Car & Wagon Co.
1883	1 S/D	Starbuck Car & Wagon Co.
1884	7 S/D	Unknown

Liveries of Bath Tramways

1880-1888	Not Known
1888-1902	Blue/Yellow

BELFAST

BELFAST STREET TRAMWAYS; ALSO RAN BELFAST & LIGONIEL TRAMWAY; SYDENHAM DISTRICT, BELFAST TRAMWAY CO; AND BELFAST & COUNTY DOWN RAILWAY

5' 3" gauge later 4' 8½"; 25 route miles; opened 1872; acquired by Belfast Corporation 1905.

The Belfast Street Tramways Company was founded in 1872 and obtained the Order-in-Council to build the 5 feet 3 inches gauge tramway and work commenced that year. The first line was opened on 28 August 1872. Additional routes were built in 1873 and 1875. Then in 1877 the company obtained another Bill to allow them to change the gauge of the tramway from 5 feet 3 inches to the standard gauge of 4 feet 8½ inches. There were further extensions in 1880 and then in 1885 a new company, the Sydenham District, Belfast Tramway Company, obtained authority to build lines in the city (with further lines in 1887 and 1889). However, they asked the Belfast Street Tramways Company to build the lines and then they rented them to BST who became the operator. Similarly when the Belfast & Ligoniel Tramway Company built a line to Ligoniel village in 1892 they rented it to the Belfast Street Tramways Company to provide the service. Then in 1894 the Belfast & County Down Railway wanted to ensure a good public service to their Queen's Quay terminus station so they built a tramway to join the Sydenham District, Belfast Tramway Company line in Bridge End into the station complex, with such a short line they rented it to the Belfast Street Tramways Company to run. These three systems, though owned by separate companies were operated with the Belfast Street Tramways Company's lines as a single system.

In 1886 Ireland was in the grip of Home Rule troubles and there were a number of clashes in Belfast and in one of them a young man on the Home Rule side was killed. During his funeral a mob rioted and attacked one of the horse tram depots. Other riots that year curtailed services but did little actual damage to tramcars. In 1889 a rival omnibus service was in direct competition with the tramways and they approached the tramway with a view to purchase it, but this was rejected by the tramway company. In 1890 the tramway company purchased six omnibuses and it is suggested this was done to impede the rival bus operator by running a tram in front of the rival buses and placing a bus behind it. This manoeuvre ensured that the rival bus had very few passengers and so the bus company's income was

Cavehill & Whitewell Tramway.

badly affected. This did little to improve relationships between the two companies.

In 1896 the company decided it was time to change to electrical operation and approached the Corporation with the idea. But the Corporation were looking to the 21-year purchase rule and set extortionate terms for agreement and the tramway company had to put aside their plans. They did get approval for extensions and the plan was to build these as electric tramways. In 1899 the Corporation obtained authority to build tramways that would extend the Belfast Street Tramways Company system and offered to rent the lines to them. This was agreed and the tramway company ran the new lines. Then in 1902 the tramway company approached the corporation with an offer to sell the tramway to them. But the corporation tried to lower the price and the shareholders refused. So instead the Belfast Street Tramways Company purchased the Sydenham District, Belfast Tramway Company and the Belfast & Ligoniel Tramway Company as was detailed in their rental agreement.

The sale went through, but at the same time the corporation informed the company that they had applied for compulsory purchase of the system. The company protested that under the 1893 Act the purchase date had been set at 1907. However the corporation were not deterred and obtained an Act to purchase the tramway in 1905, the sum to be paid to be set by an independent arbitrator. The corporation then took over the tramway in January 1905.

Routes at largest extent

Balmoral – City
Falls Park – City
Shankhill – City
Ligoniel – City
Chichester – City
York Road Station – City
Belmont – City
Oberon Street – City
Galwally Park – City

Tramcars purchased

1872	3 S/D	German
1873	16 D/D	Starbuck Car & Wagon Co.
c1875	26 D/D	Starbuck Car & Wagon Co.
1885	16 D/D	Starbuck Car & Wagon Co.
1888	2 D/D	Belfast Street Tramways
1889	7 D/D	Belfast Street Tramways
1890	11 D/D	Belfast Street Tramways
1891	8 D/D	Belfast Street Tramways
1893	10 D/D	Belfast Street Tramways
1894	2 D/D	Belfast Street Tramways
1895	2 D/D	Belfast Street Tramways
1897	21 D/D	Belfast Street Tramways
1898	7 D/D	Belfast Street Tramways
1899	12 D/D	Belfast Street Tramways
1900	16 D/D	Belfast Street Tramways
1901	10 D/D	Belfast Street Tramways
1902	13 D/D	Belfast Street Tramways

Liveries of Belfast Street Tramways

1872-1905	Blue / White

CAVEHILL & WHITEWELL TRAMWAYS CO.

4' 8½" gauge; 3 route miles; opened 1882; last horse tram 1905; acquired by Belfast Corporation 1911.

The Cavehill & Whitewell Tramway was promoted partly in order to provide a means of public transport to the Bellevue Zoo Park, a large pleasure area for Belfast citizens. Indeed it may well have had its origins in the law that on Sundays, public houses were only allowed to sell alcoholic drinks to bona fide travellers. To qualify it was necessary to have travelled at least three miles, the distance from the tramway terminus to Bellevue, so possession of a Cavehill & Whitewell tram ticket was proof of such a journey and Sundays proved to give a peak service demand (with a thriving trade for touts selling used tickets!). The tramway opened in July 1882 as a steam tramway, with just one locomotive. A second locomotive was added later in the year. Repairs to the tram locomotives were an expensive item and by 1892 they were giving trouble and the company decided to replace them with horses, with the locomotives being retained for peak demand when Bellevue had special events. Horse transport continued until 1905 when the tramway was converted for electrical operation, which commenced in February 1906. The corporation took over the system in 1911 and it became part of the Belfast Corporation system.

Route at largest extent
Glengormley – Chichester Park

Tramcars purchased

1891	3 D/D	Unknown
1893	1 D/D	Unknown
1895	1 D/D	Unknown
1899	1 D/D	Unknown

Livery of Cavehill & Whitewell Tramways Co.

1892-1906	Green / Cream

BELFAST CORPORATION TRAMWAYS

4' 8½" gauge; 25 route miles; acquired 1905 last horse tram December 1905.

The corporation continued horse tram services, albeit with considerable disruption as the tracks were made ready for electric operation. The first electric tramcars ran later in 1905 with the last horse tram running in December 1905.

Livery of Belfast Corporation Tramways

1905-1929	Bright Red / Cream (White)

BIRKDALE & SOUTHPORT TRAMWAYS COMPANY

See Southport

BIRKENHEAD

BIRKENHEAD STREET RAILWAY COMPANY, LATER BIRKENHEAD TRAMWAYS COMPANY, LATER BIRKENHEAD UNITED TRAMWAYS, OMNIBUS & CARRIAGE COMPANY INCORPORATING HOYLAKE & BIRKENHEAD RAIL & TRAMWAY CO.

4' 8½" gauge; 11 route miles; opened 1860; acquired by Birkenhead Corporation 1901.

It is generally accepted that the 1860 Birkenhead tramway is the first street tramway to be built in Britain (see Section 1 for the arguments about this) and certainly would never have come about without the entrepreneurial activities of George Francis Train. Having failed to persuade the authorities in Liverpool to agree to his laying a tramway in their city he moved across the Mersey and put the same ideas to Birkenhead Council, who agreed. So the Birkenhead Street Railway Company was established and tracks were laid in the streets of the town. The tramway opened on 30 August 1860 with a major banquet to which Train had invited all the crowned heads of Europe (though none attended). Having a step rail and no systematic definition meant that the measurement of the gauge was uncertain but it is clear that the wheels were about the same distance apart on their axles as a standard gauge tram. Train wanted to move on to London and sold his shares to the other share holders at the end of 1860. Like all step rails laid in streets the track proved a nuisance to other traffic and there was a stream of complaints and in 1864 the step rail was replaced by grooved rail. All this time

Birkenhead Street Railway Company.

the legal foundation of the tramway was slightly precarious as it had no Act of Parliament. In 1877 this was rectified by an Act that transferred the tramway to the Birkenhead Tramways Company.

Meanwhile the new tramway, the Hoylake & Birkenhead Rail & Tramway Company had been established in 1873 to run from Docks Station southwards parallel to the Mersey to Woodside Ferry to connect the Hoylake Railway with the ferry to Liverpool. The railway company leased the line to Mr W.W. Townson in 1876. In 1879 the Birkenhead Tramways Company proposed a line that would compete with the Hoylake line. So the Hoylake & Birkenhead Rail & Tramway Company opposed the idea. Discussions between the two companies led to an agreement where the Hoylake company agreed to sell its line to Birkenhead Tramways Company and this was completed the same year.

In 1886 the Mersey Railway opened its line under the Mersey from Birkenhead to Liverpool which had a massive impact on the ferry service and hence the tramway feeder to the ferry. Cutbacks were made to produce savings including putting smaller one horse cars on the Docks Station route. The local omnibus companies were having similar problems. By 1888 the tramway company declared itself bankrupt and a liquidator was appointed.

The Birkenhead Corporation purchased the tramway lines while a new company, the Birkenhead United Tramways, Omnibus & Carriage Co, was formed that purchased the rest of the tramway's assets and those of the Birkenhead & District Omnibus & Carriage Company Limited. The new company leased the tramway tracks from the council and then operated most of the public street transport in Birkenhead. In 1898 the corporation decided to purchase the tramways in Birkenhead and electrify the system. They were authorised by Act of Parliament in 1899 and purchased the Birkenhead United Tramways, Omnibus & Carriage Company in 1901.The horse tramway service continued to be run by the Birkenhead United Tramways, Omnibus & Carriage Company during the conversion process to electric tramcar operation. The last horse tram ran at the end of 1901.

Routes at largest extent
Woodside Ferry – Prenton Road
Woodside Ferry – Balls Road (Oxton)
Woodside Ferry – Docks Station

Tramcars purchased

Birkenhead Street Railway Co.

1860	2 S/D 2 D/D	John Stephenson Co. Ltd
1861	4 D/D	John Stephenson Co. Ltd
1876	8 D/D	Starbuck Car & Wagon Co.

Birkenhead Tramways Co.

1878	8 D/D	Starbuck Car & Wagon Co.
1879	8 D/D	Starbuck Car & Wagon Co. Ex Hoylake

Birkenhead United Tramways.

Hoylake & Birkenhead Rail & Tramway Co.

1873	8 D/D	Starbuck Car & Wagon Co.

Livery of Birkenhead Street Railway Co.

1860-1876	Light Green / Cream
1876-1877	Varnished Mahogany / Scarlet Red / Cream

Livery of Birkenhead Tramways Co.

1877-1889	Varnished Mahogany / Scarlet Red / Cream

Livery of Hoylake & Birkenhead Rail & Tramway Co.

1873-1879	Maroon / Cream (White)

Livery of Birkenhead United Tramways, Omnibus & Carriage Company

1889-1900	Varnished Mahogany / Scarlet Red / Cream

WIRRAL TRAMWAY COMPANY LIMITED

4' 8½" gauge; 3 route miles; opened 1877; acquired by Birkenhead Corporation 1900.

In 1874 the Wirral Tramway Company was established and applied for and obtained an Order under the 1870 Tramways Act to build a tramway between New Ferry and Woodside Ferry. Building the tramway started in 1876 and it opened for Easter 1877. The line was a success and within a couple of years the small trams needed to be replaced by larger cars, although still single-deck due to a low bridge. The new cars were heavier so in 1879 the track was relaid with heavier section rail. As part of its plans to electrify the tramways in its town, the corporation purchased the Wirral company at the end of 1899. However they were not ready to take it on and allowed the company to continue operations. In May 1900 the company informed the corporation they would cease the operation. In order to provide some service during electrification the corporation asked the Birkenhead United Tramways, Omnibus & Carriage Company to take on the service and they purchased some of the Wirral cars in order to keep the route open. The last horse car ran on 22 January 1901.

Wirral Tramway Company.

Route at largest extent

Woodside Ferry – New Ferry

Tramcars purchased

1877	7 S/D	Starbuck Car & Wagon Co.
1879	7 S/D	Starbuck Car & Wagon Co.
1880	2 S/D	Starbuck Car & Wagon Co.
1894	2 D/D	G. F. Milnes & Co.
1895	1 D/D	G. F. Milnes & Co.
1896	2 D/D	G. F. Milnes & Co.

Livery of Wirral Tramway Company Limited

1877-1900	Green / Cream

BIRMINGHAM

BIRMINGHAM & DISTRICT TRAMWAYS COMPANY LIMITED, LATER BIRMINGHAM TRAMWAYS & OMNIBUS COMPANY LIMITED, LATER BIRMINGHAM CENTRAL TRAMWAYS COMPANY LIMITED, LATER CITY OF BIRMINGHAM TRAMWAYS COMPANY LIMITED

4' 8½" gauge later 3' 6"; 37 route miles of which around 25 miles were horse operated; opened 1872; acquired by City of Birmingham Tramways Company Limited 1896.

The first proposal for a tramway in Birmingham came, unsurprisingly, from George Francis Train in 1860 as part of his campaign to introduce street tramways to as many towns and cities in England as he could. Despite pushing his ideas for over two years nothing further came of this initiative in Birmingham. Then in 1869 there were no less than three proposals to build tramways plus a suggestion from Birmingham Corporation that they would like to build their own tramway. As the Tramways Act was about to be authorised in 1870 the proposals were held in abeyance. Then in 1871 a new company was formed, the Birmingham & District Tramways Company Limited that took over the three proposals (and the Birmingham Omnibus Company). They began laying tracks to the standard gauge of 4ft 8½ inches and the first horse car ran on 20 May 1872. However the route ran from Dudley Port to the Birmingham boundary at Hockley and did not actually go into the city as the corporation had plans to lay their own tram tracks. This they did in 1872 and then leased the lines to the Birmingham & District Tramways Company Limited, with the first line in Birmingham opening in 1873. The company ran into financial problems and had to abandon one tram route and stop most of the omnibus services. A new company the Birmingham Tramways & Omnibus Company Limited took over the old company and merged it with an omnibus operation run by William Mayner.

In 1882 steam tramways came to Birmingham with a 3 feet 6 inch gauge tramway operated by the Birmingham and Aston Tramways (that never operated any horse tramways). These and new lines operated by Birmingham Central Tramways Company Limited were all 3 feet 6 inch gauge and as dual gauge tramways were not accepted by the Board of Trade it was agreed that the Birmingham Tramways & Omnibus Company Limited lines would be converted to the narrower gauge. At this time the Patent Cable Tramways Corporation wanted to build two lines for cable operation on the Handsworth and Bristol Road routes and to do so they leased the lines from the Birmingham Tramways & Omnibus Company Limited. This left the BTOCL with very few tramway routes and in 1886 they sold these and the rest of their undertaking, including the omnibus business, to Birmingham Central Tramways Company Limited. This company had, except for the Nechells horse tramway, operated steam tramways, though later they also operated accumulator cars. In 1892 electric tramways came to the Midlands through the South Staffordshire Tramways Company, and thought in Birmingham

Birmingham Tramways & Omnibus Company Limited.

turned to the new form of traction. The first proposals came in 1894 but before anything could be done a new company the City of Birmingham Tramways Company Limited was formed that took over the Birmingham Central Tramways Company Limited in 1896 with the aim of electrifying all the tramways in the city. This they did and the last horse tram ran in 1906.

Routes at largest extent of horse tramways

Colmore Row – Handsworth
Colmore Row – Villa Cross
Navigation Street – Bournbrook
Albert Street – Nechells

Tramcars purchased

Birmingham & District Tramways Company Limited

1872	12 D/D	Metropolitan Railway Carriage & Wagon Company
1873	5 D/D	Metropolitan Railway Carriage & Wagon Company
1873	5 D/D	Starbuck Car & Wagon Co.

Birmingham Tramways & Omnibus Co. Limited

1876	17 D/D	Metropolitan Railway Carriage & Wagon Company
1876	5 D/D	Starbuck Car & Wagon Co.
1876	5 S/D	Brown, Marshalls & Co.
1878	1 S/D	Brown, Marshalls & Co.
1878	2 S/D	Starbuck Car & Wagon Co.
1879	4 D/D	Ashbury Railway Carriage & Iron Co. Ltd
1880	4 D/D	Falcon Engine & Car Works Ltd

Birmingham Central Tramways Company Limited

1884	10 D/D	Falcon Engine & Car Works Ltd

City of Birmingham Tramways Company Limited

1884	10 D/D	Unknown

Livery of Birmingham & District Tramways Company Limited

1872-1876	Crimson (Midland Railway Red) / Cream

Livery of Birmingham Tramways & Omnibus Company Limited

1876-1886	Crimson (Midland Railway Red) / Cream

Livery of Birmingham Central Tramways Company Limited

1884-1890	Sage Green / Cream
1890-1896	Crimson / Pale Cream

BIRMINGHAM & MIDLAND TRAMWAYS LIMITED

See West Bromwich

BLACKBURN

BLACKBURN CORPORATION TRAMWAYS COMPANY LIMITED

4' 0" gauge 9 route miles of which around 3 miles were horse operated; opened 1887; acquired by Blackburn Corporation 1898.

The first trams to run in Blackburn were steam operated on the Blackburn and Over Darwen Tramways Company system when it opened in 1881. Horse tramways were introduced when the Blackburn Corporation Tramways Company Limited (despite the name actually a private company) built horse and steam lines in 1882. They approached the Blackburn and Over Darwen Tramways Company with a view to leasing the lines and running all the tramways in Blackburn, but were rejected. The Blackburn Corporation Tramways Company Limited ran a system comprising two steam tramway routes and two horse tramway routes. The first route to open was the steam tramway to the Church at

Blackburn Corporation Tramways Company Limited.

Blackpool Electric Tramway Company.

Intack at the Blackburn town boundary. The opening attracted a vast number of people many of whom travelled on this novel steam hauled transport. The first horse tramway route (Billinge) opened on 25 August 1888 and the second (Witton) on 26 January 1889. In 1888 the local omnibus company offered their operation for sale and it was purchased by the Blackburn Corporation Tramways Company Limited with 15 omnibuses and the stable of horses.

In 1895 the tramway's thoughts turned to conversion to electricity. An application was made to the Corporation that set up a sub-committee to look at the matter. Negotiations continued with the Corporation planning to supply the electricity for the tramway. Agreement was reached with the Corporation planning to electrify the lines (that they owned and leased to the company), but the Corporation set some conditions that the company were unhappy about. So the company countered by offering the tramway for sale to the Corporation. Negotiations were completed and the tramway was acquired by the Corporation on 24 August 1898. The new electric tram service began on 20 March 1899.

Routes at largest extent of horse tramways

Blackburn Town Centre – Billinge
Blackburn Town Centre – Griffin Inn, Witton

Tramcars purchased

1887	6 D/D	Oldbury Railway Carriage & Wagon Co. Ltd
1888	5 D/D	Falcon Engine & Car Works Ltd.

Livery of Blackburn Corporation Tramways Company Limited

1887-1897	Olive Green (Dark Green) (Dark Sage Green) / Ivory (Cream)

BLACKDOG LIGHT RAILWAY
See Strabathie

BLACKPOOL

BLACKPOOL ELECTRIC TRAMWAY CO.

4' 8½" gauge; 2 route miles; horse operated 1885, 1886 and 1893/4.

It may seem strange that the first electric tramway in Britain appears in a book devoted to horse tramways. However, on at least three occasions the Blackpool Tramway was forced to cease electric operation and use horses instead. The first time was prior to the official opening. The first track and conduit had been laid by June 1885 and Holroyd Smith had tested it using an experimental tramcar from Manchester. The Board of Trade Inspector had passed the line for public use in July, but the conduit was not completely ready and so a passenger service was operated using horses to haul the electric tramcars. This ceased on the official opening on 29 September 1885 when the electrical service was able to be operated. The conduit system had given trouble and was constantly having to be repaired, but in June 1887 the conduit failed catastrophically. But this time Holroyd Smith had moved on from Blackpool so an urgent call went out for him and he returned to find considerable damage to the conduit. While this was being seen to, the system brought in the horses again and the electric motors were removed from the tramcars and they became horse cars for three months. In September 1892 Blackpool Corporation purchased the tramway from the Blackpool Electric Tramway Company; they continued with the conduit system and in the latter part of 1893 it was evident that substantial repairs were necessary. This meant no electrical operation during the winter and instead one of the tramcars had its motors removed and the system became horse powered for about nine months.

A few years later the Corporation decided to remove the troublesome conduit and in 1899 the whole system was converted to overhead line operation and there was no further need to call on horse power.

Route at largest extent

Cocker Street, Talbot Square – Dean Street, South Shore

Electric Tramcars purchased

1885	4 D/D	Starbuck Car & Wagon Co.
1885	4 D/D 2 T/R	Lancaster Railway Carriage & Wagon Co. Ltd.
1891	2 D/D	G. F. Milnes & Co.

Livery of Blackpool Electric Tramway Company Limited

1885-1892	Olive Green / Sand / Teak

BLACKPOOL, ST ANNES & LYTHAM TRAMWAYS COMPANY LIMITED
See Lytham St Annes

BLACKROCK & KINGSTOWN TRAMWAY COMPANY
See Dublin

BOLTON

BOLTON & SUBURBAN TRAMWAYS (EDMUND HOLDEN & COMPANY)

4' 8½" gauge; 15 route miles; opened 1880; acquired by Bolton Corporation 1899.

In 1880 Bolton Corporation and Farnworth Corporations laid tramways in the town and leased them to Edmund Holden, the local omnibus operator. The initial stages of the system were completed in 1880. There were extensions in 1882 and 1889 to give the full extent of the horse tramway system. The depot was in Bradshawgate at the junction of Shiffnall Street and Carlton Street. The Corporations decided to electrify the system and like many other towns purchased the operating tramway, taking over from Edmund Holden. All routes were electrified early in 1900.

Routes at largest extent of horse tramways

Lostock Junction Lane – Halliwell
Halliwell – Farnworth
Dunscar – Daubhill Station

Tramcars purchased

1880	30 D/D	Ashbury Railway Carriage & Iron Co. Ltd
c1882	18 D/D	Ashbury Railway Carriage & Iron Co. Ltd

Livery of Edmund Holden & Company

1880-1899	Red / Cream
1880-1899	Green / Cream
1880-1899	Blue / Cream
1880-1899	Amber / Cream

Bolton & Suburban Tramways.

BRADFORD

BRADFORD TRAMWAYS COMPANY LATER BRADFORD TRAMWAYS & OMNIBUS COMPANY LIMITED

4' 0" gauge; 17 route miles of which around 2 miles were horse operated; opened 1882; acquired by Bradford Corporation 1902.

After several abortive attempts by various promoters the Bradford Corporation were persuaded by a group of entrepreneurs who formed the Bradford Tramways Company to apply under the 1870 Tramways Act to lay tracks for a horse tramway on the least hilly route out of the town centre to Lister Park. The line was leased to the company (who soon changed their name to the Bradford Tramways & Omnibus Company Limited) and the first horse tram ran on 1 February 1882. The company negotiated with the corporation to build more tramways. However, owing to the terrain the corporation refused to allow further horse-drawn tramways and instead the company agreed to use steam power. A second company, the Bradford & Shelf Tramways Company Limited, operated a line opened in 1886 from Bradford Town Hall to Wyke, this again was steam operated. In 1893 the Bradford Tramways & Omnibus Company Limited took over operation of the horse tramway in Shipley. The corporation were keen on using electrical power for the tramways and they carried out experiments in 1883, but with poor results. Nothing further was done until 1898 when the corporation built and opened its own electric tramway with two routes. These proved successful and the corporation looked to the company tramways and purchased the Bradford Tramways & Omnibus Company Limited in 1902 with the last horse tram running in May 1902.

Bradford Tramways Company.

Route at largest extent of horse tramways

Bradford Town Hall – Lister Park Gates

Tramcars purchased

1882	13 D/D	Ashbury Railway Carriage & Iron Co. Ltd
1885	4 D/D	Ashbury Railway Carriage & Iron Co. Ltd
1890	2 D/D	Unknown
1892	2 D/D	Ex-Shipley
1894	2 T/R	Unknown
1894	2 T/R	Bradford Tramways

Livery of Bradford Tramways & Omnibus Company Limited

1882-1902	Brown / Cream / Red Dashes

BRADFORD INDUSTRIAL MUSEUM

4' 0" gauge; 0.2 route miles; opened 1992, still open.

In the 1990s the Bradford Industrial Museum became home to the "Horses at Work" initiative and as part of the display of the horses a short length of track was laid alongside the museum and a replica Bradford Tramway Company tramcar was contracted from WGH Transportation Engineering Limited in 1992. This became the first wholly horse tramway to be built for over 90 years. The tramway operates sporadically, apparently there are only a couple of horses trained to haul the tram and events for each day depend on which horses are chosen for the day's demonstrations.

Route at largest extent

Depot shed – Museum entrance

Tramcars purchased

1992	1 S/D	WGH Transportation Engineering Ltd

Livery of Bradford Tramway Limited replica tram

1992-Date	Brown / Cream / Red Dashes

Bradford Industrial Museum.

BRADFORD & DISTRICT TRAMWAYS COMPANY
See Shipley

BRADFORD & DISTRICT STEAM TRAMWAY COMPANY
See Shipley

BRADFORD CORPORATION TRAMWAYS
See Shipley

BRIGHTON

BRIGHTON DISTRICT TRAMWAYS COMPANY, LATER BRIGHTON & DISTRICT TRAMWAYS COMPANY LIMITED, LATER BRIGHTON & SHOREHAM TRAMWAYS COMPANY LIMITED, LATER BRITISH ELECTRIC TRACTION COMPANY LIMITED

3' 6" gauge; 4 route miles; opened 1884; closed 1913.

The Brighton District Tramways Company were authorised in 1882 to build a tramway from Westbourne Gardens to Shoreham Station. It was intended that the tramway would be steam powered, but the Board of Trade Inspector refused to allow steam operation between Swiss Gardens and Burrell Hotel and that had to be horse operated, so three dray horses were used to haul the large bogie trailers over this section. The tramway opened on 3 July 1884. There were complaints from the public regarding the steam locomotives and in August 1884 there was a serious accident caused by horses hauling a passenger cart bolting. In 1885 the company purchased three single-deck tramcars to supplement the steam service and a further seven double-deck cars in 1886. But financially the company was getting into trouble and it went into liquidation in 1887. A new company, Brighton & District Tramways Company Limited, was formed to take over the tramway, which it did in 1888. The new company immediately withdrew steam operation and just ran with horses. Then in 1889 another new company was formed, the Brighton & Shoreham Tramways Company Limited, that took over the tramway. Most of the tramcars had been sold by the liquidator in 1887, so it had just three single-deck and one double-deck tramcars. The new company repaired the line and purchased five tramcars. The line ran at a profit for the next ten years. In 1898 the British Electric Traction Company Limited took over (though not formally until 1907) the company with the intention of rebuilding and electrifying the line with extensions to Worthing and Brighton. However Hove and Worthing councils would not agree and the proposals could not be implemented. Despite many attempts the councils barred extensions of the tramway in either direction. In 1904 negotiations opened with Hove and Portslade Councils for them to take over the tramway, but the first offer was too low for the tramway and the situation went to arbitration. The price set by the arbiter was too high for the councils and so the deal fell through. By now motor omnibus competition was growing and, as the buses could run from Brighton, through Hove to Worthing, the BET takings were affected. In 1911 Hove Council obtained an Act allowing them to introduce trolleybuses and to remove the tram tracks. This was done with haste leaving the tramway with just the line between Portslade and Shoreham. The result was the closure of the tramway in 1913.

Brighton & Shoreham Tramways Company Limited.

Route at largest extent
Westbourne Gardens – Shoreham Station

Tramcars purchased
Brighton District Tramways Company

1885	3 S/D	Oldbury Railway Carriage & Wagon Co. Ltd
1886	7 D/D	Oldbury Railway Carriage & Wagon Co. Ltd

Brighton & Shoreham Tramways Company Limited.

1891	5 D/D	Unknown
1900	3 D/D	Unknown

Livery of Brighton District Tramways Company
1884-1888 Light Brown / Cream (horse tramcars)

Livery of Brighton & Shoreham Tramways Company Limited
1884-1888 Light Brown / Cream (horse tramcars)

Livery of British Electric Traction Company Limited
1907-1913 BET Standard Dark Lake / Cream

BRISTOL

BRISTOL TRAMWAYS COMPANY LIMITED, LATER BRISTOL TRAMWAYS & CARRIAGE COMPANY LIMITED

4' 8½" gauge; 20 route miles; opened 1875; last horse trams 1900.

The Bristol Corporation sought powers to lay tramways in 1873. However, they had no company to operate the single route they were building. Then the Bristol Tramways Company Limited was founded in 1874 to run the trams. They ordered tramcars from Starbuck and were ready to commence operation. However, there was considerable consternation and opposition from many of the public. The tramway company's manager was James Clifton Robinson (later to run the London United Tramway) and he drove the first tramcar over the track. On the opening day, 9 August 1875, thousands attended the official opening. Many were most impressed by the speed of the cars and this was reflected in the high usage in the following year. Soon the company sought extensions and new routes and by 1879 there

Bristol Tramways & Carriage Company Limited.

were four routes and two more were added by 1880. In 1877 there was a trial of a steam tram locomotive. It was two years later in 1879 that seven tram locomotives were ordered and they went into service on the steepest routes in 1880. Like many such steam tramway trials the public were not happy and, no doubt influenced by high maintenance costs, the company ceased steam operation in 1881.

In 1887 the tramway company took over the local Bristol Cab Company Limited and changed its name to Bristol Tramways & Carriage Company Limited. The company saw electrical power as the future and in 1894 obtained the necessary legal powers to convert the tramway. The first route opened as an electric tramway in October 1895 and conversion continued, with the horse trams ceasing by the end of 1900.

Routes at largest extent of horse tramways

City Centre – Horfield
City Centre – Eastville
City Centre – Kingswood
City Centre – Arnos Vale
City Centre – Bedminster
City Centre – Ashton gate
City Centre – Hotwells
City Centre – Redland

Tramcars purchased

Bristol Tramways Company Limited

1875	7 D/D	Starbuck Car & Wagon Co.
1876	5 D/D	Starbuck Car & Wagon Co.
1877	33 D/D, 5 S/D	Starbuck Car & Wagon Co.
1881	21 D/D	Starbuck Car & Wagon Co.
1883	7 D/D	Metropolitan Railway Carriage & Wagon Company

Bristol Tramways & Carriage Company Limited

1892	8 D/D	G.F. Milnes & Co.
1895	18 D/D	G.F. Milnes & Co.

Livery of Bristol Tramways Company Limited

1875-?	Crimson / White
1875-1888	Dark Blue / White

Livery of Bristol Tramways & Carriage Company Limited

1888-1900	Dark Blue / White

BRITISH ELECTRIC TRACTION COMPANY LIMITED

See Brighton, South Shields, Stoke-on-Trent & West Bromwich

BURNLEY

BURNLEY & DISTRICT TRAMWAYS COMPANY LIMITED

4' 8½" gauge; 7 route miles; opened 1881; acquired by Burnley Corporation 1898; horse operated intermittently between 1882 and 1885.

Strictly speaking this system was a steam tramway with steam tram locomotives and large passenger trailers. But like many such tramways it suffered from a combination of public and corporation criticism and a greater requirement for repairs to keep the tramway running. The first trams ran on 17 September 1881, but the corporation complained about the smoke and noise from the locomotives and steam operation stopped in April 1882 and horse power was used to haul the tramcars. The replacement tram locomotive blew up on its first trip out. The tramway purchased 11 tram locomotives, but maintenance proved a problem and horses were often brought back to haul the tram-cars, though this was phased out by 1885. In 1900 the line was jointly purchased by Burnley Corporation, Nelson Corporation, Padiham UDC, Brierfield UDC and Reedley Hallows Parish Council. Plans were put forward to electrify the system and the last steam trams ran in 1901.

Burnley & District Tramways Company Limited, when it was not possible to use steam locomotives horses were used and must have had a difficult time hauling these heavy trailers.

Routes at largest extent
City Centre – Padiham
City Centre – Nelson

No dedicated horse tramcars purchased

Livery of Burnley & District Tramways Company Limited

1881-1901	Black / White

BURY

MANCHESTER, BURY, ROCHDALE & OLDHAM STEAM TRAMWAYS COMPANY LIMITED, LATER BURY, ROCHDALE & OLDHAM STEAM TRAMWAYS COMPANY LIMITED

4' 8½" & 3' 6" gauges; 30 route miles of which under 2 miles were horse operated; opened 1883; closed 1904 (horse trams ceased 1886).

The Manchester, Bury, Rochdale & Oldham Steam Tramways Company Limited was primarily a steam tramway but it did have one horse operated route from Bury town centre to Limefield, because of the narrowness of the streets. Three horse tramcars were purchased to operate the 3 feet 6 inches gauge line. After the roads had been widened in 1886 it was converted to steam power and the system did not use horses again.

Route at largest extent of horse tramways
Bury town centre – Limefield

Tramcars purchased

1883	3 D/D	Starbuck Car & Wagon Co.

Livery of Manchester, Bury, Rochdale & Oldham Steam Tramways Company Limited

1883-1886	Dark Green / Cream

Manchester, Bury, Rochdale & Oldham Steam Tramways Company Limited.

CALEDONIAN RAILWAY COMPANY
See Inchture

CAMBRIDGE

CAMBRIDGE STREET TRAMWAYS COMPANY

4' 0" gauge; 3 route miles; opened 1880; closed 1914.

In 1878 there were two proposals for laying street tramways in Cambridge from two different groups but both with the same name, the Cambridge Tramways Company. The main advantage was to provide a connection between the railway station and the town centre. As with so many tramway proposals the idea was received with very mixed feelings. The more conservative of the proposals was accepted, but with a narrower gauge than the 4 feet 8½ inches suggested. The name was also changed to the Cambridge Street Tramways Company. Construction started in July 1879 and the first trams ran in October 1880. The tramway immediately proved a success with thousands of passengers in the first few days. The tramcars were each hauled by a single horse and this led to criticism of the company for over-working them. The company struck back by demonstrating that two men could haul a tramcar, including stopping, from the station to the post office, but this did little to quieten the critics. Indeed the company was reported to the RSPCA, but they found that the horses only worked 18 hours a week and were well fed and cared for. So no action was taken. The tramway continued profitably

Cambridge Street Tramways Company.

through the 1880s and 1890s until in 1896 a new company, the Cambridge Omnibus Company, obtained licences for eight buses that would directly compete with the trams. The tramway company fought back by purchasing four omnibuses and starting their own omnibus services before the rival could start theirs. When the rival transport started it soon became evident that there were insufficient passengers to support two companies. Eventually common sense prevailed and in 1900 they reached an agreement where the omnibus company did not compete against the tram route and the tram company allowed them to operate over roads not served by trams. The omnibus company fared worst from the agreement and it ceased operating in 1902. In 1898 the British Electric Traction Company purchased shares in the company and set out proposals to electrify the system, but these were greeted with dismay by the college authorities and public opinion. So the idea was dropped and in 1904 the BET sold its shares to the Cambridge Electric Supply Company, but they fared no better. In 1905 motor buses entered Cambridge with the Cambridge Motor Bus Company and directly competed with the tramway. Revenue started to dwindle away and each year was worse than the one before. The end came when they were unable to pay the corporation the yearly maintenance charge for the track for 1912 and 1913. In 1914 the Corporation filed for compulsory winding-up of the company for non payment of rates. The last trams ran on 18 February 1914.

Cardiff Tramways Company.

Routes at largest extent
Station – Post Office
St Mary's Street – Turnstile Public House

Tramcars purchased

1880	2 D/D, 2 S/D	Starbuck Car & Wagon Co.
1885	2 S/D	Starbuck Car & Wagon Co.
1894	1 D/D	Starbuck Car & Wagon Co.
1909	1 D/D	Starbuck Car & Wagon Co.

Livery of Cambridge Street Tramways Company

1880-1892	Red / Cream / Cream Dashes
1892-1914	Red / Cream / Red Dashes

CANVEY ISLAND

CANVEY ISLAND TRAMWAY

0" gauge, monorail; 3 route miles; opened 1901; closed 1904.

There are many unusual tramways in this book, but the strangest of all must be the Canvey Island Tramway. It was built to serve a new housing and holiday resort on Canvey Island promoted by a local builder, Frederick Hester, and was meant as a temporary measure. The purpose of the monorail was to provide transport to prospective clients for the development, using a system developed by the Frenchman Monsieur Caillet. This was exhibited at the Birmingham Royal Show in 1898 and was used for both agricultural and military use in France and Egypt. Being light it would have been inexpensive to lay and operate. The tramcar (there may have been more than one car) rode on grooved wheels on a single rail and was kept in balance by stiff shafts to a horse walking alongside it, the horse providing the motive power and keeping the balance. In 1904 work began on building a conventional electric tramway and four tramcars were delivered. Unfortunately for Mr Hester 1904 had an extremely high tide and much of the land was flooded. This was enough to put off any prospective purchaser and the project was abandoned.

Canvey Island Tramway.

Route at largest extent
Benfleet Ferry – Leigh Beck

Tramcars purchased

1901	? T/R	Caillet

Livery of Canvey Island Tramway

1901-1904	Not Known

CARDIFF

CARDIFF TRAMWAYS COMPANY – PROVINCIAL TRAMWAYS COMPANY

4' 8½" gauge; 6 route miles; opened 1872; acquired by Cardiff Corporation 1902.

The first tramway to be built in Cardiff was by the Cardiff Tramways Company, a subsidiary of Provincial Tramways, opened in 1872 with two routes, one from High Street to Pier Head and from High Street to the Royal Infirmary. At this time Solomon Andrews was running omnibus services in the city. The two companies operated in reasonable harmony until 1879 when the Royal Infirmary route was extended to Broadway, Roath and a new route from High Street to Clive Road, Canton was built. This prompted Solomon Andrews to go into direct competition with the trams. In 1882 Solomon Andrews took two initiatives that really annoyed the tramway. The first was to supply tramcars, horses and drivers to the newly opened Cardiff District & Penarth Harbour Tramways Company Limited route, and the second was to take a patent for a special design of omnibus that had its wheels set exactly at the right place to run on the tramway rails, making it easier for the horses to haul the carriages. This combination reduced the revenues of the Cardiff Tramways

Company to such an extent that it was not making a profit, even though it opened a new route in 1886 from St John's Road to Cathays. Solomon Andrews offered to purchase the tramway undertaking or to sell them his omnibus business and his tramway interests in Cardiff, Portsmouth and Plymouth. This was accepted by the tramway and the transaction took place around 1888. Like many other towns the corporation was looking to electrical operation and they purchased the tramways in 1902 and the first electric tramcars were running later that year.

Routes at largest extent
Roath – Bute Docks
Canton – Bute Docks
St John's Square – Cathays
Grangetown – Adamsdown

Tramcars purchased

1872	12	Unknown
?	40	Unknown

Livery of Cardiff Tramways Company

1872-1902	Green / White (Roath route)
1872-1902	Red / White (Canton route)
1872-1902	Canary Yellow / White (Cathays route)
1872-1902	Chocolate / White Grangetown route)

CARDIFF DISTRICT & PENARTH HARBOUR TRAMWAYS COMPANY LIMITED, LATER PROVINCIAL TRAMWAYS COMPANY

4' 8½" gauge; 2 route miles; opened 1881; acquired by Cardiff Corporation 1903.

As mentioned above, the Cardiff District & Penarth Harbour Tramways Company Limited became the second tramway company in Cardiff and it opened its single route on 29 November 1881. There was an unusual arrangement where Solomon Andrews supplied the trams, horses and drivers while the company supplied the conductors and took the fares. Andrews was paid a set rate per tramcar mile. There was always a difficult relationship between the two tramway companies, particularly as Solomon Andrews also ran omnibus operations. The sale of Andrew's interests in the tramway and bus operations is given above. So around 1888 the tramway was purchased by the Provincial Tramways Company and operated as part of the Cardiff Tramways Company. When the corporation purchased the horse tramways, the sale of the Cardiff District & Penarth Harbour Tramway was delayed until February 1903 as there were arguments about the price to be paid. The corporation integrated the tramway into their electric tramway operation.

Route at largest extent
Splotlands – Lower Grangetown

Cardiff District & Penarth Harbour Tramways Company Limited.

Tramcars purchased

1881	5 D/D	Solomon Andrews & Son
1884	2 D/D	Solomon Andrews & Son
c1886	4 D/D	Solomon Andrews & Son

Livery of Cardiff District & Penarth Harbour Tramways Company Limited

1881-1903	Emerald Green (possibly)

CARSTAIRS

CARSTAIRS HOUSE TRAMWAY

2' 6" gauge; 12 route miles; opened 1889; closed c1927; horse operation 1909-c1927.

The owner of Carstairs House, Lanarkshire, Joseph Monteith, was interested in engineering and had built a water powered generator to light the house. In 1889 he laid an electric tramway, using a third rail power supply, from Carstairs West Station to the house, a distance of just over one mile. The electrical power came from the generator he had already built. This was one of the first electric tramways in Britain making Joseph Monteith a tramway pioneer. A small four-wheel tramcar was built and ran successfully carrying passengers and goods from the station to the house. Two further tramcars were added to the line as well as some goods trailers. The electrical operation is said to have ceased in 1905 when Joseph Monteith was electrocuted when he fell across the power rails. However, this appears to be a myth and it is more likely that electrical operation ceased when the house was sold in 1909. The tramway continued operating, but with horse power. It is unclear whether the passenger cars were used but hauled by horses or whether the line became goods only in operation. It is likely that the tramway ceased to be used around 1927 by which time it was mainly used to carry coal to the house and there was no passenger traffic.

Route at largest extent
Carstairs House – Carstairs West Station

Carstairs House Tramway. (Courtesy A.W. Brotchie)

Tramcars purchased
No horse tramcars were purchased. The three electric tramcars may have been used during the horse operation days.

Livery of Carstairs House Tramway

1889-1927	Teak

CAVEHILL & WHITEWELL TRAMWAY
See Belfast

CHESTER

CHESTER TRAMWAYS COMPANY, LATER CHESTER CORPORATION TRAMWAYS

4' 8½" gauge; 2 route miles; opened 1879; acquired by Chester Corporation 1902.

The idea of introducing trams to Chester came about in 1877 when T. Lloyd, Manager of the Liverpool Tramways, visited the town and thought that it looked a good proposition to bring trams to the town. The Chester Tramways Company was formed and shares were offered for sale. This was greeted with enthusiasm and the required capital was soon found. An Act of Parliament was obtained in 1878 to build two routes, one to the railway station (built over a mile from the city centre) and the other to Saltney. The lines were officially opened on 10 June 1879. The tramway ran uneventfully and profitably for 21 years. Then in 1899 the corporation had the powers (under the terms of the 1870 Tramways Act) to purchase the tramway at the 'scrap' value. This they proceeded to do. The formal transfer of the tramway took place on 1 January 1902. The corporation set about electrifying the system and in the process they relaid the track to 3 feet 6 inches gauge. The corporation continued to run the horse tramway as conversion took place and the last horse tramcar ran on 27 December 1902.

Routes at largest extent
City Centre – Railway Station
City Centre – Saltney

Tramcars purchased

1879	8 D/D	Ashbury Railway Carriage & Iron Co. Ltd.
c1880	8 D/D	Kerneen
1885	2 D/D	Starbuck Car & Wagon Co.
c1886	1 D/D	Chester Tramways John Gardner

Livery of Chester Tramways Company

1879-1902	Crimson Lake / Cream

Livery of Chester Corporation Tramways

1902-1902	Crimson Lake / Cream

Chester Tramways Company.

Chesterfield & District Tramways Company Limited.

CHESTERFIELD

CHESTERFIELD & DISTRICT TRAMWAYS COMPANY LIMITED, LATER CHESTERFIELD TRAMWAYS COMPANY, LATER CHESTERFIELD CORPORATION TRAMWAYS

4' 8½" gauge; 1 route mile; opened 1882; acquired by Chesterfield Corporation 1897; horse operation ceased 1904.

A proposal to build tramways in Chesterfield came in 1878 but was rejected by the corporation. Unlike many tramway proposals, this one was welcomed by the population and a public meeting was called that persuaded the corporation to rethink its views. An Act of Parliament was passed, but the promoters failed to start building the tramway in time and the powers lapsed and an extension of time had to be sought. The promoters formed the Chesterfield & District Tramways Company Limited and construction of the tramway began and was completed ready for opening on 8 November 1882. Despite the initial enthusiasm of the populace the tramway was not a financial success and in February 1885 the company went into voluntary liquidation. The tramway was sold to Chesterfield Tramways Company in December 1886. The new company did little better than its predecessor. The corporation sought to acquire the tramway and, as the 21-year rule did not apply, entered negotiations to purchase it as a going concern. The company must have welcomed the approach and quickly reached agreement. The corporation took over the running of the tramway in 1897 and immediately halved the price of a ticket. Although the fare was reduced the takings actually increased. Demand was such that the corporation purchased new tramcars to increase the fleet. The corporation then turned to the idea of converting the system to electrical operation. The small system was soon converted and electric cars started running a service in December 1904 and horse tram operation ceased.

Route at largest extent
Low Pavement – Brampton

Tramcars purchased

Chesterfield & District Tramways Company Limited

1882	2 D/D, 1 S/D	Ashbury Railway Carriage & Iron Co. Ltd

Chesterfield Tramways Company

1890	2 S/D	G F Milnes & Co.

Chesterfield Corporation Tramways

1898	1 S/D	G F Milnes & Co.
1899	2 S/D	G F Milnes & Co.
1903	1 D/D	Unknown

Livery of Chesterfield & District Tramways Company Limited

1882-1885	Prussian Blue / Primrose

Livery of Chesterfield Tramways Company

1886-1897	Prussian Blue / Cream

Livery of Chesterfield Corporation Tramways

1897-1904	Prussian Blue / Primrose (horse trams)
1904-1927	Carmine Red (Maroon) / Primrose

CITY OF DERRY TRAMWAYS COMPANY
See Londonderry

CITY OF WORCESTER TRAMWAYS COMPANY LIMITED
See Worcester

CITY OF YORK TRAMWAYS COMPANY LIMITED
See York

CONTINENTAL & GENERAL TRAMWAYS COMPANY
See Hull

CORK

CORK TRAMWAYS COMPANY LIMITED, LATER CORK CITIZENS' TRAMWAY COMPANY LIMITED

5' 3" gauge. 1 route mile; opened 1872; closed 1874.

Horse tramways made a relatively fleeting appearance in Cork. In fact the first proposals to build tramways in Cork came from G.F. Train in 1860, however like so many of his efforts the Cork proposals came to nothing. It was not until the Chairman of the Cork & Kinsale Junction Railway, that had its terminus on the south side of the River Lee, suggested a tramway joining his station with the Great Southern and Western terminus on the north side of the river. The Cork Tramways Company was established, with James Clifton Robinson as Manager, and the tramway was built, opening on 12 September 1872. The tramway was unusual in being a distorted 'C' shape serving just the city centre and did not extend out to the suburbs. As a result people did not use it as it did not take them where they wanted to go. Receipts were low and the tramway made losses every year. Eventually in 1874 the company allowed the tramway to fall into disuse. A new company, Cork Citizens' Tramway Company Limited was formed, that purchased the system in early 1875. The new company made efforts to revive the tramway but negotiations with the corporation failed and in October 1875 orders were issued by the corporation to have the rails removed. The tramway had ceased running in 1874 and was removed in 1875.

Route at largest extent
Albert Street Station – Lower Glanmire Road Station

Tramcars purchased

1872	6 D/D	Starbuck Car & Wagon Co.

Livery of Cork Tramways Company Limited

1872-1875	Blue / White

Cork Tramways Company Limited.

CRICH

NATIONAL TRAMWAY MUSEUM LATER CRICH TRAMWAY VILLAGE

4' 8½" gauge; 1 route mile; opened 1963 (regular horse operation to 1964); still open.

The formation of the National Tramway Museum started in 1948 when, as a result of a Light Railway and Tramway League tour of the Southampton tramway system a tramcar (number 45) was purchased for £10. The small group of LRTA members who owned the tramcar added other trams, Newcastle 102; Cardiff 131; Douglas Southern 1; Leeds 446 (Hull 132); Liverpool 429; and some tram parts. The group began to have a wish to have a permanent place to keep their trams, preferably with opportunity to drive them. The Tramway Museum Society was formally set up in 1955.

It took a further four years before a site for the museum was found. This was the quarry at Crich, Derbyshire that was available for renting. Track was laid to allow the preserved tramcars to be stored. By 1963 200 yards of running line had been laid and the museum was in a position to offer tram rides to the public. As no electrical supply was installed the motive power was a horse (Bonnie from a local farm), that hauled Sheffield 15 over the short track. This continued at weekends until June 1964 by which time the overhead line had been put up and electric tramcars took over the service. Regular horse tram service ceased, but the horse trams were operated on special occasions from that date.

Route at largest extent
Town End – Glory Mine (original horse tramway 200 yards at Town End)

Horse Trams Preserved

1873	1 S/D	Oporto number 9
1874	1 S/D	Sheffield number 15
1899	1 S/D	Chesterfield number 8

Livery of Crich Tramway Village

1963-Date	Oporto 9 – Yellow / White
1963-Date	Sheffield 15 – Red / White
1963-Date	Chesterfield 8 – Blue / White

CROYDON TRAMWAYS COMPANY
See London

CROYDON & NORWOOD TRAMWAYS COMPANY
See London

DARLINGTON

DARLINGTON STREET RAILROAD

4' 8½" gauge. 1 route mile; opened 1862; closed 1864.

The Darlington Street Railroad was the sixth and final tramway built by G.F. Train. Having built tramways in Birkenhead, three lines in London and the Potteries Train moved to the birthplace of the railways to promote a tramway in 1861. The route ran from Market Place to the Stockton & Darlington Railway Station. The tramway opened on 1 January 1862. The line was criticised by the local cab operators and those with private carriages.

However the end of the tram came about in a unique fashion. In 1864 a tramcar accidentally ran over a prize greyhound and was subsequently sued for the damages caused. The court awarded a substantial sum that bankrupted the company. The tramway ceased in 1864 and the Local Board ordered the removal of the rails in 1865.

Crich Tramway Village.

Route at largest extent
Market Place – Railway Station

Tramcars purchased

1862	2 S/D	Probably John Stephenson Co. Ltd

Livery of Darlington Street Railroad

1862-1864	Not known

STOCKTON & DARLINGTON STEAM TRAMWAYS COMPANY, LATER STOCKTON & DISTRICT TRAMWAYS COMPANY, LATER IMPERIAL TRAMWAYS

3' 0" gauge; 3 route miles; opened 1880; acquired by Darlington Corporation 1902.

Trams did not return to Darlington until 1880 when the Stockton & Darlington Steam Tramways Company opened a new tramway on 10 October 1880. Despite the name the Darlington system was always a horse tramway, it was a separate tramway in Stockton that was steam operated. The tramway was not a financial success and was liquidated in 1893 and the system was taken on by Stockton and District Tramways Company. This in turn was taken over by the Imperial Tramway Company in 1896. Initial plans to electrify the system did not come to anything when the corporation announced plans to build its own power station and a wish to convert the tramway itself. It took over the system in 1902 with horse trams continuing to operate the services during the conversion. The last horse tram ran in 1903.

Route at largest extent
Bank Top Railway Station – Cockerton

Tramcars purchased

1880	12 Mixed	Unknown

Livery Stockton & Darlington Steam Tramways Company, Stockton and District Tramways Company, Imperial Tramway Company

1880-1903	Chocolate / White

Stockton & Darlington Steam Tramways Company.

DERBY

DERBY TRAMWAYS COMPANY LATER DERBY CORPORATION TRAMWAYS

4' 0" gauge;5 route miles; opened 1880; acquired by Derby Corporation 1899, horse service ceased 1907.

The Derby Tramways Company was formed on 17 October 1877 with the purpose of building horse tramways in the city. This was roundly condemned by many of the population and the local press (the brother of the editor of the paper was an omnibus operator). This initiative was not the only one. A second group of promoters put forward plans and while the corporation was resistant it looked in 1878 that an agreement would be reached with the second group. But it did not reach a successful conclusion and the group pulled out of Derby. The original company, Derby Tramways Company, returned and were more successful, leading to an Act of Parliament authorising the building of the

Derby Tramways Company.

system passed in 1879. Construction started that year and the first tram service ran on 6 March 1880. The tramway ran profitably during the 1880s but came under financial pressures in the 1890s and the corporation decided to use its compulsory purchase powers at the first opportunity, in 1898, 21 years after the passing of the Act allowing the tramway to be built. Although the corporation could have insisted on buying the undertaking just for the scrap price, they did in fact enter negotiations and acquired the tramway the following year on the basis of an ongoing operation. The corporation continued to run the tramway while they planned its conversion to electrical operation. The last horse trams ran in Derby in 1907.

Routes at largest extent

City Centre – Windmill Hill Lane
City Centre – Normanton Hotel
City Centre – Cotton Lane
City Centre – Deadman's Lane

Tramcars purchased

Derby Tramways Company

1880	16 S/D	Starbuck Car & Wagon Co.
1887	2 D/D	Midland Railway Carriage & Wagon Co. Ltd
1894	2 D/D	Falcon Engine & Car Works Ltd

Derby Corporation Tramways

1902	3 D/D	Ex Glasgow Tramways
1903	3 D/D	Ex Glasgow Tramways

Livery of Derby Tramways Company

1880-?	Possibly route colours
?-1899	Crimson Lake / Off White
1894-1899	Scarlet Lake / Off White

Livery of Derby Corporation Tramways

1899-1902	Crimson Lake / Off White
1899-1906	Scarlet Lake / Off White
1901-1906	Dark Maroon / Cream

DERRY

See Londonderry

DEWSBURY

DEWSBURY, BATLEY & BIRSTAL TRAMWAYS COMPANY LIMITED.

4' 8½" gauge; 4 route miles (3 miles under horse operation); opened 1874; changed to steam power 1881.

In 1872 local businessmen formed the Dewsbury & Batley Tramways Company with the aim to build and operate a tramway in those towns. As the necessary capital was being sought the name of the company was changed to Dewsbury, Batley & Birstal Tramways Company Limited (using an archaic spelling of Birstall) the following year. The necessary Act was obtained in 1873 and construction of the tramway began in 1874 with the first route opening on 25 July 1875. Such was the haste that the trams ordered by the company had not been delivered, so the Board of Trade inspection and the subsequent initial service were accomplished using two tramcars borrowed from Leeds. To reduce the operating costs of the line the company experimented with steam power in 1876 and the directors were impressed. However, this was at such an early stage in the use of steam power on tramways the government was still working out the

Dewsbury, Batley & Birstal Tramways Company.

rules. The company went ahead and asked the Board of Trade inspector to examine the line as a steam operated tramway in 1878. Agreement was delayed until the Act regarding the use of steam power on tramways was passed in 1879 and the Dewsbury, Batley & Birstal Tramways Company Limited became the first tramway to convert to steam under that Act. Public steam operated service over the whole tramway began in 1881.

Routes at largest extent of horse tramway
Dewsbury Town Centre – Birstall

Horse Tramcars purchased

1874	5 D/D, 2 S/D	Starbuck Car & Wagon Co.
1880	6 D/D	Starbuck Car & Wagon Co.

Livery of Dewsbury, Batley & Birstal Tramways Company Limited

1874-1881	Bright Chrome Yellow

DICK, KERR & COMPANY LIMITED
See Bath

DOUGLAS

DOUGLAS BAY TRAMWAY, LATER ISLE OF MAN TRAMWAYS LIMITED, LATER DOUGLAS AND LAXEY COAST ELECTRIC TRAMWAY COMPANY LIMITED, LATER ISLE OF MAN TRAMWAYS & ELECTRIC POWER COMPANY LIMITED, LATER DOUGLAS CORPORATION TRAMWAYS

3' 0" gauge; 2 route miles; opened 1876; still operating.

The Douglas horse tramway is possibly the only operating street horse tramway in the world. There are short lines in museums and pleasure parks, but as a tramway open to all and running in public roads the Douglas system is the only known example still running. It was back in 1875 that Thomas Lightfoot, an engineering contractor who had retired to the Isle of Man, put forward proposals to build a horse tramway along the Douglas promenade. He applied for and was successful in getting the Douglas Bay Tramways Act passed by Tynwald in 1876 and construction began immediately. The line opened on 7 August 1876 on a route slightly shorter than the present tramway. The line was extended the following year to almost its fullest extent. A small extension to the Derby Castle and the new horse tramway depot was opened in 1877. Lightfoot was investing heavily in property and buildings along the promenade and over-extended himself leading to him selling the tramway to a new company, the Isle of Man Tramways Limited, in 1882. The new company increased the service by purchasing new tramcars and laying additional passing places. The demand from tramway passengers varied considerably between the summer, with its many holidaying visitors and the winter for the local population. So the tramway sold a large proportion of its horses in the autumn, buying new horses the following spring.

Part of the system was relaid with double track in 1888, with more in 1891 and the whole system being completed by 1893. In 1894 the horse tramway was approached by the Douglas and Laxey Coast Electric Tramway Company Limited, promoters of the new electric line from Derby Castle to Laxey. The horse tramway was sold to the new company in 1894 and following the takeover the company name was changed to the Isle of Man Tramways & Electric Power Company Limited. They applied for powers to electrify the horse tramway, but Douglas Corporation refused to agree and so it stayed as a horse operated system. Further attempts to get agreement to electrify the Douglas Bay tramway came to nought. Then in 1900 Dumbell's bank went into liquidation having a massive impact on the island. One consequence was the failure of the Isle of Man Tramways & Electric Power Company Limited that went into liquidation. The horse tramway had been financially successful and Douglas Corporation decided to purchase it and the cable tramway, both of which lay within the town boundary, and run them as a public service. The sale was completed on 2 January 1902 and celebrated with a parade of tramcars on both systems. The tramway was profitable through the years to 1914. During the First World War few people went on holiday and even fewer to the Isle of Man. The holiday industry collapsed; however, when hostilities ceased in 1918 people came flooding back to the Island. The interwar years saw the Island having over half a million visitors each summer. However, the start of the Second World War saw another drastic decline in the holiday trade. The horse tramway was closed in 1940 and stayed shut until the summer of 1946 when the service resumed. With the war ended holiday makers went back to the Island and it had another boom period. In 1956 the tramway celebrated its 80th Birthday with a brochure and a parade of cars on 7 August. Unfortunately by this time British holidays were changing and the island was no longer as popular. Visitor numbers declined and so did the number of passengers carried on the tramways. 1957 was a particularly bad year and rumours of closure had to be denied by the corporation. The future of the tramway was precarious, but it managed to continue and still make a profit for the corporation. In 1976 its centenary was celebrated, a truly remarkable landmark. In the same year the island's two bus services (run by Douglas Corporation and Isle of Man Road services) were nationalised and merged into the Isle of Man National Transport. Although there had been considerable debate as to whether the profitable horse tramway should be included, in the end it stayed under the control of Douglas Corporation. In 1927 the operation of the horse tramway became seasonal, with it closing during the winter months. The 1980s saw a steady decline in passenger numbers as the Island became less popular as a holiday resort. However, despite falling takings the horse tramway has continued to run and in 2008 the tramway operated from May to September daily 9.00am to 6.00pm.

Douglas Bay Tramway.

Route at largest extent
Victoria Pier – Derby Castle

Tramcars purchased
Douglas Bay Tramway

1876	2 D/D,1 S/D	Starbuck Car & Wagon Co.

Isle of Man Tramways Limited

1882	1 D/D	Starbuck Car & Wagon Co.
1883	2 D/D	Starbuck Car & Wagon Co.
1884	2 D/D, 2 T/R	Starbuck Car & Wagon Co.
1886	1 T/R	Starbuck Car & Wagon Co.
1887	6 D/D	Metropolitan Railway Carriage & Wagon Company ex-South Shields
1888	1 T/R	Starbuck Car & Wagon Co.
1889	2 T/R	G.F. Milnes & Co.
1890	2 T/R	G.F. Milnes & Co.
1891	4 T/R	G.F. Milnes & Co.
1892	3 S/D	G.F. Milnes & Co.

Douglas and Laxey Coast Electric Tramway Company Limited, later Isle of Man Tramways & Electric Power Company Limited

1894	2 T/R	G.F. Milnes & Co.
1896	6 C/B	G.F. Milnes & Co.

Douglas Corporation Tramways

1902	3 T/R	G.F. Milnes & Co.
1905	2 T/R	G.C. Milnes, Voss & Co.
1907	2 T/R	United Electric Car
1908	1 T/R	G.C. Milnes, Voss & Co.
1909	1 T/R	G.C. Milnes, Voss & Co.
1911	1 T/R	G.C. Milnes, Voss & Co.
1913	1 S/D	G.C. Milnes, Voss & Co.
1935	3 S/D	Vulcan Motor & Engineering Co. Ltd

Livery of Douglas Bay Tramway

1876-1882	Dark Blue / Cream / Red Dashes

Livery of Isle of Man Tramways Limited

1882-1894	Dark Blue / Cream / Red Dashes
1884-1894	Brown / Red Dashes

Livery of Douglas and Laxey Coast Electric Tramway Company Limited, later Isle of Man Tramways & Electric Power Company Limited

1894-1901	White / Cream (Yellow) / Red Dashes

Livery of Douglas Corporation Tramways

1901-1914	Yellow (Cream) / White / Red Dashes
1901-1914	Brown / Cream (white) / Red Dashes
1914-Date	All over Cream / Red Dashes
1990-Date	Maroon (Dark Red) / White (No 18)
1993-Date	Blue / White

DRYPOOL & MARFLEET STEAM TRAMWAY COMPANY LIMITED

See Hull

DUBLIN

DUBLIN TRAMWAYS COMPANY TAKEN OVER BY DUBLIN UNITED TRAMWAYS CO.

5' 3" gauge; 16 route miles; opened 1872; acquired by Dublin United Tramways Company 1881.

Proposals were made to introduce horse tramways to Dublin from 1859, including an attempt by G.F. Train. But it was not until 1867 that an Act was passed to allow the City of Dublin Tramways Company to build tramways in the city. It is possible that this company was linked to George Francis Train as it proposed to use the step rail (that had been rejected by other towns in previous years). Before anything had been done to lay any lines the City of Dublin Tramways Company was taken over by Dublin Tramways Company. However, the new company proposed using a grooved rail and not the step rail. Tramway services started on 1 February 1872 on a single route that was extended to go from Nelson's Pillar to Terenure, and by 1875 it had six routes. By now it was the largest tramway company in the city and it entered discussions with North Dublin Street Tramways Company and Dublin Central Tramways Company and the three became the Dublin United Tramways Company Limited in 1881.

Routes at largest extent
Nelson's Pillar – Terenure
Nelson's Pillar – Donneybrook
Nelson's Pillar – Sandymount
Nelson's Pillar – Clontarf
Nelson's Pillar – Park Gate Street
Harcourt Street Station – Kingsbridge Station

Tramcars purchased

1872	70 D/D	Metropolitan Railway Carriage & Wagon Company

Livery of Dublin Tramways Company

1872-1881	Red / White (possibly)
1873-1881	Yellow / White
1875-1881	Blue / White

NORTH DUBLIN STREET TRAMWAYS COMPANY TAKEN OVER BY DUBLIN UNITED TRAMWAYS CO.

5' 3" gauge; 9 route miles; opened 1873; acquired by Dublin United Tramways Company 1881.

In 1873 William Barrington, a former director of the Dublin Tramways Company set up the North Dublin Street Tramways Company and obtained powers to build three routes from Nelson's Pillar. These routes opened in 1876/7. The company was a pioneer in reducing operating expenses by having single-deck one man operated tramcars on the more lightly used routes. At first the company was at odds with Dublin Tramways Company because Barrington had built his routes over routes that it had been given powers to build but that had not been taken up. However, it seems that this was put to one side and the company joined with the Dublin Tramways Company to become the Dublin United Tramways Company Limited in 1881.

Routes at largest extent
Nelson's Pillar – Phoenix Park
Nelson's Pillar – Glasnevin
College Green – Drumcondra
Nelson's Pillar – Inchicore

Tramcars purchased

1876	8 D/D	Metropolitan Railway Carriage & Wagon Company
1877	6 S/D	Metropolitan Railway Carriage & Wagon Company
1878	6 S/D	Metropolitan Railway Carriage & Wagon Company
c1880	20 D/D	Metropolitan Railway Carriage & Wagon Company

Livery of North Dublin Street Tramways Company

1875-1881	Unknown

DUBLIN CENTRAL TRAMWAYS COMPANY, TAKEN OVER BY DUBLIN UNITED TRAMWAYS CO.

5' 3" gauge; 8 route miles; opened 1879; acquired by Dublin United Tramways 1881.

The third tramway in the city was the Dublin Central Tramways Company established in 1878 opening its first line in 1879 and having four routes by the end of the year. It joined with the

Dublin Tramways Company and the North Dublin Street Tramways Company to form the Dublin United Tramways Company Limited in 1881.

Routes at largest extent
College Green – Rathfarnham
College Green – Palmerston Park
College Green – Rathmines
College Green – Clonskeagh

Tramcars purchased

1879	22 D/D	Starbuck Car & Wagon Co.

Livery of Dublin Central Tramways Company

1879-1881	Purple / White
1879-1881	Green / White
1879-1881	Salmon / White

DUBLIN UNITED TRAMWAYS COMPANY LIMITED, LATER DUBLIN UNITED TRAMWAYS COMPANY (1896) LIMITED.

5' 3" gauge; 32 route miles; opened 1881; horse trams ceased in 1902.

The Dublin Tramways Company, the North Dublin Street Tramways Company, and the Dublin Central Tramways Company amalgamated in 1880 to form a single company, the Dublin United Tramways Company Limited, that was formally recognised in 1881. The first move was to lay interconnecting lines so that the three tramways could be operated as a single system. In 1883 the system started a parcels service that was to become one of the largest tramway parcels service in the British Isles. The company required more tramcars to serve its system and rather than buy from outside it was decided to manufacture their own tramcars at the Spa Road Workshops that had been opened in 1882. Some 181 horse tramcars were eventually built. In the 1890s the company looked to electrical operation and explored what was available and the experience of other systems. A new company, the Dublin United Tramways Company (1896) Limited, took over the Dublin United Tramways Company Limited and the Dublin Southern Tramways. Electrification had started in Dublin in 1896. More horse tram routes were converted and the last horse trams ran in 1902.

Routes at largest extent of horse tramways
Nelson's Pillar – Terenure
Nelson's Pillar – Donneybrook
Nelson's Pillar – Sandymount
Nelson's Pillar – Clontarf
Nelson's Pillar – Park Gate Street
Harcourt Street Station – Kingsbridge Station
Nelson's Pillar – Phoenix Park
Nelson's Pillar – Glasnivin
College Green – Drumcondra
Nelson's Pillar – Inchicore
College Green – Rathfarnham
College Green – Palmerston Park
College Green – Rathmines
College Green – Clonskeagh
Nelson's Pillar – Dolphin's Barn

Dublin United Tramways Company Limited.

Horse tramcars built

1882-6	181	Dublin United Tramways Co. Ltd

Livery of Dublin United Tramways Company Limited

1881-1902	Blue / White

DUBLIN SOUTHERN DISTRICT TRAMWAYS COMPANY

4' 0" and 5' 3" gauge; 8 route miles; opened 1879; acquired by Dublin United Tramways Company (1896) Limited

The Imperial Tramways Company promoted the Dublin Southern District Tramways Company to build two separate tramways to the south of Dublin. Unusually the routes were not only separate but also built to different gauges, one being the Irish standard gauge of 5' 3" the other being 4' 0". Both opened in 1879. This rather strange system became the first tramway in Dublin to convert to electrical operation. The conversion took place in 1896 and was the trigger for the Dublin United Tramways Company (1896) Limited that took over the Dublin Southern District Tramways Company, and the Dublin United Tramways Company Limited, with the intention of electrifying the whole of the Dublin tramways.

Routes at largest extent
Blackrock – Haddington Road (5' 3" gauge)
Kingstown – Dalkley (4' 0" gauge)

Tramcars purchased

1879	28 D/D	Unknown

Livery of Dublin Southern District Tramways Company

1879 -1896	Dark Green / Cream (Yellow)

BLACKROCK & KINGSTOWN TRAMWAY COMPANY

5' 3" gauge; 3 route miles; opened 1885; acquired by Dublin Southern District Tramways Company 1893.

There was a gap between the two routes of the Dublin Southern District Tramways Company lines, and a company was formed in 1883 to take advantage of that by building a tramway to connect the two. There was vigorous opposition from the Dublin, Wicklow and Wexford Railway who saw it as a direct competition for part of their route. However authority was given and the line was opened in 1885. The route was obviously attractive to the Dublin Southern District Tramways Company and they expressed an interest in purchasing it, though the final sale was not achieved until 1893.

Route at largest extent
Blackrock – Kingstown

Tramcars purchased

1885	6 D/D	Unknown

Livery of Blackrock & Kingstown Tramway Company

1885-1893	Deep Green / Cream

DUDLEY

DUDLEY, SEDGLEY & WOLVERHAMPTON TRAMWAYS COMPANY LIMITED.

4' 8½" gauge; 6 route miles (3 miles under horse operation); opened 1883; changed to steam power 1885.

The Dudley, Sedgley & Wolverhampton Tramways Company Limited was formed in 1879 with the aim of building tramways connecting Dudley with Wolverhampton. The line was opened on 7 May 1883 with horse tramcars, though the company was planning to convert the system to steam operation. Parts of the route were very steep and the journey by horse power was very slow.

The wish to start steam operation therefore was strong, but met resistance from the Board of Trade owing to the narrowness of some of the roads. This was resolved by the company agreeing to purchase narrow locomotives and trailers. It was then discovered that the rails, thought to be appropriate for steam operation were in fact unsuitable and had to be relaid. The line was closed in 1885 for the track laying and this was the last of the horse tram operation.

Route at largest extent

Dudley – Wolverhampton

Tramcars purchased

1883	7 D/D	Ashbury Railway Carriage & Iron Co. Ltd

Livery of Dudley, Sedgley & Wolverhampton Tramways Company Limited

1883-1885	Maroon / Cream

DUNDEE

DUNDEE & DISTRICT TRAMWAYS COMPANY LIMITED

4' 8½" gauge; 7 route miles; opened 1877; acquired by Dundee Corporation Tramways 1899.

A London firm of financiers and solicitors had been promoting tramways around the country and they considered Dundee another suitable town for a tramway. So Messrs Ashurst, Morris & Company applied for and obtained an Act to build horse and steam tramways in Dundee. They established a new company, the Dundee Tramway and Omnibus Company Limited. However, nothing was done until the local Police Commissioners (the equivalent of an English corporation) realised that the time limit for construction was approaching fast. In 1877, and rather in a rush, the Commissioners started construction of the first tramway line. The original entrepreneurs offered to lease the tramway, however, a group of local businessmen outbid the London firm and formed themselves into the Dundee & District Tramways Company Limited. As everything had been rushed the new company had no tramcars, horses or even stables. Two trams were hired from the Edinburgh system and three others from Glasgow. The tramway opened to the public on 30 August 1877. The service was popular and the company purchased two second-hand tramcars from Glasgow and then three new cars also from Glasgow. In 1878 the tramway company acquired the local omnibus operations and also built additional routes for the tramway system. The tramway company looked to converting the system to steam operation and in 1880 obtained authority to undertake a one year trial. A steam passenger tramcar (the Grantham type) was obtained from Dickinson, but was not a success and it was returned to the manufacturer. Horse tramcar operation continued until 1884 when another application was made for steam power trials. The steam locomotives and trailers

Dundee & District Tramways Company Limited.

were delivered in 1885. This time the steam operation was a success and reduced operating expenses considerably. The track condition on the Perth Road was very poor and the Board of Trade inspector refused to allow steam operations on it, so that service remained horse operated. To increase income a parcels service was introduced in 1888. A further route was added in 1892 with steam operation. In 1894 agreement was reached with the Post Office for letter boxes to be fitted to tramcars. Then in 1897 the corporation approached the tramway company with a view to purchasing the system. The corporation took over the tramway on 1 June 1899. The tramway company continued to run its omnibus services. The corporation set about converting the tramway to electrical power. The first electric route opened on 12 July 1900 with the last horse trams running in June 1901.

Routes at largest extent

Post Office – West Park Road (horse only)
Tay Street & Ward Road – Lochee (horse later steam)
Post Office – Stobswell (horse later steam)
Post Office – Baxter Park (horse later steam)
Meadowside – Victoria Road (steam only)
Post Office – Fairmuir (steam only)

Tramcars purchased

1877	2 D/D	Second-hand Glasgow Tramway & Omnibus Co.
1877	3 D/D	Glasgow Tramway & Omnibus Co.
1879	5 D/D	Thomas Swinton & Sons
1880	2 D/D	Thomas Swinton & Sons
1882	1 D/D	Unknown
1883	2 T/R	Possibly Thomas Swinton & Sons
1895	2 D/D	Ashbury Railway Carriage & Iron Co. Ltd
1897	2 D/D	Unknown

Livery of Dundee & District Tramways Company Limited

1877-1879	Polished Natural Mahogany
1879-1899	Dark Red / Yellow (Cream)

EAST SUFFOLK TRAMWAYS COMPANY

See Great Yarmouth

EDINBURGH

EDINBURGH STREET TRAMWAYS COMPANY LIMITED

4' 8½" gauge; 19 route miles; opened 1871; Edinburgh portion acquired by Edinburgh Corporation 1893, the Leith portion acquired by Leith Corporation 1904.

In 1870 two groups of entrepreneurs made proposals for building tramways in Edinburgh. These were the Edinburgh and Leith Tramways, and the Edinburgh Street Tramways Company Limited. The latter gained more acceptance and the promoters of the former company withdrew, allowing the Act to be passed unopposed in 1871. Building started immediately and the first line opened on 6 November 1871. More routes were opened in 1872-74. In 1876 and 1877 experiments took place with steam traction to help with Edinburgh's hilly terrain. Although the trials were successful, the authorities were not happy with the idea and blocked its use. Later the Grantham type steam passenger carriage was tried, but was also not adopted. In 1878 a parcels service was instigated. Another steam trial took place in 1881 but this time the company had permission to try out an engine for twelve months. This was more successful but the authorities again refused to allow steam operation. A further expansion of the system took place in 1881. The company applied for an Act to introduce steam operation and this was granted but with conditions. Restrictions by the authorities meant that the company had

Edinburgh Street Tramways Company Limited.

to continue with horse operation. Under the 1881 Act the company was empowered to operate omnibuses and this they started to do in conjunction with the horse tramway. Edinburgh Corporation decided in 1892 that they wanted to purchase (under the 21 year rule) the Edinburgh Street Tramways Company Limited lines in their city, in the hope that Leith Corporation would do the same for the part of the system in their territory. Leith Corporation also purchased the lines in their town, but then leased the tramway back to the Edinburgh Street Tramways Company Limited, while Edinburgh leased the lines in their city to Dick, Kerr & Company Limited and subsequently arranged a joint lease with Dick, Kerr and its subsidiary Edinburgh & District Tramways Company Limited. Relationships between the corporations and the tramway companies and between each tramway company were strained. The Edinburgh Street Tramways Company Limited tried to sell their Leith tramway but on each occasion the Leith Corporation felt the amount wanted was too high. In the meantime the Edinburgh Street Tramways Company Limited tramcars were getting old and unkempt giving rise to many complaints from the public. The Leith Corporation felt that they could not wait for the next opportunity to compulsorily purchase the tramway in 1906. So they approached the company and acquired the system in 1904 and horse tramway operation ceased later that year.

Routes at largest extent

Newhaven – Morningside Drive
Commercial Street – Marchmont Road
Bernard Street – Marchmont Road
Bernard Street – Powburn
Bernard Street – North Merchiston
Seafield – Gorgie Road
Powburn – Coltbridge
Morningside Circular
Tron Church – Tollcross
Portobello – Colinton Road

Tramcars purchased

1871	12 D/D	Tramway Car & Works Co.
1872	10 D/D	John Croall &. Sons, Edinburgh
1872	2 D/D	Drew & Bumett of Edinburgh
1872	4 D/D	Richard J. Boyall
1876	?	Richard J. Boyall
1876	10 T/R	Richard J. Boyall
1876	5 D/D, 10 T/R	Starbuck Car & Wagon Co.
1876	6 D/D	John Stephenson Co. Ltd
1880	14 D/D	Edinburgh Street Tramways
1880	5 D/D	Brown, Marshalls Birmingham
1883	1 D/D, 4 S/D	Hyslop & Co.
c1885	10 D/D	Edinburgh Street Tramways
1887	11 S/D	Edinburgh Street Tramways
1890	6 S/D	Edinburgh Street Tramways

Livery of Edinburgh Street Tramways Company Limited

1871-?	Red-Brown / Cream

1871-1883	Red / Grey
1883-1893	All White
1883-1893	Chocolate / Buff
1883-1893	Oak / White
1883-1893	Yellow / Green
1883-1904	Red / White
1883-1904	Blue / Cream (White)
1883-1904	Green / Buff
1883-1904	All Yellow
1893-1904	White / Cream
1893-1904	Orange / Buff

EDINBURGH & DISTRICT TRAMWAYS COMPANY LIMITED

4' 8½" gauge; 26 route miles; opened 1894; acquired by Edinburgh Corporation 1919; last horse tram operation 1907.

When the Edinburgh Corporation purchased the tramways in their area from the Edinburgh Street Tramways Company Limited they immediately leased the lines to Dick, Kerr & Company Limited. Dick, Kerr set up a subsidiary, the Edinburgh & District Tramways Company Limited to run the tramways. The Corporation had acquired 70 tramcars from the Edinburgh Street Tramways Company Limited as part of the deal and these were also leased to the new company. They took over the horse tram routes and started to run the operation. There was friction between the new company and the Edinburgh Street Tramways Company Limited who were still running the lines in Leith. It was through running that caused problems.

In 1884 the Edinburgh Northern Tramways Company was established and built cable tramways on the steeper northern side of the city. The cable tramway had 18 tramcars working on 3 miles of route. When the Edinburgh Corporation purchased the tramways from the Edinburgh Street Tramways Company Limited in 1893 they had plans to take over all the tramways in the city. So they set their sights on the Edinburgh Northern Tramways Company. This took a while to complete but on 31 December 1896 the lines were acquired by the Corporation and immediately leased to the Edinburgh & District Tramways Company Limited, who then purchased all the tramcars and infrastructure. The cable tramway was expanded and the horse tramway part of the system continued to run, while plans were made to convert them to cable operation. Most of the conversion took place 1899-1901, however one route remained horse powered and was not converted until 1907. Thus the last horse tramway route in Edinburgh ceased running.

Routes at largest extent

Murrayfield – Nether Liberton (horse later cable)
Pilrig – Gorgie (horse later cable)
Pilrig – Braid Hills (horse later cable)
Abbeyhill – Morningside (horse later cable)
Marchmont Road Circle (horse later cable)
Mound – Marchmont Road (cable only)
Pilrig – Churchhill (horse later cable)
Pilrig – Nether Liberton (horse later cable)
Post Office – Joppa (horse later cable)
Tollcross – Colinton Road (horse later cable)
Princes Street – Goldenacre (cable only)
Princes Street – Comely Bank (cable only)
Post Office – Gorgie (cable only)
Post Office – Morningside (horse later cable)

Edinburgh & District Tramways Company Limited.

Tramcars purchased

1893	70	Second-hand from Edinburgh Street Tramways
1894	13 D/D	Second-hand Glasgow Tramways
1895	4 D/D	Metropolitan Railway Carriage & Wagon Company
c1895	7 D/D	Edinburgh & District Tramways Co. Ltd
1896	6 D/D, 1 T/R	Edinburgh & District Tramways Co. Ltd
1897	1 D/D	Edinburgh & District Tramways Co. Ltd
1898	4 D/D	Second-hand Edinburgh Street Tramways

Livery of Edinburgh & District Tramways Company Limited

1894-1897	Blue / Cream
1894-1897	White / Cream
1894-1897	All White
1894-1897	All Yellow
1894-1897	Yellow / White
1894-1897	Dark Brown / White
1894-1897	Chocolate / Buff
1894-1897	Red / White
1894-1897	Blue / White
1894-1897	Green / Buff
1897-1919	Madder / Cream
1897-1898	Red / Cream (No 112 only)

EAST SUFFOLK TRAMWAYS COMPANY
See Great Yarmouth

EDMUND HOLDEN & COMPANY
See Bolton

EXETER

EXETER TRAMWAYS COMPANY

3' 6" gauge; 2 route miles; opened 1882; acquired by Exeter Corporation 1904.

A group of entrepreneurs proposed to lay tramways in Exeter and formed the Exeter Tramways Company in 1881 to build four tramways that were authorised under an Act of Parliament. Work on building the tramways began on 3 January 1882 and the first line was inspected on 5 April and authority was given to start public service on 6 April. All three routes were open in 1883, including an extension into the forecourt of the Great Western railway station. The tramway ran into financial problems and control was taken on by London businessmen and this allowed the tramway to continue to give service. The new owners offered to sell the tramway to the corporation in 1899, as they did not wish to invest in electrifying the system as it approached the 21-year compulsory purchase period. The corporation rejected the offer and the owners tried again in 1902. The price the corporation offered and the price the owners wanted were far apart. They agreed to go the arbitration and finally settled on the arbiter's valuation. The corporation acquired the tramway on 1 February 1904. The corporation took on the day-to-day operation of the horse tramway while it was being prepared for electrification.

Exeter Tramways Company.

The first electric trams ran in service on 4 April 1905 and that was the date of the last horse tram operation.

Routes at largest extent

City Centre – St David's Station
City Centre – Heavitree
City Centre – Pinhoe

Tramcars purchased

1882	3 S/D	Bristol Wagon & Carriage Works Co. Ltd
1883	3 D/D	Bristol Wagon & Carriage Works Co. Ltd
1884	2 D/D	Bristol Wagon & Carriage Works Co. Ltd
1896	2 D/D	Bristol Wagon & Carriage Works Co. Ltd
1900	2 D/D	Second-hand from Plymouth Corporation Tramways

Livery of Exeter Tramways Company

1882-1905	Chocolate / Yellow

FAIRBOURNE

FAIRBOURNE TRAMWAY

2' 0" gauge; 2 route miles; opened c1890; closed c1914.

The Victorian age was a period of prosperity for many people and with the money came the trend to take holidays. As a result many coastal towns were developing rapidly and an astute investor could make a profit from the rush to the seaside. One such was Arthur McDougall (more famous for his McDougall's self raising flour). He saw developments in the Mawddach estuary with Barmouth becoming a popular holiday town and the less populated south bank of the river starting to have holiday houses built on it. This he thought was an opportunity and he purchased an estate with the intention of building a holiday resort. The Cambrian Railway had built its coast line and built a station at Fairbourne, giving easy access to the area. Arthur McDougall decided to develop this area. As a cost-cutting measure he chose to set up his own brick-making factory locally and built a contractor's 2 feet gauge railway to link the brick works, the railway station and the building site, to enable materials to be moved easily. He also paid for a siding to be laid in the Cambrian Railways station and a new station building to be erected. Once houses had been built it was logical for the tramway to be used to take prospective clients to the development, so two toastrack type horse tramcars were purchased. It was also obvious to extend the tramway along the Bar to meet with the ferry connection to Barmouth. The exact date of passenger service is not known but was around 1890. Development of Fairbourne as a holiday resort went slower than McDougall liked, becoming overshadowed by Barmouth. So Arthur McDougall decided to sell his interests and the estate was taken on by the Fairbourne Estate Company in 1912. It is believed that the company continued to operate the tramway, but it fell into decline and by 1916 was described as being derelict the previous year. The line was leased by Bassett-Lowke, the miniature railway enthusiast, and re-opened in 1916 as a 15-inch gauge pleasure line. Since then until the present day it has operated as a miniature railway, though the gauge has been altered on occasions.

Route at largest extent

Fairbourne Station – Penrhyn Point Ferry

Tramcars purchased

c1890	2 T/R	Local Unknown

Livery of Fairbourne Tramway

1890-1916	Unknown

Fairbourne Tramway.

Fintona Tramway.

FINTONA

FINTONA HORSE TRAMWAY – GREAT NORTHERN RAILWAY

5' 3" gauge; 1 route mile; opened 1853; closed 1957.

In 1853 the Londonderry & Enniskillen Railway (later to become part of the Great Northern Railway) reached the small settlement of Fintona, but like so many railway connections the route of the railway passed near by not through the town. As a result the railway built a short branch line from Fintona Junction (the station on the main line) and Fintona and proposed that this would be worked by horse. A passenger service was provided using an adapted railway carriage, called by the local people the 'Van'. The Van provided the passenger service for thirty years and then it was replaced by a purpose built tramcar ordered from the Metropolitan Railway Carriage & Wagon Company, that unusually had accommodation for 1st, 2nd and 3rd Class passengers. It was this vehicle that carried passengers on the branch line for 74 years. During that time there were many horses employed, but always just one horse was used to haul the tramcar and tradition has it that the name of the horse was always 'Dick'. The tramway became very famous and when it closed it was one of only two horse tramways still operating in Europe (the second being the Douglas Bay horse tramway). The tram and a flat luggage trailer were preserved and can be seen at the Ulster Folk and Transport Museum, Cultra.

Route at largest extent

Fintona Station – Fintona Junction Station

Tramcars purchased

1853	1 D/D	Londonderry & Enniskillen Railway
1883	1 D/D	Metropolitan Railway Carriage & Wagon Co.

Folkestone, Sandgate & Hythe Tramway Company Limited.

Livery of Fintona Horse Tramway – Great Northern Railway

1853-1883	Unknown
1883-1927	Lake (Very Dark Red) / Cream (probably)
1927-1946	All Teak
1946-1957	Oxford Blue / Cream
?-1957	All Bauxite (Light Brown) (baggage truck)

FOLKESTONE

FOLKESTONE, SANDGATE & HYTHE TRAMWAY COMPANY LIMITED (SOUTH EASTERN RAILWAY)

4' 8½" gauge; 3 route miles; opened 1891; closed 1921.

The South Eastern Railway (SER) extended its lines to Dover in the 1840s to connect with cross Channel ferries and hence the continent, in doing so it by-passed Hythe. The citizens of Hythe and Sandgate pressed the railway company to build a branch to their towns and after much discussion it was built and opened in 1874. Hythe Corporation suggested that the railway might like to build a tramway to connect Hythe station with the town centre to convey goods between the two. The SER suggested that the corporation might like to join them in the project, but were turned down.

An independent company the Folkestone, Sandgate & Hythe Tramway Company Limited was established to build a tramway between those three towns, though the independence was nominal as the SER was behind the scenes ensuring that their interests were not affected. An Act was obtained in 1886 and construction of the tramway began. However, there were considerable difficulties. The Board of Trade inspection in 1889 refused authority to open the line for passengers. The main problem being that the line was laid railway style and the tops of the rails were not level with the road surface (as required in the 1870 Tramways Act). The company decided to use the tramway for goods traffic (not requiring permission from the Board of Trade) and passengers had to wait. Authority for extensions was sought but there were many objections. Objections continued even after the tramway was opened to the public on 18 May 1891, two tramcars having been purchased from G.F. Milnes & Company. An extension to Hythe town centre opened in 1892 with the final part of the line to Sandgate Hill being opened later the same year. In 1893 the SER obtained an Act to empower them to run the tramway officially, having done so unofficially for some time. In 1906 the British Electric Traction Company and the National Electric Construction Company Limited both made approaches to take over the tramway and electrify it. However, back in 1891 the SER had to agree that in future they would always object to any proposal to electrify the line with overhead wires. The National Electric Construction Company Limited agreed to lay a stud contact system, but difficulties with this type of system began to become apparent and that idea had to be dropped. As no alternative to overhead wires could be found the proposals to electrify the system were withdrawn and the tramway stayed horse operated until 1914.

In that year its horses were requisitioned for the War effort and the tramway service was suspended. In 1919 ex-army mules were bought and the tramway re-opened. The number of passengers carried declined and the system was allowed to go into disrepair and the service ceased in 1921. By 1922 it was in a very sorry state and the council issued an instruction that the tracks be lifted. In 1923 the South Eastern & Chatham Railway became part of the Southern Railway and the new railway company had the tramway rails lifted, ending all thoughts of it being re-opened.

Route at largest extent

Hythe Town Centre – Sandgate Hill

Tramcars purchased

1891	2 S/D	G.F. Milnes & Co.
1892	1 S/D, 1 T/R	South Eastern Railway
1897	1 T/R	South Eastern Railway

Livery of Folkestone, Sandgate & Hythe Tramway Company Limited (SER)

1891-1921	All South Eastern Railway Carriage Lake

GALWAY

GALWAY & SALTHILL TRAMWAY COMPANY

3' 0" gauge; 2 route miles; opened 1879; closed 1918.

After several abortive attempts a group of businessmen set up the Galway & Salthill Tramway Company and obtained an Act of Parliament in 1877, however, it was not completed and ready for opening until 1879. The line linked the seaside resort of Salthill with Galway railway station. Salthill was a popular residential area for the wealthier people of Galway and so the tramway aimed to provide a source of travel for those residents. It also wanted to take holiday makers going to the seaside, having travelled into the area by train. The line continued to work profitably and in 1909 five new tramcars were purchased. But the line was to be overcome by events far away. The First World War in 1914 meant that the tramway horses were requisitioned and sent to France. The tramway company struggled on but with a stable of too few and second grade horses combined with falling visitor numbers due to the conflict meant that the system closed in 1918. It had the honour of being the most westerly tramway in Europe.

Route at largest extent

Galway Station – Salthill

Tramcars purchased

1879	6 D/D	Starbuck Car & Wagon Co.
1880	1 D/D	Starbuck Car & Wagon Co.
1888	1 S/D	Starbuck Car & Wagon Co.
1909	5 D/D	United Electric Tramway Co. Ltd

Livery of Galway & Salthill Tramway Company

1879-1918	Red / White

GENERAL TRAMWAYS COMPANY

See Portsmouth

GEORGE GRAY & SONS

See Glenanne

GLASGOW

GLASGOW TRAMWAYS & OMNIBUS COMPANY LIMITED

4' 7¾" gauge; 31 route miles; opened 1872; acquired by Glasgow Corporation 1894.

In 1870 two separate groups of promoters made proposals to introduce tramways to Glasgow and both set out to gain Acts of Parliament. The Glasgow Corporation stepped in and said that they would oppose the proposals unless the two groups amalgamated their initiatives into one proposal. They had to do this or see their efforts brought to a halt. A new company the Glasgow Street Tramways Company Limited was formed. However before anything could be done the corporation said that they themselves would seek powers to build and operate the tramway (in contravention of the 1870 Tramways Act). When the corporation realised they were not allowed to operate tramways they supported the formation of the Glasgow Tramways & Omnibus Company Limited in 1871 and the company started building the tram lines. Agreements were reached with the local omnibus operators and Andrew Menzies, one of the omnibus proprietors, was appointed as Managing Director and the tramway company then purchased the omnibus company. The whole proposal was taken on by the British & Foreign Tramways Company, with the directors of the Glasgow Tramways & Omnibus Company Limited being on the board of the new company. It set up another company the Tramway Car & Works Company Limited to manufacture 200 tramcars for the new tramway. However, the new company was not in a position to manufacture tramcars until the summer of 1872. These were sent as fast as possible to enable the tramway to open on 19 August 1872. Originally just 2 miles of track were opened, but the company extended the system quickly and by 1875 there were 16 route miles. The first tramcars were painted in a livery of the Menzies tartan (no doubt the decision was influenced by the Managing Director, Andrew Menzies). Expansion continued over the years and at the end the company were running over 31 route miles. The company was the first in the country to introduce route colours for their trams, a feature copied by many other systems. The relationship between the company and the Glasgow Corporation was acrimonious and remained so throughout the life of the company. When the company sought authority to build lines in the city that would be remunerative the corporation refused while the corporation wanted the company to open lines to sparsely populated (hence financially unviable) suburbs, which the company refused. In 1892 the company approached the corporation offering to sell all their interests in the tramway, including tramcars and horses, on the basis of a going concern, but without any sum for 'goodwill'. The corporation were not so inclined and took back the track that was theirs in 1894 and then told the public that the company refused to sell the trams, horses and depots. So the corporation purchased a new fleet of tramcars, depots and horses, leaving the

Galway & Salthill Tramway Company.

Glasgow Tramways & Omnibus Company Limited.

company to sell their tramcars on the second-hand market or to scrap them. The company did operate the Glasgow to Ibrox line for a further two years before selling the lease to the corporation. The Company still operated the omnibuses and took advantage of the Corporation's lack of tramcars and made handsome profits in 1894. But once the Corporation replaced the fleet of cars they undercut the omnibus fares and the Company ceased trading in 1908.

Routes at largest extent

City Centre – Paisley Road Toll
Paisley Road Toll – Govan & Linthouse
City Centre – Whiteinch
City Centre – Kelvinside
City Centre – Maryhill
City Centre – Rockvilla
City Centre – Duke Street Station
City Centre – Parkhead
City Centre – Dalmarnock
City Centre – Crosshill
City Centre – Queen's Park
City Centre – Shawlands

Tramcars purchased

1872-6	114 D/D	Tramway Car & Works Co.
1875	54 D/D, 2 S/D	John Stephenson Co. Ltd.
c1880	47 D/D, 2 S/D	Glasgow Tramway and Omnibus Co. Ltd
1884	24 D/D	Metropolitan Railway Carriage & Wagon Company
1886	24 D/D	Metropolitan Railway Carriage & Wagon Company

Livery of Glasgow Tramways & Omnibus Company Limited

1872-1875	Menzies Tartan / White (Cream)
1875-1894	Cream / Route Colour – Red, White, Blue, Green, Brown, Yellow, Menzies Tartan
1894-1896	Brown / Cream

GLASGOW & IBROX TRAMWAY COMPANY LIMITED

4' 7¾" gauge; 2 route miles; opened 1879; acquired by Govan Commissioners 1891.

This short line was built in Govan to link the Glasgow Tramways & Omnibus Company Limited line at the Paisley Road Toll with the railway station at Ibrox. It was formed as the Glasgow & Ibrox Tramway Company Limited in 1877 with the tramway opening on 18 July 1879. With just four tramcars the tramway had a precarious existence, even though at the Paisley Road Toll it met both the Glasgow tramways and the Vale of Clyde Tramway. Throughout its life it was a financial failure, constantly making losses. Like the Glasgow Tramways & Omnibus Company Limited it suffered from the enmity of the Glasgow Corporation. The company frequently attempted to overcome its financial difficulties by getting agreement to through running into Glasgow city. But the corporation would have nothing of this and refused every application. So the company offered the tramway for sale to the corporation, but again met with refusal. Then in 1891 the Govan Commissioners approached the tramway with an offer to purchase it. While these negotiations were proceeding a gang of workmen appeared one night and connected the Ibrox line with the Glasgow tramways. This was entirely unofficial and surprised the corporation. By the time they discovered what had happened the Glasgow Tramways & Omnibus Company Limited were running through tramcars along the Ibrox line and had effectively taken over its operation. The tramway later became part of the Glasgow Corporation system.

Route at largest extent

Paisley Road Toll – Ibrox Station

Tramcars purchased

1879	2 D/D	Ashbury Railway Carriage & Iron Co. Ltd
1880	1 D/D	Ashbury Railway Carriage & Iron Co. Ltd
c1880	1 S/D	Ashbury Railway Carriage & Iron Co. Ltd

Livery of Glasgow & Ibrox Tramway Company Limited

1879-1891	Blue / Cream

VALE OF CLYDE TRAMWAYS COMPANY

4' 7¾" gauge; 7 route miles; opened 1873; Govan section acquired by Govan Commissioners 1893; Gourock section acquired by Gourock Commissioners in 1894.

The Vale of Clyde Tramways Company is an example of one of

The tramcar on the left is from the Glasgow & Ibrox Tramway Company Limited.

Vale of Clyde Tramways Company.

those companies that operated two small tramways isolated from each other. The first was in Govan and the other in Greenock and both lines were opened in 1873. The closeness of the company with the Glasgow Tramways & Omnibus Company Limited is illustrated by the fact that both companies shared the same solicitors, parliamentary agents and construction engineer. Indeed the Glasgow company provided the horses to run the Govan line and wanted to have through running, as did the Vale of Clyde company, but the Glasgow Corporation refused to agree. It was the Vale of Clyde Tramways that set the unusual gauge for all Glasgow tramways. The docks either side of the Govan line suggested that they could use the tramway to take railway wagons from the railway goods station to their premises in the docks area. After experiments it was determined this could be achieved if the tramway gauge was set at 4' 7¾", thus the rails were laid at that gauge. As there were plans to link all the tramways in and around Glasgow that became the gauge to use. The Govan line ran from Paisley Road Toll joining onto the Glasgow Tramways & Omnibus Company Limited line, and going parallel with the Clyde to the Clydeside dockyards. The Govan line was horse operated until 1877 when the company leased steam tram locomotives and horse operation ceased. The Govan Commissioners indicated in 1893 that they wished to purchase the line in their area and acquired the line soon after. The commissioners leased the line to the Glasgow Tramways & Omnibus Company Limited who operated a horse tram service. The Greenock line connected with the Greenock & Port Glasgow Tramways Company line and it was inevitable that the Vale of Clyde line would be taken over and this happened in 1894. This was the end of tram operation for the Vale of Clyde Tramways Company.

Routes at largest extent

Paisley Road Toll – Govan & Linthouse
Port Glasgow – Ashton

Tramcars purchased

1873	12 D/D	Starbuck Car & Wagon Co.
1874	2 D/D	Unknown

Livery of Vale of Clyde Tramways Company

1878-1893 Brown / Cream

GLASGOW CORPORATION TRAMWAYS

4' 7¾" gauge; horse tramways: 31 route miles; acquired Glasgow Tramways & Omnibus Company Limited lines in 1894; electrified in 1898; horse tramway operation ceased 1902.

As has been described above the Glasgow Corporation had an acrimonious relationship with the Glasgow Tramways & Omnibus Company Limited and this came to a head when the company approached the corporation in 1890 with a view to extending the lease of the tramway lines. The corporation had aspirations to run the tramways in the city and set impossible conditions on a new lease, making the company give up their tramway operation. The company offered to sell the corporation the tramcars, horses, depots and stables. But the corporation not only wanted to pay just scrap value, they also set conditions to prevent the company from operating omnibuses in competition with the corporation trams. The result was that the corporation took over the tramway lines but had no trams, horses, depots or stables. The corporation publicly stated that the company refused to sell the tramcars to them and went ahead to order enough tramcars to run the tramway, leaving the company with hundreds of useless tramcars that were offered for sale to other tramways around the country. In 1893 the corporation purchased sample tramcars and in 1894 ordered 200 trams from three manufacturers. Then the next year they bought another 170 and built a further 29 in their own workshops. This was a massive boost to the horse tramcar manufacturing industry at a time when orders for horse trams were declining rapidly. The first corporation owned tramcars began operation on 1 July 1894. During this time the corporation were planning for the electrification of the tramways, having rejected the idea of cable operation. The first electric tramcars began public service on 13 October 1898. A program of replacing horse trams with electric cars continued until the last horse tram ran on 14 April 1902.

Routes at largest extent

City Centre – Paisley Road Toll
Paisley Road Toll – Govan & Linthouse
City Centre – Whiteinch
City Centre – Kelvinside
City Centre – Maryhill
City Centre – Rockvilla
City Centre – Duke Street Station
City Centre – Parkhead
City Centre – Dalmarnock
City Centre – Crosshill
City Centre – Queen's Park
City Centre – Shawlands

Tramcars purchased

1893	3 D/D	North Metropolitan London
1893	1 D/D	G.F. Milnes & Co.
1893	2 D/D	Falcon Engine & Car Works Ltd
1894	90 D/D	Brown, Marshalls & Co. Ltd
1894	20 D/D	Midland Railway Carriage & Wagon Co. Ltd
1894	90 D/D	Metropolitan Railway Carriage & Wagon Company
c1895	45 D/D	Brown, Marshalls & Co. Ltd
c1895	60 D/D	Midland Railway Carriage & Wagon Co. Ltd
c1895	65 D/D	Metropolitan Railway Carriage & Wagon Company

Glasgow Corporation Tramways.

c1895	29 D/D	Glasgow Corporation Tramways
1896	20 D/D	Ex-Glasgow Street Tramways

Livery of Glasgow Corporation Tramways

1894-1902	Crimson Lake / Cream + Route Colour – Red, White, Blue, Green, Brown, Yellow, Menzies Tartan

GLENANNE

GLENANNE – LOUGHGILLY HORSE TRAMWAY (GEORGE GRAY & SONS)

1' 10" gauge; 3 route miles; opened 1897; closed c1918.

George Gray and Sons owned linen mills in the village of Glenanne and used the Great Northern Railway (Ireland) station at Loughgilly to transport its goods. However the link to the station was by a lengthy road using horse and carts. In 1897 the company built a more direct road between the mills and the station, the GNR(I) assisting by moving the station to a new site half a mile along the line. The company then laid a tramway along the road to assist in the movement of their goods. The purpose was to supply the mills with coal and take finished linen to the station. They also decided to operate a passenger service for the local population. A simple single-deck knifeboard seating tramcar was purchased for the service and it was even named, being called "Carew" after a local family. The tramcar met with each passenger train that stopped at the station. The tramway had an uneventful life until the First World War when the company had increasing difficulty in hiring horses for the service. A petrol lorry was purchased to carry the goods traffic and the tramway ceased running around 1918.

Route at largest extent

Loughgilly station – Glenanne Factory Gates

Tramcar purchased

1897	1 S/D	Local Unknown

Livery of Glenanne – Loughgilly Horse Tramway

1897-1919	Unknown

GLOUCESTER

GLOUCESTER TRAMWAYS COMPANY LIMITED, LATER CITY OF GLOUCESTER TRAMWAYS COMPANY LIMITED, LATER GLOUCESTER CORPORATION TRAMWAYS

4' 0" gauge; 3 route miles; opened 1879; last horse tram 1904.

Imperial Tramways, a company specialising in promoting tramways in towns around the country, set up the Gloucester Tramways Company Limited in 1877 to build a horse tramway in the city. The Act of Parliament was obtained in 1878 and the first passenger service ran on 24 May 1879. The venture was not a success and two routes were closed then for a short while the whole system closed. The Gloucester Tramways Company Limited was sold to the City of Gloucester Tramways Company Limited on 2 July 1881 and re-opened, though the Kingsholme line remained closed. The new company managed to run the system successfully and even built an extension to Tuffley Avenue in 1897. In 1899 the company approached the corporation with a view to extending and electrifying the system. The corporation initially agreed, however during detailed discussions they could not agree on the price of electricity the corporation would charge the company or the price it would pay to purchase the system. After a period of stalemate discussions were renewed and agreement was reached on the price the corporation would pay the company to purchase the system. The purchase was completed on 29 September 1902, but the company continued to run the operation while the corporation rebuilt the tramway for electric operation. The last horse tram ran on 17 March 1904.

Glenanne – Loughgilly Horse Tramway.

Routes at largest extent

City centre – Fleece Inn, Wotton
City centre – India Road
City centre – Theresa Place
City centre – St Nicolas Church
City centre – Tuffley Avenue
Eastgate Street – Railway stations

Tramcars purchased

Gloucester Tramways Company Limited		
1879	6 S/D	Bristol Wagon & Carriage Works Co. Ltd
1879	6 S/D	Falcon Engine & Car Works Ltd.
City of Gloucester Tramways Company Limited		
1881	6 S/D	Starbuck Car & Wagon Co.
1886	4 S/D	Gloucester Railway Carriage & Wagon Company
Gloucester Corporation Tramways		
1902	4 S/D	Gloucester Railway Carriage & Wagon Company

Livery of Gloucester Tramways Company Limited	
1879-1881	Unknown
Livery of City of Gloucester Tramways Company Limited	
1881-1902	Blue / Cream
1881-1902	Red / Cream
Livery of Gloucester Corporation Tramways	
1902-1904	Crimson Lake / Cream

GLYN VALLEY

GLYN VALLEY TRAMWAY COMPANY

2' 4¼" gauge; 5 route miles; opened 1873 goods and 1874 passengers; last horse tram 1886.

The industrial revolution saw an enormous increase in the demand for minerals and one area rich in slate, granite and coal was the Ceiriog Valley near Chirk. Quarries opened around the area, but they were only able to supply to local destinations as transport was difficult. In 1848 the railway arrived at Chirk and wider distribution was available. However, many quarries were some distance from the railway and roads were primitive. An attempt was made in 1861 to gain parliamentary authority to extend an existing road and build a roadside railway to link the quarries with the station. But this was rejected and things had to wait until the 1870 Tramways Act was passed. The quarry owners realised this would give them the opportunity to built a tramway to provide the essential link and the Glyn Valley

Gloucester Tramways Company Limited.

Tramway Act was passed in the same year. Raising the necessary capital proved difficult and the tramway was not laid until 1873 with just goods working to begin with. The gauge chosen, 2' 4¼" was unique in British tramways and is thought to have been chosen as half standard gauge. In 1874 an open single-deck tramcar was purchased from Ashburys and passenger service began on 1 April, though the principle function of the tramway was to transport goods. The steepness of the line meant that heavy mineral trains had to be kept small to allow the horses to haul them up the hill. The expenditure on horse power was enormous and meant that there was nothing left for profit. The line ran at a loss every year. Eventually thoughts turned to changing to steam operation and authority to make the change was obtained in 1885. The conversion work started in 1886 the tramway continued to take goods traffic, but the passenger service ceased and this was the last of the horse passenger tramway.

Route at largest extent

Pontfaen – Glyn (Llansantffraid Glynceiriog)

Tramcars purchased

1874	1 T/R	Ashbury Railway Carriage & Iron Co. Ltd
c1874	2 S/D	Ashbury Railway Carriage & Iron Co. Ltd

Livery of Glyn Valley Tramway Company

1873-1886	Unknown

Glyn Valley Tramway Company.

GOSPORT

GOSPORT STREET TRAMWAYS COMPANY, LATER PORTSMOUTH STREET TRAMWAYS COMPANY

3' 0" gauge; 3 route miles; opened 1882; last horse tram 1905.

The Provincial Tramways Company Limited promoted the Portsmouth Street Tramways Company in 1873 and then looked across the entrance of Portsmouth Harbour to Gosport as another opportunity. The Gosport Street Tramways Company was formed as a subsidiary and obtained an Act in 1879 to build tramways in that town. However construction was delayed and the tramway did not open until 17 July 1882. The route ran from Gosport Hard to St Ann's Hill and then was extended to Brockhurst in 1883. In August 1883 the Gosport company was amalgamated with the Portsmouth Street Tramways Company. In 1900 the Gosport and Alverstoke Urban District Council approached the tramway wanting to purchase the tramway under its rights according to the 1870 Act. The Provincial Tramways Company Limited responded by saying that the council were not acting in accordance with the 1870 Act as they had not given the required notice period and the purchase was dropped. Then in 1901 the Provincial company offered to sell the tramway to the council, but the offer was not taken. So the Provincial company applied for authority to electrify and extend the system and gained an Act in 1901. Work started in 1903 and as the system was modified the gauge was altered from 3' 0" to 4' 7¾". The new electric trams ran on 24 January 1906. It is probable that the last horse trams operated in 1905 until the narrow gauge rails were lifted.

Route at largest extent
Gosport Hard – Brockhurst

Tramcars purchased

1882	8 S/D	Unknown
1883	4 D/D	Unknown

Livery of Gosport Street Tramways Company

1882-1905	Emerald Green / Cream

GRAVESEND

GRAVESEND, ROSHERVILLE & NORTHFLEET TRAMWAYS COMPANY LIMITED

3' 6" gauge; 2 route miles; opened 1883; last horse tram 1901.

The Gravesend, Rosherville & Northfleet Tramways Company Limited was formed in 1881 with the passing of an Act authorising tramways to be built in Gravesend. The necessary capital was

Gosport Street Tramways Company.

Gravesend, Rosherville & Northfleet Tramways Company Limited.

found and construction was started in 1882 with the first horse trams carrying passengers on 15 June 1883. The horses for the service were hired from a local farmer who also hired horses to Gravesend Town Council. Part of the conditions of hire was that the tramway horses had to be available to pull the fire engines when required. When there was a fire alarm it was the practice to stop the tram nearest the fire station and remove the horses and attach them to the fire engine. An extension of the tramway was sought in 1884 and authorisation was obtained. The extension was not constructed immediately. Seeking to reduce costs the company looked at electric operation and in 1888 allowed the Series Electric Traction Company to take on the extension to test their system of electrical operation. The extension was built to the same gauge so that horse trams could operate over the line. Experiments continued for eighteen months and then the Series company withdrew the tramcars and the horse tramway took over operations. Horse operation continued until 1899 when the Drake & Gorham Electric Power & Traction Syndicate Limited (later to become the National Electric Traction Company Limited) purchased controlling interest in the Gravesend tramway. They applied for authority to electrify the system, but once getting the necessary legal powers they did nothing. In 1901 they sold the tramway to the British Electric Traction Company The name of the tramway was changed to the Gravesend & Northfleet Electric Tramways Limited. The BET set about converting the system for electrical operation, including changing the gauge to 4' 8½". This required the horse tramway to cease operating and the last horse tram ran on 30 June 1901.

Route at largest extent
Huggins College – King Street Clock Tower

Tramcars purchased

1883	4 S/D, 1 T/R	Unknown
1898	4 D/D	North Metropolitan Tramways

Livery

1883-1901	No uniform livery

GREAT GRIMSBY STREET TRAMWAYS COMPANY
See Grimsby

GREAT NORTHERN RAILWAY
See Fintona

GREAT YARMOUTH

EAST SUFFOLK TRAMWAYS COMPANY, LATER YARMOUTH & GORLESTON TRAMWAYS COMPANY LIMITED, LATER GREAT YARMOUTH CORPORATION TRAMWAYS

4' 8½" gauge to 1882 then 3' 6" gauge; 3 route miles; opened 1875; acquired by Great Yarmouth Corporation 1905.

In 1870 the East Anglian Tramway Company proposed building tramways in Great Yarmouth and obtained the necessary Act in 1871. Construction of the tramway started the following year, by which time the East Suffolk Tramways Company had taken over the scheme. The tramway was built to the 4' 8½" gauge and opened on 25 March 1875. Operation continued uneventfully until 1878 when the undertaking was purchased by the Yarmouth & Gorleston Tramways Company Limited. Authority for an extension was granted in 1882 and at the same time the system was relayed to 3' 6" gauge. Before and after the change of gauge the line was worked by ten tramcars, whether these were the same cars rebuilt for the new gauge or if they were new cars is not known. The tramway was not a great success, making a loss over a six-year period. In 1900 the British Electric Traction Company acquired almost all the shares of the tramway, with the intention of extending and electrifying it. However, the corporation had aspirations to run the tramway and vetoed any attempts by BET to gain the necessary authority. The corporation built new routes for electrical operation, while the company continued to run the horse tramway. The corporation then purchased the horse tramway in March 1905. The horse lines were then converted so the last horse trams ran in 1905.

Greenock & Port Glasgow Tramways Company.

Routes at largest extent
Southtown Station – Brush Quay

Tramcars purchased
East Suffolk Tramways Company

1875	10 D/D	Midland Railway Carriage & Wagon Co. Ltd

Yarmouth & Gorleston Tramways Company Limited.

1882	10 D/D	Midland Railway Carriage & Wagon Co. Ltd

Livery of East Suffolk Tramways Company
1875-1878 Unknown

Livery of Yarmouth & Gorleston Tramways Company Limited
1878-1900 Red / Cream
1878-1900 Green / Cream

Livery of Great Yarmouth Corporation Tramways
1902-1933 Maroon / Cream

Yarmouth & Gorleston Tramways Company Limited.

GREEN (PRITCHARD) & COMPANY
See Worcester

GREENOCK

GREENOCK & PORT GLASGOW TRAMWAYS COMPANY

4' 7¾" gauge; 7 route miles; opened 1889; horse tramway operation ceased 1901; tramway closed 1929.

In 1886 three businessmen in Greenock proposed a tramway for the town to connect Greenock with Port Glasgow. They gained permission from the relevant authorities and an Act was passed in 1887 authorising a 2½-mile tramway, including purchasing the part of the Vale of Clyde Tramways Company line in the parish of Inverkip. The new company was called the Greenock & Port Glasgow Tramways Company. The line was built and opened on 29 November 1889. In 1894 the lease of the Vale of Clyde Tramways Company for the line in Greenock expired and the Greenock & Port Glasgow Tramways Company succeeded in out bidding the former lessees and were able to extend their line to Gourock. In 1898 the British Electric Traction Company showed an interest in electrifying the line and they purchased the company and obtained agreement from the authorities to go ahead with their proposals. The first electric tramcars ran in October 1901 and a month later the last horse tram was withdrawn.

Route at largest extent
Victoria Road, Gourock – Port Glasgow

Tramcars purchased

1889	11 D/D	G. F. Milnes & Co.
1894	6 D/D	Starbuck Car & Wagon Co. and Tramway Car & Works Co.
1900	3 D/D	G. F. Milnes & Co.

Livery
1889-1901 Red / Cream

Great Grimsby Street Tramways Company.

GRIMSBY

GREAT GRIMSBY STREET TRAMWAYS COMPANY

4' 8½" gauge; 6 route miles; opened 1881; horse tramway operation ceased 1901; part acquired by Grimsby Corporation 1925, remainder by Cleethorpes UDC 1935.

The Provincial Tramways Company proposed building a tramway in Grimsby in 1876, but this came to nothing. They tried again in 1878 in competition with the Imperial Tramways Company and the corporation chose Provincial who applied for the necessary legal authority with an Act passed in 1879. Public service started on 4 June 1881. In 1886 the company gained powers to extend the tramway and this was built in 1887. This itself was extended to reach the seafront in 1898. The company then thought about electrifying the system and conversion started in 1899. The horse trams continued to work the service while the conversion was taking place, with the horse trams working over the heavier new rails. The conversion took place with the last horse tram running on 6 December 1901.

Routes at largest extent

Wheatsheaf – Cleethorpes sea front
Tasburgh Street – Cleethorpes sea front
Tasburgh Street – Wheatsheaf

Tramcars purchased

1881	7 D/D	Unknown
1882	2 D/D	Unknown
1886	2 T/R	Unknown
1888	2 T/R	Unknown
1890	1 D/D	Unknown
1892	3 D/D	Unknown
1893	2 D/D	Unknown
1899	4 D/D	Electric Railway & Tramway Carriage Works

Livery of Great Grimsby Street Tramways Company

1881-1905	Emerald Green / Cream

HARDING, W. & COMPANY LIMITED

See Preston

HARLECH

HARLECH TRAMWAY

2' 0" gauge (believed); 1 route mile; opened 1878; closed c1890.

Mr Samuel Holland, MP for Merionethshire, promoted a short tramway in Harlech that ran from 600 yards south of the Cambrian Railway station by Quarry Cottage to the beach. It was opened in 1878 with just one tramcar and ran in the summer months to take holiday makers from the town to the beach where a refreshment room and bathing machines had been constructed. It is possible that the tramway used the track bed of a previous mineral railway, but information is scarce and no photographs exist. The tramway ran from 7.30am to 8.30pm and probably lasted for 12 years closing in or around 1890.

Route at largest extent

Quarry Cottage – Beach

Tramcar purchased

1878	1 T/R	Rees Evans

Livery

1878-1890	Not Known

HARROW ROAD & PADDINGTON TRAMWAYS COMPANY

See London Section

HASLAR

HASLAR ROYAL NAVAL HOSPITAL TRAMWAY

4' 8½" gauge; less than 1 route mile; opened 1877; closed c1920.

Perhaps this tramway should not be in this book as strictly it was not a horse tramway, the motive power always being human. However, it is included as the tramcar was based on horse trams. Haslar Hospital was opened in 1753 to care for injured and ill seamen. In 1877 a standard gauge tramway was built to convey seriously ill patients (and on occasions dignitaries) from a jetty to the hospital buildings. There was also a longer eighteen-inch gauge goods tramway. Having just one tramcar the tramway continued in operation until the end of the First World War and then closed around 1920.

Haslar Royal Naval Hospital Tramway.

Route at largest extent

Jetty – Hospital buildings

Tramcar purchased

1877	1 S/D	Metropolitan Railway Carriage & Wagon Company

Livery

1877-1920	Unknown

HAWORTH PATENT PERAMBULATING SYSTEM

See Salford

HEATON PARK HERITAGE TRAMWAY
See Manchester

HERNE BAY

HERNE BAY PIER

Unknown gauge; less than 1 route mile; opened c1830; closed c1862.

Herne Bay pier opened in the early 1830s and was designed by Thomas Telford, though the work was probably done by Thomas Rhodes. A single-track tramway was incorporated into the pier that had small wagons to carry luggage and goods from one end of the pier to the other. These trucks were pushed by men. Sir Henry Oxenden was connected with the pier and when he was a student at Cambridge he built an ice yacht that was powered by the wind. This was developed into a land yacht and he suggested a similar concept could be used on the pier. A flat truck, possibly one of the existing goods wagons, was fitted with a mast and sail and it was used first on 13 June 1833. The trial was successful and the vehicle was given the name "Old Neptune's Car" and it was used in normal use when there was a suitable wind and there is a sketch showing the truck in full sail hauling open and enclosed passenger cars. In October 1862 the steam boat service to the pier ceased and without that trade the pier closed. It was sold for scrap in 1871. A new pier was built in 1873 but with an electric tramway; the rare sail-powered tram was never seen again.

Route at largest extent
Pier Entrance – Pier Head

Tramcars purchased

1874	3 S/D	Unknown

Livery

c1830-1862	Unknown

HOYLAKE & BIRKENHEAD RAIL & TRAMWAY COMPANY
See Birkenhead

HUDDERSFIELD

HUDDERSFIELD CORPORATION TRAMWAYS

4' 7¾" gauge; 22 route miles (2 route miles horse operated); opened 1883 (horse tram service opened 1885; horse tramway operation ceased 1902).

In 1877 the London Tramways and General Works Company approached Huddersfield Corporation with the proposal that the company build tramways in the town. The corporation were reluctant and decided that any tramways should be built and controlled by themselves and so refused permission. Then in 1879 the corporation put forward its own Bill and this was passed as an Act in 1880. The corporation began laying tram tracks in the town's streets. Their intention was to lease the tramways to a private company who would operate the system. However, they were unable to find any company willing to take on all the tramways. So the corporation decided to run the tramways themselves and duly applied to parliament for the necessary authority. This was granted and the corporation then decided that their tramway would be steam operated and not, as was more common, horse powered. A steam locomotive and trailer were purchased and public service began on 11 January 1883. Further steam locomotives and trailers were purchased as new routes opened. However, one route, that from St George's

Huddersfield Corporation Tramways.

Square to Moldgreen, passed through a very narrow street and the corporation decided that steam trams were not appropriate and that route would be horse worked. This opened on 9 May 1885 using two horse trams specially purchased and using horses hired from a local supplier. Then in August the corporation decided that the Fartown route should also be horse worked and a further two tramcars were purchased. In 1899 the corporation decided to electrify their system like many other tramways. Conversion started in 1900 and over the next two years the system was re-built for electric tramcars and the last horse trams ran in 1902.

Horse tram routes at largest extent
St George's Square – Moldgreen
St George's Square – Fartown

Tramcars purchased

1885	4 D/D	Ashbury Railway Carriage & Iron Co. Ltd

Livery of Huddersfield Corporation Tramways

1885-1902	Dark Indian Red / Cream

HULL

CONTINENTAL & GENERAL TRAMWAYS COMPANY, LATER HULL STREET TRAMWAYS COMPANY LIMITED, LATER HULL CORPORATION TRAMWAYS

4' 8½" gauge; 21 route miles (7 route miles horse operated); opened 1875; closed 1945 (horse tramway operation ceased 1899).

Proposals to lay tram tracks in Hull streets came soon after the 1870 Tramways Act when the Continental & General Tramways Company submitted a Bill to Parliament. After some changes due to representations from critics the Act was passed in 1872. Construction started and the first trams ran in passenger service

Hull Street Tramways Company Limited.

on 1 January 1875. Very soon the tramway system was sold to Hull Street Tramways Company Limited on 16 October 1876. The tramway continued to operate but gradually competition from waggonettes reduced the profitability of the tramway and it was making a loss by 1887. The lack of money meant that the track was getting into disrepair and causing the corporation concerns. They pressed the tramway company to make repairs, but without money the company was not able to. Things reached a height in December 1889 when the tramway company went into liquidation. In 1891 the Holderness Road (to Crown Inn) section was sold to the Drypool and Marfleet Steam Tramways Company who, despite their name, continued to operate that section under horse power. After lengthy negotiations, during which various entrepreneurs and companies put forward proposals before pulling out from the negotiations, the corporation purchased the remainder of the tramway in October 1899. By this time the corporation had put in place plans to electrify the system, as all the track needed renewing anyway. Construction started promptly and the first electric trams ran on 5 July 1899, with the last horse tram operating on 30 September.

Horse tram routes at largest extent
Town Centre – Dairycoates
Town Centre – Newington
Town Centre – Botanic Gardens
Town Centre – Haworth Arms
Town Centre – Crown Inn
Town Centre – Pier

Tramcars purchased
Continental & General Tramways Company
1875 2 S/D Unknown

Hull Street Tramways Company Limited
1878 1 S/D Possibly Belgium
1878 6 D/D, 6 S/D Unknown
1879 3 D/D, 4 S/D Unknown
1882 12 D/D Unknown

Livery of Continental & General Tramways Company
1875-1876 Dark Reddish Brown / White
Livery of Hull Street Tramways Company Limited
1876-1896 Dark Reddish Brown / White
Livery of Hull Corporation Tramways
1896-1899 Dark Reddish Brown / White (horse tramcars)

DRYPOOL & MARFLEET STEAM TRAMWAY COMPANY LIMITED, LATER HULL CORPORATION TRAMWAYS

4' 8½" gauge; 2 route miles (1 route mile horse operated); opened 1889 (horse operation from 1891); closed 1945 (horse tramway operation ceased 1900).

The Drypool & Marfleet Steam Tramway Company Limited opened on 21 May 1889 as a one-route steam operated tramway in Hull going from Great Union Street to Lee Smith Street, near Alexandra Dock. It became involved in horse tramways when the Hull Street Tramways Company Limited went into liquidation and the steam tramway purchased the Holderness Road route from the liquidators. This route continued as a horse operated route probably because the track was in a poor condition and would have needed relaying to take the greater weight of the steam locomotives, and the Drypool & Marfleet Steam Tramway Company Limited was in financial difficulty and could not afford it. So they operated it as a horse tramway until the whole system was sold to the corporation on 31 January 1900. While the corporation operated the steam route for another year it is likely that the horse route was incorporated into the electrification programme and the last horse trams would have run on it in 1900.

Horse tram route at largest extent
Town Centre – Crown Inn

Tramcars purchased
1891 Unknown Unknown

Livery
1891-1900 Possibly continued to have the Hull Street Tramways colours or may have repainted them into the company colours of Deep Crimson / White

---

IMPERIAL TRAMWAYS
See Darlington and Middlesbrough

INCHTURE

INCHTURE HORSE TRAMWAY (CALEDONIAN RAILWAY COMPANY)

4' 8½" gauge; 2 route miles; opened 1849; closed 1917.

Inchture Tramway.

The Dundee and Perth Railway opened in 1847 and like many railways of its time the stations were not necessarily close to the communities they were named after. One such was the village of Inchture. Inchture Station was some two miles from the village and the local population suggested to the railway that a branch be built to provide a closer connection. The railway agreed and in 1849 the short branch was opened and in addition to the goods traffic a passenger service was provided using a horse-drawn coach as a tramcar. This was replaced in 1895 by a purpose built tramcar made in the St Rollox works of the Caledonian Railway. The branch gave service to the village until the First World War when it was formerly closed on 1 January 1917. The rails were lifted and sent to the war effort in France, however, the ship sank and they now lie on the ocean bed.

Horse tram route at largest extent
Inchture Station – Inchture Village

Tramcars purchased
1849 1 S/D Caledonian Railway
1895 1 S/D Caledonian Railway

Livery of Inchture Horse Tramway
1849-1917 Crimson Lake / White

IPSWICH

IPSWICH TRAMWAY COMPANY, LATER IPSWICH CORPORATION TRAMWAYS

3' 6" gauge; 4 route miles; opened 1880; acquired by Ipswich Corporation 1901; horse tramway operation ceased 1903.

Ipswich Tramway Company.

In 1879 entrepreneurs from London proposed building a tramway in the town of Ipswich and they set about getting the necessary agreements and authority. The tramway opened on 13 October 1880 and the Ipswich Tramway Company was established in 1881. The system was completed in 1884 with the opening of the link from Cornhill to Majors Corner. The tramway ran smoothly until November 1893 when the tram services were withdrawn for two weeks following an argument with the corporation about road maintenance. This was resolved and services resumed. In 1897 the corporation successfully applied for authority to electrify the tramway, though they did not reach agreement over purchasing the company's tramway until 1901. During the reconstruction of the system for the electric trams the horse trams were operated by the corporation. Finally the horse trams had to cease working in order to allow the tracks to be relaid and the last car ran on 6 June 1903.

Routes at largest extent

Derby Road Station – Norwich Road
Derby Road Station – Ipswich Station
Ipswich Station – Norwich Road

Tramcars purchased

1880	2 S/D	Starbuck Car & Wagon Co.
1881	1 D/D	Unknown
1882	4 S/D	Unknown
1884	1 D/D	Unknown
1889	1 D/D	Unknown

Livery of Ipswich Tramway Co.
1880-1901 Mahogany Brown / Cream
Livery of Ipswich Corporation Tramways
1901-903 Maroon / Cream

ISLE OF MAN TRAMWAYS & ELECTRIC POWER COMPANY LIMITED
See Douglas

JOSEPH SPEIGHT
See Shipley

JOYCE GREEN HOSPITALS TRAMWAYS, METROPOLITAN ASYLUMS BOARD
See London

KEIGHLEY

KEIGHLEY TRAMWAYS COMPANY LIMITED, LATER KEIGHLEY CORPORATION TRAMWAYS

4' 0" gauge; 2 route miles; opened 1889; acquired by Keighley Corporation 1901 (horse tramway operation ceased 1904).

The first scheme to build tramways in Keighley came in 1885, but the corporation soon intervened to stop it when they discovered that the promoters only had experience of two tramways that they were unable to afford to operate. Though a failure, this prompted local businessmen to promote their own scheme. Keighley Tramways Company Limited was established and received the blessing of the corporation (not surprising as for the most part they were the same people). The Parliamentary Order was obtained in 1888 and construction began in 1889. The first line from the town centre to Ingrow opened with a ceremonial journey on 8 May 1889. The second line to Utley opened in December. In 1891 all bar one of the horses contracted 'pink eye' forcing the company to stop all services for two months. When services resumed the company set about increasing its revenue by purchasing several waggonettes and running a bus service. They also agreed with the Keighley fire brigade that when needed the tramway horses could be commandeered to take the fire engine to the fire, much to the annoyance of the passengers left on a tramcar with no horse power. Like so many small horse tramways the Keighley line did not yield any profit and it was not possible to establish a fund to relay tracks when they wore out. So in 1896 the company suggested to the corporation that they might like to buy the tramway system. The corporation agreed to

Keighley Tramways Company Limited.

buy the tram tracks and lease them back to the company. As they needed extensive repairs the corporation paid a nominal £5, far less than the actual value of the tracks. In 1898 the corporation sought to acquire powers to electrify the system and made an offer for the whole of the tramways. This was accepted and the corporation took over the tramway on 21 September 1901. The company retained the waggonette side of the business and these and the related horses were sold by auction, the lots including a hearse and two mourning coaches. The corporation took over running the tramway and set about the conversion to electric operation. This took a while and the horses continued the service until 28 May 1904 when the service was stopped to allow the relaying of tracks. Just four days later the tramcars, horses and all the equipment were sold by auction.

Routes at largest extent
North Street – Utley
North Street – Ingrow

Tramcars purchased

1889	7 D/D	Starbuck Car & Wagon Co.

Livery of Keighley Tramways Company Limited
1889-1901 Unknown

Livery of Keighley Corporation Tramways
1901-1904 Unknown

LANCASTER

LANCASTER & DISTRICT TRAMWAYS COMPANY LIMITED

4' 8½" gauge; 4 route miles; opened 1890; closed 1921.

Although there were already two main line railway connections between Lancaster and Morecambe (the Midland Railway and the London & North Western Railway) some local entrepreneurs proposed to link the towns with a horse tramway and so the Lancaster & District Tramways Company Limited was formed in 1888. The tramway from Morecambe to Stonewell in Lancaster was opened on 2 August 1890. It appeared that the tramway was not in competition with the railway as the whole journey by tram took 35 minutes and cost 4d compared to the journey by train that took 15 minutes and cost 3d. Like many 'holiday' type tramways the company sold most of the horses in the autumn, ran a skeleton service during the winter and purchased horses in spring ready for the summer rush. Income was sufficient to keep the system operating but as time passed it was clear that horse operation was obsolete, however the company did not have sufficient capital to pay for the conversion to electric power. It had never connected with the tramways in Lancaster or Morecambe and thus was rather isolated. So the horses continued. In 1914 the tramway company merged with a local bus operation. Then in 1921 it made overtures to the corporations with a view to selling the tramway to them. Unfortunately they were not interested, so the company decided to close the tramway completely and the last tram ran in 1921.

Route at largest extent
Lancaster – Morecambe

Tramcars purchased

1890	14 D/D	Lancaster Railway Carriage & Wagon Co. Ltd

Livery
1890-1921 Unknown

Lancaster & District Tramways Company Limited.

LANDPORT & SOUTHSEA TRAMWAYS COMPANY
See Portsmouth

LEA BRIDGE, LEYTON & WALTHAMSTOW TRAMWAYS COMPANY
See London Section

LEA BRIDGE, LEYTON & WALTHAMSTOW TRAMWAYS COMPANY LIMITED
See London Section

LEAMINGTON

LEAMINGTON & WARWICK TRAMWAYS & OMNIBUS COMPANY LIMITED, LATER LEAMINGTON & WARWICK ELECTRICAL COMPANY LIMITED

4' 8½" gauge; 3 route miles; opened 1881; changed name to Leamington & Warwick Electrical Company Limited in 1902, (horse tramway operation ceased 1905).

In 1872 the first proposals for building a tramway between Warwick and Leamington were discussed, but nothing happened until 1878 when a Bill was placed before parliament to gain authority to construct such a tramway. There were considerable discussions with the local authorities concerned and finally all objections were withdrawn and the way was clear for the Act to be passed, which it did in 1879. However, the original promoters decided not to go ahead and they sold the scheme on to a locally formed company, the Leamington & Warwick Tramways & Omnibus Company Limited. Construction was not smooth, agreements with several contractors proved abortive and the actual building of the line did not start until 1881. The tramway opened to the public on 21 November 1881. In 1897 the newly formed British Electric Traction Company approached the company with a proposal to electrify the system. As a result the BET took over the tramway in 1898 and set about getting the necessary agreements and authority to convert the system to electrical operation and at the same time convert the gauge to 3' 6". Repeating the experiences when the tramway was first built, the corporations raised objections and needed persuading to reach a point where objections were withdrawn. In 1902 the name of the tramway was changed to reflect the proposals and it became the Leamington & Warwick Electrical Company Limited. Reconstruction started early in 1905 and in order to enable the tracks to be relaid the horse tram service ceased.

Route at largest extent

Warwick – Leamington Station

Tramcars purchased

1881	2 D/D	Brown, Marshalls & Co. Ltd
1881	2 D/D	Metropolitan Railway Carriage & Wagon Company
1882	1 D/D	Second-hand ex Birmingham & District
1882	2 D/D	Metropolitan Railway Carriage & Wagon Company
1895	3 D/D	Falcon Engine & Car Works Ltd.
1899	3 D/D	Metropolitan Railway Carriage & Wagon Company

Livery of Leamington & Warwick Tramways & Omnibus Company Limited.

1881-1902	Bright Red / Cream

Livery of Leamington & Warwick Electrical Company Limited.

1902-1905	Bright Red / Cream

LEEDS

LEEDS TRAMWAY COMPANY, LATER LEEDS CORPORATION TRAMWAYS

4' 8½" gauge; 14 route miles; opened 1871; acquired by Leeds Corporation Tramways 1894, (horse tramway operation ceased 1901).

The first proposal for a street tramway in Leeds came, not surprisingly, from G.F. Train. In 1861 he wrote to the corporation offering to lay a mile of track in Wellington Street or any other place the corporation would like. The corporation took no action and the proposal faded away. Two further proposals from different entrepreneurs came in 1869, but without the support of the corporation they too fell by the wayside. However, two local businessmen laid a short length of track on private ground and invited the councillors to inspect its operation. This changed the mood and the corporation began to accept that perhaps Leeds should be looking to having a tramway. But they decided that they should have control and lay the tramway lines themselves and lease the operation to a private company. However, once they successfully stopped the private initiatives the corporation did nothing. Then two brothers, William and Daniel Busby promoted a Bill to lay tramways in Leeds. After heated meetings the view of the corporation started to move towards having a tramway. This was seen by other businessmen and further schemes were submitted. The corporation had four proposals and chose to support the Busby brothers. An Act was obtained in 1871 and construction of the tramway began and it opened on 16 September 1871. In the same year the Busby brothers obtained an Act setting up the Leeds Tramway Company to acquire the tramway. Over the following years the tramway expanded with new or extended routes being opened. In 1877 the company looked for an alternative to horse traction and experimented with steam power. Trials took place and the results were favourable.

Leamington & Warwick Tramways & Omnibus Company Limited.

Leeds Tramway Company.

So orders were placed and steam locomotives replaced the horses on the Headingley and Wortley routes in 1880. Originally they hauled horse tramcars, but in 1882 new bogie trailers were purchased. In 1890 the corporation had laid tracks on a route in Roundhay and were approached by the Thomson Houston Company who offered to run the Roundhay line with electric tramcars. The corporation agreed and the Roundhay line became the first in the country to operate with overhead electrical supply. The tramway company's 21-year period, under the 1870 Act, was due to expire in 1892 and the corporation started negotiations with the company in 1889. No agreement was reached, but by this time, and in common with many other horse tramways, the track desperately needed relaying and the company did not have the money to do so. As usual the biggest problem was agreeing a price. The two parties finally agreed to allowing a Board of Trade Arbiter to act as a referee. However, the arguments carried on over many years and it was not until 1894 that the corporation finally purchased the tramway and the Leeds Tramway Company was wound up the following year. The corporation had decided that electric traction was the future for the tramways and so plans were put forward to make the necessary changes. In the meantime the horse and steam services continued, but under corporation control. As electrification expanded the horse tram service was withdrawn and the last horse tram in Leeds ran on 13 October 1901.

Routes at largest extent
City Centre – Wortley
City Centre – Kirkstall
City Centre – Headingley
City Centre – Chapeltown
City Centre – Hunslet
City Centre – Primrose

Tramcars purchased
Leeds Tramway Company

1871	4 D/D	Starbuck Car & Wagon Co.
1871	10 D/D	John Stephenson Co. Ltd.
1873	8 D/D, 2 S/D	Starbuck Car & Wagon Co.
1874	9 D/D, 9 S/D	Starbuck Car & Wagon Co.
1875	13 S/D	Starbuck Car & Wagon Co.
1876	6 S/D	Starbuck Car & Wagon Co.
1879	3 T/R	Leeds Tramways Co.
1883	3 D/D	Ashbury Railway Carriage & Iron Co. Ltd
1885	1 D/D	Leeds Tramways Co.
1887/8	2 D/D, 4 S/D	G.F. Milnes & Co.

Leeds Corporation Tramways

1897	4 D/D	G.F. Milnes & Co.
1898	10 D/D, 10 S/D	G.F. Milnes & Co.

Livery of Leeds Tramway Company
1871-1894 Chocolate / Primrose / White
Livery of Leeds Corporation Tramways
1894-1901 Chocolate / White

LEICESTER

LEICESTER TRAMWAYS COMPANY LIMITED, LATER LEICESTER CORPORATION TRAMWAYS

4' 8½" gauge; 9 route miles; opened 1874; acquired by Leicester Corporation Tramways 1901, (horse tramway operation ceased 1904).

Proposals to build a tramway in Leicester came in 1873 when two entrepreneurs gained agreement from the corporation and obtained an Act of Parliament in the same year. The Leicester Tramways Company was established and building the tramway started. The first line, from the Clock Tower to the Folly Inn, was

Leicester Tramways Company.

opened on 24 December 1874. Additional routes were opened the following year with a considerable increase in the number of tramcars. In 1876 trials were carried out with a steam tram locomotive, but this seemed to be prone to derailment and one round trip of 3½ miles took 1½ hours. The locomotive went back to its maker, Hughes, and nothing further was attempted with steam operation. 1877 saw extensions to the system. In 1888 the company purchased the omnibus company owned by Solomon Andrews and then had a virtual monopoly on public transport in the city. Operation was successful, generally with a regular payment of dividend to the shareholders. They were even able to keep the tracks maintained and renewed where necessary. The 21 years of the 1870 Act came up in 1895, but the corporation did not exercise their purchasing powers until 1901 and then they took over the operation of the tramway. The conditions of service for tramway employees were improved with fewer hours of work and proper breaks. The corporation then set about converting the system for electric operation. During the major disruption on the road temporary tracks were laid to keep the horse tram service going. As the conversion proceeded electric tramcars replaced the horse cars with the last horse tram running on 31 October 1904.

Routes at largest extent
Clock Tower – Belgrave
Clock Tower – Uppingham Road
Clock Tower – Knighton Drive
Clock Tower – Grace Road Cricket Ground
Clock Tower – Woodgate

Tramcars purchased
Leicester Tramways Company Limited

1874	27 D/D, 3 S/D	Starbuck Car & Wagon Co.
c1876	16 ?	Unknown

Leicester Corporation Tramways

1902	4 D/D	Ex-Nottingham

Livery Leicester Tramways Company Limited
1875-? Red / White
1875-? All Green
?-1901 Grey / Biscuit
Livery Leicester Corporation Tramways
1901-1904 Grey / Biscuit

LEITH

LEITH CORPORATION TRAMWAYS

4' 8½" gauge; 9 route miles; opened 1904; absorbed by Edinburgh Corporation 1920 (horse tramway operation ceased 1905).

As detailed in the Edinburgh entry in 1870 two groups of entrepreneurs made proposals for building tramways in Edinburgh. These were the Edinburgh and Leith Tramways and the

Leith Corporation Tramways.

Edinburgh Street Tramways Company Limited. The latter gained more acceptance and the promoters of the former company withdrew allowing the Act to be passed unopposed in 1871. Building started immediately and the first line opened on 6 November 1871. For details on the Edinburgh Street Tramways Company Limited see the Edinburgh entry. When the Edinburgh Corporation proposed acquiring the company's line within their boundaries the Leith Corporation became concerned. The arrangements where the one company operated all the system were good for Leith, giving access for Edinburgh people to Leith and vice versa. So the Leith Corporation suggested a joint purchase, but Edinburgh were determined to go it alone. Leith entered an agreement with the company to allow them to continue to operate the tramways within the Leith boundary. Eventually through running agreements were made, though the Edinburgh Street Tramways Company Limited had to share with the newly formed Edinburgh & District Tramways Company Limited.

The Leith Corporation could see that the future for tramways was electric traction and so they approached the company in 1903 with an offer to buy the tramway. This was accepted and the formal transfer took place on 23 October 1904. Work to convert the system to electric operation began and the horse trams continued to give service as the routes were converted. The final horse tramcar ran on 2 November 1905.

Routes at largest extent

Leith – Edinburgh
Bernard Street – Newhaven
Bernard Street – Pilrig
Foot of Leith Walk – Seafield Place
Foot of Leith Walk – Newhaven

Tramcars purchased

1904	28 D/D	Purchased from Edinburgh Street Tramways Co. Ltd

Livery of Leith Corporation Tramways

1904-1905	Blue / Cream

LEYTON UDC TRAMWAYS
See London Section

LINCOLN

LINCOLN TRAMWAYS COMPANY LIMITED

3' 6" gauge; 2 route miles; opened 1882; acquired by Lincoln Council 1904 (horse tramway operation ceased 1905).

The Lincoln Tramways Company was formed in 1880 with the intention of building four miles of tramway in the city. Proposals were put forward for three tramway routes (only one was actually built). At the same time the Lincolnshire Tramways Company proposed a tramway on a different route. An Act was passed in 1881 authorising all the routes. Work started on the first tramway and it opened to the public on 8 September 1882. The tramway continued to work steadily until 1889 when the corporation explored the possibilities of providing electric tramway routes to other areas of the city. After extensive consideration and advice from experts nothing came from this initiative. Then the corporation looked to the horse tramway with a view to changing it to electrical operation. The corporation went ahead to purchase the tramway and in July 1904 became the owners of the tramway system. The conversion did not start until the following year, but when it did it was necessary to close the tramway as it was just one route. So the last horse tram ran on 22 July 1905 and without any delay the tramcars and horses were auctioned on 25 July. There was a proposal to build a cable tramway on the funicular principle up Steep Hill, but the corporation would not support the idea.

Routes at largest extent

Gatehouse Hotel – St Benedict's Church

Tramcars purchased

1882	2 S/D	Ashbury Railway Carriage & Iron Co. Ltd
1883	2 S/D	Ashbury Railway Carriage & Iron Co. Ltd
1884	1 S/D	Ashbury Railway Carriage & Iron Co. Ltd
1885	1 S/D	Ashbury Railway Carriage & Iron Co. Ltd
1889	2 T/R	Ex Gravesend
1900	2 S/D	Falcon Engine & Car Works Ltd.

Livery

1882-1905	Red / Cream

Lincoln Tramways Company.

LINE OF DOCKS RAILWAY
See Liverpool

LIVERPOOL

LINE OF DOCKS RAILWAY

4' 8½" gauge; 3 route miles; horse tramway opened 1859; closed c1872.

In 1856 William Curtis patented an idea allowing horse omnibuses to run on rails as well as road by using a separate flange on each wheel that could be raised when travelling on the road. He sought to promote this idea and persuaded a local

Liverpool omnibus firm to gain permission to run the vehicles on the Liverpool docks railway. This was agreed for 1859 without charge by the Docks Board. In 1860 the Docks Board decided that payment should be made for use of their track. The omnibus owners refused on the basis that they could not afford to pay. The Board expected the bus owners to discuss their receipts and operating costs in order to reach an agreed sum. But the bus operators refused and so the Docks Board withdrew permission to use their rails. It was agreed that in 1861 the rail/bus operators would pay a flat fee per journey and the service resumed. How much longer it worked is unclear but it was running up to 1872 and may have run for many years after that.

Route at largest extent
Brunswick Dock – Huskisson Dock

Tramcars purchased

1859	? S/D	Unknown

Livery of Line of Docks Tramway

1859-1872	Unknown

LIVERPOOL ROAD & RAILWAY OMNIBUS COMPANY LIMITED (OLD SWAN TRAMWAY)

4' 8½" gauge; 2 route miles; opened 1861; closed 1862.

At the same time as the Line of Docks Railway experiment Liverpool Corporation was approached by proposals from both George Francis Train and the Busby brothers. However, there were objections and nothing further came from this. The Busby brothers realised that there would be a long delay if they ever got a response from Liverpool Corporation and so negotiated with the Liverpool and Prescot Turnpike Trust to lay a tramway on the road from the Liverpool boundary to the Old Swan, where the brothers had a bus route. This part of the road was outside the control of the Liverpool Corporation. The brothers established the Liverpool Road & Railway Omnibus Company Limited in 1861. The tramway was built using a step rail and it opened on 2 July 1861. The plans were to extend the line to the Liverpool docks when the corporation agreed, however, they decided not to support the extension. By the end of 1861 the track was giving trouble. It may have been badly laid or may have had inherent design faults but the Turnpike Trust considered that it was causing danger and damage to other road users. So the track was removed by the Trust in May 1862. In 1871 the company was taken over by the Liverpool Omnibus and Tramways Company Limited.

Route at largest extent
Liverpool boundary – Old Swan

Tramcars purchased

1861	1 D/D	Oldbury Railway Carriage & Wagon Co. Ltd

Livery of Liverpool Road & Railway Omnibus Company Limited

1861-1862	Unknown

LIVERPOOL TRAMWAYS COMPANY, LATER LIVERPOOL UNITED TRAMWAYS & OMNIBUS COMPANY LIMITED

4' 8½" gauge; 43 route miles; opened 1869; acquired by Liverpool Corporation 1897 (last horse tram ran 1902).

The Liverpool Tramways Company Limited was established on 12 December 1865 with the aim to operate tramways in the city. After difficulties with the omnibus proprietors, who objected to tramways, an Act was passed in 1868 authorising the building and operating of tramways. Construction started the following year and the first tramway opened on 1 November 1869. In the ensuing years new routes were opened, but always with great opposition from the omnibus lobby and many thousands of pounds were spent on litigation. The tramways company promoted the Liverpool Tramways Act 1871 that authorised the building of a comprehensive tramway network in the city. The same year the Liverpool Omnibus and Tramways Company Limited was formed and took over the Liverpool Road & Rail Omnibus Company. The new company was formed to acquire the Liverpool Tramways Company Limited. However, this did not happen. Like many such horse tramways the track deteriorated and the corporation worked with the company to rebuild the track at the company's expense. The tramway finances were unsatisfactory and this led them to negotiate with the omnibus company to amalgamate. In February 1876 the Liverpool Omnibus and Tramways Company Limited merged with the Liverpool Tramways Company Limited to become the Liverpool United Tramways & Omnibus Company Limited and created a near monopoly in street public transport. Rationalisation was implemented with competition between omnibus and tram routes being removed. Further expansion of the routes took place in 1877. In 1880 the company agreed to sell the tram tracks to the corporation in return for them being leased back to the company. However, the contract was biased to the corporation and was to prove a financial burden to the company. Despite this there was further expansion of the routes in the 1880s.The company experienced problems from other omnibus operators and this affected the profits so much that in 1884 they set about purchasing rivals. Once again the company had a near monopoly of public transport. At around this time the company sought less expensive methods of power to replace the horses. They examined steam, cable, compressed air and electricity. There were disadvantages for all the different methods and it was decided that the risks and costs were too great for the company. In 1896 the company was extremely concerned at the lack of maintenance carried out by the corporation on the tracks and complained. The corporation admitted nothing and called on the company to provide proof of their allegations. As a result hundreds of photographs of the damaged track were taken and expert testimonials obtained. This showed beyond doubt that the corporation were negligent in keeping the track in good repair. The cost to remedy the situation was enormous so the corporation took an easier option by purchasing the company and converting the tramway to electrical operation. The negotiations reached an agreement where the tramway was sold to the corporation on 1 January 1897, but the company continued to operate it until 31 August. On 1 September 1897 the corporation took over operation of the system and conversion began. The last horse tramcar ran on 6 December 1902.

Liverpool Omnibus and Tramways Company Limited.

Routes at largest extent
Pier Head – Seaforth
Pier Head – Litherland
Pier Head – Linacre
Pier Head – Princes Park
Pier Head – Wavertree

Pier Head –Old Swan
Pier Head – West Derby
Pier Head – Clubmoor
Pier Head – Everton
Pier Head – Aintree
Pier Head – Fazakerley

Tramcars purchased
Liverpool Tramways Co.

1869	24 D/D	John Stephenson Co. Ltd
1869	18 D/D	Starbuck Car & Wagon Co.

Liverpool Omnibus & Tramways Company Limited

1871	6 D/D	John Stephenson Co. Ltd

Liverpool United Tramways & Omnibus Company Limited

1876	6 D/D	John Stephenson Co. Ltd
c1878	50 D/D	John Stephenson Co. Ltd
1882	10 D/D	Starbuck Car & Wagon Co.
c1883	55 D/D	Ashbury Railway Carriage & Iron Co. Ltd
1884	24 D/D	Liverpool United Tramways & Omnibus Co.
1885	175	Liverpool United Tramways & Omnibus Co.

Livery of Liverpool Tramways Co.

1869-1876	Maroon / White

Livery of Liverpool United Tramways & Omnibus Company Limited

1876 -1884	Maroon (Crimson Lake) / White (Cream)
1884-1891	Buff (Yellow) / White
1884-1891	Blue / White
1884-1891	Light Brown / White
1884-1897	Tartan / White
1884-1897	Green / White
1884-1897	Red / White
1891-1897	Light Red / White
1891-1897	Dark Blue / White
1891-1897	Light Blue / White
1891-1897	Brown / White
1891-1897	Dark Brown with Buff band / White

LLANELLY

LLANELLY TRAMWAYS COMPANY LIMITED, LATER LLANELLY & DISTRICT ELECTRIC LIGHTING & TRACTION COMPANY

3' 0" gauge (4' 8½" gauge from 1908); 6 route miles (horse tramway 1 route mile); opened 1882; closed 1933 (last horse tram ran 1911).

The first proposals for a tramway in Llanelly came in 1877 when solicitors from London suggested a tramway to the local corporation. This idea was deferred and quietly lost by the corporation. The next approach came from a civil engineer, Charles Winby from Nottingham, who put proposals to the corporation. An Act giving authority was passed in 1880 and the Llanelly Tramways Company Limited. was established. The gauge chosen, 3' 0" was unusual and may have been chosen to deter omnibus operators from running their buses using the rails to give a smoother passage. The tramway opened for public service on 28 September 1882. Unfortunately for the company James Andrews, brother of Solomon Andrews, was running an omnibus service along the tram route. In 1883 he started using the Solomon Andrews patent omnibus where the wheels were set at just the right distance to run on the tram rails and benefit from the rails without any of the costs of upkeep. The tramway took out a court action, but lost as it was the public highway and the buses did not have flanged wheels. In 1905 the Llanelly

Llanelly Tramways Company Limited.

Tramways Company Limited was taken over by the British Power Company Limited. The tramway continued under its original name, but the British Power Company Limited made application to convert the tramway to electrical operation and re-gauge to 4' 8½", resulting in the Llanelly & District Light Railway Order, passed in 1907. Conversion started in 1908 and the electric tramway opened on 12 June 1911. As the track gauge needed to be changed the old horse trams were withdrawn as the new track was laid. This created complaints from the public as the tramway service had ceased. The company solved this by purchasing three second-hand ex-London County Council tramcars that were standard gauge and continued to run the service until 11 June 1911, the day before electric tram operation commenced.

Route at largest extent
Railway Station – Woodend

Tramcars purchased
LlanellyTramways Company Limited

1882	3 S/D	Unknown
c1885	2 S/D	Unknown

Llanelly & District Electric Lighting & Traction Company

1908	3 D/D	Ex LCC tramcars

Livery of Llanelly Tramways Company Limited

1882-1908	Unknown

Livery of Llanelly & District Electric Lighting & Traction Company

1908-1911	Unknown (horse trams)

LONDON, CAMBERWELL & DULWICH TRAMWAY COMPANY
See London Section

LONDON COUNTY COUNCIL TRAMWAYS
See London Section

LONDON, DEPTFORD & GREENWICH TRAMWAY COMPANY
See London Section

LONDON SOUTHERN TRAMWAYS COMPANY
See London Section

LONDON STREET TRAMWAYS COMPANY
See London Section

LONDON TRAMWAYS COMPANY LIMITED
See London Section

LONDON UNITED TRAMWAYS LIMITED
See London Section

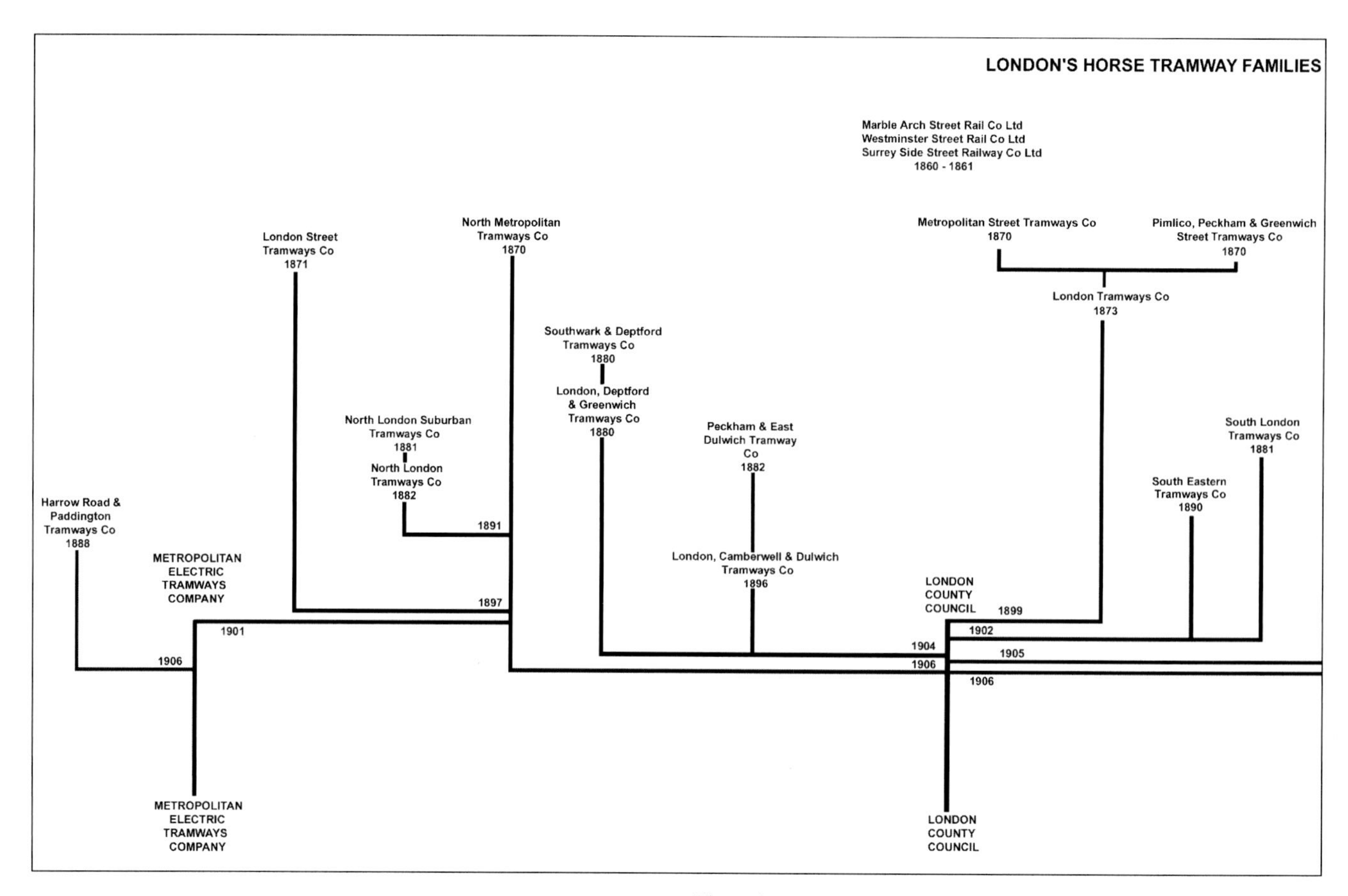

LONDON

At the time of the horse tram London was the largest city in the world. It is not surprising that it was the target of many promoters and that it had the room for many tramways and the population to ensure that they were profitable. This makes it difficult for the historian. In this book the section on London includes every tramway that was in the area that later became part of greater London. To make as much sense as possible from the plethora of tramways they have been grouped according to which of the large electric tramways absorbed the horse tramway system. Those horse tramways that were not converted to electric operation are examined in the first part of the section.

TRAIN'S TRAMWAYS
MARBLE ARCH STREET RAIL COMPANY LIMITED

George Francis Train had set his sights on London as the proper place for his horse tramways. Following the introduction of the tramway in Birkenhead, he travelled to London and after some set-backs he managed to get agreement to lay three tramway routes.

Marble Arch Street Rail Company Limited.

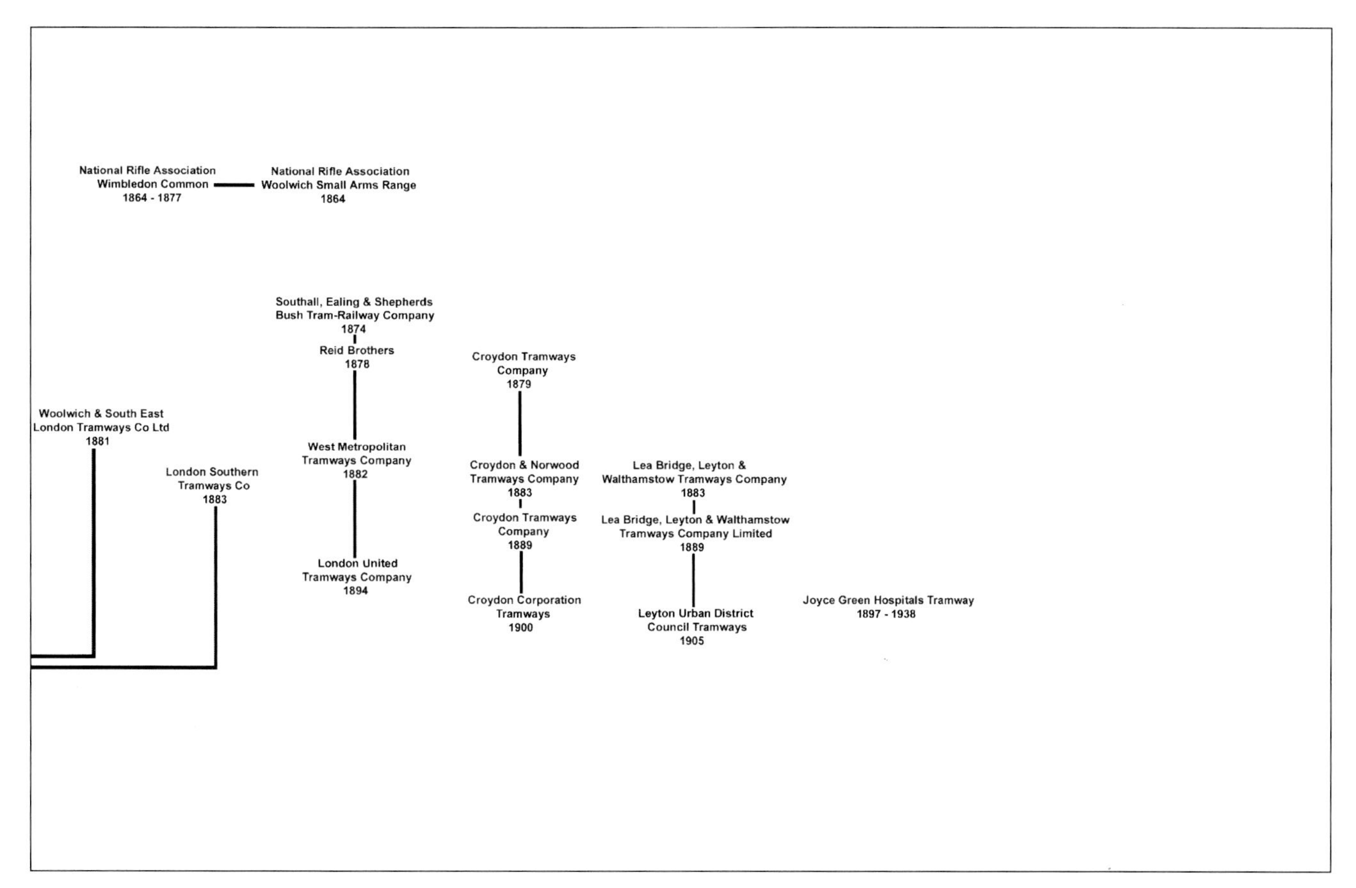

The Marble Arch Street Rail Company Limited was formed in January 1861 and rails laid in the Bayswater Road from Marble Arch to Porchester Terrace. The tramway opened on 14 April 1861. Most histories quote that the tramcars came from John Stephenson, but a magazine (The Engineer) report at the time says that one of the tramcars (it calls an omnibus) was made by the Railway Carriage and Wagon Company of Birmingham, though it is not clear if the tramcar was completed in time or was only ready after the London lines closed. The local magistrates took exception to the tramway and charged Train with unlawfully breaking up the road. He was fined 1 shilling with costs. He was then given until 1 October to remove the rails.

Route at largest extent
Marble Arch – Porchester Terrace

Tramcars purchased

1861	2 S/D	John Stephenson Co. Ltd

Livery of Marble Arch Street Rail Company Limited

1861-1862	Unknown

WESTMINSTER STREET RAIL COMPANY LIMITED

4' 8½" gauge; 1 route mile; opened 1861; closed 1862.

This was the second of Train's London tramways and ran from Victoria Station to Parliament Square. It opened on 15 April 1861, but again had many complaints and had to remove the rails in 1862.

Route at largest extent
Victoria Station – Parliament Square

Tramcars purchased

1861	1 S/D	John Stephenson Co. Ltd

Livery of Westminster Street Rail Company Limited

1861-1862	Blue / White (possibly)

SURREY SIDE STREET RAIL COMPANY LIMITED

4' 8½" gauge; 1 route mile; opened 1861; closed 1862.

This was the third and last of Train's London tramways and it opened on 15 August 1861. Once again the authorities did not like the line and Train had to appear in court on 7 April 1862 where he was ordered to close the line. He continued operating until the Sheriff of Surrey ordered a gang to remove the rails. This was the end of Train's London enterprises.

Route at largest extent
Westminster Bridge – Kennington Gate

Tramcars purchased

1861	2 S/D	John Stephenson Co. Ltd

Livery of Surrey Side Street Rail Company Limited

1861-1862	Yellow / Cream (possibly)

NATIONAL RIFLE ASSOCIATION WIMBLEDON COMMON TRAMWAY

3' 6" gauge; 1 route mile; opened 1864; closed 1889 (horse operation ceased 1877).

The National Rifle Association held its annual competitions on Wimbledon Common from early in the 1800s. The then Secretary of the NRA was impressed by the narrow gauge railway in Woolwich that ran for munitions purposes. This included a line from the firing point of the 1,000 yard range to the target. He brought back the idea and the NRS purchased a temporary 3' 6" gauge tramway with six horse tramcars. The line was laid each year from summer 1864. When not required the tramway track and cars were stored at the NRA farm on Wimbledon Common. The tramway was opened in 1864 by the Prince of Wales, making it probably the first tramway in Britain to be opened by royalty. In the first years of its use the initial six tramcars were simple single-deck open cars with knifeboard seating hauled by a cavalry soldier on his horse. Later the knifeboard tramcars were replaced with similar single-deck open cars, but with toastrack seating. The use of horses ceased in 1877

National Rifle Association, Woolwich Small Arms Experimental Range Tramway.

when a steam locomotive was tried out and proved a success so it was purchased. The competition moved from Wimbledon Common to Bisley Camp in 1890 and trams were not seen again on Wimbledon Common.

Route at largest extent
Tibbet's Corner – Firing Ranges & NRA offices

Tramcars purchased

1864	6 S/D	Unknown

Livery of Wimbledon Common Tramway

1864-1877	Unknown

WOOLWICH SMALL ARMS EXPERIMENTAL RANGE TRAMWAY

3' 6" gauge; 1 route mile; opened 1864; closed 1864.

In December 1864 the National Rifle Association held a competitive trial of rifles on the small arms experimental ranges in the Woolwich Arsenal. At the trial the NRA laid a temporary tramway that was described as similar to the one used for the Grand Rifle Meeting held in Wimbledon a few months earlier. It is not stated, but in all probability this was the same tramway, moved to Woolwich from its store in Wimbledon. The two drawings that exist of the tramways actually show a different design of tramcar at Wimbledon from that at Woolwich. The competitive trial actually turned out to be something of a farce. There were only two manufacturers as entrants and one was disqualified for having rifles that had a bore that was one thousandth of an inch below the regulation size. The remaining competitor was given the prize by default. To entertain the audience a demonstration shoot was given. But to complete the day it was cold and rainy and the venue described as a dreary spot with much discomfort. It is not known if this competition was held again and whether the tramway was ever erected at Woolwich on other occasions.

Route at largest extent
Firing position – Small Arms Targets

Tramcars purchased

1864	6 S/D	Unknown

Livery of Woolwich Range Tramway

1864-1864	Unknown

JOYCE GREEN HOSPITAL

Joyce Green Hospitals Tramways, Metropolitan Asylums Board 4' 0" gauge; 3 route miles; opened 1897; closed 1938 (horse tramway operation ceased 1925).

The London Metropolitan Asylums Board decided that the use of hulks of ships on the Thames to contain smallpox and other highly contagious diseases was unsatisfactory and they built a new hospital complex on the marshes at Dartford. This was opened in 1897 and it had a horse tramway system to move patients from the river (having been brought by boat) to the hospital wards. Special tramcars able to carry stretchers were purchased. As electric tramways were being developed around the country the hospital considered changing the motive power on a number of occasions. However nothing was done until 1925 when an experiment was carried out using one of the LCC petrol ambulances to haul a tramcar. This was a success and as a result the use of horses ceased that year.

Routes at largest extent
Pier – Long Reach Hospital
Pier – Joyce Green Hospital
Pier – Orchard Hospital

Tramcars purchased

1902	2 S/D	Second-hand ex-Harrow Road & Paddington Tramways
1902	4 D/D	Second-hand steam tram trailers ex Burnley and Huddersfield Tramways
1905	1 S/D	Electric Railway & Tramway Carriage Works Ltd
1908	4 S/D	Electric Railway & Tramway Carriage Works Ltd

Livery of Joyce Green Hospitals Tramways

1897-1905	Red
1905-1938	Navy Blue / White

Joyce Green Hospitals Tramways.

London County Council

METROPOLITAN STREET TRAMWAYS COMPANY, LATER LONDON TRAMWAYS COMPANY LIMITED

4' 8½" gauge; 24 route miles; opened 1870; acquired by London County Council 1899.

Following the removal of Train's tramways in 1861, the idea of tramways was not raised for 8 years. Then in 1869 three proposals were put forward and all obtained Acts of Parliament to build their lines. The Metropolitan Street Tramways Company built tramways south of the river in the Elephant and Castle, Southwark and Lambeth areas. Construction began in 1870 with the first line opening on 2 May 1870. At the same time as the Metropolitan Street Tramways Company, the Pimlico, Peckham & Greenwich Street Tramways Company was authorised to build tramways in South London. The two companies agreed that it was in their interests to combine and the London Tramways Company Limited was established in 1873 and authorised to purchase the two tramways under the London Tramways

London County Council tramcar in 1910 in pristine condition. John Prentice collection.

London Tramways Company Limited.

Company Limited Purchase Act 1873. For the history of the company see the Pimlico, Peckham & Greenwich Street Tramways Company below.

Metropolitan Street Tramways Company routes at largest extent

Westminster Bridge – Stockwell
Waterloo Bridge – Camberwell
Waterloo Bridge – Clapham

Tramcars purchased

1870	?	Starbuck Car & Wagon Co.
1870	?	John Stephenson Co. Ltd
1870	?	Metropolitan Railway Carriage & Wagon Co. Ltd
1870	?	The Danish firm of Rowan of Randers

Livery of Metropolitan Street Tramways Company

1870-1873 Blue / White

PIMLICO, PECKHAM & GREENWICH STREET TRAMWAYS COMPANY, LATER LONDON TRAMWAYS COMPANY LIMITED

4' 8½" gauge; 24 route miles; opened 1870; acquired by London County Council 1899.

This was the second of the three tramway proposals in 1869. The Pimlico, Peckham & Greenwich Street Tramways Company had also proposed to build tramways south of the river. The first of the tramways opened 13 December 1870, however it had to close a few days later as there was a massive snow storm that closed all traffic until 7 January 1871. As mentioned above the Metropolitan Street Tramways Company had been building tramways in the same area. They agreed it would be best for them to be under one management. So the London Tramways Company Limited was established in 1873 and authorised to purchase the two tramways under the London Tramways Company Limited Purchase Act 1873. Thoughts immediately turned to extensions as both earlier companies had applied for extensions and new routes. These had been authorised and construction began as soon as possible. The new company had troubled times in 1877 as the tram tracks were wearing out and needed replacement. It took a while and there were still arguments in 1880 when the company tried to re-capitalise in order to get funds to build extensions. One extension was to go up Brixton Hill that was too steep for horses. So a cable tramway was built and the horses unhitched at the bottom with the horse tramcar being hauled up the hill by cable regaining horses at the top of the hill for the final journey to Streatham. In 1889 the staff became very unsettled and there were a number of meetings to complain about wages and working conditions, all refuted by the company. However, at one meeting there were members of the London County Council. This may have prompted them to make overtures to the company in 1892 to purchase the tramway, in accordance with the powers in the 1870 Act. The company prevaricated and would not reach agreement. As the tramway had been opened over a number of years it would not be until 1898 that the LCC could purchase it all. So the LCC reached an agreement to acquire the tramway on 1 January 1899. From that date the LCC took control of all of the London Tramways Company Limited operations.

Pimlico, Peckham & Greenwich Street Tramways Company routes at largest extent

Elephant & Castle – Greenwich
Elephant & Castle – Woolwich
Elephant & Castle – Vauxhall Bridge
Vauxhall Bridge – Victoria Station
Elephant & Castle – Westminster Bridge
Elephant & Castle – Blackfriars Bridge
London Tramways Company Limited routes at largest extent
Westminster Bridge – Tooting
Waterloo Bridge – Camberwell
Waterloo Bridge – Streatham

Elephant & Castle – Greenwich
Elephant & Castle – Woolwich
Elephant & Castle – Vauxhall Bridge
Vauxhall Bridge – Victoria Station
Elephant & Castle – Westminster Bridge
Elephant & Castle – Blackfriars Bridge

Tramcars purchased
Pimlico, Peckham & Greenwich Street Tramways Company

1870	9 D/D	Drew & Bumett
1871	?	John Stephenson Co. Ltd

London Tramways Company Limited

c1878	?	John Stephenson Co. Ltd
c1878	?	London Tramways Co.

Livery of Pimlico, Peckham & Greenwich Street Tramways Company

1870 – 1873	Unknown

Livery of London Tramways Company Limited

1873 – 1899	White / Route Colours; Green, Blue, Red, Yellow, Chocolate Brown, Light Green, All White, Dark Green or Dark Blue

---

SOUTH EASTERN METROPOLITAN TRAMWAYS COMPANY

4' 8½" gauge; 3 route miles; opened 1890; acquired by London County Council 1902.

In 1884 the South Eastern Metropolitan Tramways Company gained authority to build a tramway from Greenwich to Catford. Nothing was done and a similar Act was authorised in 1888, though construction was delayed until 1890. The line was completed for inspection on 5 August 1890 using borrowed tramcars from the North Metropolitan Tramways Company. Before the public service could begin the company needed the tramcars that had been ordered. These did not arrive until October and the service started on 11 October 1890. The company was unusual in its recognition of its employees and each year had an outing for the staff. In 1899 the company applied for authority to electrify the line and got an Act of Parliament in 1900. This was more a negotiating ploy with the LCC than a serious move to electrify the system. The LCC made an agreement with the company and the tramway was sold to them on 1 April 1902. The LCC took over operation of the system.

Route at largest extent
Greenwich – Catford

Tramcars purchased

1890	10 D/D	North Metropolitan Tramways

Livery of South Eastern Metropolitan Tramways Company

1890-1902	All White

SOUTHWARK & DEPTFORD TRAMWAY COMPANY, LATER LONDON, DEPTFORD & GREENWICH TRAMWAY COMPANY

4' 8½" gauge; 7 route miles; opened 1881; acquired by London County Council 1904.

The Southwark & Deptford Tramway Company was authorised in 1879 to build tramways in the Bermondsey and Rotherhithe area. The first tramway was opened on 5 June 1881 and the remainder later in the year. Extensions were authorised and built. The tramway was renamed the London, Deptford & Greenwich Tramway Company in 1893. In 1900 the LCC gave notice that they were to compulsory purchase the first lines to be authorised, although the company protested and suggested that the council should wait two years and then they could purchase the whole tramway. However, the LCC went ahead and gave formal notice of intent to buy. The purchase was formally completed on 7 July 1904 and the LCC took on the operation of the tramway.

Route at largest extent
Bricklayers Arms – Tooley Street
Bricklayers Arms – Deptford
Canal Bridge – Rotherhithe
Tooley Street – Deptford
Canal Bridge – Tooley Street

Tramcars purchased

1880	28 D/D, 6 S/D	Metropolitan Railway Carriage & Wagon Co.
1904	10 D/D	Unknown

Livery of Southwark & Deptford Tramways Company

1879-1893	Blue / White
1879-1893	Green / White
1879-1893	All White

Southwark & Deptford Tramway Company.

London, Deptford & Greenwich Tramway Company.

Livery of London, Deptford & Greenwich Tramway Company

1893-1904	Blue / White
1893-1904	Green / White
1893-1904	All White

PECKHAM & EAST DULWICH TRAMWAYS COMPANY, LATER LONDON, CAMBERWELL & DULWICH TRAMWAY COMPANY

4' 8½" gauge; 3 route miles; opened 1896; closed 1900, acquired by London County Council 1904.

Authority was given in 1882 for the Peckham & East Dulwich Tramways Company to build tramways in the Peckham and Dulwich areas. The tramway was built over many months, but when completed there was no request for inspection as the company had no tramcars, no horses and no staff. This did not prevent it from successfully applying for an extension to the route and again this was built, but not opened. In 1887 the name of the company was changed to the London, Camberwell & Dulwich Tramway Company; indeed the tramway did not open for public service until 1896. However, this service was not to run for long. It ended in 1900 and the authorities tried to get the company to remove the tracks. In the end the LCC offered to purchase the lines, but by the time the sale was completed the tramway was in the hands of the receivers.

Routes at largest extent

Plough Inn – Hollydale Road
Plough Inn – Heaton Arms

Tramcars purchased

1896	4 T/R	Midland Railway Carriage & Wagon Co. Ltd

London, Camberwell & Dulwich Tramway Company.

Livery of Peckham & East Dulwich Tramways Company

1882-1887	Unknown

Livery of London, Camberwell & Dulwich Tramway Company

1887-1904	Unknown

WOOLWICH & SOUTH EAST LONDON TRAMWAYS COMPANY LIMITED

3' 6" gauge. 5 route miles; opened 1881; acquired by London County Council 1905.

The Woolwich & Plumstead Tramways Company obtained authority by an Act in 1880 to build a tramway to connect Plumstead & Woolwich with East Greenwich. Having obtained the Act the company immediately sold out to the Woolwich & South East London Tramways Company Limited. The tramway was opened on 4 June 1881 reaching Nile Street by the Woolwich ferry. The same year a successful application was made to extend the line to reach the London Tramways Company Limited line at East Greenwich. This tripled the length of the tramway. The major employer in Woolwich was the Royal Arsenal. To serve the workers special lunchtime 'express' tramcars ran from Woolwich to Plumstead and back. They were only for workmen, ladies and well dressed gentlemen were not allowed on the cars. The line was cleared of all other tramcars and the express trams went along the route non-stop. Passengers had to jump off the moving car when approaching their homes, eat their dinner and jump back on the moving return tram to get back to work. Timing was such that the wives could rely on the tram to deliver their husbands at the same precise time each day. In 1902 the LCC gave notice that they were to compulsory purchase the tramway, even though they knew they would have to relay the track to the standard gauge. The matter went to arbitration and the transfer took place on 1 June 1905. The LCC took over the horse tramway operation.

Woolwich & South East London Tramways Company Limited.

Route at largest extent

Plumstead Church – East Greenwich

Tramcars purchased

1881	6 D/D	Metropolitan Railway Carriage & Wagon Co.
1882	6 D/D	Metropolitan Railway Carriage & Wagon Co.
1884	10 D/D	Metropolitan Railway Carriage & Wagon Co.
1895	5 D/D	Metropolitan Railway Carriage & Wagon Co.
1900	6 D/D	Metropolitan Railway Carriage & Wagon Co.
1902	2 D/D	Metropolitan Railway Carriage & Wagon Co.

Livery of Woolwich & South East London Tramways Company Limited

1881-?	Light Blue / Primrose (Yellow)
?-1905	Deep Maroon / Cream

SOUTH LONDON TRAMWAYS COMPANY

4' 8½" gauge; 13 route miles; opened 1881; acquired by London County Council 1902.

In 1878 and 1879 proposals were put forward by three groups to lay tramways along the broad strip along the south bank of the Thames. Of the three, the South London Tramways Company won support and an Act authorising their scheme was passed in 1879 and opened on 5 January 1881. In the meantime further authority was obtained in 1880, 1881 and 1882 to extend the tramways. This included buying the rights from the City of London & Metropolitan Tramways Company Limited, a company that had been given powers to construct a tramway in St George's Road. The company went through a turbulent time in 1885 when financial difficulties led to the shareholders voting the Chairman and a Director off the Company Board. While the political events seem to have been settled the company still failed to make profits up to 1891. That year the company leased a loss-making line to the London Tramways Co, who connected it to one of their lines. This was still not enough and they abandoned another loss-making route. The LCC acquired the Waterloo line of the South London Tramways Company on 1 January 1899. However they allowed the company to continue to operate the line for another year and then bought out the rights of the company in 1900. The LCC decided to purchase the rest of the tramway, but the company resisted, seeking to delay the purchase until the whole of the tramway came under the 21-year rule in 1903. The debate continued with neither side seeming to be in a hurry to settle the situation. Finally the LCC acquired the whole undertaking on 21 November 1902.

Routes at largest extent

Wandsworth – London Bridge
Wandsworth – Hop Exchange
Wandsworth East Hill – London Bridge
Wandsworth – Westminster Bridge
Wandsworth – Waterloo
Wandsworth East Hill – Waterloo
Wandsworth – Elephant & Castle
Hop Exchange – Elephant & Castle

Tramcars purchased

1881	14 D/D, 14 S/D	Lancaster Railway Carriage & Wagon Co. Ltd
1884	? D/D	John Stephenson Co. Ltd
c1885	63 D/D	London Southern Tramways Co.

Livery of South London Tramways Company

1879-1902	Green / White
1879-1902	Brown / White
1879-1902	Yellow / White
1879-1902	Blue / White
1879-1902	Red / White
1879-1902	Chocolate / White

South London Tramways Company.

London Southern Tramways Company.

LONDON SOUTHERN TRAMWAYS COMPANY

4' 8½" gauge; 6 route miles; opened 1883; acquired by London County Council 1906.

In 1880 the London Southern Tramways Company proposed building tramways in the Camberwell Green, Vauxhall, Brixton and West Norwood areas. The necessary Act of Parliament was passed in 1882 and the first line opened on 7 November 1883. The line operated without difficulties until 1903, when the LCC had the right to compulsory purchase the lines. However, the LCC decided that the tracks were in a deplorable condition and said that they would only purchase the system if it was relaid for electrical operation. After some negotiations the LCC did decide to purchase the lines. The LCC took over operation of the line on 2 October 1906, but the formal transfer did not take place until 20 December.

Routes at largest extent

Vauxhall Station – Camberwell Green
Camberwell Green – Loughborough Junction
Vauxhall Station – West Norwood
Camberwell Green – West Norwood
Camberwell Green – Brixton

Tramcars purchased

1883	?	Falcon Engine & Car Works Ltd
c1890	?	London Southern Tramways
1895	? D/D	'Lowbridge' cars. Unknown manufacturer

Livery of London Southern Tramways Company

1883-1906	Red / Cream
1883-1906	Blue / Cream
1883-1906	Brown / Cream

NORTH METROPOLITAN TRAMWAYS COMPANY

4' 8½" gauge; 57 route miles; opened 1870; part acquired by Metropolitan Electric Tramways Company 1901 part by London County Council 1906.

Originally referred to as the Metropolitan Tramways Company the company obtained an Act in 1869 to allow it to lay tramways in Middlesex. Later that year the name changed to the North Metropolitan Tramways Company, and this was the beginning of the largest company owned horse tramway in London. Once the 1870 Tramways Act had been passed the company applied again to Parliament to bring its authorised lines within the ambit of the new Act. The first 2½ miles of tramway were opened to the public on 14 May 1870. Expansion continued with Acts in 1871, 1873, 1874 and 1877. In 1875 the London Street Tramways Company was in considerable financial difficulties and asked the North Metropolitan Tramways Company for help. Various ideas were discussed including the purchase of the London Street Tramways Company by the North Metropolitan Tramways

North Metropolitan Tramways Company.

Company and the leasing of the lines to the latter company. In the end all were rejected for various reasons, but the two companies agreed to join their lines and instigate through running. Under the North Metropolitan Tramways Act of 1885 the company was authorised to build tramcars for itself and other undertakings and over 300 tramcars were built by the company. Like so many other tramways of the time, the problem of deteriorating track raised itself as an issue. After much prevarication, the trackwork was slowly repaired. Further lines were authorised in 1880, 1882, 1884, 1885, 1887 and 1888. Like the other tramways in the LCC area the company were given notice that the LCC wanted to compulsory purchase the line authorised in 1870. The company objected, rightly pointing out that to take a short section of an operating tramway was unfair and the LCC should wait until all the tramways within its boundaries were available for compulsory purchase. (The area covered by the North Metropolitan Tramways Company included Middlesex as well as that within the LCC boundary.) To add to the confusion the North Metropolitan Tramways Company took over the London Street Tramways Company in 1897 (see below). The company complained to the Board of Trade about the LCC proposals to buy parts of their system as they came under the compulsory purchase dates. The company also suggested that the LCC purchase the lines and then rent them back to the North Metropolitan Tramways Company. No agreement was reached and so both parties said they would abide by the recommendations of an arbiter if negotiations failed. In fact there was movement on both sides and it was agreed that the LCC would purchase all the lines in 1896 within their area and that they would lease the lines back to the company for operation. This was carried out with the LCC finally deciding to take over the operation of the lines in their area in April 1906.

In 1894 the Metropolitan Tramways and Omnibus Company Limited was formed with the intention of building electric tramways in the north of London (now the north of Greater London). But little happened until 1901 when the British Electric Traction Company took over the company and changed the name to Metropolitan Electric Tramways Company. At the same time the newly named company purchased the lines of the North Metropolitan Tramways Company in Middlesex, but leased them back to the horse tram company. Other parts of the North Metropolitan system were compulsory purchased by East Ham, West Ham and Leyton local authorities who went on to electrify their sections of tramway.

Routes at largest extent

Highgate – Moorgate
Finsbury Park – Moorgate
Manor House – Moorgate
Stamford Hill – Moorgate
Stamford Hill – Holborn
Seven Sisters Road – London Docks
"Swan" Clapton – Dalston Lane
Lea Bridge – Bloomsbury
Well Street – Aldgate
Canning Town – Plaistow
South Hackney – West India Docks
Leytonstone – Aldgate
Manor Park – Aldgate
Poplar – Bloomsbury

North Metropolitan Tramways Company.

Tramcars purchased

1870	10 D/D	John Stephenson Co. Ltd
1871	20 D/D	John Stephenson Co. Ltd
1873	4 D/D	John Stephenson Co. Ltd
1875	6 D/D	John Stephenson Co. Ltd
1875	5 D/D	Starbuck Car & Wagon Co.
1876	4 D/D	John Stephenson Co. Ltd
1878	30 D/D	John Stephenson Co. Ltd
1879	19 D/D	John Stephenson Co. Ltd
1879	9 D/D	Falcon Engine & Car Works Ltd
1881	7 D/D	Starbuck Car & Wagon Co.
1881	5 D/D	Falcon Engine & Car Works Ltd
1882	14 D/D	Falcon Engine & Car Works Ltd
1882	5 D/D	Starbuck Car & Wagon Co.
1885	66 D/D	North Metropolitan Tramways
1887	44 D/D	North Metropolitan Tramways
1888	20 D/D	North Metropolitan Tramways
1889	18 D/D	North Metropolitan Tramways
1890	38 D/D	North Metropolitan Tramways
1891	26 D/D	North Metropolitan Tramways
1892	42 D/D	North Metropolitan Tramways
1893	32 D/D	North Metropolitan Tramways
1894	36 D/D	North Metropolitan Tramways
1895	48 D/D	North Metropolitan Tramways
1896	50 D/D	North Metropolitan Tramways
1897	22 D/D	North Metropolitan Tramways
1898	40 D/D	North Metropolitan Tramways
1899	40 D/D	North Metropolitan Tramways

Livery of North Metropolitan Tramways Company

1870-1912	Blue / White
1870-1912	All White
1870-1912	Red / White
1870-1912	Brown / White
1870-1912	Yellow / White
1870-1912	Green / White
1870-1912	Light Blue / White

LONDON STREET TRAMWAYS COMPANY

4' 8½" gauge; 13 route miles; opened 1871; acquired by North Metropolitan Tramways Company 1897.

The London Street Tramways Company put forward proposals in 1870 to build tramways in the Kings Cross, Camden Town, Hampstead and Holloway areas. This was not without challenge as the North Metropolitan Tramways Company, the Metropolitan Street Tramways Company, the Pimlico, Peckham & Greenwich Street Tramways Company and the North London Tramways Company all had ideas of laying tramways in the same areas. However, the London Street Tramways Company gained the agreement of the authorities and an Act authorising the building of the tramways was passed in 1870, with the tramway opening to the public on 27 November 1871. Unfortunately the company secretary had omitted to get the line inspected and the company hurriedly requested an inspection. This took place on 7 December and, no doubt to the grave embarrassment of the company, the inspector refused to grant approval. He stated that at one point there was so much mud he could not find the rails! The company then said that the Act did not require an inspection, so they continued to operate a service. After discussions with the Board of Trade a further inspection was carried out on 5 January 1872, by which time repairs had been carried out, and a certificate approving the line was issued. Authority to extend the tramways was obtained in 1874, 1877, 1879, 1882, 1884, 1885, 1887 and 1888. The LCC looked at the lines with interest and kept a record of when the lines would reach their 21-year compulsory date. They intended to purchase them as soon as possible. This raised concerns in the company that were justified in 1891 when the LCC gave notice of intent to purchase the first lines within their area. Like many of the purchases by the LCC the company objected and suggested an arbiter look at the situation. The arbiter agreed with the LCC that they could purchase the first tramways and recommended a purchase price, but also said that the lines should be leased back to the company. The company objected and took the matter to court. This went against them, so they appealed and this too went against them. So the earliest parts of the company's tramway system were sold to the LCC in 1894 and leased back to the company. At this point the North Metropolitan Tramways Company proposed that the LCC should take over all the lines owned by themselves and the London Street Tramways Company, then lease them all back to the North Metropolitan Tramways Company who would operate them all as a single system. This was agreed and the London Street Tramways Company sold all their tramcars, horses, stables etc. to the North Metropolitan Tramways Company in 1897. As described above the LCC took over operation of the tramways in April 1906.

Routes at largest extent

Euston Road – Hampstead
Euston Road – Archway Tavern
Holborn – Parliament Hill
Holborn – Archway Tavern
Holborn – Holloway
Farringdon – Holloway
Farringdon – Parliament Hill
Angel Islington – Parliament Hill
Angel Islington – Archway Tavern

Tramcars purchased

1871	20 D/D	Starbuck Car & Wagon Co. & Metropolitan RC&W Co Ltd
1873	75 D/D	John Stephenson Co. Ltd., Metropolitan RC&W Co Ltd and Falcon Engine & Car Works Ltd
c1880	44 D/D	Unknown

Livery of London Street Tramways Company

1871-1897	White (Cream) / Red (Vermilion)
1871-1897	White (Cream) / Pink (Light Red)
1871-1897	White (Cream) / Other Route Colours

LONDON COUNTY COUNCIL TRAMWAYS

4' 8½" gauge; 167 route miles (120 route miles horse tramway); LCC operation started 1899; electric operation started 1903 (horse tramway operation ceased 1914).

The long-term aim of the London County Council was to acquire all the tramways in its area and then to convert them all to electrical operation. It was necessary to purchase the existing tramways and this took from 1899 to 1908. As the tramways were purchased, the LCC took over the operation. Generally the service continued with little change. The LCC did reduce fares where possible and introduced uniforms and better conditions for staff. The horse tramcars were repainted when necessary with a standard livery of deep purple lake and primrose. Electrification started on the Tooting lines with the event being celebrated by the opening of the line by the Prince and Princess of Wales. While conversion was taking place the horse trams continued running until being replaced by electric cars as each route was rebuilt. The final route to be horse worked by the LCC was the Victoria Park line in East London between West India Docks and Cassland Road, South Hackney via Burdett Road and Grove Road. The line closed on 19 August 1914 when the War Office requisitioned the horses, but had to wait until after the war for electrification in 1921.

Routes at largest extent

Westminster Bridge – Stockwell
Waterloo Bridge – Camberwell
Waterloo Bridge – Clapham
Elephant & Castle – Greenwich

Elephant & Castle – Woolwich
Elephant & Castle – Vauxhall Bridge
Vauxhall Bridge – Victoria Station
Elephant & Castle – Westminster Bridge
Elephant & Castle – Blackfriars Bridge
Westminster Bridge – Tooting
Waterloo Bridge – Camberwell
Waterloo Bridge – Streatham
Elephant & Castle – Greenwich
Elephant & Castle – Woolwich
Elephant & Castle – Vauxhall Bridge
Vauxhall Bridge – Victoria Station
Elephant & Castle – Westminster Bridge
Elephant & Castle – Blackfriars Bridge
Greenwich – Catford
Bricklayers Arms – Tooley Street
Bricklayers Arms – Deptford
Canal Bridge – Rotherhithe
Tooley Street – Deptford
Canal Bridge – Tooley Street
Plough Inn – Hollydale Road
Plough Inn – Heaton Arms
Plumstead Church – East Greenwich
Wandsworth – London Bridge
Wandsworth – Hop Exchange
Wandsworth East Hill – London Bridge
Wandsworth – Westminster Bridge
Wandsworth – Waterloo
Wandsworth East Hill – Waterloo
Wandsworth – Elephant & Castle
Hop Exchange – Elephant & Castle
Vauxhall Station – Camberwell Green
Camberwell Green – Loughborough Junction
Vauxhall Station – West Norwood
Camberwell Green – West Norwood
Camberwell Green – Brixton
Highgate – Moorgate
Finsbury Park – Moorgate
Manor House – Moorgate
Stamford Hill – Moorgate
Stamford Hill – Holborn
Seven Sisters Road – London Docks
"Swan" Clapton – Dalston Lane
Lea Bridge – Bloomsbury
Well Street – Aldgate
Hackney – Aldersgate
South Hackney – West India Docks
Bow – Aldgate
Poplar – Aldgate
Poplar – Bloomsbury
Euston Road – Hampstead
Euston Road – Archway Tavern
Holborn – Parliament Hill
Holborn – Archway Tavern
Holborn – Holloway
Farringdon – Holloway
Farringdon – Parliament Hill
Angel Islington – Parliament Hill
Angel Islington – Archway Tavern

Tramcars purchased

1900	c500	The LCC may have made some tramcars

Livery of London County Council

1896-1903	Chocolate / Cream
1896-1903	Green / Cream
1896-1903	Red / Cream
1896-1903	Light Green / Cream
1896-1903	All White
1896-1903	Yellow / Cream
1896-1903	Blue / White
1896-1903	Dark Green / Cream
1896-1903	Dark Blue / Cream
1896-1914	Deep Purple Lake / Primrose

Metropolitan Electric Tramways Company

NORTH METROPOLITAN TRAMWAYS COMPANY

4' 8½" gauge; 57 route miles; opened 1870; part acquired part by Metropolitan Electric Tramways Company 1901 part by London County Council 1906.

See above for the history of this company that was purchased part by the London County Council and part by the Metropolitan Electric Tramways.

LONDON STREET TRAMWAYS COMPANY

4' 8½" gauge. 13 route miles; opened 1871; acquired by North Metropolitan Tramways Company 1897.

See above for the history of this company that was purchased by the North Metropolitan Tramways Company and then part of which was purchased by the London County Council and part by the Metropolitan Electric Tramways.

NORTH LONDON SUBURBAN TRAMWAYS COMPANY, LATER NORTH LONDON TRAMWAYS COMPANY

4' 8½" gauge; 8 route miles; opened 1881; acquired by North Metropolitan Tramways Company 1891.

The North London Suburban Tramways Company was established in 1878 to build steam operated tramways in Middlesex. It received authority to construct its tramways in 1879 and the first part of the tramway opened on 12 April 1881, but only for horse operation. The second part was opened on 7 January 1882, but the company was in serious financial difficulty and by the end of January it went bankrupt. It was taken over by the North London Tramways Company and extensions to the system were authorised in 1883. The intention had been to run the system as a steam tramway and after some arguments with the Metropolitan Board, who objected, authority was given for steam operation over the whole system, though the company kept horse tramcars and ran horse services. The system ran into financial trouble again in 1889 and was liquidated in 1890. It continued to run under the management of the liquidator until the North Metropolitan Tramways Company was asked to operate the lines as a horse tramway, the steam tram locomotives having been withdrawn. Rather than just operating the tramway the North Metropolitan Tramways Company decided to buy the system for themselves and this was formally achieved on 12 April 1892.

North London Tramways Company.

Routes at largest extent
Stamford Hill – Ponders End
Finsbury Park – Ponders End
Manor House – Wood Green
Finsbury Park – Wood Green

Tramcars purchased

1878	12 S/D	Ashbury Railway Carriage & Iron Co. Ltd
1881	8 S/D	Ashbury Railway Carriage & Iron Co. Ltd

Livery of North London Suburban Tramways Company
1878-1882 Unknown
Livery of North London Tramways Company
1882-1891 Dark Green / White

HARROW ROAD & PADDINGTON TRAMWAYS COMPANY

4' 8½" gauge; 3 route miles; opened 1888; acquired by Metropolitan Electric Tramways Company 1906.

There were several proposals from 1874 onwards to build tramways in the Harrow Road and Paddington areas. It was not until 1886 that authorisation was obtained by the Harrow Road & Paddington Tramways Company to build a line along the Harrow Road to Lock Bridge. The line opened on 7 July 1888 and in 1891 further authorisation was given to extend the line. The situation was unusual as when the tramway was authorised and built it was almost wholly in Middlesex, but when the London County Council was created in 1889 it was mainly in the new LCC area. By this time the Cambridge Road route was uneconomic and so the company just ran a 'statutory' tram once every three months with token fare paying passengers to keep their rights on the line. In 1903 the track was purchased by the LCC and the Metropolitan Electric Tramways (on behalf of Middlesex County Council) though the company continued to operate the horse trams. The line was electrified and the LCC leased its tracks to the Metropolitan Electric Tramways to operate.

Routes at largest extent
Royal Oak, Harlesden- Lock Bridge
Lock Bridge – Cambridge Road

Tramcars purchased

1888	12 D/D	G.F. Milnes & Co.
1890	9 D/D	Falcon Engine & Car Works Ltd

Livery of Harrow Road & Paddington Tramways Company
1886-1906 Red / White
1886-1906 Brown / White

Harrow Road & Paddington Tramways Company.

METROPOLITAN ELECTRIC TRAMWAYS COMPANY

4' 8½" gauge; 54 route miles (41 route miles horse tramway); MET acquisitions started 1901; electric operation started 1904 (horse tramway operation ceased 1905).

To be strictly correct the Metropolitan Electric Tramways Company did not operate a horse tramway. When it purchased systems for electrification it allowed the horse company to continue operating the tramway while the conversion to electric power was undertaken. The MET only took over the operation when the electric tramcars entered service. Therefore it is not appropriate to list the routes, it did not purchase any new horse tramcars and did not have a livery for horse trams.

London United Tramways Limited

SOUTHALL, EALING & SHEPHERDS BUSH TRAM-RAILWAY COMPANY, LATER THE REID BROTHERS, LATER WEST METROPOLITAN TRAMWAYS COMPANY LIMITED, LATER LONDON UNITED TRAMWAYS LIMITED

4' 8½" gauge; 10 route miles; opened 1874; electric operation started 1901 (horse tramway operation ceased 1912).

The Southall, Ealing & Shepherds Bush Tram-Railway Company was established in 1870 to promote the building of a tramway between Shepherds Bush and Acton. It gained the agreement of the authorities and was authorised to build the tramway in 1873. The first tram ran in public service on 1 June 1874, despite having failed the inspection and not having a certificate of fitness. Despite pressure from the Board of Trade and threats of court action the tramway continued to operate. More threats were issued, but it was another problem that caused the line to close. The engineers who had constructed the line, the Reid brothers, had not been paid and they put in a court action to liquidate the tramway company. The court appointed a liquidator and the company ceased trading. The last tramcar ran on 23 February 1874. The liquidator failed to find a buyer and finally the Reid brothers agreed to operate the tramway and complete the full length of the line on behalf of the liquidator. An inspection by the Board of Trade resulted in a certificate of fitness being issued on 21 September 1875 with the passenger service starting again on the same day. After much debate and argument the tramway was sold to the Reid brothers on 25 January 1878. The tramway continued to run under the management of the Reid brothers until they sold all their tramway interests to the West Metropolitan Tramways Company Limited on 6 March 1882. Extensions to the tramway system were opened in 1882 and 1883 including a short route from Richmond to Kew Bridge that was separated from the rest of the system by the River Thames. The financial management of the company deteriorated up to 1892, when the debenture holders called in the receiver and the company was liquidated in 1893. The system was put up for public auction as a going concern, but failed to attract any bidders. Following this a private sale was agreed and the liquidator sold the tramway to an agent of the Imperial Tramways Company, who set up a new company the London United Tramways Limited to run the system, the formal date of purchase being 20 August 1894. The LUT had plans to electrify the tramway and to expand its operations under the management of Clifton Robinson. In the meantime horse operation continued with the tracks being repaired and maintained and some new tramcars being purchased. The first electric trams ran on 4 April 1901 and the last horse trams ceased running on 20 April 1912.

Routes at largest extent
Acton – Shepherds Bush

West Metropolitan Tramways Company Limited.

Shepherds Bush – Kew Bridge
Hammersmith – Kew Bridge
Richmond – Kew Bridge

Tramcars purchased

Southall, Ealing & Shepherds Bush Tram-Railway Company

1874	2 D/D	Starbuck Car & Wagon Co.
1877	1 D/D	Starbuck Car & Wagon Co.
1878	1 D/D	Starbuck Car & Wagon Co.

West Metropolitan Tramways Company Limited

1882	9 S/D	Falcon Engine & Car Works Ltd
1882	10 D/D	John Stephenson Co. Ltd
1883	4 S/D	Falcon Engine & Car Works Ltd
1883	6 D/D	Unknown
1886	4 D/D	Falcon Engine & Car Works Ltd
1887	1 S/D	Falcon Engine & Car Works Ltd
1894	15 D/D	G.F. Milnes & Co.

London United Tramways Limited

1895	15 D/D	G.F. Milnes & Co.
1897	10 D/D	London United Tramways

Livery of Southall, Ealing & Shepherds Bush Tram-Railway Company

1874-1882	Unknown

Livery of West Metropolitan Tramways Company Limited

1882-1894	Yellow / Ivory
1882-1894	Brown / Yellow
1882-1894	Blue / Cream

Livery of London United Tramways Limited

1901-1912	Chocolate (Brown) / Cream

Croydon

CROYDON TRAMWAYS COMPANY, LATER CROYDON & NORWOOD TRAMWAYS COMPANY, LATER CROYDON TRAMWAYS COMPANY

4' 8½" gauge; 7 route miles; opened 1879; acquired by Croydon Corporation 1900.

Local businessmen in Croydon decided in 1877 to set up the Croydon Tramways Company to promote a horse tramway in the town. Agreement was reached with the Local Board and an Act of Parliament obtained in 1878 with track laying starting the same year. The first route was ready the following year with the tramway opening on 9 October with extensions and further routes opening in the following three years. In 1882 a new company was established to open tramways in Norwood called the Norwood and District Tramways Company which started laying track in 1883. The Croydon Tramways Company approached the new company and it was agreed that the two systems would merge, the new company being called the Croydon & Norwood Tramways Company. The system was then leased to the Steam Traction Company with the intention of running steam trams. As no steam locomotives had been purchased the system continued to be horse-drawn. In 1884 the steam company purchased six Hohenzollern fireless steam locomotives from Germany. These were not a success and the steam company gave up the lease and operation reverted to the Croydon & Norwood Tramways Company. The fireless steam locomotives were returned to Germany. The new Norwood lines proved to be a financial embarrassment to such an extent that the company went into liquidation in 1887. The liquidator continued to run the tramway, but the Norwood route was closed and after complaints from the corporation the rails were lifted. The remainder of the system was sold to a new company in 1889, confusingly with the same name as the original company "Croydon Tramways Company". In 1898 the British Electric Traction Company became interested in the system and started talks with a view to taking it over and electrifying it. Later that year the corporation decided to make their own approach and indicated to the tramway company that they would take it over when the lease expired. The takeover was completed in 1900. During the conversion horse services continued with the last horse tram running in 1902.

Routes at largest extent

Red Deer South Croydon – Thornton Heath Pond
Thornton Heath – Thornton Heath Pond
South Norwood – West Croydon
Addiscombe – West Croydon

Croydon Tramways Company.

Tramcars purchased
Croydon Tramways Company (original)

1879	5 S/D	Starbuck Car & Wagon Co.
1880	2 S/D	Starbuck Car & Wagon Co.

Croydon & Norwood Tramways Company

c1883	4 D/D	Various
c1883	3 D/D	Birmingham Railway Carriage & Wagon Co.

Croydon Tramways Company (second)

c1890	4 D/D	Falcon Engine & Car Works Ltd
c1890	1 D/D	Birmingham Railway Carriage & Wagon Co.
c1890	2 D/D	John Stephenson Co. Ltd
1897	8 D/D	Falcon Engine & Car Works Ltd

Livery of Croydon Tramways Company (Original)

1879-1883	Dark Green / White
1879-1883	Blue / White
1879-1883	Red / White

Livery of Croydon & Norwood Tramways Company

1883-1890	Green / White
1883-1890	Blue / White
1883-1890	Red / White

Livery of Croydon Tramways Company (Second)

1890-1900	Green / White
1890-1900	Blue / White
1890-1900	Red / White

Leyton

LEA BRIDGE, LEYTON & WALTHAMSTOW TRAMWAYS COMPANY, LATER LEA BRIDGE, LEYTON & WALTHAMSTOW TRAMWAYS COMPANY LIMITED, LATER LEYTON UDC TRAMWAYS

4' 8½" gauge; 5 route miles; opened 1883; acquired by Leyton UDC Tramways 1905.

In 1882 the Epping Forest was opened to the public. A group of businessmen saw the opportunity to build a tramway to take the public to this new open area and also provide links to the two nearest railway stations at Hoe Street and Leyton. They put forward their ideas in 1879, set up the Lea Bridge, Leyton & Walthamstow Tramways Company and obtained authority to construct the line in 1881. The public tramway service started on 12 May 1883. From the very beginning the tramway had financial problems, as receipts were well below what had been expected. The contractor who had built the line had not been paid and applied to the courts for the company to be wound-up. The tramway ceased running and a liquidator was appointed on 15 January 1885. All those interested in purchasing the line found insurmountable difficulties and the tramway lay dormant. The condition of the trackwork deteriorated rapidly. Finally a group set up the Lea Bridge, Leyton & Walthamstow Tramways Company Limited in 1888 and purchased the tramway from the liquidator. The new owners repaired the trackwork and re-opened the tramway service in May 1889. The new company managed to run the tramway at a profit, though this may have been due to the omnibus services that it also ran. In 1898 the first parts of the tramway became available to Leyton Council under the compulsory purchase provisions of the 1870 Act. It was clear that splitting the tramway in this way would not be sensible for either the company or the council. So the company suggested that the council should purchase the whole tramway. The subsequent negotiations were protracted and it was not until 13 April 1905 that the purchase was completed. The council wanted to electrify the line and entered into an agreement where the company continued to run the tramway until October 1905 when the council took over operating the tramway. Conversion of the tramway continued with the electric trams beginning on 1 December 1906. The last horse tram ran on 9 December 1908.

Routes at largest extent

Upper Clapton – Rising Sun, Whipps Cross
Upper Clapton – Leyton Station
Leyton Station – Rising Sun, Whipps Cross

Tramcars purchased
Lea Bridge, Leyton & Walthamstow Tramways Company

1883	10 S/D	Merryweather & Sons Ltd

Lea Bridge, Leyton & Walthamstow Tramways Company Limited

1883	10 S/D	Merryweather & Sons Ltd
1888	12 D/D	Second-hand North Metropolitan
1892	6 D/D	Second-hand
1899	D/D	Electric Railway & Tramway Carriage Works Limited

Leyton UDC Tramways

1905	22 D/D	Transferred from company
1905	6 D/D	Second-hand from company

Livery of Lea Bridge, Leyton & Walthamstow Tramways Company

1881-1884	Bright Red (Brown)/ White

Livery of Lea Bridge, Leyton & Walthamstow Tramways Company Limited

1888-1905	Bright Red / White

Livery of Leyton UDC Tramways

1905-1908	Bright Red / White

LONDONDERRY (DERRY)

CITY OF DERRY TRAMWAYS CO

4' 8½" gauge; 2 route miles; opened 1897; closed 1919.

In the late 1900s Londonderry had four railway stations, all

Lea Bridge, Leyton & Walthamstow Tramways Company Limited.

Leyton Urban District Council Tramways.

City of Derry Tramways Co.

termini. Three were close together near Carlisle Bridge and the centre of the city, while the fourth was at Graving Dock some 1½ miles from the centre. The latter was the terminus of the Londonderry & Lough Swilly Railway (LLSR) a 3' 0" gauge system and they had an agreement with the Londonderry Port & Harbour Commission to run goods and passenger trains over their private railway to Middle Quay. However, the agreement was terminated by the Commission in 1887 and the LLSR had to terminate at Graving Dock leaving passengers to find their own way to the town centre. It was clear that some form of public transport was needed and, after an omnibus service demonstrated shortcomings, the City of Derry Tramways Company Limited was established in 1892 to build a tramway between Graving Dock and the city centre.

After difficulties in raising the necessary capital the tramway opened on 3 December 1897. The system came close to being sold to the British Thomson Houston Company which was interested in electrifying the system, but at the last moment the negotiations failed. A second proposal came from Messrs J.G. White & Company Limited in 1906, but again this came to nothing. In 1919 the tram employees union demanded increased wages and threatened strike action. The company responded by saying they had no money, receipts were so poor, but the Union continued to call the strike. The tramway ceased running and the company put up the horses for auction and the tramway never ran again. The service was replaced by motor buses operated by the corporation.

Route at largest extent

Carlisle Bridge – Graving Dock Station

Tramcars purchased

1897	2 D/D	Starbuck Car & Wagon Co.
1900	2 D/D	G.F. Milnes & Co.
1903	2 D/D	G.F. Milnes & Co.
1905	3 D/D	Second-hand from Belfast Tramways
1910	1 D/D	Unknown

Livery of City of Derry Tramways Company

1897-1905	All dark Red
1905-1919	Red / Cream (ex Belfast trams)

LYTHAM ST ANNES

BLACKPOOL, ST ANNES & LYTHAM TRAMWAYS COMPANY LIMITED.

4' 8½" gauge; 2 route miles; opened 1896; acquired by Lytham St Annes Corporation 1920, closed 1937; horse tram operation 1900-1901.

In 1892 the Blackpool Corporation extended their tramway to Station Road, along Lytham Road. This encouraged Lytham promoters to propose a tramway from Lytham to meet with the Blackpool tramway and so provide a direct route between the two towns. They resurrected the earlier Blackpool, St Annes & Lytham tramway schemes and the first stretch of tramway was opened on 11 July 1896. The company had leased the line to the British Gas Traction Company and they operated it using gas trams. As the line extended, so further gas trams were added to the fleet. However, things were not well and the gas company went into liquidation in 1899, though they had ceased operations on the Lytham system in 1898. The Blackpool, St Annes & Lytham Tramways Company was floated as a public company in 1898 and with some of the proceeds it purchased the British Gas Traction Company. In 1900 the number of gas trams available could not meet the service requirements and so 20 horse trams were purchased second-hand from Farnworth and a mixed gas and horse operation was started. Plans were made to electrify the system, as the public compared the efficient and quiet electric trams in Blackpool with the inefficient and noisy Lytham gas trams. Work started on converting the tramway in 1903. By this time it was clear that the gas trams would be of no use to anyone after the conversion so they were kept to run the system during conversion. The horses and horse trams were taken out of service in 1901 and sold. This was the end of the very short lived horse tramway operation in Lytham St Annes.

Route at largest extent
Lytham Cottage Hospital – Starr Gate

Tramcars purchased

1900	17 D/D	Ex-Farnworth UDC, Ashbury Railway Carriage & Iron Co. Ltd built cars
1900	3 D/D	Ex-Blackburn & Over Darwen

Livery of Blackpool, St Annes & Lytham Tramways Company Limited

1900-1901	Royal Blue / Cream

MANCHESTER

MANCHESTER AND SALFORD TRAMWAYS, LATER MANCHESTER CARRIAGE COMPANY LIMITED, LATER MANCHESTER CARRIAGE & TRAMWAYS COMPANY LIMITED

4' 8½" gauge; 42 route miles; opened 1877; acquired by Salford Corporation and Oldham Corporation 1901; Ashton Corporation and Manchester Corporation 1903.

The Manchester Carriage Company Limited was the major omnibus concern in Manchester and in 1869 indicated it was interested in promoting tramways in the city. As the government was developing the 1870 Tramways Act they decided to wait until the details became public. The first formal advances were made in 1874 and the corporation (with Salford Corporation) obtained an act to build a line from Pendleton to Kersal. In accordance with the Act they could not run the tramways themselves, so they invited tenders from private companies. Surprisingly the Manchester Carriage Company Limited did not tender and the corporations leased the line to two businessmen, Daniel Busby and William Turton under the title Manchester and Salford Tramways. As the tramway was being constructed the businessmen were in discussion with the Manchester Carriage Company Limited and this resulted in the line being sold to the company on 26 April 1877, with the tramway itself opening on 17 May. Expansion took place, but all the while there was co-operation with the Manchester Suburban Tramways Company and soon most of the directors managed both companies. So it was natural that this situation would be regularised and in 1880 the two companies merged to become Manchester Carriage & Tramways Company Limited. Between 1880 and 1882 the system was expanded to meet the travel needs of the population of Manchester. From 1882 there were minor additions, but the main system had been laid by that year.

The manager of the Manchester Carriage Company Limited carriage works (later Manchester Carriage & Tramways Company Limited) was John Eades. He designed a lightweight reversible tramcar where the body was turned on the chassis at the terminus. This was adapted by the Manchester tramways and, after much interest was shown by other tramway systems, the patent was licensed to the Ashbury Railway Carriage & Iron Company Limited. They built many tramcars using the patent, while the Manchester tramways built their own trams to the same design.

The Manchester Corporation started to show interest in acquiring the tramway for electrification in 1895. But no firm action was taken until 1901 when the tramway started to become available under the compulsory purchase sections of the 1870 Act. The company asked for an extension of their lease until 1906. The company ran routes across corporation boundaries and it took a while for the authorities to determine how the purchase and electrification was to proceed. They finally agreed to have four arrangements, each with its own tramway system. They

Manchester Carriage & Tramways Company Limited.

each made their own agreements with the company. Manchester agreed that there would be a gradual transfer to be completed in 1903. Salford and Oldham on the other hand wanted a big bang with all the company tramways in their area being purchased on 27 April 1901 and 31 October respectively and Ashton Corporation on 31 March 1903. The last horse tram ran in Manchester on 31 March 1903.

Routes at largest extent
Albert Square – Cheetham Hill
Albert Square – Hightown
Deansgate – Pendleton
Deansgate – Swinton
Deansgate – Peel Green
Deansgate – Cross Lane
Deansgate – Higher Broughton
Deansgate – Lower Broughton
Exchange – Belle Vue
Exchange – Palatine Road
Exchange – Burlington Street
Exchange – Princess Road
Exchange – Brook's Bar
Exchange – Alexandra Park
Exchange – Stretford
High Street – Harpurhey
Piccadilly – Old Trafford
Piccadilly – Princess Road
Piccadilly – Denton
Piccadilly – Stockport
Piccadilly – Fallowfield
Piccadilly – Miles Platting
Piccadilly – Ashton-under-Lyne
Piccadilly – Greenheys
Hollinwood – Oldham
Ashton-under-Lyne – Stalybridge
Rusholme – Seymour Grove

Tramcars purchased

Manchester Carriage Company Limited

1877	30 D/D	Starbuck Car & Wagon Co. Ltd

Manchester Carriage & Tramways Company Limited

1880	24 S/D	Manchester Carriage & Tramways Co.
1884	326 D/D	Manchester Carriage & Tramways Co.
1888	56 S/D	Manchester Carriage & Tramways Co.
1890	385	Most Manchester Carriage & Tramways Co.
1895	515 D/D, 84 S/D	Manchester Carriage & Tramways Co.

Livery of Manchester Carriage Company Limited

1877-1900	Red / Cream

Livery of Manchester Carriage & Tramways Company Limited

1880-1903	Red / Cream

MANCHESTER SUBURBAN TRAMWAYS COMPANY

4' 8½" gauge; 7 route miles; opened 1877; merged with Manchester Carriage Company Limited 1880.

After Daniel Busby and William Turton had sold the Manchester and Salford Tramways to the Manchester Carriage Company Limited, they applied for powers to construct tramways in Stretford and Gorton under the newly formed company called the Manchester Suburban Tramways Company. The first line opened on 30 July 1877. The company expanded its system, then in 1880 the Manchester Suburban Tramways Company merged with the Manchester Carriage Company Limited to become the Manchester Carriage & Tramways Company Limited, see above for details.

Routes at largest extent

See above

Tramcars purchased

1878	2 D/D	Manchester Carriage & Tramways Co.
1878	4 S/D	Starbuck Car & Wagon Co.

Livery of Manchester Suburban Tramways Company

1877-1880 Red / Cream

HEATON PARK HERITAGE TRAMWAY

4' 8½" gauge; 1 route mile; opened 1979; still open, horse tram first operated 2008.

The Heaton Park Heritage Tramway opened in September 1979 using the original rails that were laid in the park in the early 1900s. These old rails were still intact beneath modern tarmac. The short line has been restored and extended to provide an operating tramway with restored tramcars from Manchester and other cities. One such tramcar is number L53, an Eades design reversible car. This tramcar was built in the 1880s and was recently used as an annex to a hairdresser and as part of a fish and chip shop. It was taken to the depot at Heaton Park and has been completely restored to operating condition. It is used on special occasions.

Route at largest extent

Park Gates – Lakeside

Tramcar

c1880	1 D/D	Manchester Carriage & Tramways Co.

Livery of Manchester Carriage & Tramways Company Limited

2008-Date Red / Cream

Heaton Park Heritage Tramway. (Alan Kirkman)

MARBLE ARCH STREET RAIL COMPANY LIMITED

See London Section

MAURICE JONES

See Shipley

METROPOLITAN ASYLUMS BOARD, JOYCE GREEN HOSPITALS TRAMWAYS

See London Section

METROPOLITAN ELECTRIC TRAMWAYS COMPANY

See London Section

METROPOLITAN STREET TRAMWAYS COMPANY

See London Section

MIDDLESBROUGH

MIDDLESBROUGH & STOCKTON TRAMWAYS COMPANY, LATER MIDDLESBROUGH, STOCKTON & THORNABY ELECTRIC TRAMWAYS (IMPERIAL TRAMWAYS)

4' 8½" gauge; 3 route miles; opened 1874; closed 1934 (horse tram operation ceased 1897).

As a pioneer of railed passenger transport it would have been expected that Stockton would embrace the tramway. However, the local authority had quite the opposite attitude and when local individuals put forward proposals to link Stockton with Middlesbrough they opposed the schemes. As a result the promoters reduced the ideas to just Middlesbrough and Acts were passed in 1873 and 1875 giving powers to construct tramways in the town. Construction of the first line started in 1874 and it was opened in November. The Middlesbrough & Stockton Tramways Company was formed to run the tramway. However, the Imperial Tramways Company took over the controlling interest in the tramway company in August 1878, while keeping the original name. A second route was opened in 1880 and a third in 1882, by which time the horse tramway was at its greatest extent. By this time Stockton Council had changed their mind about tramways and allowed the Stockton and Darlington Steam Tramways Company to build lines in the town. The Imperial Tramways Company acquired the company in 1896 and put forward proposals to join up and electrify the Middlesbrough and Stockton systems. In converting the tramways a new, unusual, gauge of 3' 7" was chosen for the rebuilt lines. As the tracks had to be completely relaid the horse tramway had to be closed and the last horse tramcars ran in 1897.

Middlesbrough & Stockton Tramways Company.

Routes at largest extent
Town Centre – Calvert Street, Newport
Town Centre – Linthorpe
Town Centre – Clarence Ferry (now the transporter bridge)

Tramcars purchased

1874	2 D/D, 2 S/D	Starbuck Car & Wagon Co.
1879	6 D/D	Ashbury Railway Carriage & Iron Co. Ltd
1883	3 D/D	Starbuck Car & Wagon Co.
1894	4 D/D	Unknown

Livery of Middlesbrough & Stockton Tramways Company
1874-1878 Red / Cream
Livery of Middlesbrough, Stockton & Thornaby Electric Tramways (Imperial Tramways)
1878 - 1897 Red / Cream

MORECAMBE

MORECAMBE TRAMWAYS COMPANY, LATER PART ACQUIRED BY MORECAMBE CORPORATION TRAMWAYS

4' 8½" gauge. 4 route miles; opened 1887; closed 1924.

With the coming of the railway in 1848 the small seaside village of Poulton (later to be called Morecambe) started to become popular as a holiday resort. By the mid 1880s there were around 40,000 visitors each year. Local businessmen saw an opportunity for a tramway to serve the visitors. A prospectus was issued in 1886 and later that year an Act was passed enabling the Morecambe Tramways Company to build tramways in the town. The tramway opened on 3 June 1887 and was well received by the public. Income continued to increase and dividends were paid to the shareholders. The system was extended in 1892 and ran smoothly until George Balfour arrived in 1906 who wanted to acquire the tramway. The corporation stepped in and in 1909 purchased those parts of the system that came up for compulsory purchase. Having purchased the part of the system running between the Battery Inn and Bare the corporation took over the running, leaving the company with the remainder. Although the idea of conversion to electrical operation was often talked about (the first as early as 1887) nothing ever came of it and the corporation ran the system with horse trams until it closed on 6 October 1926, the last horse tramway to operate on the mainland of Britain outside of museums.

The Morecambe Tramways Company was left with a 1¼-mile route from the Battery Inn to Strawberry Gardens and had lost all but three of their tramcars to the corporation. They continued to operate the tramway with horse trams until 1912 when they purchased four petrol tramcars. The horse tram operation ceased that year and operation with petrol trams continued until 1924 when they were withdrawn at the end of the season and the company tramway closed.

Routes at largest extent
Strawberry Gardens – Bare
later
Strawberry Gardens – Battery Inn (Company operation)
Battery Inn – Bare (Corporation operation)

Tramcars purchased
Morecambe Tramways Company

1887	2 D/D, 2 T/R	Lancaster Railway Carriage & Wagon Co. Ltd
1888	2 D/D	Lancaster Railway Carriage & Wagon Co. Ltd
1889	1 D/D	Lancaster Railway Carriage & Wagon Co. Ltd
1897	4 D/D	Lancaster Railway Carriage & Wagon Co. Ltd
1898	4 D/D	Second-hand?
1901	2 D/D	Lancaster Railway Carriage & Wagon Co. Ltd

Morecambe Corporation Tramways

1919	1 D/D, 1 T/R	English Electric Co. Ltd
1922	1 D/D, 1 T/R	English Electric Co. Ltd

Morecambe Tramways Company.

Livery of Morecambe Tramways Company

1887-1912	Maroon / Teak / White
1912-1924	Maroon / White (Cream)
?-1924	Green / White

Livery of Morecambe Corporation Tramways

1909-1924	Maroon / White

MURCAR RAILWAY
See Strabathie

MARBLE ARCH STREET RAIL COMPANY LIMITED
See London Section

MAURICE JONES
See Shipley

METROPOLITAN ASYLUMS BOARD, JOYCE GREEN HOSPITALS TRAMWAYS
See London Section

METROPOLITAN ELECTRIC TRAMWAYS COMPANY
See London Section

METROPOLITAN STREET TRAMWAYS COMPANY
See London Section

NEATH

NEATH & DISTRICT TRAMWAYS COMPANY, LATER NEATH CORPORATION TRAMWAYS

4' 8½" gauge. 4 route miles; opened 1875; Neath Corporation operated the line from 1916; closed 1920 (horse operation from 1875 to 1899).

Neath gained a horse tramway in 1875 when the Neath & District Tramways Company opened its line from Skewen to Briton Ferry. The authorisation had been given in the Act passed in 1873. There is surprisingly little information about the horse operation as it has been overshadowed by the gas operation that came later. The original company was acquired by the Neath Corporation in 1897 who operated it using horses, but the corporation decided that gas traction was better and the tramway was leased to the British Gas Traction Company Limited to be operated using their gas trams. Horse operation ceased in August 1899, when sufficient trams were available to run the gas operation. Unfortunately the British Gas Traction Company Limited went into liquidation less than two months later. It took a while to sort out the situation and it was not until 1902 that the Provincial Gas Traction Company Limited took over the tramway. Gas tram services continued until 1916 when it too went bankrupt. The corporation decided to take over operation itself and it purchased the assets of the company for a sum just enough to pay off the debtors. The trams were in a deplorable condition and the corporation was only able to use four of them, even so they were completely worn out by 1919. The corporation had decided against electrical operation and so the only option they had was to close the system. Thus in August 1920 the line was closed.

Route at largest extent
Skewen – Briton Ferry

Tramcars purchased

1875	11?	Unknown

Livery of Neath & District Tramways Company

1875-1896	Unknown

Neath & District Tramways Company.

NEWCASTLE-UPON-TYNE

NEWCASTLE & GOSFORTH TRAMWAYS & CARRIAGE COMPANY LIMITED

4' 8½" gauge; 12 route miles; opened 1878; acquired by Newcastle Corporation 1901 when horse operation ceased.

Newcastle Corporation obtained authority in 1878 to construct tramways in the city, but under the 1870 Tramways Act they were not permitted to operate the system. Therefore they leased the tracks to the Newcastle & Gosforth Tramways & Carriage Company Limited. The company then obtained authority to build an extension to the system that was outside the city boundary and reached out to Gosforth. In 1899 the lease ran out and the corporation gave notice that they would take over the tramway. The usual acrimonious debate took place and it was not until 13 April 1901 that the corporation took control of the tramway. The company refused to continue operating as a horse tramway and the corporation closed the tramway on that date to allow conversion to electric power. The corporation then compulsorily purchased the line in Gosforth and incorporated it in the Newcastle Corporation tramway system.

Routes at largest extent
City Centre – Gosforth
City Centre – Scotswood Road
City Centre – Elswick
City Centre – Arthur's Hill
City Centre – Osborne Road
City Centre – Byker

Tramcars purchased

1875	?	Ashbury Railway Carriage & Iron Co. Ltd
1875	?	Midland Railway Carriage & Wagon Co. Ltd
c1880	?	Newcastle & Gosforth Tramways & Carriage Co. Ltd

Newcastle & Gosforth Tramways & Carriage Company Limited.

Livery of Newcastle & Gosforth Tramways & Carriage Company Limited

1878-1901	Unknown

NEWPORT

NEWPORT (MON) TRAMWAYS COMPANY, LATER SOLOMON ANDREWS LATER NEWPORT CORPORATION TRAMWAYS

4' 8½" gauge; 1 route mile; opened 1875; acquired by Newport Corporation 1894; horse operation ceased 1903.

The first proposals to build a tramway in Newport came in 1870, but were rejected by the council. From that point the idea of having a tramway in the town came up as a regular issue (one of the councillors being the major promoter). Each time there were objections. It was not until December 1872 that the council supported an application, from a different promoter. Objections from others led to a Board of Trade enquiry that found in favour of the tramway. The promoter obtained authorisation through the Newport (Mon) Tramways Act 1873, setting up the Newport (Mon) Tramways Company and construction began in April 1874 with the tramway opening on 1 February 1875. The service was a success from the start with good dividends being paid to the shareholders. The tramway was prevented from extending the route through the High Street because it was too narrow. In 1881 the company's lease for the provision of horses expired and they decided to cease running the tramway themselves and leased the line to Mr Perry for an annual rental. This lease ended in 1885 and the Newport Tramways Company chose to take on the operations themselves. The council became a corporation in 1891 and at the same time they applied for authority to built extensions to the tramway and convert it to electric power. The Newport (Mon) Tramways Company was served with notice and they ceased running the tramway on 28 July 1894. The corporation had entered into an agreement with Solomon Andrews to lease the tramway to him to operate. As the lines were to be re-laid Solomon Andrews replaced the tram service with a bus during the conversion. When the extensions had been built and the old route re-laid service began again with horse trams. Solomon Andrews' lease expired in 1901 and the corporation then took over running the horse trams. The corporation then used their powers to electrify the system with the first electric trams running on 8 September 1901. The whole system except the short Church Road route was electrified, Church Road being still horse operated. Interestingly this last horse tram service did not charge fares. It was expected that after using the horse car customers would board an electric tram for the rest of their journey and then pay a fare. It was found that some passengers used the free tram and then walked the rest of the way. This generous gesture finished when the Church Road service was withdrawn on 3 November 1903, the last horse tram service in Newport.

Newport (Mon) Tramways Company.

Routes at largest extent

Tredegar Place – Pillgwenlly Station
Westgate Square – Malpas Road
Westgate Square – Caerleon Road
Westgate Square – Church Road
Westgate Square – Chepstow Road
Westgate Square – Corporation Road

Tramcars purchased
Newport Tramways Company

1874	4 S/D	Starbuck Car & Wagon Co.
1890	4 D/D	Unknown

Solomon Andrews

1894	23?	Unknown
1901	3 D/D	Ex-Liverpool

Livery of Newport Tramways Company

1875-1894	Green / Cream

Livery of Newport Corporation Tramways

1894-1903	Green / Cream

NORTH DUBLIN STREET TRAMWAYS COMPANY
See Dublin

NORTH LONDON SUBURBAN TRAMWAYS COMPANY
See London Section

NORTH LONDON TRAMWAYS COMPANY
See London Section

NORTH METROPOLITAN TRAMWAYS COMPANY
See London Section

NORTH SHIELDS & DISTRICT TRAMWAYS LIMITED
See Tynemouth

NORTH SHIELDS & TYNEMOUTH DISTRICT TRAMWAYS LIMITED
See Tynemouth

NORTH STAFFORDSHIRE TRAMWAYS COMPANY LIMITED
See Stoke-on-Trent

NORTHAMPTON

NORTHAMPTON STREET TRAMWAYS COMPANY, LATER NORTHAMPTON CORPORATION TRAMWAYS

3' 6" gauge; 5 route miles; opened 1881; acquired by Northampton Corporation 1901; horse operation ceased 1904.

In 1879 a London firm of tramway contractors decided that Northampton would be an ideal place to build a tramway. The corporation agreed and so the Northampton Street Tramways Company was established and an Act of Parliament giving authority to build the tramway was passed in 1880. A contract for the construction, equipping and operating the tramway was made between the company and the tramway contractors and so the first section was completed by May 1881. The tramway opened on 4 June 1881 and extensions were built in 1883. The contract for the building and operating of the tramway expired on 2 January 1884 and the Northampton Street Tramways Company took over running the system. In 1883 the company had experimented with a gas engine and a strange man-powered pedal scheme. There was local resentment when the company took over the operations as they were all from the London area, and this was compounded when there was no dividend for shareholders for several years. After a major row some local businessmen were appointed as directors and the fortunes changed, with a small profit being made. But some changes were not popular, particularly when all the conductors were sacked and replaced by 14-16 year-old boys who were much cheaper. Some of the double-deck cars were rebuilt as small, light weight single-deck cars, needing only one horse. A further extension was authorised in 1892. The corporation were beginning to think about electrification and approached the company in 1898. The usual arguments began culminating in a compulsory purchase bid in 1901. The purchase was delayed by legal processes following a fatal

Northampton Street Tramways Company.

crash in 1901 while claims for compensation were being settled. The corporation acquired the tramway on 21 October 1901. They took over the operation of the horse trams while the conversion to electrical operation took place. The last horse tramcar ran on 19 August 1904.

Routes at largest extent

All Saints Church – Kingsley Park
All Saints Church – Abington Park
All Saints Church – Franklin's Gardens
All Saints Church – Kingsthorpe

Tramcars purchased

1881	8 D/D	Birmingham Carriage & Wagon Company
1883	2 D/D	Birmingham Carriage & Wagon Company
1893	4 S/D	Birmingham Carriage & Wagon Company
1893	2 D/D	Falcon Engine & Car Works Ltd
1899	7 D/D	Falcon Engine & Car Works Ltd

Livery of Northampton Street Tramways Company

1880-1901	Dark Green / Cream
1893-1901	Red / Cream
1893-1901	Blue / Cream

Livery of Northampton Corporation Tramways

1901-1904	Dark Green / Cream
1901-1904	Red / Cream
1901-1904	Blue / Cream

NOTTINGHAM

NOTTINGHAM & DISTRICT TRAMWAYS COMPANY LIMITED, LATER NOTTINGHAM CORPORATION TRAMWAYS

4' 8½" gauge; 8 route miles; opened 1878; acquired by Nottingham Corporation 1897; horse operation ceased 1904.

The Nottingham & District Tramways Company Limited was established to build tramways in Nottingham authorised by the Act of 1877. The tramway routes were built and the first two lines opened on 17 September 1878. A further route was opened in the following year and a fourth in 1881. Nottingham Corporation gave notice in 1897 that it would purchase the first lines as they were about to come to the 21-year period defined in the 1870 Act. A sum of £80,000 was agreed for the whole system and the corporation found themselves in possession of a well kept and efficient system. Their thoughts immediately turned to electrifying the tramway. In the meantime the horse trams were being operated by the corporation, who had changed the route liveries of the company to a uniform maroon and cream livery. The conversion of the tramway coincided with many such schemes throughout the country and Nottingham found itself in a position where their chosen tramcar manufacturer, Dick, Kerr Company, had such a full order book that delivery was slow. The first electric trams ran in public service on 1 January 1901 and the last horse tramcars ran in 1902 and were then sold.

Routes at largest extent

Market Place – Basford
Market Place – Carrington
St Peter's Church – Trent Bridge
St Peter's Church – London Road

Tramcars purchased

Nottingham & District Tramways Company Limited.

1878	8 S/D	Starbuck Car & Wagon Co.
1879	3 D/D, 1 S/D	John Stephenson Co. Ltd
1880	5 S/D	Starbuck Car & Wagon Co.
1881	5 S/D	Starbuck Car & Wagon Co.
1883	2 S/D	Starbuck Car & Wagon Co.
1884	2 T/R	Starbuck Car & Wagon Co.
1885	1 D/D, 2 S/D	Starbuck Car & Wagon Co.
1887	1 D/D	Ex Manchester Tramways
1888	4 D/D	Ex Horse buses from Andrews of Carrington
1891	2 T/R	Unknown
1892	4 D/D	G.F. Milnes & Co.
1895	3 D/D	G.F. Milnes & Co.

Livery of Nottingham & District Tramways Company Limited

1878-1897	All Yellow
1879-1897	Red /White
1881-1897	Dark Blue / White
1882-1887	All Brown
1884-1897	All Green

Livery of Nottingham Corporation Tramways

1897-1902	Maroon / Cream (horse trams)

OLD SWAN TRAMWAY

See Liverpool

OXFORD

CITY OF OXFORD & DISTRICT TRAMWAYS COMPANY LIMITED, LATER CITY OF OXFORD ELECTRIC TRAMWAYS LIMITED

4' 0" gauge. 5 route miles; opened 1881; closed 1914.

Some London tramway promoters set up the Oxford Tramways Company Limited in 1879 with the intention of building a tramway in Oxford. Having obtained the agreement of the city authorities a Bill was placed before parliament and this became an Act in the same year. While negotiations were taking place the original company was wound up and replaced by the City of Oxford & District Tramways Company Limited. The necessary funding was obtained and building commenced with the first part of the tramway opening on 1 December 1881. The trams were well patronised by the public and the company turned profits each year. In 1907 the 21-year period (the last extension being authorised in 1886) expired and the council indicated their wish to purchase the system compulsorily. Though the ratepayers of the city had no wish for the tramway to be purchased by the council, they went ahead and acquired the tramway. The council invited tenders to operate the system and convert it to electric operation. Only two companies were interested, the horse tramway company and the National Electric Construction Company Limited. The latter was awarded the lease and they set up the City of Oxford Electric Tramways Limited to extend and convert the system to electric operation. The City council insisted that there could be no overhead electric supply in the centre of the

City of Oxford & District Tramways Company.

city and the proposals were to use the Dolter stud system. But by the time the electric company was ready to convert the tramway it was clear that the Dolter stud system was not successful and some other means would be required. The company suggested using overhead wires in the suburbs and either conduit or petrol electric trams in the centre. It is also felt that the company was in financial difficulties in funding these expensive options. To add to the company's woes the council demanded the financial penalties built into the contract for failing to electrify the system in the time given. Throughout this time the horse trams continued to operate, but were getting more opposition from motor buses. The public saw the motor bus as a modern and reliable transport. The tramway company recognised this and suggested to the council that the company should operate a bus service and close the tramway. Despite obstruction from the council a bus service was instigated by William Morris (of Morris Motors) in 1913. Immediately the trams were emptied as passengers preferred the bus. The success of the buses was obvious to the tramway and another bus operator Thomas Tilling and they both applied to run buses. The council yielded to the inevitable and granted licences to all three. The three operators soon realised that co-operation was better than competition and an agreement was formed in 1914 where the tramway company ran all the bus services in the city. This saw the end of the tramway and it closed in August 1914, the company being renamed the City of Oxford Motor Services Limited.

Routes at largest extent

Railway Stations – Cowley Road
Carfax – Kingston Road
Carfax – Summertown
Summertown – New Hinksey

Tramcars purchased

City of Oxford & District Tramways Company Limited

1881	4 S/D	Starbuck Car & Wagon Co.
1882	8 S/D	Starbuck Car & Wagon Co.
c1890	8 D/D	G. F. Milnes & Co.
1900	2 D/D	Unknown
c1903	12 D/D	Second-hand from London companies

City of Oxford Electric Tramways Limited

1909	2 D/D	Ex London County Council

Livery of City of Oxford & District Tramways Company Limited

1881-?	Dark blue / White
?-1914	Maroon / White

OYSTERMOUTH TRAMROAD

See Swansea

PAISLEY

PAISLEY TRAMWAYS COMPANY LIMITED, LATER PAISLEY DISTRICT TRAMWAYS COMPANY

4' 7¾" gauge; 2 route miles; opened 1885; acquired by Paisley District Tramways Company 1903; horse operation ceased 1903.

The Paisley Tramways Company Limited was incorporated on 24 December 1884 and soon applied to parliament for authority to build tramways in Paisley. As the proposals did not have any opposition the application became an Act in 1885. The promoters obviously felt that at some time the system would be linked to the Glasgow tramways as the gauge chosen was 4' 7¾". The first trams ran in service on 30 December 1885. The system expanded and ran at a profit until 1892 when a poor year meant losses. In 1894 Glasgow Corporation took over the tramways in its city, but did not have any tramcars. Paisley helped out by hiring two trams to Glasgow, they soon found that they could operate a good service without those two cars so they sold them to Glasgow. In 1897 the British Electric Traction Company proposed purchasing the system with intent to electrify and extend it. Paisley Corporation opposed the scheme, preferring to wait until Glasgow Corporation offered to take over the tramway. So the BET took the matter to parliament and became the first company to obtain an Act where the local authorities objected. The BET set up the Paisley District Tramways Company that took over the horse tram company on 3 January 1903. Conversion was to start soon and the last horse tram ran on 21 November 1903.

Paisley Tramways Company Limited.

Route at largest extent
East End – West End

Tramcars purchased

1885	5 D/D	Metropolitan Railway Carriage & Wagon Co.
1887	2 S/D	Glasgow Tramway & Omnibus Co.
1890	2 S/D	Glasgow Tramway & Omnibus Co.
1901	2 D/D	Glasgow Tramway & Omnibus Co.

Livery of Paisley Tramways Company Limited

1885-1887	Brown / White
1887-1903	Bright Red / White

PATENT CABLE TRAMWAYS CORPORATION
See Bath

PECKHAM & EAST DULWICH TRAMWAYS COMPANY
See London Section

PERTH

PERTH & DISTRICT TRAMWAYS COMPANY LIMITED, LATER PERTH CORPORATION TRAMWAYS

3' 6" gauge; 5 route miles; opened 1895; acquired by Perth Corporation 1903; horse operation ceased 1905.

The first proposal for tramways in Perth came in 1880 when the traffic on the Perth to Scone horse bus encouraged promoters to suggest laying a tramway between the two towns. But nothing came of this until 1893 when the Perth & District Tramways Company Limited was established and a provisional order obtained to authorise a tramway to be built. An early act of the new company was to purchase the Scone & Perth Omnibus Company and start operating the buses from May 1894. Construction of the tramway started in the same year and the first service trams ran on 17 September 1895. The tramway was a financial success with dividends being paid each year to shareholders. Two additional routes were added in 1898. The following year the company applied for authority to run mechanical traction in order that they could convert the system to electric operation. This came to the notice of the council and after debating the matter the council decided to purchase the tramway. Negotiations took two years before an agreed purchase price was determined and the tramway was sold to the council on 7 October 1903. While deciding on which form of mechanical traction would be best the council continued to operate the horse tram service. Conversion to electrical operation started in 1904 with the electric cars taking over from the horse cars on the afternoon of 31 October 1905, the last horse car running around 2.30pm.

Routes at largest extent
High Street – Scone
Cherry Bank – The Cross
Craigie – The Cross

Tramcars purchased

1895	4 D/D, 1 T/R	Brown Marshalls
1898	4 D/D	Unknown

Livery of Perth & District Tramways Company Limited

1895-1898	Dark Crimson / Pale Cream
1898-1903	Dark Red-Brown / Yellow

Livery of Perth Corporation Tramways

1903-1905	Dark Red-Brown / Yellow

PIMLICO, PECKHAM & GREENWICH STREET TRAMWAYS COMPANY
See London Section

PLYMOUTH

PLYMOUTH, STONEHOUSE & DEVONPORT TRAMWAYS COMPANY

4' 8½" gauge; 3 route miles; opened 1872; closed 1922; horse operation ceased 1901.

The Plymouth, Stonehouse & Devonport Tramways Company was one of the first tramways to be approved after the passing of the 1870 Tramways Act with its first tramcars running on 18 March 1872. It was extended in Devonport in 1874. At the turn of the century the company decided that electrical power was the future and they obtained the appropriate powers. At the same time they decided to change the gauge to 3' 6" to match the other tramways in the area. The conversion took place in 1901 and the last horse trams stopped running and the electric cars began running the same year.

Routes at largest extent
Derry's Clock, Plymouth – Fore Street, Devonport
Pier Street – Theatre

Perth & District Tramways Company Limited.

Plymouth, Stonehouse & Devonport Tramways Company.

Plymouth, Devonport & District Tramways Company.

Tramcars purchased

1872	8 D/D	Unknown
?	12 D/D	Unknown

Livery of Plymouth, Stonehouse & Devonport Tramways Company

1872-1901	Bright Emerald Green / White

PLYMOUTH, DEVONPORT & DISTRICT TRAMWAYS COMPANY, LATER PLYMOUTH TRAMWAYS COMPANY LATER PLYMOUTH CORPORATION TRAMWAYS

3' 6" gauge; 18 route miles; opened 1884; closed 1945; horse operation from 1886 to 1907; acquired by Plymouth Corporation 1892.

The Plymouth, Devonport & District Tramways Company had a very short but eventful life. The company was established in 1882 under the Plymouth, Devonport & District Tramways Act that authorised the building of seven tramways that were to use steam power. In order to ensure that the tramways were all built the Act incorporated a provision that the corporations could not consent to the opening of any part unless the whole system was opened. The tramway was part built when inspected and the Board of Trade inspector refused to allow steam operation on the narrow streets in the town centre. The company opened two routes on 7 November 1884 with steam operation, though it is possible that some horse trams were also used. As no tracks had been laid in Devonport the corporation took out an injunction on 14 November preventing the company from running its trams.

Plymouth Corporation Tramways.

The company went into liquidation in 1885. The tramway was purchased by the Plymouth Tramways Company who decided to operate it using horse tramcars from 1886 (though the company was not incorporated until 1889). Plymouth Corporation decided to acquire the line and an Act authorising the acquisition was passed in 1892 and the purchase was completed on 11 March 1893, with horse operation continuing. The corporation electrified the system having gained authority to do so in 1898 with the first electric trams running on 22 September 1899. Horse trams continued to run on the West Hoe route until 1907 when the last of the horse trams were withdrawn.

Routes at largest extent

Fore Street – Tor Lane
Fore Street – Stuart Road
Morice Square – Tor Lane
Morice Square – St Budeaux
Stuart Road – South Keyham

Tramcars purchased

Plymouth Tramways Company

1885	12 D/D	Bristol Wagon Co.

Plymouth Corporation Tramways

1894	6 D/D	Bristol Wagon Co.
1894	3 D/D, 2 S/D	G. F. Milnes & Co.
1895	2 D/D	G.F. Milnes & Co.
1897	4 D/D	G.F. Milnes & Co.
1897	2 S/D	Bristol Wagon Co.
1898	2 D/D	Midland Railway & Carriage Co.
1898	2 S/D	Bristol Wagon Co.

Livery of Plymouth, Devonport & District Tramways Company

1882-1885	Brown / White

Livery of Plymouth Tramways Company

1885-1892	Red / Cream

Livery of Plymouth Corporation Tramways

1892-1907	Vermilion / White (horse trams)

PONTYPRIDD

PONTYPRIDD & RHONDDA VALLEY TRAMWAYS COMPANY, LATER PONTYPRIDD UDC TRAMWAYS

3' 6" gauge; 3 route miles; opened 1887; acquired by Pontypridd & Rhondda Councils 1904; horse operation ceased 1903.

A group of local businessmen established the Pontypridd & Rhondda Valley Tramways Company in 1882 to build a tramway between Pontypridd and Treherbert. The tramway was opened in March 1888 and had financial difficulties even before the service started. The operation was not helped by a low railway bridge that forced the line to terminate short of the town centre and that the other terminus only reached the town boundary near Borth some eight miles short of Treherbert. The company was in disarray, unable to pay the building contractors or buy sufficient tramcars to run the system. The tramway was saved when Solomon Andrews agreed to operate the line for three years. With his extensive experience of horse omnibus and tramway operation, plus his coach and tramcar factory he was able to keep the concern going. Though it continued to have finance problems, such that track maintenance was minimal and the local authorities complained that in places the rails were three inches above

Pontypridd & Rhondda Valley Tramways Company.

the road surface. In 1890 the company went into liquidation and the liquidator reached an agreement with Solomon Andrews to run the tramway while a buyer was sought. The South Wales Property, Machinery and Carriage Company (a company owned by Solomon Andrews) purchased the system. In 1898 the British Electric Traction Company purchased the line with a contract that prohibited Solomon Andrews from competing against the tramway. The BET then approached the council with a proposal to electrify and extend the line. But the council objected and the proposals failed. So the company continued with horse operation until February 1902 when an outbreak of glanders killed most of the horses. The company offered the system for sale to the council, who reminded the company that they would have compulsory powers to buy anyway in 1903. Eventually a price was agreed and the sale went through on 31 October 1904. The council set about the necessary preparations for converting the system to electrical operation. Rebuilding work started in 1903 and the tramway was re-opened on 5 March 1905. It is likely that the last horse trams ran up to the purchase by the council, it is unlikely the council ran any horse tram services.

Route at largest extent
Rhondda Road – Victoria Bridge

Tramcars purchased

1888	1 D/D	Unknown
1888	6 D/D, 2 S/D	Solomon Andrews

Livery of Pontypridd & Rhondda Valley Tramways Company

1888-1903	Unknown

PORTSMOUTH STREET TRAMWAYS COMPANY
See Gosport

PORTSMOUTH

LANDPORT & SOUTHSEA TRAMWAYS COMPANY, LATER PURCHASED BY PROVINCIAL TRAMWAYS COMPANY, LATER PORTSMOUTH STREET TRAMWAYS COMPANY LATER PORTSMOUTH CORPORATION TRAMWAYS

4' 7¾" gauge; 2 route miles; opened 1865; acquired by Portsmouth Corporation 1901; horse operation ceased 1903.

Portsmouth has the honour of being the first town to have a legal tramway, that is one properly authorised by an Act of Parliament. This was the Landport & Southsea Tramways Act of 1863. The track was laid and the first services began on 15 May 1865. The tramway had some small extensions added but remained very small. In February 1878 it was purchased by the Provincial Tramways Company Limited, managed as a single tramway by the Portsmouth Street Tramways Company and this was regularised in November 1882 when it name was changed to become Portsmouth Street Tramways Company. For the remainder of its history see below.

Routes at largest extent
See Portsmouth Street Tramways Company

Tramcars purchased

1865	2? S/D	Unknown

Livery of Landport & Southsea Tramways Company

1865-1882	Unknown

PORTSMOUTH STREET TRAMWAYS COMPANY (PROVINCIAL TRAMWAYS COMPANY), LATER PORTSMOUTH CORPORATION TRAMWAYS

4' 7¾" gauge; 15 route mile; opened 1874; acquired by Portsmouth Corporation 1901; horse operation ceased 1903.

The Provincial Tramways Company was set up on 10 July 1872 to be a holding company for a variety of tramway companies around the country. It promoted the Portsmouth Street Tramways Company in 1873 to build and operate tramways in Portsmouth. It gained its Act in 1874 with the authority to build its tramways. In February 1878 the Provincial Tramways Company Limited purchased the Landport & Southsea Tramways Company and the General Tramways Company and managed the three tramways as a single system. This was regularised in November 1882 when the Provincial Tramways Company Limited got authority to combine four tramways that it owned: the Landport & Southsea Tramways Company; the Portsmouth Street Tramways Company; the General Tramways Company; and the Gosport Street Tramways Company, under the umbrella of the

Portsmouth Street Tramways Company.

Portsmouth Street Tramways Company. In 1897 the corporation decided that they wished to purchase the tramway system with the intension of converting it to electric operation and extending it. It advised the Portsmouth Tramways Company that it intended to compulsorily purchase those lines that were 21 years old. The necessary authority was obtained in 1898 and the corporation gave the company twelve months notice of transfer. Later in 1898 the corporation agreed to purchase the whole of the system and negotiations took place leading up to the formal transfer of the system to the corporation on 31 December 1899. There was a hiccup as the tramway company also had horse buses and they insisted that they were all part of the deal (thus requiring compensation for them) while the corporation was only interested in the trams.

The matter ended up in the courts, only during the hearing a compromise was reached with an extra payment by the corporation to the company for agreeing to the conditions. Conversion of the tramway began on 23 February 1901 and the first electric tramcars ran in public service on 24 September 1901. The last horse tram route was the Cosham service and the use of horse trams ended in May 1903.

Routes at largest extent

North End – Clarence Pier
North End – Victoria Road
North End – South Parade Pier
North End – Cosham
North End – Floating Bridge
Dockyard – South Parade Pier
Dockyard – Copnor Railway Gates
Dockyard – Strand
Point – Eastney

Tramcars purchased

1874	65	Unknown
1893	10 D/D	North Metropolitan Tramways
1894	10 D/D	Dick, Kerr & Co Ltd

Livery of Portsmouth Street Tramways Company

1874-1899	Yellow / White
1874-1899	Green / White
1874-1899	Chocolate / White

Livery of Portsmouth Street Tramways Company

1899-1903	Yellow / White
1899-1903	Green / White
1899-1903	Chocolate / White

GENERAL TRAMWAYS COMPANY, LATER PURCHASED BY PROVINCIAL TRAMWAYS COMPANY, LATER PORTSMOUTH CORPORATION TRAMWAYS

4' 7¾" gauge; 3 route mile; opened 1878; acquired by Portsmouth Corporation 1901; horse operation ceased 1903.

In 1875 a new company was formed called the General Tramways Company of Portsmouth Limited. Its proposals were subject to objections and so a public enquiry was held and most of the planned routes were supported. In February 1878 it was purchased by the Provincial Tramways Company Limited, managed as a single tramway by the Portsmouth Street Tramways Company and this was regularised in November 1882 when its name was changed to become Portsmouth Street Tramways Company. For the remainder of its history see above.

Routes at largest extent

See Portsmouth Street Tramways Company

Tramcars purchased

1878	?	Unknown

Livery of General Tramways Company

1878-1882	Unknown

PRESTON

PRESTON TRAMWAYS COMPANY, LATER W. HARDING & COMPANY LIMITED, LATER PRESTON CORPORATION

3' 6" gauge; 7 route mile; opened 1879; acquired by Preston Corporation 1886; horse operation ceased 1903.

The first tramway was promoted by the Preston Tramways Company who obtained authority to build a tramway in the town with an Act passed in 1876. The tramway opened to the public on 20 March 1879. Three years later the council extended the system and they constructed the tracks. These two new routes were leased to W. Harding & Company Limited, a local omnibus operator. With such a small system the Preston Tramways Company sold their tramway to the corporation in 1886, giving the corporation ownership of all the tramways in the town. They also leased this line to W. Harding & Company Limited. As the date approached for the end of the lease in 1903 the corporation looked to converting the system to electric operation and running it themselves. When the lease ran out on 31 December 1903 horse tram services ceased. While the system was being converted the Harding company provided a temporary horse bus service.

Routes at largest extent

Fishergate Hill – Farrington Park
Ashton – Town Hall

Preston Tramways Company.

Tramcars purchased

1879	6 S/D	Unknown
1882	8 D/D	Unknown

Livery of Preston Tramways Company

1879-1903	Yellow / Cream

PRITCHARD GREEN & COMPANY
See Worcester

PROVINCIAL TRAMWAYS COMPANY
See Portsmouth

PWLLHELI

WEST END TRAMWAY, LATER PWLLHELI & LLANBEDROG TRAMWAY (S. ANDREWS & SON)

3' 0" gauge; 4 route miles; opened 1896; closed 1927.

The small town of Pwllheli was unusual in having two separate horse tramways, one company-owned and the other owned by the corporation. The town itself had been a busy fishing port that had declined in Victorian times. Although the railway reached the town in 1867 it had done nothing to improve matters. In the summer of 1893 Solomon Andrews was holidaying in Llandudno when he saw an advertisement for land for sale at Pwllheli. He attended the sale, liked the area and purchased land bordering the sea south west of the town. He saw the potential of building property to turn the town into a holiday resort. He used a quarry nearby to supply the stone for the buildings and he laid a mineral tramway to carry the stone to the building site. Once it had fulfilled that purpose Solomon Andrews saw that it could be used to carry passengers from the town to the properties. He lengthened it to go all the way along the sea front and closer to the railway station. His carriage works in Cardiff built the trams and it is believed the tramway first carried passengers in the summer of 1896. It was called the West End Tramway and linked with a horse bus that took passengers to the railway station. In 1896 Solomon Andrews purchased a mansion in Llanbedrog, just a little further along from his development and made it into pleasure gardens with a roller skating rink, art gallery, gardens and tea rooms. The tramway was extended one end to Llanbedrog and the other end along Cardiff Road to a point in the town near the railway station. At this time it took a new name, the Pwllheli & Llanbedrog Tramway. The tramway helped the town prosper and in doing so prospered itself. Then on 28 October 1927 the town was hit by a very severe gale and high tide that damaged the tram track and even sweeping some of it into the sea, never to be seen again. As the tram service could be replaced inexpensively by buses the decision was taken to abandon it and trams no longer ran in Pwllheli.

Route at largest extent
Pwllheli – Llanbedrog

Tramcars purchased

c1894	8 T/R, 4 S/D	Solomon Andrews & Son
1897	2 T/R	Solomon Andrews & Son
1899	1 S/D, 1 T/R	Solomon Andrews & Son
1921	1 S/D, 2 T/R	Midland RC&W Co Ltd Ex Pwllheli Corporation

Livery of Pwllheli & Llanbedrog Tramway

1896-1927	Dark Red / Cream

PWLLHELI CORPORATION TRAMWAYS

2' 6" gauge; 1 route mile; opened 1899; closed 1919.

Having seen the success of the Solomon Andrews tramway, the Pwllheli Corporation were prompted to built a tramway along the harbour wall to South Beach as part of the developments of that area. A one-mile line was built from the railway station and it opened on 24 July 1899.

One strange fact is that the line appears to have been built without any parliamentary approval and hence no Board of Trade inspection. While the Solomon Andrews line also had no parliamentary approval it was built on private land and so did not need an Act. But the corporation line was built in the roadway and strictly speaking was illegal. Operation was very quiet, with just two tramcars and the service operating only in the summer

Pwllheli & Llanbedrog Tramway.

Pwllheli Corporation Tramway.

season. The corporation had grand ideas to extend the tramway (hence the original use of the plural tramways in its name), but nothing further was ever achieved. In 1910 the corporation advertised the line to be leased but there was no interest so they approached Solomon Andrews to ask if he would run the tramway in conjunction with his line. He was not interested so the corporation continued to run the line. In 1917 Mr T.J. Williams asked if he could run the tramway and this was allowed on payment of a small sum as rental and taking the entire responsibility for the upkeep of the line.

The same arrangement was made in 1918, Mr Williams being the only person interested in renting the tramway. By 1919 the tram track was in a dreadful state and the rails needed replacing, something the corporation could not afford. So they advertised for a bus service instead and the tramway was closed and the rails sold and removed. This ended one of the country's smallest tramways.

Route at largest extent
Pwllheli Station – South Beach

Tramcars purchased

1899	1 S/D 1 T/R	Midland Railway Carriage & Wagon Co. Ltd
1901	1 T/R	Midland Railway Carriage & Wagon Co. Ltd

Livery of Pwllheli Corporation Tramways

1899-1920	Blue / White

RAMSGATE

RAMSGATE AND MARGATE TRAMWAYS COMPANY

3' 6" gauge; 1 route mile; never opened.

In 1879 the Ramsgate and Margate Tramways Company succeeded in obtaining an Act to build tramways on the Isle of Thanet. Initially authority was given to build a tramway six miles long to 2 feet 6½ inches gauge to connect Ramsgate with Margate. A second Act was passed in 1882 allowing the company to use steam power and altering the track gauge to 3 feet 6 inches. A mile of track was laid from St Peter's Church to the railway station at Broadstairs. An order for six tramcars was placed with the Metropolitan Railway Carriage & Wagon Company and one was delivered. By this time the company had been having difficulties with the two councils, who opposed the idea of having a tramway. It appears that the company ran out of money and the tramway was abandoned and the company wound up. The tramcar was tested on the track that had been laid, but it is not known if any passenger service was given. The tramcar was sold to South Shields and then on to Douglas where it can be seen today as number 18 in the fleet.

Routes at largest extent
St Peter's Church – Broadstairs Railway Station

Tramcars purchased

1883	1 D/D	Metropolitan Railway Carriage & Wagon Company

Livery of Ramsgate and Margate Tramways Company

1883-1883	Unknown

READING

READING TRAMWAYS COMPANY LATER READING CORPORATION TRAMWAYS

4' 0" gauge; 2 route miles; opened 1879; acquired by Reading Corporation 1901; horse operation ceased 1903.

The Reading Tramways Company (a subsidiary of Imperial Tramways Company) was formed in 1878 to build tramways in the town. Authority was given in an Act of 1878 and the tramway opened on 5 April 1879. Like many of the small company owned tramways Reading tramway was the recipient of many complaints from the corporation and the general public about the lack of service, overloading and the condition of the tracks. An attempt in the 1880s to extend the tramway was rejected owing to the complaints of influential residents along the proposed route. The tramway indicated to the corporation that they would like to electrify the system including an offer to pay the expenses for a corporation visit to see the electric trams in Bristol. The corporation did not accept the offer as they had ideas to purchase the tramway and electrify it themselves. In 1899 the corporation gave notice of intent to purchase the tramway compulsorily. The company objected and took the matter to court, but their arguments were rejected. The company appealed, but when a similar case that had reached the House of Lords was dismissed the company withdrew their appeal. So the corporation went ahead with the purchase that was accomplished on 31 October 1901.

Reading Tramways Company.

While the conversion process was going through the horse tramway continued to provide service. As the discussions over the purchase price took far longer than expected the electric tramway conversion was delayed. It was not until 21 July 1903 that the last horse tram ran in Reading.

Routes at largest extent
Barracks – Town Centre
Town Centre – Cemetery Junction

Tramcars purchased

1879	6 S/D	Unknown
1879	1 S/D	Hughes (Falcon Engine & Car Works Ltd)
1880	6 D/D	Unknown

Livery of Reading Tramways Company
1879-1901 Unknown

REID BROTHERS
See London Section

ROTHESAY

ROTHESAY TRAMWAYS COMPANY LIMITED

4' 0" gauge later 3' 6" gauge; 2 route miles; opened 1882; acquired by British Electric Tramways Company 1902; horse operation ceased 1902.

At a meeting in Rothesay Town Hall a group of businessmen suggested that it was time for the town to have a tramway and that they would form themselves into a committee. The town council did not object and the Rothesay Tramways Company Limited was formed that obtained an Act in 1879 to lay tramways in the town. The proposals were supported by the local people, though the Marquess of Bute at first objected stating that Bute was no place for tramways. The line was to connect Rothesay Pier with Port Bannatyne and was laid with a gauge of 4' 0". The line opened on 1 June 1882. In 1892 the then manager was asked to resign as there was disquiet over the conduct and discipline of the staff. A clue as to the cause was given when the Directors announced that they hoped that the next manager would be a total abstainer. The first twelve tramcars were purchased from Savile Street Foundry, Sheffield, but subsequent additions all came from local coach builders or carpenters. In 1897 the British Electric Traction Company approached the company suggesting that they could introduce electric power to the system, but the company was not ready, the horse tramway was quite profitable. After a couple of years of continued contact the tramway company gave way and they sold the system to BET in July 1899. So the Rothesay Tramways Company Limited became a subsidiary of BET. Horse tram operation continued while plans were being made for the conversion of the system to electric power. The BET decided at the same time as the conversion the gauge would be changed to 3' 6". Work started on 3 March 1902 and the horse tramway was suspended and replaced by horse buses during the reconstruction. To reinstate a tramway service before the electrical power was used ten of the horse trams were regauged to 3' 6" and they went back in service on 17 May 1902. The last day of the horse trams was 18 August 1902 with the first electric tram services beginning the next day.

Route at largest extent
Rothesay Pier – Port Bannatyne

Tramcars purchased

1882	4 S/D, 8 T/R	Savile Street Foundry & Engineering Co. Ltd of Sheffield
1882	2 T/R	James McBride
1891	2 T/R	William Lauder
1894	2 T/R	William Lauder
1897	1 T/R	William Lauder

Livery of Rothesay Tramways Company Limited
1882-1902 Maroon / Cream

Rothesay Tramways Company.

RYDE, ISLE OF WIGHT

RYDE PIER

4' 8½" gauge; 1 route mile; opened 1864; closed 1969; horse operation ceased 1889.

Ryde gained its first pier in 1814 but it was not until 29 August 1864 that a tramway was opened on the pier to carry passengers and their luggage to and from the ferries. A steam locomotive had been tried prior to the opening, but its weight set up potentially damaging vibrations and the trials were halted very quickly and the locomotive sent back to its makers. So the pier tramway opened using horse power. At this time the Island's railway only reached St John's Station the other side of the town from the pier. Though there was some opposition, the pier company gained the authority to build an extension of the line to the station and this was opened on 7 August 1871. The tram rails were connected to the railway track so that the railway company could operate through running of goods vans from the station to the pier end (all hauled by horses). In 1880 the railway line was extended from St John's Station along the route of the tramway on to a new pier built alongside the old one. So passengers for the ferries no longer needed to change at St John's, but they could stay on the train all the way to the ferry. The town part of the pier tramway was closed and the tramway just worked on the pier. The pier company continued to look for an alternative power to horses and in 1885 Siemens were asked to electrify the pier tramway. The first line opened in March 1886 and proved a success, so the second line was converted in 1889 and horse tram operation ceased.

Ryde Pier Tramway.

Route at largest extent
St John's Station – Pier Head

Tramcars purchased

1864	1 S/D	T.B. Ayshford
1865	1 S/D	T.B. Ayshford
1867	1 S/D	Harvey
1871	5 D/D	Starbuck Car & Wagon Co.
1871	1 S/D	Local
1871	1 S/D	John Knapp

Livery of Ryde Pier

1864-1889	Vermilion / Blue (horse tramcar)
1867-1889	All Brown (trailer No. 4)

ST HELENS

ST HELENS & DISTRICT TRAMWAYS COMPANY, LATER ST HELENS & DISTRICT TRAMWAYS COMPANY LIMITED

4' 8½" gauge; 9 route miles; opened 1881; closed 1936; horse operation ceased 1890.

In 1878 St Helens found it considering three proposals to build tramways in the town. After consideration the project by the group promoting the St Helens & District Tramways Company was supported by the corporation and an Act was passed in 1879 giving authority to build the tramway. Construction was delayed by a slow response to the sale of shares and arguments with the corporation over the type of track to be used. So an extension to the two year limit for construction had to be obtained. Construction began in October 1880 and things became fraught with arguments between the corporation, company and contractor over the quality of the construction and materials used. The first part of the tramway was opened on 5 November 1881 and the next part was started with a different contractor with the final part opening in August 1882. The financial side of the operation was somewhat precarious. The company blamed the hilly nature of the town requiring additional horses to haul the tramcars. So they decided to explore steam power. However, the company did not have enough capital to buy steam tram locomotives. Poor management may well have been a factor as an investigation found drunkenness, theft of fare money by conductors, and allowing people to travel free. Action improved revenue, but this was needed just to maintain the system. On 20 March 1889 the company sold the system to a new company, the similarly named St Helens & District Tramways Company Limited. The new company purchased six steam tram locomotives and steam operation arrived and started running in April 1890. There was then a mixture of horse and steam operation. Horse tram operation ceased on 12 May 1890 when the whole system was operated by steam locomotives.

St Helens & District Tramways Company.

Route at largest extent
Town Centre – King's Arms
Town Centre – Denton's Green
Town Centre – Peasley Cross
Town Centre – Haydock Railway Station

Tramcars purchased

1881	6 D/D	Ashbury Railway Carriage & Iron Company Ltd
1882	3 S/D	Oldbury Railway Carriage & Wagon Co. Ltd
1882	3 D/D	Metropolitan Railway Carriage & Wagon Co.
1888	1 S/D	G.F. Milnes & Co.

Livery of St Helens & District Tramways Company

1881-1889	Unknown

Livery of St Helens & District Tramways Company Limited

1890-1890	Unknown

SALFORD

HAWORTH PATENT PERAMBULATING SYSTEM

c5' 0" gauge; 1 route mile; opened 1861; closed 1872.

A short history of this pioneering line was given in Section 1 "Tramway Pioneers". John Haworth patented a system where two flat metal strips about three inches wide were fixed to the road and in order to keep the tramcar on the top of the strips a third grooved rail was laid centrally between the running strips and a guide wheel kept the wheels on the flat strips. With another businessman, John Greenwood, he demonstrated the system to Salford Council who agreed to him laying about one mile of route. It was single track as when two tramcars met head on one would raise its guide wheel and it became effectively an omnibus. While this method did not spread to any other towns, nor was it extended in Salford, it did last until 1872, so was a partial success. No doubt one factor leading to its lack of complete success was the ease with which other road users, in particularly omnibuses, could also make use of the smooth surface of the strips, while Mr Haworth had to pay for the maintenance of them and the road surface between the strips and 12 inches either side.

Haworth Patent Perambulating System.

Route at largest extent
Broad Street, Pendleton – Albert Bridge, Salford

Tramcars purchased

1861	? D/D	Unknown

Livery of Haworth Patent Perambulating System

1861-1872	Unknown

MANCHESTER AND SALFORD TRAMWAYS, LATER MANCHESTER CARRIAGE COMPANY LIMITED, LATER MANCHESTER CARRIAGE & TRAMWAYS COMPANY LIMITED, LATER SALFORD CORPORATION

4' 8½" gauge; 42 route miles; opened 1877; acquired by Salford Corporation and Oldham Corporation 1901; Ashton Corporation and Manchester Corporation 1903.

The history of the Manchester Carriage & Tramways Company Limited is detailed above under Manchester. Because the horse tramway was laid in four towns, when the corporations decided to purchase the parts in their areas the tramway was split. The Salford part was purchased in 1901. The corporation had the right to compulsory purchase the tramways in its area in 1898, but in agreement with Manchester Corporation, Salford deferred it until 1901, when the Manchester leases ran out. The tramway company sought a new power source and experimented with a steam tramcar and an accumulator car, but without adopting either system.

The corporation took over the company lines on 28 April 1901 with special arrangements for those tramcars running through to Manchester. To run the lines in their area the corporation purchased 94 trams and 900 horses from the company, with the company continuing to repairs the tramcars. Owing to last minute disagreements about the sums to be paid for the tramcars and horses the tram services ceased on 28 April. Hasty negotiations saw an agreement reached and the services recommenced on 1 May. Problems for Salford were not over, as Manchester Corporation proved difficult about through running arrangements as Salford felt that Manchester was trying to control their tramway. Relationships were fraught. The next task for Salford was to convert the tramway to electric operation. The electric tramway was formally opened on 20 November 1901 with the last horse trams running on 25 March 1903.

Route at largest extent
See Manchester Carriage & Tramways Company Limited above

Tramcars purchased
See Manchester Carriage & Tramways Company Limited above

Livery of Manchester Carriage Company Limited

1877-1900	Red / Cream

Livery of Manchester Carriage & Tramways Company Limited

1880-1901	Red / Cream

Livery Salford Corporation Tramways

1901-1903	Red / White

SALTAIRE

SALTAIRE EXHIBITION TRAMWAY

1' 8" gauge; 1 route mile; opened 1887; closed 1887.

1887 was Queen Victoria's Golden Jubilee year and there were celebrations over the whole country. The town of Saltaire hosted the Royal Yorkshire Jubilee Exhibition which featured exhibits from all over the world. It seemed to be a combination of trade exhibits showing the best of manufacturing and a fun fair for the public. The latter included an early switch-back railway (roller-coaster). To move visitors around the exhibition a horse tramway was built. There were six open toastrack tramcars on the service. When the exhibition closed a local businessman Sam Wilson bought the tramcars and opened a pleasure tramway around Glen Pond using two of the tramcars, the other trams were dismantled and parts used in the construction of the Shipley Glen Cable tramway that opened in 1895. The switch back railway used at the exhibition was dismantled and moved to the top of Shipley Glen as part of an amusement fair constructed there.

Route at largest extent
Around the exhibition

Tramcars purchased

1887	6 T/R	Unknown

Manchester and Salford Tramways.

Livery of Saltaire Exhibition

1887-1887	Unknown

SHEFFIELD

SHEFFIELD TRAMWAYS COMPANY, LATER SHEFFIELD CORPORATION TRAMWAYS

4' 8½" gauge; 9 route miles; opened 1877; acquired by Sheffield Corporation 1896; horse operation ceased 1902.

In 1870 the Sheffield Carriage Company wrote to the corporation proposing to run a tramway in the city. The company suggested that the corporation construct the lines and lease them to the company, but nothing came of this idea. Then in 1871 a group of local businessmen wrote suggesting a tramway, but the carriage company claimed prior rights. The corporation decided to request authority to build a tramway, but at the same time another businessman reached an agreement with local omnibus operators and also applied for authority to build tramways. A deal was struck where the corporation withdrew their application in return for the company putting conditions into their proposals. An Act was passed in 1872 and the Sheffield Tramways Company was established. The first trams ran in public service on 7 October 1873, with further routes opening until the company system was at its maximum in 1877. The company suffered competition from omnibuses and their revenue was hit. Trials with steam tram locomotives were made, but nothing further came from them. Things seemed to pick up when horse omnibus competition was withdrawn. But in 1879 a general depression reduced revenue and the company removed children's half fares. There was a court case that determined that the company was within its rights to do so. The public decided to walk rather than use the tram and revenue fell further. So the company cut the wages of staff by nearly 25%. The children's half fares were reinstated, but that did not attract people back on to the trams. As so frequently happens with horse tramways the relationship between the company and the corporation deteriorated and the corporation decided it should take control of the tramways and operate them itself. In 1895 the corporation applied for authority to operate the tramways by electricity, this coinciding with very strong public opinion that the company trams should be taken over by the corporation. The authority was given after the matter went to the House of Lords giving the corporation the right to operate the tramways. The transfer of the tramway took place on 11 July 1896 and Sheffield became the first corporation to take over a tramway under new rules and have full tenure of the system. The horse tram service continued while the corporation determined what would be the best power source for the tramway. The overhead electrical system was chosen and conversion started on 3 January 1898 with the first electric trams carrying passengers on 5 September 1899. Combined horse and electric tram operation continued while more routes were converted with the last horse trams operating in 1902.

Route at largest extent

West Bar – Hillsborough
Waingate – Brightside
Waingate – Carbrook
High Street – Walkley
High Street – Hunters Bar
High Street – Abbeydale Road
Moorhead – Nether Edge
Moorhead – Healey

Tramcars purchased

Sheffield Tramways Company

1873	12 D/D	Starbuck Car & Wagon Co.
1874	8 D/D	Starbuck Car & Wagon Co.
1875	8 S/D	Starbuck Car & Wagon Co.
1876	1 D/D	Falcon Engine & Car Works Ltd
1877	18 D/D, 5 S/D	Starbuck Car & Wagon Co.
1883	7 D/D	Starbuck Car & Wagon Co.
1884	4 S/D	Ashbury Railway Carriage & Iron Co. Ltd
1886	2 D/D	Ashbury Railway Carriage & Iron Co. Ltd
1887	2 D/D	Ashbury Railway Carriage & Iron Co. Ltd

Sheffield Tramways Company.

Sheffield Corporation Tramways

1896		Took over Sheffield Tramways with 44 cars
1896	12 D/D	G.F. Milnes & Co.
1896	12 T/R	G.F. Milnes & Co.

Livery of Sheffield Tramways Company

1873-1896	Crimson Lake / Cream
1874-1896	Dove Grey / White
1875-1896	Red / Cream
1877-1896	Dark Blue / Cream
1877-1896	Carminette / Cream
1877-1896	Dark Green / Cream

Livery of Sheffield Corporation Tramways

1896-1899	Crimson Lake / Cream (horse tramcars)
1896-1900	Red / Cream (White) (horse tramcars)
1896-1902	Dark Blue / Cream (horse tramcars)
1896-1900	Carminette / Cream (horse tramcars)
1896-1899	Royal Blue / Cream (horse tramcars)

SHIPLEY

JOSEPH SPEIGHT, LATER MAURICE JONES, LATER BRADFORD & DISTRICT STEAM TRAMWAY COMPANY LIMITED, LATER BRADFORD & DISTRICT TRAMWAYS COMPANY, LATER BRADFORD CORPORATION TRAMWAYS

4' 0" gauge; 2 route miles; opened 1882; last horse trams ran in 1891.

The history of tramways in Shipley is a series of unsuccessful operators with a series of liquidations. It began in 1873 with an unsuccessful application by the Bradford Tramways Company. Then Joseph Speight, a tramway contractor from Prescott, gained authority in 1880 to build a horse tramway from the Rosse Hotel, Saltaire to Fox and Hounds, Shipley. The line was built and opened in 1882. The line was not a success and went bankrupt in 1883. The tramcars and horses were sold and later the tramway route was taken on by Maurice Jones from Liverpool who applied to the Local Board for permission to run it as a steam tramway. In order to get the tramway running Jones purchased new light tramcars and started the service in 1884. Jones applied for a new route from the Rosse Hotel, Saltaire to

Frizinghall in 1885. However, Jones had no more success than before and the service ceased in 1885 before the new line could be built. Jones transferred the tramway to the Bradford & District Steam Tramways Company Limited in July 1885. Despite its name the new company never ran trams in Bradford nor did it use steam trams. They started a service again in 1885, but ceased operating by 1887. But it was running again for the Royal Yorkshire Jubilee Exhibition held in Saltaire in May 1887 and the tramway benefited from the large number of visitors to the exhibition. But the Bradford & District Steam Tramways Company Limited went into liquidation in September 1887. In 1888 a new company, the Bradford & District Tramways Company Limited, purchased the tramway. This company built the route to Frizinghall, several years after the authority had been obtained. In 1891 the tramway was taken over by a receiver and the service stopped in October and the horses and tramcars sold by auction. The lines stayed closed for two years then, in March 1893, the Shipley Local Board agreed to purchase the tramway and leased the routes to the Bradford & District Tramways Company and operations started later that month, but using steam power. The last horse trams to run in Shipley were those that ran in 1891.

Routes at largest extent
Rosse Hotel, Saltaire – Fox & Hounds, Shipley
Rosse Hotel, Saltaire – Frizinghall

Tramcars purchased
Joseph Speight
1882 1 D/D, 1 S/D Oldbury Railway Carriage & Wagon Co. Ltd
Maurice Jones
1884 2 S/D Unknown
Bradford & District Tramways Company Limited
1888 3 S/D Unknown

Livery of all Shipley Tramways
1882-1891 Not known

SHIPLEY GLEN POND TRAMWAY

1' 8" gauge (possibly); less than 1 route mile; opened c1887; closed c1910.

In May 1887 the Royal Yorkshire Jubilee Exhibition was held in Saltaire. In the exhibition grounds a horse-drawn tramway had been laid to convey people around the grounds. When the exhibition closed a local businessman, Sam Wilson, purchased the six toastrack tramcars used on the tramway. He stored four of the tramcars and used the final two to run on a circular track he built around the Glen Pond that was part of the grounds of the entertainment area at the top of Shipley Glen. Information is very limited but it is thought that the tramway opened around 1887/8. Sam Wilson also built the Shipley Glen Tramway, a funicular that runs from Higher Coach Road to the top of the glen. He may have used the four stored tramcars to build the tramcars for the funicular. The end of the Pond tramway has not been recorded but was probably sometime before the First World War.

Shipley Glen Pond Tramway.

Route at largest extent
Circular route around Shipley Glen Pond

Tramcars purchased
1887 6 T/R Unknown

Livery of Shipley Glen Pond Tramway
c1887-c1910 Not known

SKEGNESS

SKEGNESS TRAMWAY

Unknown gauge. Below 1 route mile; opened c1880; closed c1882.

Little is know about this short-lived tramway. It opened around 1880 to carry holiday makers from Grand Parade to a fun fair and the beach. There were two open toastrack tramcars with canvass awnings. No doubt it only ran during the summer season and even then only for a few years. It is believed to have closed around 1882. Nothing is known about the origins or disposal of the tramcars.

Skegness Tramway.

Route at largest extent
Grand Parade – Fun fair and Beach

Tramcars purchased
1880 2 T/R ?

Livery of Skegness Tramway
1880-1882 Unknown

SOLOMON ANDREWS

See Newport & Pwllheli

SOUTH EASTERN METROPOLITAN TRAMWAYS COMPANY

See London Section

SOUTH LONDON TRAMWAYS COMPANY

See London Section" immediately below Solomon Andrews.

South Shields Tramways Company.

SOUTH SHIELDS

SOUTH SHIELDS TRAMWAYS COMPANY LATER SOUTH SHIELDS TRAMWAYS & CARRIAGE COMPANY LATER BRITISH ELECTRIC TRAMWAYS COMPANY

3' 6" gauge. 3 route miles; opened 1883; acquired by South Shields Corporation 1906, last horse trams ran in 1906.

After several proposals from different groups the corporation decided in 1880 to apply for authority to build tramways in the town and they obtained authority in 1881. After some investigation the corporation decided to construct the line to 3' 6" gauge and started building the lines in 1882. Unfortunately the Board of Trade inspector noticed the gauge was different to the 4' 8½" authorised and refused to approve the line until the change had been given parliamentary sanction. To get out of a difficult position the corporation got agreement for a complex Bill that would allow the tramway to open and give agreement to join with the Jarrow and Hebburn Tramways Company and change the gauge if needed. This was authorised in 1883, so South Shields could run their tramway and it opened on 1 August 1883. The tramway had been leased to the South Shields Tramways Company. The company soon ran into financial difficulties and the company went into liquidation on 31 March 1886. It ran on for a month then on 31 April 1886, at night, the tramcars were hauled off the track and into a timber yard and the horses were sold by auction. The tramcars turned up a year later working on the Douglas Bay Tramway, Isle of Man. The corporation and town were stunned to find they had no tram service. Many thought this was temporary, but it took a year for the tramway to start again. A new company was formed, the South Shields Tramways & Carriage Company Limited to operate the line and new trams were ordered. The service was restarted on 28 March 1887 and the company also branched out with omnibus operation. Unlike the first company the new company was able to run at a profit. They caught the eye of the British Electric Traction Company and the BET made a handsome offer to buy the system, with a view to electrifying it. The transfer took place in July 1899. The corporation gave notice to the company that they were ending the lease on 1 February 1906 and that they were compulsorily purchasing the system. With the end of the company lease the tramway closed on 31 January 1906 and South Shields once again had no tramway. The corporation went ahead and converted the system to electric operation and changed the gauge to 4' 8½". The electric tramway opened on 23 June 1906.

Route at largest extent
Pier Head – Tyne Dock

Tramcars purchased
South Shields Tramways Company

1883	1 D/D	Metropolitan Railway Carriage & Wagon Co, ex Ramsgate & Margate Tramways
1883	5 D/D	Metropolitan Railway Carriage & Wagon Co.

South Shields Tramways & Carriage Company Limited

1887	4 D/D, 6 S/D	G. F. Milnes & Co.
c1890	6 S/D	Ashbury Railway Carriage & Iron Co. Ltd
c1890	6 D/D	G.F. Milnes & Co.

Livery of South Shields Tramways Company
1883-1886 Unknown
Livery of South Shields Tramways & Carriage Company Limited
1887-1899 Unknown

SOUTHALL, EALING & SHEPHERDS BUSH TRAM-RAILWAY COMPANY
See London Section

SOUTHAMPTON

SOUTHAMPTON TRAMWAYS COMPANY, LATER SOUTHAMPTON CORPORATION TRAMWAYS

4' 8½" gauge; 5 route miles; opened 1879; acquired by Southampton Corporation 1898; horse operation ceased 1901.

The British and Foreign Tramway Company was set up by a group of businessmen and lawyers to promote tramways in Britain and Europe. In 1872 they approached Southampton Corporation with proposals to build tramways in the city. However, local businessmen were apprehensive at letting 'outsiders' build a tramway in their city and the corporation were also less than enthusiastic and turned down any idea of laying tramways in the High Street and Above Bar and this was enough to deter the company from going any further. A few years later the corporation realised that it was falling behind as many similar cities and towns were getting this most modern public transport. They supported local businessmen in the formation of the Southampton Tramways Company with proposals that were very similar to the ones rejected four years earlier. The required Act was passed in 1877 and the first trams ran in public service on 5 May 1879. The company chose to run services on Sunday so there was the inevitable opposition, but the company held its ground arguing that the takings showed that there was a real demand for Sunday operation. The Annual General Meeting in 1881 was eventful as the shareholders discovered that the manager had gone to America and that no dividend would be paid. They dismissed the board of directors and replaced them with their own choice of directors. Things were a little better the next year as only the manager was sacked for "irregularities in the forage account". Things got better and the company was able to pay a regular attractive 8% dividend. The usual acrimony existed between the corporation and the company regarding the

Southampton Tramways Company.

maintenance of the track and roadway, and the corporation also had an eye to modernising the system by converting it to electric power. So when the 21 years elapsed from the passing of the Act the corporation gave notice to the company that it was to purchase the system compulsorily. The transfer took place on 30 June 1898, though arguments over the price carried on for over a year. The conversion was started and the first public services with electric tramcars started on 22 January 1900. Horse tram operation continued while the conversion work carried on and the last horse tram ran on 2 August 1901.

Routes at largest extent

Stag Gates – Floating Bridge
Stag Gates – Terminus Station
Prospect Place Junction – Shirley

Tramcars purchased

1879	9 S/D	Bristol Wagon Co.
1879	7 D/D	Starbuck Car & Wagon Co.
1881	4 D/D	Starbuck Car & Wagon Co.
1893	7 D/D	North Metropolitan Tramways

Livery of Southampton Tramways Company

1879-1898 Unknown

SOUTH EASTERN RAILWAY

See Folkestone

SOUTHEND

SOUTHEND PIER TRAMWAY

3' 6" gauge; 1 route mile; opened c1850; horse operation ceased 1881.

The first Southend Pier, an all-wood construction, was opened in 1830 and was only half a mile long, which left it well away from the sea during low tide. So in 1846 the pier was extended to reach deep water and allow vessels to be boarded all day. It was now 1¼ miles long and was the longest pier in Europe. To allow an easier passage for baggage a track (with wooden rails) was laid on the pier and two flat wagons were used to carry baggage and were pushed by hand. There was also another truck that had a mast and sail and when the wind was favourable it would travel up and down the pier using wind power. In 1875 the wooden rails were replaced with iron rails and three passenger cars and a flat truck were hauled by a pair of horses the length of the pier. An entertainment tent was erected over the pier and the horse tram would travel through the tent, even when there were concerts playing. The operation using horses had its dangers, as the hooves of the horses were prone to breaking through the more rotted parts of the decking. It became so unsafe that the tramway was closed in 1881. In 1885 it was decided to build a new pier of iron and that the new pier would have an electric tramway on it and horses were not seen again on the pier.

Route at largest extent

Pier Entrance – Pier Head

Tramcars purchased

1874	3 S/D	Unknown

Livery of Southend Pier Tramway

c1850-1881 Unknown

SOUTHPORT

SOUTHPORT TRAMWAYS COMPANY LIMITED

4' 8½" gauge; 6 route miles; opened 1873; acquired by Southport Corporation 1896; horse operation ceased 1902.

The Southport Tramways Company Limited was formed in 1871 to build and operate tramways in Southport. The authorisation was given in an Act of 1872 with the tramway opening on 31 May 1873. The original route was extended in 1875 and a second route added in 1878. In 1888 Southport Corporation decided to purchase all the lines within their territories. This galvanised

Southend Pier Tramway.

Birkdale & Southport Tramways Company.

Birkdale UDC to do likewise. Negotiations took eight years and it was not until 1896 that the corporations purchased the tramways. The corporation and UDC then leased the lines back to the Southport Tramways Company Limited for a period of 21 years. The corporation electrified the company lines, though the company was to run the services and pay rent to the corporation. The first company electric trams ran in service on 11 August 1901 and the last horse tramcars ran in 1902, when the final electric routes opened.

Routes at largest extent

Botanic Gardens – Birkdale Station
Winter Gardens – Botanic Gardens

Tramcars purchased

1873	6 D/D	Starbuck Car & Wagon Co.
1878	16 D/D	Starbuck Car & Wagon Co.
1886	?	Unknown

Livery of Southport Tramways Company Limited

1873-1878	Green / White
1878-1901	Green / Yellow / White
1878-1901	Green / Brown / White

BIRKDALE & SOUTHPORT TRAMWAYS COMPANY, LATER SOUTHPORT CORPORATION TRAMWAYS

4' 8½" gauge; 4 route miles; opened 1883; acquired by Southport Corporation & Birkdale UDC 1899; horse operation ceased 1900.

In 1879 a second company was formed, the Birkdale & Southport Tramways Company which obtained the authority to build a tramway that opened on 12 May 1883. As described above the Southport Corporation and Birkdale UDC purchased all the lines within their territories in 1896. The corporation set about converting the Birkdale & Southport Tramways Company lines for electric operation. The new electric trams first ran on 18 July 1900 and all the horse trams were withdrawn.

Routes at largest extent

London Square – Kew Gardens
Kew Gardens – Crown Hotel

Tramcars purchased

1883	3 D/D	Ex St Helen's and District
1883	9 D/D	Ex Birkenhead Street Railway
1887	7 D/D	G.F. Milnes & Co.

Livery of Birkdale & Southport Tramways Company

1883-1902	Varnished Mahogany / Cream / Bright Red Window Pillars

SOUTHWARK & DEPTFORD TRAMWAY COMPANY

See London Section

SPEIGHT (JOSEPH)

See Shipley

STAFFORDSHIRE POTTERIES STREET RAILWAY COMPANY LIMITED

See Potteries

Southport Tramways Company Limited.

STIRLING

STIRLING & BRIDGE OF ALLAN TRAMWAY COMPANY LIMITED

4' 8½" gauge; 4 route miles; opened 1874; closed 1920.

Stirling Town Council found itself considering two proposals to build tramways in the town in 1871. After considerable debate the council gave support to the Stirling & Bridge of Allan Tramway Company Limited that wished to build a tramway between the town centre and the Bridge of Allan and the necessary Act was passed in 1872. The tramway opened on 27 July 1874. There was a slight setback on 30 January 1877 when the tramway's stables caught fire. The situation was not helped when fire brigades from both Stirling and Bridge of Allan turned up and then argued about whose fire it was. The building was saved, but the company lost a tramcar, an omnibus and three horses. The company experimented with a steam passenger tram in 1878, but there were objections from the authorities and the vehicle was banned from the road. A parcels service was started in 1892 leading to a strange accident where the horses hauling the parcels van bolted and collided with a tramcar, derailing the car, the horses of which bolted. An extension was opened to St Ninians in 1898. Unusually for a small horse tramway the system was financially sound and it attracted the attention of other promoters with plans to convert it to electrical operation. Talks went on for many years and during this the council moved from being in favour to being anti and opposing all proposals. So the tramway continued to operate under horse power and unusually made a comfortable profit. In 1908 fixed stopping places were introduced and studiously ignored by the public who still hailed the tramcars anywhere they liked. With no prospect of using electrical power the company experimented with a petrol tramcar in 1913. Later that year Balfour Beatty approached the company with proposals to introduce electrical supply and this time discussions were positive and it looked like the system would be converted. However, just after agreement was reached the First World War started and everything was put on hold. When it was raised again in 1918 the costs had risen too high to be considered. Now the tramway was running with aged tramcars using the outdated horse power. Motor buses were becoming more efficient and reliable and it was not long before the tramway found itself with serious competition and it was decided to close it. The last horse tram ran on 5 February 1920 and that was the end of tramways in Stirling.

Routes at largest extent

St Ninians – King Street, Stirling
King Street, Stirling – Causewayhead
Causewayhead – Bridge of Allan

Stirling & Bridge of Allan Tramway Company Limited.

Tramcars purchased

1874	2 D/D, 1 S/D	Tramway Car & Works Co.
1877	1 D/D	Tramway Car & Works Co.
1885	3 T/R	Unknown
1887	1 D/D	Ashbury Railway Carriage & Iron Co. Ltd., possibly second-hand from Edinburgh
1888	? D/D	Ashbury Railway Carriage & Iron Co. Ltd.
1894	1 T/R	Unknown
1894	1 D/D	G.F. Milnes & Co.
1895	1 D/D	Second-hand from Glasgow
1900	3 D/D	Second-hand from Edinburgh
1902	3 D/D	Second-hand from Edinburgh
1905	2 D/D	Second-hand from Leith

Livery of Stirling & Bridge of Allan Tramway Company Limited

1877-1910	Flaming Red
1888-1910	Chocolate Brown / Cream
1902-1910	All White
1902-1910	Blue / White
1902-1910	Red / White
1910-1920	Red Brown / Cream
1913-1920	Dark Green / Cream

STOCKPORT

STOCKPORT & HAZEL GROVE CARRIAGE & TRAMWAYS COMPANY LIMITED

4' 8½" gauge; 3 route miles; opened 1890; acquired by Stockport Corporation 1905; horse operation ceased 1905.

The first trams in Stockport were those of the Manchester Carriage and Tramways Company when it opened a line in 1880 connecting Stockport town centre with Manchester. The detailed history of the company is given above under Manchester. In 1888 there were proposals to build another tramway in Stockport. This was from the Stockport & Hazel Grove Carriage & Tramways Company Limited and it was given authority to do so by an Act in 1889 and the tramway opened on 29 March 1890. A new route was built to Edgeley opening in December 1891. Stockport Corporation decided that the town needed electric trams and applied for powers to build and operate its own tramways in 1899, gaining authority to do so in 1900. The electric tramway opened on 26 August 1901. During this time the company horse tramway continued to operate between St Peter's Square to Hazel Grove and to Edgeley. But the corporation had its eye on the system as it wanted to convert it to electrical operation and to incorporate it into the rest of the electric tramway system. As this was before the 21-year term expired the corporation had to agree a sale price with the company on the basis of a going concern. Purchase of the tramway took until 24 January 1905, when the system passed into the hands of the corporation. Conversion to electric operation began three months later and the horse trams continued to run while the conversion took place, with horse buses covering those parts of the routes actually impassable due to rail replacement. The last horse tram operated on 4 July 1905.

Routes at largest extent

St Peter's Square – Hazel Grove
St Peter's Square – Edgeley

Stockport & Hazel Grove Carriage & Tramways Company Limited.

Tramcars purchased

1890	16 D/D	Manchester Carriage & Tramways Co.
1890	3 S/D	Unknown
1890	1 T/R	Unknown

Livery of Stockport & Hazel Grove Carriage & Tramways Company Limited

1890-1905	Vermilion / Cream (Not reliable, taken from tinted postcard)

STOCKTON & DARLINGTON STEAM TRAMWAYS COMPANY

See Darlington

STOCKTON & DISTRICT TRAMWAYS COMPANY

See Darlington

STOKE-ON-TRENT

STAFFORDSHIRE POTTERIES STREET RAILWAY COMPANY LIMITED, LATER NORTH STAFFORDSHIRE TRAMWAYS COMPANY LIMITED (LATER PURCHASED BY BRITISH ELECTRIC TRACTION COMPANY)

4' 8½" gauge later 4' 0" gauge; 7 route miles of which 2 miles were horse tramways; opened 1862; closed 1928; horse operation ceased 1884.

The Staffordshire Potteries Street Railway Company Limited was one of George Francis Train's pioneering street tramway lines. It opened on 11 January 1862 with a line just short of two miles and laid using the step rail so favoured by Train. The line was leased to Edward Brassington from 1862 to 1865 when G.B. Bradford took over the lease. It is thought that some time around 1863 the line was re-laid with grooved rail, coinciding with the relaying of the Birkenhead tramway with grooved rail. The North Staffordshire Tramways Company Limited was formed in 1878 and obtained an Act in 1879 authorising them to build and run a steam tramway in the Potteries area. In order to have control of all the tramways in the area the new company purchased the Staffordshire Potteries Street Railway Company Limited on 8 November 1879. It ran the old tramway with horse trams at the same time as building a 4' 0" gauge steam tramway along the same roads. Trials were carried out with three different manufacturers' steam trams. The Act specified that two of the routes could not be operated using steam power and so the company had to use horse trams. This continued until 1884 when authority was obtained to convert them to steam operation. With the introduction of steam traction on these two routes the use of horse trams ceased entirely.

Horse tram routes at largest extent

Market Place, Burslem – Foundry Street, Hanley
London Road – Glebe Street

Tramcars purchased

Staffordshire Potteries Street Railway Company Limited

1862	2 S/D	Starbuck Car & Wagon Co.
1866	5 S/D	Unknown

Staffordshire Potteries Street Railway Company Limited

1881	20 D/D	Starbuck Car & Wagon Co.
c1882	4? D/D	Unknown

Livery of Staffordshire Potteries Street Railway Company Limited

1862-1879	Unknown

Livery of North Staffordshire Tramways Company Limited

1879-1884	Dark Green

STRABATHIE

STRABATHIE & BLACKDOG LIGHT RAILWAY

3' 0" gauge; 1 route mile; opened 1899; closed 1951; horse operation ceased c1924.

Around 1898 the Seaton Brick & Tile Company Limited moved to a new clay pit north of Aberdeen near Strabathie. Around 100 people were employed and the factory produced 5 million bricks and 1,750,000 drainpipes each year. The finished products from the factory were carried by horse and cart to Aberdeen. This was an inefficient and costly method so the company decided to lay a tramway from Blackdog to the Bridge of Don. A 3' 0" gauge line was laid in 1899 on private land, hence not needing parliamentary approval. A saddle tank locomotive was purchased to haul the wagons along the line. The company also purchased four second-hand horse tramcars from Aberdeen Corporation and, after conversion from double-deck to single-deck, these were used to take workers to and from the brick factory. It is likely that the tramcars were hauled by both horses and the locomotive depending on what was most convenient on the day. In 1909 land alongside the line was acquired by the Murcar Links Golf Club Company Limited who built a new course. The golf course reached an agreement with the brick company to allow the club to run their own tramcar on the line. To begin with the golf club paid for the brick company to haul two trams using the locomotive. This was extremely popular and a regular Saturday service was established. In 1910 the golf club purchased a petrol railcar and this was used to run the passenger service for club members. During the First World War the golf course was used by the Admiralty and the brick company carried the personnel to and from the clubhouse.

The clay pit became exhausted around 1924 and was closed and the tramway was purchased by the golf club. From this point onward the line was worked entirely by the railcar and horse operation ceased.

Route at largest extent

Bridge of Don – Blackdog Brickworks

Tramcars purchased

1899	4 S/D	Ex Aberdeen Tramways

Livery of Strabathie & Blackdog Light Railway

1899-1924	Unknown

STRATFORD UPON AVON

STRATFORD-ON-AVON AND MORETON-IN-THE-MARSH TRAMWAY

4' 8" gauge; 19 route miles; opened 1826; closed c1880.

The people of Stratford upon Avon had always been able to use the river to transport goods to and from the town. However, it did not give an easy link to the manufacturing centre in the Black Country. To remedy this, the Stratford Canal was built and opened in 1816 and a more direct route was available. Local businessmen realised that a rail link between Stratford and Moreton in the Marsh would reduce the price of coal to that town by 8s a ton, a considerable sum in those days. Authority to build the line was given in the Stratford and Moreton Tramroad Act of 1821 and again in 1825. However, the latter prohibited the use of steam locomotives over six miles of the route, so horse power had to be used over the whole line. The line opened on 5 September 1826 and carried coal, other minerals and farm produce. At this stage there was no passenger service. The gauge was probably 4' 8", the standard gauge for tramroads of this time, as the track usually spread slightly and soon became 4' 8½" or even 4' 9", the width of the wheels being wide enough to accommodate this. Around 1830 the tramway carried passengers, the exact date is not known but fees were set in 1834 regarding carrying passengers and it is likely that this had been the practice for some while. Speculative illustrations show passengers being carried in open wagons. In 1845 the Oxford, Worcester and Wolverhampton Railway had authority to build their railway and an agreement was reached whereby the OWWR would lease the tramway from 1847 and operate it. The tramway proved a liability, losing money every year. So the OWWR purchased the whole line intending to introduce steam operation. The company approached I.K. Brunel for advice. His view was that the part of the line near Stratford could not be so worked unless there were radical alterations, but the rest of the line could be changed. The OWWR had opened its line as far as Moreton in 1853. The OWWR contracted a Mr Bull for him to operate a service over the tramway so that passengers could continue their journey to Stratford. He used an ordinary railway coach adapted for horse power.

In 1863 the line was acquired by the Great Western Railway who in 1886 decided to convert the southern section of the tramway into a branch line railway and this was completed on 1 July 1889. The northern section to Stratford was allowed to continue using horse traction. But this was not to last for long and the tramway to Stratford closed around 1904, with the rails being lifted in the First World War.

Stratford-on-Avon and Moreton-in-the-Marsh Tramway.

Route at largest extent

Stratford upon Avon – Moreton in the Marsh

Tramcars purchased

c1830	1 S/D	Smith & Willey Windsor Foundry Liverpool
1853	1 S/D	Unknown

Livery of Stratford-on-Avon & Moreton-in-the-Marsh Tramway

1830-1889 Unknown

Livery of Great Western Railway

1889-1904 Unknown

SUNDERLAND

SUNDERLAND TRAMWAYS COMPANY LATER SUNDERLAND CORPORATION TRAMWAYS

4' 8" gauge; 6 route miles; opened 1879; acquired by Sunderland Corporation 1900; horse operation ceased 1901.

The Sunderland Tramways Company was established in 1878 to operate horse trams in Sunderland. The necessary authority came with the Sunderland Tramways Act of 1878 allowing construction of the tramways. The first tram ran on 28 April 1879. Later that year new routes were opened and extra tramcars purchased. The corporation then stepped in and in 1880 obtained authority to build additional routes that when completed were leased to the tramway company. There was a brief experiment with steam traction in 1880 and 1881, but the reliability was poor and the locomotives were sent back to their manufacturers. In 1894 the company proposed building extensions and new routes but wanted the corporation to agree to grant them a further 21-year lease for the whole system, but the corporation was unwilling to give up their option of purchasing the tramway. Indeed in 1899 the corporation gave the necessary notice to the company for compulsory purchase in 1900 and then applied for an Act authorising them to purchase the company.

The formal purchase took place on 1 January 1900. The corporation immediately set about preparing to electrify the system. The first electric trams ran in public service on 15 August 1900. While the conversion was taking place the horse trams continued to give as much service as possible with the last horse tram operating on 19 February 1901.

Routes at largest extent

Roker – Christ Church
City Centre – Docks
City Centre – Southwick

Tramcars purchased

1879	2 D/D, 3 S/D	Unknown
c1880	28 D/D	Ashbury Railway Carriage & Iron Co. Ltd

Livery of Sunderland Tramways Company

1879-1899 Unknown

Livery of Sunderland Corporation Tramways

1900-1901 Unknown

SURREY SIDE STREET RAIL COMPANY LIMITED

See London Section

Sunderland Tramways Company.

SWANSEA

OYSTERMOUTH TRAMROAD

4' 0" gauge; 5 route miles; opened 1806; closed 1826; horse operation 1807-1827.

As described in the first section of this book the Oystermouth Tramroad has the great distinction of being the first public passenger railed transport in the world. To be absolutely accurate it was a plateway rather than a railway as the wheels of the tram and wagons ran on 'L' shaped angle iron fixed to blocks of granite with spikes. Originally a mineral tramroad the line opened in 1806 to transport goods from quarries in the Mumbles area. The reason it is in this book is that in 1807 the company agreed to allow Benjamin French to run a coach for passengers between Swansea and Oystermouth Church. Although the end of the passenger service is not known, it is believed that it continued until 1827 when a turnpike road was built along the same route. The competition from road vehicles closed the tramroad.

Oystermouth Tramroad, replica of the second tramcar.

Route at largest extent

Swansea – Oystermouth Church

Tramcars purchased

1807	1 S/D	Benjamin French
c1815	1 S/D	Benjamin French

Livery of Oystermouth Tramroad

1807-1827	Replica tramcar painted Yellow / Black

SWANSEA AND MUMBLES RAILWAY

4' 8½" gauge; 5 route miles; opened 1860; closed 1960; horse operation 1860-1877.

By 1855 the Oystermouth Tramroad was derelict when part of it was relaid with edge rails and to standard gauge to convey coal from the Rhydydefid colliery in the Clyne Valley to Swansea. Five years later a passenger service was introduced between Swansea and Black Pill. This was operated by George Morris from 27 July 1860. Later that year the line was relaid to Oystermouth and the passenger service extended the whole length of the line on 10 November. Four horse tramcars were used, two double-deck and two toastrack. On 1 July 1877 the Swansea Improvements & Tramways Company took over oper-

Swansea and Mumbles Railway.

ating the line and decided to change to steam power. The horse trams were withdrawn on 16 August 1877 and steam tramway operation began the following day. From that date the line was worked by steam traction and later electric tramcars.

Route at largest extent
Swansea – Oystermouth Church

Tramcars purchased

1860	2 D/D, 2 T/R	Unknown

Livery of Swansea and Mumbles Railway

1860-1877	Unknown

SWANSEA IMPROVEMENTS & TRAMWAYS COMPANY

4' 8½" gauge. 5 route miles; opened 1878; closed 1937; horse operation 1878-1900.

The Swansea Improvements & Tramways Company was established in 1873 and the promoters applied for an Act to authorise them to build tramways in Swansea. Interestingly the 1874 Act was called the Swansea Improvements & Tramways Act and it established the Swansea Improvements & Tramways Company that had the powers to build the tramway, the first company being there to raise the necessary capital. Construction was delayed by a variety of reasons and the tramway did not open until 12 April 1878 with ten tramcars made in America by Stephenson. The company had constant arguments with the Aberdyberthy Bridge Turnpike Road Trust. The tramway passed through the toll gate to reach the bridge. The toll payable depended on the number of passengers on each tramcar. The tramway company had two tactics to avoid paying. The first was to terminate the journey at the toll gate leaving passengers to walk the rest of the way. The other method was to stop at the toll gate, ask all the passengers to alight and walk through the gate, the tram then drove through empty, picking up all the passengers on the other side. Finally the two organisations agreed that the tramway company should pay a small sum per tramcar, though there was always antagonism between the two bodies. The company had another irritation at Prince of Wales Road where a property stood in the way of the tramway getting to the High Street. For two years the trams had to stop either side of the property and passengers walked around it to board the car waiting on the other side. Finally the issue was resolved by the owner selling the site to the tramway company. The company experimented with steam tram operation on the Morrison route but withdrew it after two years. As the time approached to the 21-year mark the corporation sought powers to purchase the system and convert it to electrical operation. On legal advice the company did the same and both proposals went to parliament. Surprisingly the Corporation's proposals were rejected and the company obtained the authority in 1897.

The British Electric Traction Company was interested in purchasing the company, but when the tramway company obtained authority to convert to electric power the shares rose almost three times their previous value, so the BET decided to gain a majority holding rather than buying it outright. Conversion started in 1898 with the first electric trams starting operation on 30 June 1900. The start of electric services coincided with all the horse tramcars being offered for sale.

Routes at largest extent
High Street – The Duke, Morriston
High Street – Cwmbwria
Gower Street – St Helens
Alexandra Road – Docks

Tramcars purchased

1878	10 S/D	John Stephenson & Co.
c1880	57	Swansea Improvements & Tramways Co.

Livery of Swansea Improvements & Tramways Company

1878-1900	Yellow / Cream

SYDENHAM DISTRICT, BELFAST TRAMWAY COMPANY
See Belfast

TRAMWAY TRUST COMPANY
See Worcester

TYNEMOUTH

TYNEMOUTH & DISTRICT TRAMWAYS LIMITED, LATER NORTH SHIELDS & DISTRICT TRAMWAYS LIMITED, LATER NORTH SHIELDS & TYNEMOUTH DISTRICT TRAMWAYS LIMITED, LATER TYNEMOUTH & DISTRICT ELECTRIC TRACTION COMPANY LIMITED

3' 0" gauge; 3 route miles; opened 1880; closed 1930; horse operation 1880-1883.

The Tynemouth & District Tramways Limited was established in 1878 and obtained authority to build tramways in the town with an Act of 1879. The tramway opened on 30 June 1880 but the company did not last long, going bankrupt in 1881. The North Shields & District Tramways Limited was founded in 1882 to purchase the tramway. They extended the line to Prudhoe Street in Tynemouth and replaced the horse trams with steam operation. So the last horse trams ran in 1883. The new company had little greater success and in 1886 it too went bankrupt. It was purchased by the North Shields & Tynemouth District Tramways Limited in 1890 who continued the steam tram operation. The tramway was then purchased by the British Electric Traction Company in 1897 and the name was changed in 1899 to the Tynemouth & District Electric Traction Company Limited in preparation for the conversion to electrical operation. At the same time the tramway was rebuilt to 3' 6" gauge.

Route at largest extent
Camden Street, North Shields – Grand Parade, Tynemouth

Tramcars purchased

1880	? D/D, ? T/R	Unknown

Livery of Tynemouth & District Tramways Limited

1880-1881	Unknown

Swansea Tramways & Improvements Company.

Wallasey Tramways Company.

Livery of North Shields & District Tramways Limited

1882-1886	Unknown

Livery of North Shields & Tynemouth District Tramways Limited

1890-1897	Unknown

Livery of Tynemouth & District Electric Traction Company Limited

1897-1930	Unknown

VALE OF CLYDE TRAMWAYS COMPANY

See Glasgow

W. HARDING & COMPANY LIMITED

See Preston

WALLASEY

WALLASEY TRAMWAYS COMPANY, LATER WALLASEY UNITED TRAMWAYS & OMNIBUS COMPANY LIMITED, LATER WALLASEY CORPORATION TRAMWAYS

4' 8½" gauge; 3 route miles; opened 1879; closed 1933; horse operation ceased 1902.

In 1870 a group of local businessmen got together to build a tramway in Wallasey and to promote the Wallasey Tramways Bill in 1870. As the 1870 Tramways Act was soon to come into being they waited until 1871 as it was far less expensive to obtain authority under the general Act than by a special individual Act. So they applied in 1871 and were duly authorised to set up the Wallasey Tramways Company and to build their tramway. However, the promoters had difficulty raising the necessary funding and the company was wound up in 1874 without building anything. The next venture came in 1876 and was led by the Busby brothers. They were successful in getting the Wallasey Tramways Act of 1878 passed with a new company, the Wallasey Tramways Company. The tramway was officially opened on 28 June 1879. A rival bus company set up services between the Docks Station and New Brighton, but the tramway company retaliated by setting up its own bus company in 1885 and running in competition. As so often happened relationships between the company and the local authorities were poor with arguments over the amount of rent demanded by the local authority and the state of the track. In 1891 the tramway and bus companies decided to formalise their situation and they merged to become the Wallasey United Tramways & Omnibus Company Limited. In the 1890s Wallasey had a major expansion and this led to the local authorities deciding to acquire and electrify the tramways. The original Act allowed the local authorities to purchase the system compulsorily after 15 years rather than the usual 21. They applied for and obtained the Wallasey Tramways and Improvements Act 1899. It was one thing having the Act it was another acquiring the tramway system. Because the council had missed purchasing the tramways after the 15-year period, the tramway company said that they had forfeited the right to purchase the line compulsorily. The council disagreed and asked the Board of Trade to appoint an arbiter. This was done and the tramway was sold to the council on 30 March 1901. Work on the conversion started later that year and the first electric tram services started on 17 March 1902 and the last horse trams ran on 19 March 1902.

Route at largest extent

Seacombe – New Brighton

Tramcars purchased

Wallasey Tramways Company

1879	7 S/D	Starbuck Car & Wagon Co.
1880	5 D/D	Ashbury Railway Carriage & Iron Co. Ltd

Wallasey United Tramways & Omnibus Company Limited

1893	7 D/D	G.F. Milnes & Co.

Wallasey Corporation Tramways

1901	3 D/D	Ex Liverpool

Livery of Wallasey Tramways Company

1879-1891	Red / Ivory

Livery of Wallasey United Tramways & Omnibus Company Limited

1891-1901	Maroon / Cream

Livery of Wallasey Corporation Tramways

1901-1902	Unknown (horse trams)

WANTAGE

WANTAGE TRAMWAY COMPANY LIMITED

4' 8½" gauge; 2 route miles; opened 1875; closed 1925; horse operation 1875-1876.

When the Great Western Railway built its line from London to Bristol (opened in 1841) it missed Wantage by 2½ miles. Naturally Wantage was keen to have a direct link with the railway and speculators in London promoted in 1866 such a line, but failed to raise sufficient funding. After the passing of the Tramways Act in 1870, local businessmen promoted a tramway, to be laid along the side of the road (making it a tramroad), from the centre of the town to Wantage Road Station on the mainline. The Wantage Tramway Company was established in 1873 and the necessary authority was gained in 1874. Construction was started the same year and the tramway was ready to open on 1 October 1875 with the passenger service starting on 11 October. The Act empowered the company to operate using horse power. A double-deck open top tramcar had been purchased from the Starbuck Car & Wagon Company. This was joined later in the year by a single-deck tramcar from the same manufacturer. However, later that year the company obtained the steam tramcar made by John Grantham for trials. After initial problems and many adjustments, the company was impressed and so sought powers to operate the tramway using steam power. This was

Warrenpoint & Rostrevor Tramways Company.

granted in 1876 and the Grantham tramcar was put into regular public service from 1 August 1876 making it the first tramway in the British Isles to use steam traction. The horse service was removed once the steam tramcar was used.

Route at largest extent
Market Place, Wantage – Wantage Road Station

Tramcars purchased

1875	1 D/D, 1 S/D	Starbuck Car & Wagon Co.

Livery of Wantage Tramway Company Limited

1875-1876	Unknown

WARRENPOINT

WARRENPOINT & ROSTREVOR TRAMWAYS COMPANY

3' 0" gauge; 3 route miles; opened 1877; closed 1915.

The Newry, Warrenpoint and Rostrevor Railway opened in 1849 linking Newry with Warrenpoint, but the railway never did get extended to Rostrevor. The railway was linked to the main Belfast to Dublin line in 1854 giving a boost to Warrenpoint. The people of Rostrevor wanted to take advantage of the railway and for many years sought to have the railway extended, but without any success. Later local entrepreneurs promoted the Warrenpoint & Rostrevor Tramways Company that obtained authority to build the tramway which opened in July 1877. The gauge is uncertain, sources give both 3' 0" or 2' 10" as the gauge. The line ran steadily mainly providing service to holiday makers during the summer. Originally the system had seven tramcars and as the demand on the tramway grew more cars were added. Possibly the most unusual was the "Band-car" a large open car used to carry military and other bands to the skating rink at Rostrevor where they would entertain the crowds. The line looked as if it would continue for many years, but in February 1915 the town suffered severe gales that damaged the tramway track. Competition from motor buses meant that it was not financially viable to reconstruct the tramway and so the system was closed.

Route at largest extent
Warrenpoint – The Quay, Rostrevor

Tramcars purchased

1877	3 S/D, 4 T/R	Unknown
?	5 T/R	Unknown
?	1 Open	Unknown the "Band-car"

Livery of Warrenpoint & Rostrevor Tramways Company

1877-1915	Yellow / White
1877-1915	Red / White
1877-1915	Blue / White

WEST BROMWICH

BIRMINGHAM & MIDLAND TRAMWAYS LIMITED, LATER BRITISH ELECTRIC TRACTION COMPANY

3' 6" gauge; 12 route miles (3 miles under horse operation); opened 1883; horse operation 1893-1903.

The Birmingham & Midland Tramways Limited was formed to take over the powers given to the Birmingham and Western Districts Tramways Company Limited, the company that built the tramways under the Birmingham & Midland Tramways Act.

B. Crowther (Birmingham & Midland Tramways Limited).

The system was opened on 6 July 1885 and was entirely steam operated. It linked Birmingham with the Black Country. Two short branches were found to be unprofitable and so they were closed in 1893 and arrangements were made with a Mr B. Crowther for him to run the service using horse trams. The new services started on 20 May 1893. The horse trams continued to operate, even though the company had been taken over by British Electric Traction Company Limited in 1900. The BET had planes to electrify the system and work on this progressed. The horse trams ceased running on 3 November 1903 when the electric tramcars took over the lines.

Routes at largest extent

West Bromwich – Spon Lane,West Smethwick
West Bromwich – Bromford Lane, Oldbury

Tramcars purchased

1893	2 D/D	B. Crowther
1895	2 D/D	Metropolitan Railway Carriage & Wagon Co.

Livery of Birmingham & Midland Tramways Limited

1885-1890	Dark Green / Cream
1890-1900	All Dark Green
1890-1900	Dark Green / Cream
1900-1903	Munich Lake (Crimson)

WEST END TRAMWAY
See Pwllheli

WEST METROPOLITAN TRAMWAYS COMPANY LIMITED
See London Section

WESTMINSTER STREET RAIL COMPANY LIMITED
See London Section

WIGAN

WIGAN TRAMWAYS COMPANY LIMITED

3' 6" gauge; 5 route miles; opened 1880; acquired by Wigan Corporation 1902; horse operation 1880-1885.

The first proposals for a tramway in Wigan came from a group led by the Liverpool entrepreneur William Busby (one of the Busby brothers) who put up the idea in 1878. Despite having a number of councillors in the group, the group found themselves having long and protracted discussions with the corporation. Finally the group obtained authority to build on 11 August 1879. With the authority agreed, the group established the Wigan Tramways Company Limited on 13 September 1879. The necessary funding was gathered and construction began with the first services starting on 31 July 1880. It was soon realised that the route was too hilly for horse operation and an alternative was sought. On 5 November 1881 experiments with a steam tram and trailer took place. The company considered them to be successful and from February 1882 steam traction gradually took over the horse operation, though a few horses were kept to cover when a steam tram locomotive was being repaired or extra trams were required.

On 29 December 1883 a runaway tram engine crashed into the rear of the preceding tram and trailer, killing the coroner for West Derby. This accident led to the steam trams being withdrawn and horse trams were reinstated. However, the steep hill still proved difficult and steam trams were brought back in 1884, though horses were kept in reserve for emergencies. The company was having financial difficulties and in 1885 the remaining horses were sold, thus ending horse tramway operation in Wigan.

Routes at largest extent

Market Place – Black Bull, Pemberton
King Street – Market Street, Hindley

Tramcars purchased

1880	8 D/D	Ashbury Railway Carriage & Iron Co. Ltd

Livery of Wigan Tramways Company Limited

1880-1885	Dark Red / Cream

WIMBLEDON COMMON TRAMWAY
See London Section

WIRRAL TRAMWAY COMPANY
See Birkenhead

Wigan Tramways Company Limited.

Wolverhampton Tramways Company.

WOLVERHAMPTON

WOLVERHAMPTON TRAMWAYS COMPANY LATER WOLVERHAMPTON CORPORATION TRAMWAYS

4' 8½" gauge. 10 route miles; opened 1878; acquired by Wolverhampton Corporation 1900; horse operation ceased 1903.

In 1876 the corporation received a letter from a group of "influential gentlemen" proposing the building of a tramway in the town. This led to the incorporation of the Wolverhampton Tramways Company on 14 December 1876 and obtaining authority to build the tramway on 23 July 1877. The Act allowed Wolverhampton Corporation to purchase the tramway compulsorily at any time within the first 10 years after opening and then after 21 years. The Act also stipulated that traction could only be by horse power. The tramway was to be standard gauge (4' 8½") and not the narrow gauge adopted by the other Black Country tramways. Construction of the tramway started soon after and the first services ran on 30 April 1878. In 1880 the company applied for authority to run steam tram locomotives and were successful. Steam operation began on 17 May 1881. Despite being popular with the local people it was not well received by the corporation and they refused to allow any further operation. So the steam locomotive had to be withdrawn in September and the system ran only on horse power from then onwards. The corporation did not exercise its compulsory purchase option during the first ten years.

The next opportunity came up after another eleven years and the corporation now felt it was time for them to take over the tramway. The usual arguments took place over the purchase price, eventually settled by an arbitrator. The transfer date was 1 May 1900. The corporation then operated the horse tramways within its boundary. Plans for electrification were drawn up, the corporation having decided on the Lorain stud contact system and a change of gauge to 3' 6". Although stud contact operation on other systems proved difficult and were swiftly removed, the Wolverhampton system successfully ran on the stud for many years. As the electrification proceeded so horse trams were removed from service, the last horse-drawn tramcar ran in 1903.

Routes at largest extent

Queen Square – Newbridge
Queen Street – Willenhall
Queen Street – Moxley

Tramcars purchased

Wolverhampton Tramways Company

1878	4 S/D	John Stephenson Co. Ltd
1878	4 D/D	Falcon Engine & Car Works Ltd
c1880	12 D/D	Falcon Engine & Car Works Ltd
1892	4 D/D	Falcon Engine & Car Works Ltd
1895	1 D/D	G.F. Milnes & Co.

Wolverhampton Corporation Tramways

1902	3 D/D	Ex North Metropolitan Tramways
1902	? D/D	Ex Liverpool Tramways

Livery of Wolverhampton Tramways Company

1878-1900	Nut Brown / White

Livery of Wolverhampton Corporation Tramways

1900-1903	Nut Brown / White
1900-1903	Yellow / White (ex-North Metropolitan Tramways Co. Limited)
1901-1903	Maroon / Cream (ex-Liverpool)

WOOLWICH & SOUTH EAST LONDON TRAMWAYS COMPANY LIMITED

See London Section

WOOLWICH SMALL ARMS EXPERIMENTAL RANGE TRAMWAY

See London Section

WORCESTER

TRAMWAY TRUST COMPANY, LATER CITY OF WORCESTER TRAMWAYS COMPANY LIMITED, LATER PRITCHARD GREEN & COMPANY, LATER WORCESTER TRAMWAYS LIMITED, LATER WORCESTER ELECTRIC TRACTION COMPANY LIMITED

3' 0" gauge; 3 route miles; opened 1884; closed 1928; horse operation ceased 1903.

Worcester Tramways Limited.

In 1879 a number of schemes to build tramways in the city were put before the council and they chose to support the one promoted by the Tramway Trust Company. Authority was obtained and the first trams started running on 18th February 1884 on the unusual gauge of 3' 0". The venture was a financial failure and the company soon went into liquidation; it continued operating in this state until being sold by the liquidator in 1889 to the City of Worcester Tramways Company Limited which unfortunately fared little better and in 1892 it too went into liquidation. In the following year the system was purchased by Pritchard Green & Company with the intention of selling it on, which it did in 1894 to Worcester Tramways Limited. The new company appointed Richard Fairbairn as manager and he introduced horse bus services to the surrounding countryside. In 1897 the company proposed to the corporation that the system be extended and electrified. The corporation considered the situation and proposed to purchase the system and electrify and operate it themselves. However, in 1899 the British Electric Traction Company came on the scene and proposed electrifying and extending the system. The corporation agreed and BET purchased the horse tram company. Work started on the conversion in 1901 and with the gauge conversion was described as the siege of Worcester. It was not possible to run horse trams so replacement horse buses ran the services. The last horse trams ran on 28 June 1903.

Routes at largest extent

The Cross – Portobello Inn, Bransford Road
The Cross – Vine Inn, Ombersley Road
St Nicholas Street – Shrub Hill Station

Tramcars purchased

Tramway Trust Company

1884	6 D/D	Falcon Engine & Car Works Ltd

Worcester Tramways Limited

1900	2 D/D, 2 S/D	Falcon Engine & Car Works Ltd
1901	2 D/D	Unknown

Livery of Tramway Trust Company
1884-1889 Unknown

Livery of City of Worcester Tramways Company Limited
1889-1893 Unknown

Livery of Pritchard Green & Company
1893-1894 Unknown

Livery of Worcester Tramways Limited
1893-1903 Unknown

WREXHAM

WREXHAM DISTRICT TRAMWAYS COMPANY, LATER WREXHAM TRAMWAYS LIMITED, LATER WREXHAM & DISTRICT ELECTRIC TRACTION COMPANY

3' 0" gauge; 3 route miles; opened 1876; closed 1927; horse operation ceased 1901.

Wrexham Tramways Limited.

The Wrexham District Tramways Company was formed in 1874 and obtained permission to build tramways in the town. Gathering funding was very slow and so work on laying tracks took time and the first tram did not run until 1 November 1876. As the town was hilly the company had thoughts of using steam power, but this was frowned on by the Board of Trade; nothing more came of it and the two horse cars continued to give service. The company had been given authority to build over six miles of tramway but because of lack of funding had only constructed three miles. So in 1878 it changed its name to Wrexham Tramways Limited, tacitly admitting that the routes would stay within the town. In 1884 a local businessman, Fred Jones, rented the line for £100 a year and set about building himself an extra tramcar. He appears to have copied tram number 2 but made his new car slightly larger. Unfortunately he forgot to check the height of the archway leading out from his workshop and was forced to remove the upper deck to get the tram out and had to re-assemble it in the road. Operation continued until 1900 when the company was acquired by the British Electric Traction Company who registered the name as Wrexham & District Electric Traction Company Limited. The BET proposed converting the system to electric operation and change the gauge to 3' 6". They closed the horse tram service on 26 April 1901 and a replacement horse bus service was implemented for the next two years until the electric tramway opened.

Route at largest extent
New Inn, Johnstown – Red Lion Inn, Wrexham

Tramcars purchased
Wrexham District Tramways Company

1876	1 D/D, 1 T/R	Starbuck Car & Wagon Co.

Wrexham Tramways Limited

1884	1 D/D	Frederick Jones, Wrexham

Livery of Wrexham District Tramways Company
1876-1878 Dark Brown / Cream
Livery of Wrexham Tramways Limited
1878-1901 Dark Brown / Cream

YARMOUTH & GORLESTON TRAMWAYS
See Great Yarmouth

YORK

YORK TRAMWAYS COMPANY, LATER CITY OF YORK TRAMWAYS COMPANY LIMITED, LATER YORK CORPORATION TRAMWAYS

4' 0" gauge; 3 route miles; opened 1880; acquired by York Corporation 1909; horse operation ceased 1909.

A proposal to build tramways in York came in 1878 and the Corporation gave their assent so an application for authorisation was sought and gained by Act in 1879 that also established the York Tramways Company. Construction of the line started the next year and the first tram service ran on 26 October 1880. The company soon decided that they would be able to provide a better service using steam traction. They applied to the corporation for permission to carry out trials and this was agreed. Two such vehicles were tried, the first having had too many problems. The trial was to last six months but the steam tramcars disappeared before the end of the period and nothing is known about what happened to them and the company carried on using horse power. In 1885 the Imperial Tramways Group formed the City of York Tramways Company Limited to purchase the York Tramways Company which it did on 1 January 1886. The Corporation approached the company in 1899 with a proposal to purchase the system. However, when the corporation sounded the views of the townspeople they found that most were against the corporation running the tramway. The situation changed a few years later when the condition of the tramways had deteriorated and the corporation decided to purchase the system. The purchase took place on 27 February 1909 and the Corporation started running the horse tramway while conversion to electric power, with a change of gauge to 3' 6", took place. The last horse trams ran on until later that year when they had to be withdrawn to allow the conversion to take place.

Route at largest extent
Knavesmire – Fulford Village

Tramcars purchased
York Tramways Company

1880	3 S/D	Starbuck Car & Wagon Co.
1881	3 S/D, 2 T/R	Starbuck Car & Wagon Co.
1882	2 S/D	Starbuck Car & Wagon Co.

City of York Tramways Company Limited

1905	5 D/D	Second-hand

Livery of York Tramways Company
1880-1886 Chocolate / White
Livery of City of York Tramways Company Limited
1886-1909 Chocolate / White

City of York Tramways Company Limited.

Section 4

THE SEARCH FOR BETTER MOTIVE POWER

THE PROBLEM

As has been detailed previously the heaviest cost on any horse tramway system were the horses. Their working time was restricted, so each two horse tramcar required ten horses to keep it operating. Each horse required stabling, fodder, stable hands and veterinary care. They had to be cared for when they were ill and an epidemic in the stable could lay low the majority of the horses. So the search for an alternative power source was a preoccupation of not only tramway operators, but also every person who fancied themselves as inventors. The Victorian age was a time of invention and innovation and the period from around 1870 to 1900 was a fascinating time with all kinds of sensible and improbable ideas of improving tramway propulsion being promoted. As all were novel, the tramway operators had the unenviable task of working out which would be reliable and which of those would be the most cost effective. This was made more difficult by inventors making claims that their inventions would reduce costs at a stroke and putting forward optimistic, if not fictional, cost benefit calculations. Though in more recent times I can recall people being promised that electricity from nuclear power would be so cheap it would not be worth putting in meters in homes.

Such was the pressure to find an alternative to horse power for tramways that in 1872 the Society of Arts (the organisation responsible for the Great Exhibition of 1851) offered the Howard Medal for the design of a traction engine that could replace horse power on tramways. The specification included the requirement that the steam engine had to be part of a carriage that carried passengers. The winner was John Grantham for a steam carriage used on the Wantage tramway. Unfortunately John Grantham died in 1874, during trials of his engine at Wantage, and the medal was awarded posthumously in 1875.

The search for a better power source was not purely seeking a cheaper form. Indeed often the alternative was more costly per car mile to run. The equation for the operators was a complex balance of cost versus income. The horse tramcar had a defined limit on the number of passengers that could be carried in each tramcar. The maximum for a system that was generally level with no steep hills was 20 passengers in the saloon and 22 on the upper deck, giving a total of 42 passengers. A steam trailer could carry around 60 seated passengers, though the restrictions on the use of steam power meant that the speed of the journey was not much faster than the horse tramcar. However, the comfort level improved as steam trailers were given enclosed upper saloons. So in inclement weather passengers remained dry no matter which part of the tramcar they rode on. With the introduction of electric traction travel on trams became far more popular. The tramcars were clean, the routes were extended so that they were able to serve a greater area and the journey time was reduced. It is hard for us, from our perspective, to understand what an impact these vehicles had on the general population. Passenger transport up to that point had almost always consisted of a power source hauling a trailer, whether it be a horse tramcar, horse omnibus, horse and cart or steam tramcar. Then the electric tramway came along, with tramcars much larger than any horse-drawn vehicle, moving almost silently with no obvious engine or motors. Even more astonishing was the fact that they would

The New Orleans City Railroad experimented with this man powered tramcar, without success.

The London Tramways Company used mules in order to keep the trams running. This photograph shows three mules replacing two horses.

climb steep hills without needing additional help, stopping and starting with no more problems than on level ground. The first electric tramcars carried around 60 seated passengers and later this increased to around 80 (the largest capacity tramcar in Blackpool today has seats for 98 passengers). Also the cost per car mile was generally lower than either horse or steam. Operators were able to reduce fares and see an increased income as more people used the tramcars.

This period of change and progress was not welcomed by everyone. The tramway companies were often at the receiving end of complaints, some directly to them, others to council officers. Here the public was often aided by the Board of Trade regulations. The By-Laws stated that *"No steam or smoke shall be emitted from the engines, and no hot air shall issue in a way to annoy passengers."* For a steam tram locomotive this requirement was difficult. The engine had to consume its own smoke, which meant burning expensive high grade coal. The steam had to be removed by passing the exhaust gases through condensing pipes, though the water recaptured could be returned to the water tank. On at least one occasion a steam tram locomotive burst a steam pipe. The driver was forced to wait for engineers from the depot to bring another engine to tow him back. He then found he was prosecuted for emitting steam contrary to the By-Laws. His plea of being unable to do anything about it because a pipe had burst was not accepted by the judge. The decision was that the By-Laws banned any emission of steam no matter what the circumstances and the unfortunate driver found himself having to pay a fine. Local hackney cab and omnibus operators also saw the new tramcars as a threat to their trade. It was not unknown for the rails on hills to have soft soap rubbed over the running surface, to encourage the steam locomotives to slip. This was particularly popular when the Board of Trade were present to inspect the new form of power. Stones would also be wedged in the groove of the rails, again to interrupt the passage of the cars.

However the pressure on tramway operators to reduce costs was great. As has been described in the previous chapter many systems ran on a hand to mouth basis, gave little or no return to their shareholders and had no funds to repair or replace worn out track. In such circumstances they were willing to consider any alternative to the horse. So, many trials were carried out all over the country, the operators being cautious enough to ensure that the trials were at the cost of the particular inventor and no purchase was required unless the operators were fully satisfied.

ALTERNATIVE ANIMALS

The 1870 Tramways Act gave authority for authorised tramways to use animal power, so one possibility was to replace the horse with a cheaper source of power. In fact the options were very limited. Herne Bay and Southend piers and the Haslar Naval Hospital used tram cars pushed by manpower. They all had common factors, the tramway was very short, on the flat and had small tramcars. Northampton Street Tramways experimented in 1883 with a manual power engine. This unique locomotive was invented by John William Graham from Lincoln and made locally in Northampton. It appears to have been a four-wheel cycle type of machine with a drive having two gears. The driver had to operate foot treadles to drive the machine with the tramcar hooked on the back. The two gears were called 'power', presumably a low gearing to start off and 'speed' an optimistic title for a higher gear. There is no record of how the machine and the driver faired during the experiments and the machine disappeared without trace. The New Orleans City Railroad experimented with a tramcar powered by the driver. A handwheel on the driver's platform was turned and this drove two long beams on the roof of the tramcar. These in turn powered a wheel on which was set spokes with blocks of wood on the ends. These turned and thrust against the ground, pushing the tramcar along. The vehicle never progressed beyond initial testing.

For practical purposes the only replacement for the horse was either buffalo, oxen or mules. There were experiments with the

A contemporary drawing of the Herne Bay Pier tramway using sail power.

Some light railways also used sail power. Here the Spurn and Kilnsea Railway uses wagon fitted with a sail. No doubt the proximity of the sea had an influence on making the sail power work.

Lytham St Annes used gas tramcars as an alternative to horse power.

former on lines with steep hills as the buffalos and oxen could haul greater loads than horses, but they were very slow and their feet were not suited to the hard road surface. It was soon realised that there was no real suitable alternative to the horse. Mules were not slow, but they were extremely difficult to control. Drivers had great problems with them and if they refused to haul a tramcar there was little the driver could do to persuade them. Also they had no value when they reached the end of their tram hauling days. The only real use of mules came when horses were very scarce, such as during epidemics or at wartime when the War Department had requisitioned fit horses.

SAILING ON RAILS

The pier trams at Herne Bay and Southend used their maritime connections to use wind power to move tramcars. On each a flat wagon was fitted with a mast and a simple sail attached. When the wind was in the right direction the wagon would move up and down the pier using wind power. In 1807 the Mumbles Railway used a sail-powered wagon; whether this was an authorised experiment or a bit of fun by staff is not clear, but it was reported as having run the full length of the tramway. A similar wagon was used on the Festiniog Railway in the late 1800s and a replica wagon has recently been built and run along the Cob. It was able to move at a speed in excess of 20mph relying entirely on the wind. However as a means of powering town street transport the wind was not a viable possibility.

CLOCKWORK

A Belgian inventor, Edward Henry Leveaux, patented a clockwork tramcar in 1873. The following year an experimental tramcar locomotive was built to his design by Thomas Middleton & Co. of Loman Street, Southwark, London and tested in 1875 at the Metropolitan District Railway Lillie Bridge Depot. It was able to haul a five-ton tramcar at 7mph for a distance of half a mile before needing winding up. The winding was accomplished using a stationary steam engine to wind up the springs by means of an extending shaft from the engine. The inventor took out British and American patents for his ideas on clockwork trams. Similar proposals were made in America with George Jiencke patenting a clockwork tramcar in 1883. The patent was taken up by the American Spring Car Motor Company of Camden, New Jersey. However, nothing came of either of these ventures and Britain and America never saw clockwork trams in regular service on their streets.

INTERNAL COMBUSTION ENGINES

These days the internal combustion engine would seem to have been a practical alternative. However the internal combustion engine was not invented until 1876 by Nikolaus August Otto (1832-1891), using a mixture of town gas and air as the fuel. The first gas tramcar appears to be a tram locomotive designed by Messrs Grose, L. Moore and O. Mobbs in 1882 and built by Mobb's Vulcan Ironworks, Northampton. This was given trials on the Northampton horse tramway and used town gas to power an Otto engine. It is possible that this locomotive was the first example of the internal combustion engine being used for road transport in Britain. As with a new type of power the machine needed modifications and even so it is likely that it was soon withdrawn as no further record exists of its subsequent history.

The Connelly Oil Motor was an early form of internal combustion engine. Experiments were undertaken in Deptford and Croydon.

The Morecambe Tramways Company used four petrol tramcars.

The gas tramcar was also tried in Switzerland and Germany with cars by Messrs Guilliéron and Amrein being used in Neuchâtel and those by Luhrig of Dresden operating on the Dessau tramway. Rights to the latter were obtained by the Electric Traction Syndicate Limited when the original inventor died. The Electric Traction Syndicate Limited persuaded the Croydon Tramways Company to undertake trials with a tramcar in 1893. The tramcar was powered by ordinary town gas that was pumped under pressure into reservoirs and used to power a small two cylinder internal combustion Otto engine. Though improve-

An experimental petrol tramcar was used on the Stirling and Bridge of Allan tramway.

The petrol railcar built by John B. Duff for the Murcar Links Golf Club, running on the Strabathie and Blackdog Light Railway.

The LCC used a few petrol tramcars to save the cost of laying conduit on a lightly used route.

ments were made to the tramcar, the corporation were unhappy at experiments being held on their streets and after around a year the tram was removed.

The gas tram next surfaced when the British Gas Traction Company, formed in 1896 to exploit the Luhrig gas trams, was given a seven-year lease to operate the Lytham St Annes tramway. They proposed using the Luhrig gas tramcar and operation with two tramcars began in July 1896. The British Gas Traction Company sought expansion and introduced gas trams to Trafford Park in July 1897 and Neath in August 1899. However, the Lytham service was in severe financial difficulties and the company had to cease their operations there in 1898 and then went bankrupt in November 1899. The Lytham system was taken on by a new company that purchased the British Gas Traction Company in order to control all aspects of the gas trams. The system required more gas trams than were available so they had to introduce horse trams as well and finally electrified the system in 1903 after the depot had been blown down in a gale. The Trafford Park tramway was taken on by the Trafford Park Estate and continued operation finally withdrawing the gas trams in 1908. In Neath the Provincial Gas Traction Co. Ltd took over the tramway and operated the gas trams until 1916 when it too went bankrupt. Neath Corporation took over the operation of the tramway but the system was in a bad condition and as they had no wish to electrify it the tramway closed in August 1920. So while gas trams did have a long life, they were restricted to just a few systems and never caught on for more general use.

The use of the petrol internal combustion engine as a power source for tramways first came in 1892 with the trials of the Connelly oil motor. The motor was rather like a small steam 'dummy' that hauled a passenger carrying trailer (a horse tramcar). The motor had a primitive type of internal combustion engine using mineral oil as a fuel that had to be heated using the exhaust gases in order for it to fire in the cylinders and requiring a flywheel to keep it moving. It was first tried on the London Deptford and Greenwich Tramway when the Board of Trade gave permission for trials to take place for a total of 18 months. It appears that the motor did perform running over 5,000 miles and carrying in excess of 40,000 passengers. But there was no further application for the trial and the motor was removed. It made an appearance in Croydon in 1893 where after a demonstration it was allowed to operate in service. However little else is known and the oil motor disappeared without any further record.

Internal combustion did not make another appearance until 1904, by which time technology had developed considerably and the chosen fuel was petrol. The Scottish Motor Engineering Company Ltd of Edinburgh built an experimental petrol tramcar and offered it to the Perth tramways and the Leith tramways. Both systems were at the stage where the horse tramway was old and outdated, but conversion to electric operation would be extremely costly. The councils dithered and the Scottish motor company offered a cheap way of modernising their tramways. As it was Leith decided to dig into the ratepayer's pockets and electrify their system. Perth decided to try out the petrol tramcar. To begin with the petrol engine was found to be underpowered and it

One of the petrol electric tramcars used on the Dublin & Blessington tramway.

was replaced by a larger engine and this was satisfactory. However, although the tramcar performed well it was too heavy and too large for the old track. To compound the problems the track had been forced out of gauge by the action of a road roller. Then the engine was found to need frequent maintenance by expert engineers and the trial ended with the tramcar being sent back to the manufacturer.

An early example of a petrol tramcar was on the unusual Strabathie and Blackdog Light Railway when, in 1910, the Murcar Links Golf Club used a John B. Duff petrol railcar to carry members to and from the club. The car gave good service and in 1932 a Wickham petrol railcar joined it. Both cars worked on until 1950 when the tramway service to the club ceased and the two railcars scrapped.

The first street tramway to use the petrol tramcar in regular service was the Morecambe tramway in 1914. This short and level tramway came about when the Morecambe Corporation purchased part of the Morecambe Tramways Co. system compulsorily and decided to operate it themselves. The Morecambe Tramways Co. was left with just a mile of route that proved very expensive to run using horses. So in 1912 they purchased four single-deck petrol tramcars, three enclosed and one open. On the lightly trafficked line they proved their worth and continued to give service to 1924.

Another petrol tramcar was employed on the Stirling & Bridge of Allan horse tramway. In an attempt to reduce costs the company had one of its horse trams fitted with a petrol engine by the Lanarkshire Motor Company in 1913. On return it entered service and appeared to be successful, if rather noisier than the horse trams. It is possible that more conversions might have taken place but for proposals for conversion to electric operation that fell through at the start of World War One. By 1920 buses were too much competition for the tramway and it closed.

In 1912 the LCC was pondering what to do with a short line between West India Docks and South Hackney. It was horse worked but needed to be electrified, but the local authority refused to allow overhead wires to be erected. The LCC felt that the cost of conduit track was too high for a lightly used route. So an alternative was sought and the LCC experimented in 1913 with a petrol-electric tramcar. Tilling-Stevens had been successful with petrol-electric buses and it was decided to use the same technology on these trams. The experimental tramcar started its trials and a second tramcar joined it. But the LCC was dissatisfied and withdrew both cars; the third car ordered was never used for the trials. Stored for a while, the trams were then allocated to Marius Road Depot. They had their bodies removed and couplings attached and they became depot shunters, moving trailer cars around the depot – a job they did until the use of trailer cars ceased.

The next system to use petrol-electric tramcars was Hastings. They had opened a seafront line using the Dolter stud contact system, as the corporation had refused permission to erect overhead. This proved to be the wrong solution, constantly breaking down and being extremely costly. The situation got so bad the tramway staff went on strike in 1911 insisting that the Dolter studs be removed. The final blow came from the Board of Trade who ordered the removal of the studs. The corporation still refused to allow overhead and having heard of the petrol-electric trams being tried by the LCC they converted some of their trams with this power source and they went into service in 1914. The new power source proved problematic, the tramcars being low powered, unreliable, noisy and smelling of exhaust fumes. As only part of the system was precluded from using the overhead the trams would switch to the overhead when it left the overhead free area. Even so the public protested about the poor service and the corporation had to relent and finally in 1920 they allowed overhead wires to be put up. The new overhead route opened in 1921 and the petrol-electric units removed from those trams that were fitted with it.

A further experiment was carried out with petrol-electric power when the Dublin & Blessington tramway sought to save

A rare photograph of a driver using a starting handle on a tramcar.

costs against their steam operation. Two large double-deck cars were ordered from Hurst Nelson with Westinghouse electrical equipment. The trams had very low gears to allow them to climb the steep hills on the line. This meant that they were very slow. When delivered in 1915 the engines were requisitioned for use in submarines and the company had to argue forcibly to get replacements. The tramcars proved to be underpowered for the heavy gradients they faced and far more expensive than promised, costing 4d a mile versus the predicted ⅛d per mile. The tramcars were relegated to a siding and saw little further service.

The final example of internal combustion being used in passenger service is the Joyce Green hospital complex. Here horse tramcars were used to transport patients from the jetty on the River Thames to the various hospitals and these continued until 1925 when experiments with hauling the trams using petrol ambulances proved successful. So the horses were withdrawn and the petrol engine became dominant. There was one further similar example but not in public service. In the Charlton Depot of London Transport there was no conduit or overhead wire. So to shunt tramcars around the depot area petrol tractors were used to push and pull the cars.

COMPRESSED AIR

To solve the problems of emitting no smoke or steam some inventors turned to using compressed air. This is similar to steam in that cylinders are used to power the tramcar. However instead of the pressure of a steam boiler, the tram used a cylinder of compressed air that was used to propel the car. However it does mean that highly pressurised air had to be compressed into the cylinder and when the air pressure in the cylinder fell, so did the performance of the tramcar. The up side was that there was no smoke and the only discharge from the tramcar was ordinary air. The name we hear the most in connection with compressed air trams is Frenchman Louis Mékarski, who in 1872 and 1873 took out patents for his system with trials in France in 1875. In the same year William Dundas Scott-Moncrieff built a compressed

A contemporary drawing of the experimental Beaumont compressed air locomotive trialled in Leyton.

A drawing giving a close view of the Mékarski compressed air system, here on a Paris tramcar.

The Mékarski compressed air tramcar in Paris, hauling a trailer.

air tramcar and tested it on the Vale of Clyde steam tramway. The tramcar had six reservoirs to hold the compressed air, however it could only manage three miles between recharging. Trials continued on occasions to 1877, by which time the experimental nature of the tramcar was demonstrated in the expense of running it due to its poor reliability. On withdrawal it was replaced with steam tram locomotives.

The Beaumont Compressed Air Locomotive Company built a tram locomotive and trailer using the patent compressed air system designed by Colonel F.E.B. Beaumont. Trials took place on the North Metropolitan Tramways Company rails between Stratford and Leytonstone. The first runs took place on 14 August 1881. The locomotive had an air reservoir pressurised to 1,000 lb per sq.in. The air was used to power a small piston engine that drove the wheels through gearing. It was effectively a steam engine driven by compressed air. The air was pressurised using a stationary compressor and fed to the locomotive through a pipe and it took fifteen minutes to refill the tank. The tank was sufficient for the 44-minute five-mile return trip. How long the trials lasted is not known and probably the usual teething problems caused the locomotive and trailer to be removed from the line. Colonel Beaumont used his compressed air locomotives in the construction of tunnels where the method of power was a distinct advantage. In 1883 he was working on the Mersey tunnel and asked the Liverpool tramways if he could trial his compressed air tram locomotive. It worked successfully, however the cost of running the locomotive was not sufficiently lower than the horse tramcars. So the project was halted and the tram locomotive removed.

The Chester tramway used a Hughes and Lancaster compressed air tramcar without success.

Compressed air was also used by Mékarski and two of his locomotives (built by the Compressed Air Engine Co. of London) were given trials on the Wantage tramway in 1880. The system required the building of a stationary engine to pressurise the air for refilling the locomotive reservoir. Though the trials were proclaimed a success it was found that the stationary engine used 24cwt of coal compared to 5cwt used by the line's steam locomotives and the compressed air locomotives were removed from Wantage. The next appearance of the Mékarski tramcar was on the Caledonian Road, London in 1883, 1885 and 1888 for four months. Mékarski had more success in Paris where 208 of his tramcars were used, some lasting to 1914. The system used a technique where the air was heated by steam before it entered the cylinders making some believe they were steam trams. In 1886 in Chester a horse tramcar (number 9) was loaned to the Hughes & Lancaster Engineering Company who fitted a compressed air engine. This had compressed air reservoirs under the tramcar that operated a four cylinder engine. The tramcar was beset with problems, it being said that it lost more air through leakage than it used in the engine. To keep the air pressure up there were supply points along the route. These would automatically connect with the tramcar and recharge the reservoirs in ten seconds. The leakage issue proved insurmountable and even after the drastic move of removing the upper deck to make it lighter, the tramcar was not a rival to the horse trams and it eventually disappeared from the system.

CABLE

Hauling tramcars by cable was an alternative. The cable haulage of railed transport has a long history going back to the mineral lines where the only way to move heavy wagons up or down inclines was to use a cable where a stationary steam engine could haul up or lower down rakes of wagons. The use of cable for trams came into eminence when San Francisco built its famous cable car tramway system that opened in 1873. The system consists of a continuous cable running in a channel in the road. There is a gripper that is fixed to the tramcar and that protrudes down through a slot in the road to the cable. To move the driver operates a lever that brings together two grips either side of the cable. As they tighten the tramcar accelerates until it reaches the speed of the cable. To stop, the gripper is released and the driver uses the brake to stop the tramcar. This is a simplistic explanation as it needs highly complex engineering to ensure it operates properly.

There were two lines in London using the same technology to overcome hills that were too steep for horse traction. The Highgate Hill Cable Tramway opened in 1884 and was the first cable operated tramway in Europe. The second line was the London Tramways cable line on Brixton Hill that opened in 1892, where initially tractor cars (or dummies) would take horse trams up and down the hill. Later horse-drawn tramcars were fitted with gripper gear to enable them to be pulled up the hill without the need for a tractor car. Both London lines were removed when electric operation was introduced.

The largest network of cable tramways was found in Edinburgh. Horse trams were having difficulty with the steep hills in the city and the Edinburgh Northern Tramways eventually persuaded the corporation to allow them to build a cable tramway. This opened in 1888 and was found to be far less

The Highgate Hill cable tramway.

The whole of the Constitution Hill tramway funicular.

London had another cable tramway on the Brixton Hill route.

The Great Orme used the funicular on its cable tramway. (Author)

expensive to operate than the horse tramways. When the corporation purchased the horse lines in the city compulsorily they decided to convert them to cable operation. These ran until 1922 when the corporation realised that the system was very out of date and the tramways were converted to electric operation. There was a smaller line in Birmingham, which again was replaced by electric power. The two small lines in Matlock (1893-1927) and Douglas, Isle of Man (1896-1929), closed as motor bus technology improved and buses had the power to drive easily up the hills.

Cable power had a major difficulty in that if there was a breakdown in the cable system or the power house, then the whole of that line was affected. The public became disenchanted with the frequent breakdowns that were associated with the technology of the period. With the horse trams if a horse became unable to haul a tramcar it was soon replaced by another. The cable system could be out of action for hours and often days.

FUNICULARS

The difference between cable tramways and funiculars is that the latter have just two tramcars, one fixed at each end of the cable. As one tram goes up the hill the other goes down. There were two funiculars that operated in the street, the Swansea

Matlock also had a cable tramway.

In America one inventor came up with this steam horse locomotive, without success.

Constitution Hill Incline Tramway Company that was less than ¼-mile long, all in the street, and the Great Orme Tramway just over 1-mile long with some street running. The former opened in 1898 and closed in 1901, while the latter opened in 1902 and is still running.

AMMONIA GAS ENGINE

Dr Emile Lamm (from New Orleans) used the chemical properties of sal ammoniac (ammonium chloride) to power a passenger carrying tramcar in 1871. When sal ammoniac is heated in the presence of hydrate of lime (caustic lime) it produces ammonia gas (a toxic gas). On Dr Lamm's tramcar a hot water reservoir on the roof contained a cylinder of liquid ammonia gas. The heat pressurised the gas and this was directed to pistons driving the wheels of the tramcar. The exhaust gas was discharged into the reservoir of water where it condensed and in doing so heated up the water. Unfortunately the gas had to be kept within the confines of the mechanism, any escaping gas not only smelt obnoxious, but it was also toxic. The engineering standards of the time could not ensure there was no gas escape and so no further tramcars were built.

STEAM

The use of steam power was the most tried and tested alternative to the horse. Steam locomotives had been used successfully by the railways for over 30 years when the first horse tramcars ran in Britain. So it was inevitable that operators would look to steam as an alternative. However, the demands of a tramway are quite different from a railway. On a railway a locomotive must take a large number of carriages, travel at speed and stop at points several miles, or more, apart. The tramway needs a locomotive that hauls one or two tramcars, has to stop frequently, travel at the slow speed of the rest of the traffic and reverse at the terminus of the route.

The history of steam power on tramways has been well documented, particularly in the seven-volume work by David Gladwin *"The History of the British Steam Tram"*. It is not intended to repeat that work in this book, so this is a very short summary of the key aspects of the attempts to replace horse traction by steam power. The first application of steam power to tramways took place in Cincinnati in 1859 when a steam carriage capable of carrying eighty passengers was built by a Mr Latta. By the next year five or six steam carriages were being used on American tramways. Even G.F. Train thought this may be the way forward as he patented a steam carriage in 1860.

In Britain the first use of a steam locomotive working on a tramway was in 1863 when the Ryde Pier tramway operators tested a Manning, Wardle locomotive. However it was found that the construction of the pier was not strong enough to take the weight and vibration of the steam locomotive and it was sent back to the manufacturers. The use of steam on tramways increased and by the late 1870s it was recognised by the government that steam power was becoming a favoured way of powering the tramways. The 1870 Act had not addressed that issue, at the time there were no steam tramways, so in 1879 the Use of Mechanical Power on Tramways Act was passed that empowered the Board of Trade to grant licences and issue regulations for the use of steam or other mechanical power on tramways. The same year the Board of Trade issued a "Model Form" for use by tramway promoters to use to obtain authority under the 1870 Act to use steam power. These placed certain restrictions on the use of steam.

The Grantham steam tramcar as used on the Wantage tramway.

Dublin and Lucan Tramway used the Perrett steam tramcar without success.

A photograph of a demonstrator steam tram locomotive made by Merryweather.

BOARD OF TRADE REGULATIONS FOR THE USE OF STEAM POWER ON TRAMWAYS

Regulations

I. The engine or engines to be used on the Tramways shall comply with the following requirements, that is to say:—

(a) They shall be fitted with an efficient brake, and a governor shall be attached to each of them so arranged that at any time when the engine attains a speed of [ten] or more miles an hour it shall cause the steam to be shut off and the brakes applied.

(b) Each engine shall be numbered, and the number shall be shown in a conspicuous part thereof.

(c) They shall be fitted with an indicator by means of which the speed is shown; with a suitable fender to push aside obstructions; and with a special bell [or whistle, or other apparatus] to be sounded as a warning when necessary.

(d) Arrangements shall be made enabling the driver to command the fullest possible view of the road before him.

(e) They shall be free from noise produced by blast or clatter of machinery; the machinery shall be concealed from view at all points above four inches from the level of the rails, and all fire used on such engines shall be concealed from view.

II. Every carriage used on the Tramways shall be so constructed as to provide for the safety of passengers and for their safe entrance to, exit from, and accommodation in, such carriages, and for their protection from the machinery of any engine used for drawing or propelling such carriages.

As well as the ill-fated toastrack horse tramcars for Rothesay tramways the Savile Street Foundry made a steam tramcar, but it was not a success.

The Hohenzollern fireless steam tram locomotive, this particular drawing is of the locomotive that was made for Java, but the Croydon example was of a similar design.

III. The Board of Trade and their officers may, from time to time, and shall on the application of the Local Authority of any of the districts through which the said tramways pass, inspect such engines or carriages used on the Tramways and the machinery therein, and may, whenever they think fit, prohibit the use on the Tramways of any of them which in their opinion are not safe for use.

IV. The speed at which such engines and carriages shall be driven or propelled along the Tramways shall not exceed the rate of eight miles an hour, and the speed at which such engines shall pass through movable facing-points shall not exceed the rate of four miles an hour.

By-Laws

I. The special bell [or whistle, or other apparatus] shall be sounded by the driver of the engine from time to time when it is necessary as a warning.

II. No steam or smoke shall be emitted from the engines, and no hot air shall issue in a way to annoy passengers.

III. Whenever it is necessary to prevent impending danger, the engine shall be brought to a standstill.

IV. The entrance to and exit from the carriages shall be by the hindermost or conductor's platform.

V. The engines and carriages shall be brought to a standstill immediately before reaching the following points:-

VI. The Company shall place and keep placed, in a conspicuous position inside of each carriage in use on the Tramways, a printed copy of these Regulations and Byelaws.

STEAM PASSENGER TRAMCAR

These regulations set the criteria for using steam power and were the major influence on the design and operation of steam power. On the railways of the time the steam motor carriage was a popular vehicle and it was thought that this was the way forward. As was previously mentioned in 1872 the Society of Arts offered the Howard Medal as a prize for a design of a traction engine that could replace horse power on tramways. The engine had to be contained within the vehicle that carried the passengers. The prize was awarded posthumously to John Grantham in 1875 for his experiments on the Wantage Tramway with a tramcar of his design with a body built by the Oldbury Railway Carriage and Wagon Co. Others also took the steam tramcar route including Edward Perrett who experimented with a steam tramcar in 1876 and sold one to the Dublin & Lucan Tramway in 1881. In the same year Beyer Peacock manufactured a steam tramcar for the North Staffordshire Tramways (Potteries), but this was the only such vehicle they constructed, all their other steam tramway vehicles were locomotives. In 1878 Messrs Robertson and Henderson of Glasgow had a steam tramcar built to their design in Birkenhead. The tramcar was taken to Scotland and had trials on the Glasgow, Greenock, Edinburgh and Stirling systems. However, once the trials had been completed nothing further is known about the tramcar, which has to be considered a failure. Another manufacturer to make just one steam tramcar was the Savile Street Foundry which trialled it in Sheffield in 1886, but without success.

STEAM TRAM LOCOMOTIVE

By this time it was becoming clear that a steam tramcar was not the way forward. Taking another leaf from the railways the preferred option was to have an independent steam locomotive that hauled carriages. It was possible to have a very small locomotive that had the power to haul a large passenger trailer. Initially it was often the practice to haul more than one trailer, rather like a railway train. However, there were a number of fatalities when passengers fell between the trailers. The Board of trade did not ban such operation but they did deter operators from running multi-trailer trains. The other problem with steam tramways was the size of the trailers. These were much larger than the horse trams. They were longer, usually with bogies and while the width was restricted to six feet the overhang on curves meant that the swept path was much greater than a horse tram. As a result the Board of trade would only issue permission to run steam in the streets if the road was wide enough. They would ban them from narrow roads. This resulted in some operators having to run horse trams over the narrower streets. As these were frequently in the centre of towns, the ruling caused a major disruption, with either passengers having to transfer vehicles or having steam and horse cars sharing the same tracks.

However a number of towns did have successful steam tramways and some well known locomotive manufacturers built considerable numbers of steam tram locomotives for this country and abroad. Until it was demonstrated that electrical power was the most cost effective means of propelling tramcars, steam was the viable alternative. However even here there were some cul-de-sacs.

FIRELESS TRAM LOCOMOTIVE

Dr Emile Lamm, of New Orleans, USA, in 1872 designed a fireless steam locomotive which he tested pulling trams at Carrollton. In 1876 in France, Léon Francq took this design and improved it to produce a prototype for the Rueil to Marly-le-Roi tramway, to the west of Paris. The fireless locomotive had an advantage over the normal steam tram locomotive as it did not have a fireman. However, it was found that the locomotive had to be recharged with steam every 15 kilometres. The first fireless steam tram locomotive in Britain was used on the Croydon &

Another early manufacturer was the Yorkshire Engine company.

The Liquid Fuel Engineering Company (Lifu) made mainly omnibuses, but did trial an experimental tramcar on Portsmouth tramways.

Norwood Tramways Company in 1884 and it was built by the Hohenzollern company in Dusseldorf to the Lamm & Francq design but using Joy's valve gear. The company had built similar locomotives for Java. Six such locomotives were supplied and they had large boilers that were charged with high pressure steam from a stationary boiler. The steam would then be used in the normal way. They were not a success and horses had to replace them.

LIQUID FUEL

In the 1890s the Liquid Fuel Engineering Company, based in Cowes, Isle of Wight, was building steam yachts and wanted to

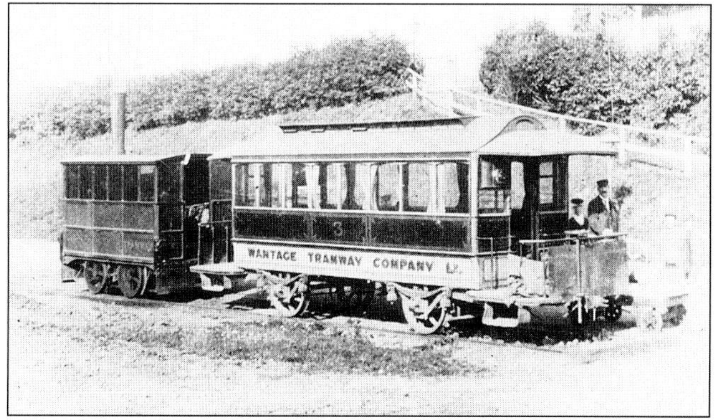

An early steam dummy was made by the Hughes company for the Wantage tramway.

When steam tram locomotives were first used they would haul horse tramcars, like this Yorkshire Engine company.

Elieson was another inventor ready to try battery propulsion.

expand into steam omnibuses, automobiles, lorries, charabancs and wagonettes. They registered the trade name "Lifu" from the words "liquid fuel". The selling point of their steam engines was that they were fuelled using liquid paraffin oil sprayed under pressure into the boiler, using pressurised air in the fuel tank. Three Lifu steam buses were used between Dover and Deal by the Dover & East Kent Motor Bus Company Ltd but the company failed and the fate of the buses is not known.

A Lifu tramcar was built for Portsmouth Tramways and it is believed to be the only such tramcar that was ever built. The tram was first used in 1896 on the horse tramway, but was restricted to a short route as it required operating points, while the horse trams had open points, the horse hauling the tram in the desired direction, something not possible with the Lifu tramcar. The tramcar was a combined unit with the steam boiler and engine being part of a double-deck passenger car. It would haul one or two horse trailers, to give a far higher passenger carrying capability than any one horse tram. The Lifu was painted blue and appeared to have been, if not a success, at least tolerated by the tramway. It was in service from 1896 to 1901 and when withdrawn the body continued to give service as an office in the depot.

Reckenzaun experimented with battery power at Kew.

Another experiment was this Lironi battery tramcar.

ACCUMULATOR ELECTRICITY

The history of the development of electric traction on tramways has been examined in detail in Pioneers of Electric Railroading edited by John Stevens. The first demonstration of electrically powered passenger transport was a short line made by Werner von Siemens for the Berlin Trade Fair in 1879. Like many new developments it was not obvious how well electrical power could be used on tramways. One early problem was how to get the electricity to the tramcar. One solution was to take it with the tram in the form of batteries or accumulators. Indeed the very first electric tramcar to run in the British Isles was a Faure accumulator car (a horse car with an electric motor and accumulators under the seats) built at the North Metropolitan Union Road works at Leytonstone in 1882. In the following year an Anthony Reckenzaun tramcar was given trials at Kew on the West Metropolitan Tramways. The tramcar had 50 wet accumulators, but unfortunately failed on its first day of testing and was removed and not seen again. An Elieson battery locomotive was tested on the North Metropolitan tramway in 1886 and the locomotive was used for around two years before the North Metropolitan decided it was not worth continuing to use it. The final experiment in London was in 1889 when six battery tramcars built by the General Electric Traction & Power Co. to the design of Mr Lironi were used on the Canning Town to Plaistow route. They gave service for three years, though their cause was not helped by an explosion in one of the trams. However it was found that the weight of the trams damaged the track and they were withdrawn in 1892.

Now very much in vogue for pollution free motoring, the early accumulator cars had their own particular problems. The batteries of the day were heavy wet batteries with lead plates and full of sulphuric acid. In order to provide sufficient power, racks of batteries had to be fitted and the only place was beneath the

Birmingham had an extensive battery system as well as horse, steam and cable.

The Swansea and Mumbles tramway experimented with battery power with this very large tramcar.

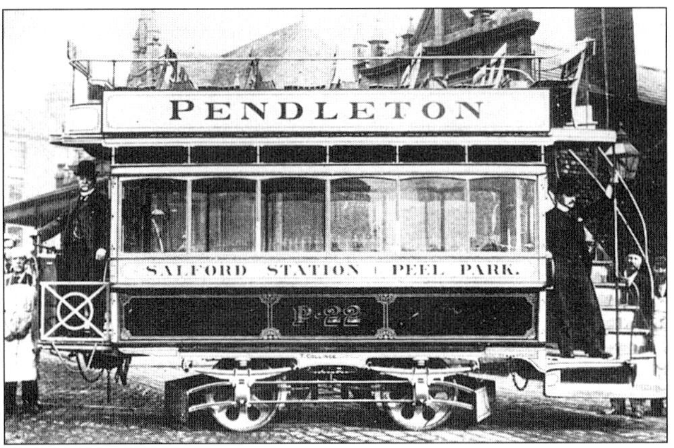

Even John Eades experimented with battery power on his reversible tramcars.

A London change pit showing the plough being placed to slide under the tramcar.

The third rail supply can clearly been seen in the foreground of this photograph of the Giants Causeway tramway.

It is generally recognised that the first use of electrical power to haul passengers was Siemens locomotive at the Berlin Trade Fair of 1879.

lower deck seats. The staff had to take care not to cover themselves in acid each time the batteries were changed for re-charging, while the unfortunate passengers would complain of odious fumes and sue the tramway operator for clothes damaged by acid splashes. Even so fourteen accumulator tramcars were used for eleven years in Birmingham. In 1898 John Eades, Workshop Manager for Manchester tramways, adapted one of the reversible tramcars (number P22) by adding electric motors and putting batteries under the seats. Although initially well received the batteries and motors were removed from the tramcar and it returned to being hauled by horses and no further battery cars were made for Manchester. The Swansea and Mumbles tramway had several battery powered tramcars in 1902, but they were not successful and the idea was abandoned in 1903, and the cars were used as trailers, with the electrical equipment being removed. There have been two more recent examples with the first electric operation on the Seaton Tramway in 1970 being an electric tramcar powered by a flat trailer loaded with batteries. This was a purely temporary measure until the overhead wiring had been installed. Then in 2005 a new battery powered tramcar was built for use on the Southport Pier tramway, a short level tramway with just one tramcar.

CONDUIT ELECTRICITY

The first electric tramways had difficulties with getting the electricity to the tramcars. The Giant's Causeway tramway used a third rail, as it ran on the side of the road and was able to have a raised third rail supply. Blackpool used a conduit supply system that had a tendency to flood at high tide. The Series Electrical Traction System was a system using a side conduit and unusual connections so that the tramcars picked up electrical power in series, rather than the now usual parallel. Trials were held in Northfleet in 1888, but they were not a success. Others used a stud system. All these were replaced by the more practical overhead wire supply. However, in London the conduit system was successfully used until the closure of the tramway in 1952.

ELECTRICITY

Once the overhead system of electrical supply was developed it became clear that this was the way forward and most tramways were built or converted for this type of operation.

Inevitably electric tramways overtook the horse ones and for a short time they both ran at the same time.

Blackpool in the early days of the conduit operation.

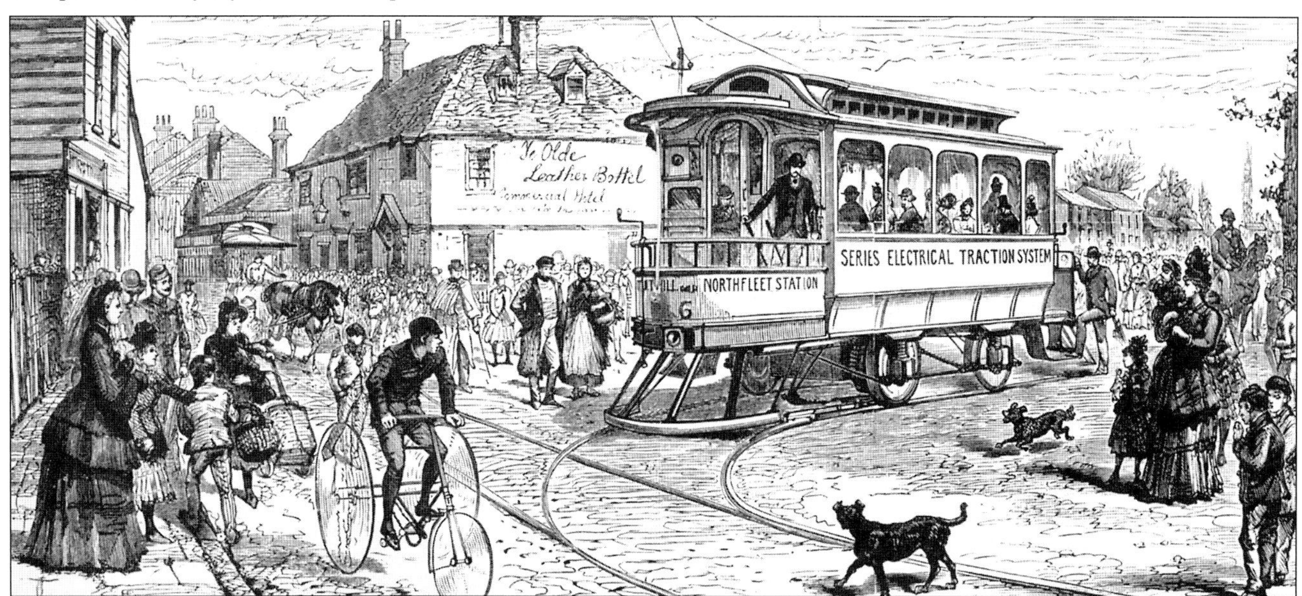

The Series Electrical Traction System had trials in Northfleet.

THE DEMISE OF THE HORSE TRAMWAY

The cold statistics seem to indicate a situation where tramway operators placed all their faith in the horse tram, with some moving to steam operation, until around 1900 when there was a complete shift and everything went to electric tramways. Appendix 1 demonstrates that the use of steam tramways was a transport cul-de-sac for tramways. There were relatively few steam tramways and of those hardly any were direct replacements of horse operation, the vast majority were introduced on new tramways. However, they too succumbed to the electric tramcar.

By 1890 electric tramcar development in America was starting to provide reliable and economic cars. Wanting to develop new markets many American companies sold tramcars to Britain and also set up British associates to exploit the technology. The development of electric tramways is demonstrated by the table of electric tramways opened each year (There were no electric tramway openings in the years omitted from the table).

Once the electric trams came along, horse trams became redundant. One Dutch line solved the problem of what to do with the old tramcar bodies, Three have been converted to make an articulated petrol tramcar. The control is from the centre car, set at right angles to its former position. The other two tramcars had been attached with one wheel set of each removed.

While the technical achievements were the catalyst for the change the timing was dominated by the effects of the 1870 Tramways Act. The Act enabled the local authorities to purchase tramways compulsorily in their area at scrap price 21 years after the initial authority to build the tramway. As new horse tramways had the greatest development from the mid 1870s to the mid 1880s, the purchase opportunities really expanded from the mid 1890s to the mid 1900s. This is reflected in the table on the left. The Act meant that existing horse tramways were reluctant to invest large amounts of capital in converting to electric power, when in a few years the local authority could buy it all at a fraction of the cost. Some applied to the local authority to get a long lease if they converted the system, but usually this was rejected as the municipalities now wanted to run their own tramways, having been given authority to do so in 1896. This led to the significant change to electric power.

Number of Electric Tramways opened each year

YEAR	1883	1885	1892	1893	1895	1896	1897	1898	1899
NUMBER	1	2	1	2	3	3	3	7	8

YEAR	1900	1901	1902	1903	1904	1905	1906	1907	1908
NUMBER	13	27	17	27	25	13	7	5	3

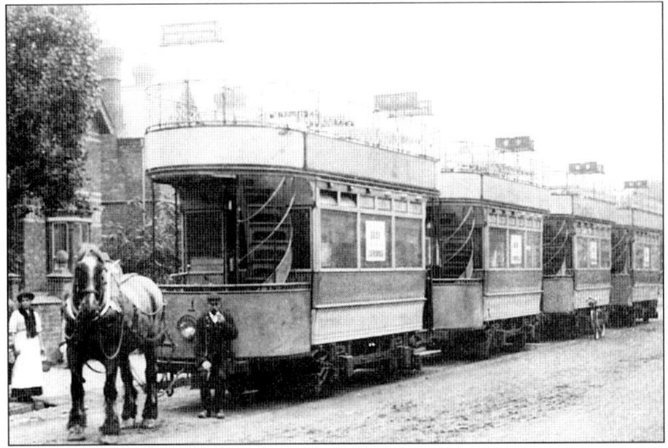

The driver seems to miss the irony of a horse dragging in the new electric tramcars for the Lincoln system.

At this time some horse tramcars were converted for electrical operation, as this Glasgow scene shows.

The major user of the stud contact system was the Wolverhampton tramway.

The economics of electric traction meant that it was inevitable that all horse tramways, apart from some oddities, would be converted. What was surprising was the astonishing rate of change. Over a period of ten years public transport in towns moved from being dominated by the horse to electric traction. The change over the next ten years saw a similar move from horse omnibuses to mechanical buses. The tramways now had a strong competitor for moving the public on the roads, just as many years later the bus had to compete against the car.

Appendix 1

COSTS OF RUNNING A HORSE TRAMWAY

In the 1860s and 1870s the horse was the only source of power available to tramways. Even when alternative power sources were being explored the horse remained the favourite. It was only the development of the electric tramcar, with a separate power house and overhead wiring that the horse started to be replaced. The development of horse tramways can be gauged by the number of horses working on tramways in the British Isles. The figures come from the Board of Trade returns and are only available from 1878:

Year	1878	1880	1885	1890	1895
Number of horses	9,222	12,392	23,308	27,719	32,273

Year	1900	1905	1910	1918	1920
Number of horses	37,481	13,357	1,880	92	116

NOTES:
The number of horses is not entirely reliable as no definition is given for that number. Some systems may take the average number over the year, others may give the number on the date the return was completed. It is additionally complicated by some systems selling horses in the autumn and running a smaller stud during the winter months, increasing the number in the spring. Some may also include horses used for omnibus work, where the company operated both trams and buses.
The maximum number of horses was given in 1899 with 44,171 horses being used on tramways.
There is no figure for 1915 as no returns were required during the 1914-1918 conflict.

In 1870 the cost of a two-horse double-deck tramcar was around £200. With a stud of eleven horses per tramcar the total capital tied up in operating one tramcar was £530 (the costs of a similar electric tramcar in 1903 was £500). In 1899 the total capital sum for all tramways that was invested in horses and tramcars was £2.6 million (equal to £1.3 billion at today's values), this at a time when the average wage for a worker was around £1 per week. The tramway working life of a horse was around four years and the resale value was £20 unless it was one of the majority that died in service, when the carcass would be sold for 10s.

There is a steady expansion of the number of horses up to 1899, even though during the 1880s steam operation was being used. It appears that steam power supplemented horse tramways rather than replaced them. However, once electric operation really got going from 1899 onwards the decline in horse powered tramways is dramatic. Within five years the number of horses dropped by over two-thirds. In the same period the route mileage went from 1,122 miles to 2,117 miles (almost 90% increase). The reason for this major change was the economy of electric tramway operation.

The costs of operating a horse tramway were many and various but the major expenses were the upkeep and replacement of horses and repairing and replacing tramcars. Less frequent but costly was the replacement of track. For the very early tramways the initial rails were experimental and generally technology meant they were lightly constructed. So replacements were required after a few years, by which time rails had improved and they usually lasted with maintenance until needing to be replaced by heavier section rail for electric operation. The costs of horses are shown for 1890 and compared with steam operation.

The average cost of running horses is around 5d per car mile, while the steam traction shows expenses of less than half, at 2.15d. This demonstrates the attractiveness of steam traction to operators, though the initial capital costs were high.

The policy of 'always a tram in sight' is demonstrated by this Liverpool view.

Two very full tramcars in Glasgow, showing the popularity of the trams with the public.

This Stockport tram fills up and is ready to go with two more trams taking a break before following on.

A full complement of passengers has given this Stirling tramcar a decided back heavy appearance.

Revenue from advertising can be very useful and this Cambridge tramcar even uses the seat backs to bring in extra money.

As well as the high costs of keeping horses there was another major problem for the operators and that was the uncertainty associated with the provender for the horses. The fodder consisted of maize, oats, beans, bran, hay and clover. The price of all of these was dependent upon the harvest. A poor harvest would restrict the availability of feed and, given the demand by all horse users, the prices would increase. It was not unusual for prices to double from one year to another, then drop again. This is an issue for the operator because, like all businesses, forward planning depends on having some understanding of what future costs will be. While there was some possibility to purchase fodder from abroad if the home harvest failed, such was the demand that prices would rise. Effectively Europe was a single market for horse fodder. Once electric operation replaced the horse the fuel costs were the electric power and often the operators also owned the generating power, while coal was far less subject to variation.

The table shows the costs at a time when steam traction was not new but was still undergoing considerable technical development. The higher costs of the steam rolling stock (0.55d for steam stock compared to 0.39d for horse tramcars) reflects the more technical requirements of the steam tram locomotives and the larger size of the tram trailers.

To make a real comparison between the costs of the different modes the overall costs need to be compared to the overall receipts to give the profit. To enable different sized systems to be compared the figures have been rationalised per car mile.

This shows that the costs for steam operation are above those for horse tramways and while the receipts are slightly higher, giving overall profit figures that favour the steam operation, it is not a significant amount. 1890 is a very early date for electric operation and figures are not so easy to obtain. Overall profit is only available for Blackpool and this shows a profit per mile run double that of horse or steam operation. Costs are available for three other operators and these show a significant reduction (roughly half) on the costs for horse and steam operation. It was estimated that the costs to run one horse tram with its horses for a period of four years was £1,000, while the costs of running an electric tramcar for the same period was £500

Fair Fares

Horse tramway operators always had the tricky task of balancing the fares they charged with the effect on revenue. This is most graphically demonstrated by the Chester Tramway when the Corporation purchased the system compulsorily in 1902. Prior to the purchase the operator charged flat fares of 3d for those travelling in the saloon and 2d for those on the exposed upper deck. When the Corporation took over they decided to significantly cut the fares to a two stage structure, charging 1d per stage. Effectively those travelling to or from the town centre would pay 1d, the higher fare was for passengers travelling across town. To see what impact this had on the revenue they made direct comparisons between the then current income and the income for the same week a year previously. The results were:

W/E 1 February 1902	15,286 passengers	revenue £71 13s 1d
Same week 1901	5,427 passengers	revenue £61 3s 1d
W/E 1 March 1902	17,282 passengers	revenue £80 5s 4d
Same week 1901	6,961 passengers	revenue £71 13s 3d

This shows that while the fares were reduced by between a half and two thirds, the additional numbers of passengers more than made up the cut and the revenue was increased. The additional benefit as far as the Councillors were concerned was the goodwill of the passengers, now having an affordable town transport.

Similar reductions in fares occurred in other towns when the tramways were municipalised, including the London County Council.

Track and Motive Power Costs 1890

NOTE: All figures are given in pre-decimal coinage

Horse

System	Maintenance of road and track	Number of horses	Cost of maintaining horses	Cost of replacing horses	Cost per car mile run
Gloucester	£71	32	£877	£172	1.8d
York	£95	37	£1,086	£70	2.3d
London Street	£6,708	1,127	£40,126	£4,984	4.4d
Sheffield	£4,774	316	£14,346	£1,825	5.6d
Edinburgh	£6,371	992	£31,820	£4,361	5.8d
Newcastle	£590	278	£11,550	£1,174	5.0d

Steam

System	Maintenance of road and track	Number of locos	Cost of maintaining locos	Cost per car mile run
Accrington	£1,880	14	£2,228	2.1d
Blackburn	£953	10	£1,267	2.8d
Burnley	£1,370	14	£1,372	1.6d
Huddersfield	£1,746	18	£1,803	2.1d

Cost of Repairing Tramcars 1890

System	Number of tramcars	Annual miles per car	Total maintenance bill	Cost per car	Cost per car mile run
Horse					
Gloucester	10	13,661	£56	£5.6	0.10d
York	8	15,126	£70	£8.75	0.14d
London Street	124	19,753	£3,401	£27.4	0.33d
Sheffield	46	15,039	£1,150	£25.0	0.34d
Edinburgh	76	19,753	£3,833	£50.4	0.61d
Newcastle	30	20,201	£1,537	£51.2	0.61d
Steam					
Blackburn	15	10,538	£165	£11.0	0.25d
Burnley	13	15,085	£315	£24.2	0.39d
Accrington	14	17,960	£596	£42.6	0.61d
Huddersfield	19	11,239	£840	£44.2	0.94d

Overall Cost per Car Mile 1890

System	Year	Total costs £	Annual miles	Cost per car mile run	Receipts per car mile	Profit per car mile
Horse						
Sheffield	1883	32,623	658,536	11.89d	12.25d	0.36d
Gloucester	1890	2,523	136,614	4.43d	5.04d	0.61d
York	1890	2,660	121,007	5.28d	7.14d	1.86d
Newcastle	1890	25,197	606,046	9.98d	12.07d	2.09d
London Trwys	1884	207,143	5,580,436	8.91d	11.18d	2.27d
Glasgow	1884	82,847	1,966,713	10.11d	12.50d	2.39d
London Street	1890	101,081	2,449,436	9.90d	12.39d	2.49d
Dublin	1884	84,591	2,097,312	9.68d	12.68d	3.00d
North Met	1883	220,971	4,729,490	11.21d	14.49d	3.28d
Sheffield	1890	28,789	691,810	9.99d	13.60d	3.61d
Liverpool	1883	57,526	1,203,317	11.47d	16.09d	4.62d
Edinburgh	1890	68,948	1,501,253	11.02d	16.54d	5.52d
Steam						
Accrington	1890	11,887	251,451	11.35d	12.30d	0.95d
Blackburn	1890	6,630	158,077	10.07d	14.58d	4.51d
Burnley	1890	9,582	196,109	11.73d	15.73d	4.00d
Huddersfield	1890	11,564	213,546	13.00d	17.76d	4.76d
Electric						
Blackpool	1890	3,136	95,368	7.89d	16.53d	8.64d
Bessbrook & Newry	1890	346	23,468	3.54d		
Guernsey	1890			5.79d		
Leeds	1890	2,382	102,914	5.55d		

It looks as if the passenger on the stairs is going to be unlucky at getting a seat for his trip into Greenock.

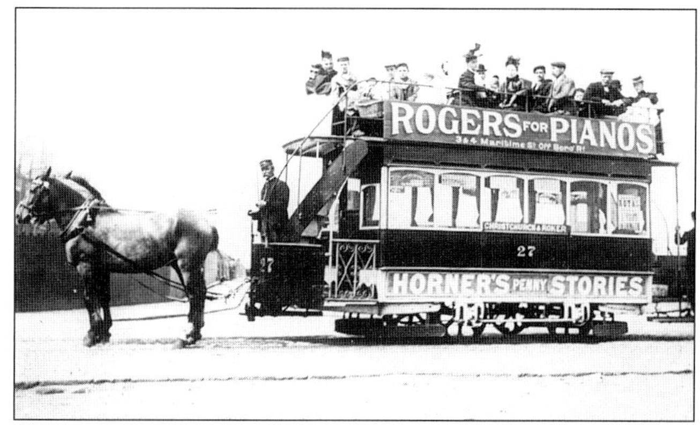

The upper deck is very popular, with no one inside, on this Sunderland tram.

Competitors for passengers. Both the wagonette and the tramcar have a full load of passengers. By the look of the Sunday Best attire it is probably a holiday day.

There seems no tradition of always sitting facing the direction of travel, as the upper deck passengers filling this Birkenhead tramcar demonstrate. One passenger has even made the handrail an extra seat.

Compare the empty omnibus with the very full tramcar in Glasgow.

Appendix 2

HORSE TRAMWAY TOKENS AND PASSES

This Appendix is a short history of transport tokens and passes used by horse tramway operators in the British Isles. Firstly is the need to explain what tokens and passes are. Tokens are a stamped or moulded piece of metal or plastic resembling a coin. Like a coin they have a value marked on them. They are issued by an individual or a company and the public can exchange them for money, goods or services to the marked value. Passes are a document or a stamped or moulded piece of metal or plastic, without any marked value, that allows the holder to travel for no payment, or a lower than normal payment, and that may be subject to restrictions. The most recent examples are the National Transport Tokens and the National Bus Pass. The National Transport Tokens were coin like tokens stamped with a value. They were given or sold at a subsidised rate to eligible members of the public, who could then use them to exchange or part exchange for public travel to the value marked on the token. The National Bus Pass is a plastic enclosed document that when shown in accordance with the rules allows the bearer to travel free on buses. The main difference to the holder is that the token has to be given up in exchange for a ticket, while the bus pass is shown, but retained by the holder. According to the procedure of the bus company they may or may not issue a ticket (with nil monetary fare).

Transport tokens began around the late 1700s with tokens being produced with pictures of stagecoaches. It is not clear if these were used as tickets or as tokens for the pre-payment of the fare. The most frequently found state that they are payable in London on the obverse and that they are a token of gratitude on the reverse. With the rise of horse omnibuses tokens were used and they appear to be able to be purchased prior to journeys, possibly at a discount for purchasing a number at once. The token would be exchanged for a ride on the appropriate omnibus.

The first tramway 'tokens' were produced by G.F. Train and were souvenirs. They were brass oval medallions made for the opening of his various tramways and given to passengers on the first day of operation. They did not have any value. He also produced a similar design special silver token with his name on it for use as a pass for travel at any time on his tramway.

After tramways became more common then more tokens were used, though not all tramway companies issued them. The types of tokens are numerous and each is explored bellow:

Tokens for pre-payment by the public

This type of token could be purchased prior to travel and may well have been sold at a small discount. For example six tokens could be purchased for the price of five. The stamped design would include the value of the ticket for which the token could be exchanged. Most horse tramway tokens were made of brass, though the Glasgow Tramway and Omnibus Company Limited did use celluloid (an early form of plastic) to mould hard wearing pre-payment tokens.

Concessionary tokens

Some tramway systems issued tokens to blind members of the public to allow them to have free travel. The only examples that have been seen are from the Glasgow Corporation tramways and

◀ The first travel tokens were issued by stagecoach operators in the 18th century.

▲ Pre-payment omnibus token issued by John Menzies in Glasgow.

Following the practice on the Birkenhead tramway George Train produced a souvenir token for passengers on the first day of operation of the Potteries tramway. He produced similar tokens for all his tramways. The Birkenhead token is the earliest British tramway token, having been made in 1860. ▶

▲ Paisley District Tramways used an unusual octagonal pre-payment ½d token.

▲ The first use of celluloid was seen on the Glasgow Tramway and Omnibus Company with this 1d token.

◀ A pre-payment 1d token issued by the Bradford tramways.

these have a value stamped on them, so would be exchanged for a ticket. It is assumed that the tokens were issued free by the Corporation to blind people to use on the tramway.

The other category of concessionary fares were those issued to schoolchildren. The process would be similar to the Blind tokens. Presumably the rationale behind using tokens is that the token could only be used by children when travelling to and from school. They could not be taken by wayward parents and used to buy alcohol and would not have any value to trade because of their very specific use. There is an example from the Blackburn and Over Darwen Tramways Company. This not only specified that it was a scholars ticket it also specified "Only available in going to or returning from school between Hollins Grove and Blackburn".

Employee passes

The tramway company also usually allowed their own staff to travel free to and from work. Most used the pay check as identity and on production of the pay check the individual would be allowed free journeys. But some would issue a pass for employees and one that has been seen is from Huddersfield. There is an unusual 'Sand' pass example from the Glasgow Tramway and Omnibus Company Limited. This was given to employees who had to go to another depot to pick up bags of dry sand that was used to fill the sand boxes on the dashes of the tramcars. The sand was thrown onto the rails by the driver when the brake was applied on the tram.

Public service passes

Many tramway operators had agreements with some of the public services to enable their employees, when on duty, to travel free of charge on the tramcars. Bradford City Tramways issued a free pass to District Nurses. These were marked 'Only to be used when on duty'. Presumably the conductors were told that only nurses in uniform were allowed to use the pass.

The Glasgow Tramway and Omnibus Company Limited had two passes for workers in the General Post Office. One was marked 'Letter Carrier in Uniform' and the other 'Telegraph Boy in Uniform'.

After the horse trams

The use of tokens on trams developed further with the expansion of electric tramways. It is not within the scope of this book to explore this aspect, however the use of tokens and passes continues until today. Local rules allow certain National Bus Passes to be used on current public tramways.

◀ Driver's pay check used by the Glasgow Corporation as a travel pass to and from work. The depot and employee's number are stamped on the back.

The Blackburn and Over Darwen tramways issued this 1½d token for schoolchildren, with all its restrictions plainly stamped on the token. ▶

▲ Huddersfield unusually used enamelled metal for its employee passes.

The Glasgow Tramway and Omnibus Company issued this pass for employees to journey from one depot to another to collect bags of sand.

District Nurses in Bradford were able to use this pass to travel in the course of their work. ▼

Glasgow Tramway and Omnibus Company accepted these passes for letter carriers for the GPO. ▼

▲ There were similar passes for Telegraph Boys.

▲ The Glasgow Corporation rectangular 1d token for blind persons.

The ½d tokens for blind persons were oval in shape. ▶

Appendix 3

SPECIFICATION OF HORSE TRAMWAY CARS

Minute of Agreement and Specification in 1882 for 8 open tramway cars and 4 closed single deck tramway cars for The Rothesay Tramways Company (Limited) to be supplied by the Savile Street Foundry & Engineering Company (Limited). The original document is entirely hand written and has proved difficult to reproduce. This transcription is offered with the exact wording, spelling and punctuation of the original document.

Minute of Agreement between The Rothesay Tramways Company (Limited) hereinafter called the parties of the first part and The Savile Street Foundry and Engineering Company (Limited) carrying on business at Savile Street East Sheffield, hereinafter called the parties of the second part.

The parties hereto considering that the parties of the second part have made offer to make and supply the parties of the first part with tramway cars for the purpose of their undertaking, which offer the parties of the first part have agreed to accept and that on the terms and conditions afterwritten Therefore the parties have agreed and hereby agree as follows viz.

First The parties of the second part bind and oblige themselves and their successors and representatives whomsoever to make and supply to the parties of the first part eight open tramway cars, each car not to exceed twenty six hundredweights in weight and to be seated for twenty four passengers allowing a space of sixteen inches of sitting room for each passenger, and that at the price of eighty five pounds sterling for each such car; and four closed tramway cars each car not to exceed thirty-hundred weights in weight and to be seated for twenty passengers allowing a space of sixteen inches of sitting room for each passenger, and that at the price of One hundred and ten pounds sterling for each closed car

Second The parties of the second part bind and oblige themselves and their foresaids to make the whole of the said cars, both open and closed, in a good sufficient and workmanlike manner conform to the Drawings and of materials of the quality and description set forth in the Specifications which are subscribed by the parties as relative thereto, and are hereby declared to be incorporated with these presents

Third The parties of the first part shall be at liberty to have the work of constructing the foresaid cars inspected continuously or from time to time by such person or persons as shall be appointed by them for that purpose

Fourth The parties of the second part further bind and oblige themselves and their foresaids to have the whole of the said eight open cars completed and delivered on the tramways lines of the parties of the first part at Rothesay and that free of expense to the parties of the first part as follows viz. two cars on or before the ninth day of May Eighteen hundred and eighty two and the remaining six cars on or before the fifteenth day of May Eighteen hundred and eighty two, and to have the whole of the four closed cars completed and delivered on the tramway lines of the parties of the first part at Rothesay and that free of expense to the parties of the first part on the twenty ninth day of May Eighteen hundred and eighty two; Declaring that in the event of the parties of the second part failing to complete and deliver the [page break – signed by James Lindsay, John M. Cook and R.E.Dickinson] the [sic] cars as aforesaid they hereby agree to make payment to the parties of the first part of the sum of one pound sterling per car per day in name of liquidated [sic] and agreed on compensation for each day the said cars or any of them shall remain incompleted and undelivered after the said respective dates

Fifth The parties of the first part shall on delivery of the said cars make payment to the parties of the second part of the agreed on price thereof in cash or in the option of the parties of the first part by bills at three months from the dates of delivery of the cars, with power to them to renew the said bills on their reaching maturity for other three months, they paying the discount thereon

Sixth In the event of any difference of opinion arising as to the true intent and meaning of these presents or as to the manner of construction of the foresaid cars or the materials employed therein or as regards the implementing or carrying into effect of the provisions herein contained both parties hereby submit and refer such difference or differences to the determination of John Macrae, Civil Engineer, Edinburgh, whose decision shall be final and binding on both parties notwithstanding his being connected with the parties of the first part in any way whatsoever

Lastly Both parties hereto bind and oblige themselves to perform their respective parts of the premises [sic] to each other under the penalty of One hundred pounds sterling to be paid by the party failing to the party performing or willing to perform over and above performance In Witness whereof these presents written upon this and the preceding page by Robert Kennaway Sutherland, clerk to Paterson Cameron and Company, Solicitors before the Supreme Courts of Scotland, Edinburgh, are together with a duplicate hereof subscribed by the parties hereto as follows, viz. on behalf of the said The Rothesay Tramways Company (Limited) by James Lindsay of Drydenbank, Merchant, Edinburgh, one of the directors and John Macfarlane Cook Accountant, Edinburgh, the Secretary, both of the said The Rothesay Tramways Company (Limited) duly empowered to subscribe these presents on behalf thereof and on behalf of the said The Savile Street Foundry and Engineering Company (Limited) by Richard Elihu Dickinson residing at One hundred and seventy three Ellesmere Road, Sheffield, duly authorised and empowered to subscribe these presents on behalf thereof, all at Edinburgh upon the twentieth day of March in the year Eighteen hundred and eighty two before these witnesses Sarah Newton Forbes, residing at Four Manor Place, Edinburgh, and Duncan Wilhu Paterson solicitor before the Supreme Courts of Scotland there.

Signed by S.N.Forbes – witness, and
D.W.Paterson witness, James Lindsay, John M.
Cook Secretary, R.E.Dickinson

In the margin:
I the within named and designed
John Macrae hereby Accept of the
Office of Arbiter conferred on me
by the within Minute of Agreement
and so Hereby Nominate and appoint
Mr. John Innes, Solicitor, Edinburgh,
to be Clerk and Legal Assessor to
the Reference; In Witness Whereof
this minute written by John Gibb
Glendinning, Clerk to Millar Robson
& Innes, Law Agents and Conveyancers
in Edinburgh, is subscribed by me the
said John Macrae, at Edinburgh, upon
upon the thirteenth day of December
in the year Eighteen hundred and eighty
two before these witnesses James
Proudfoot and Peter Howie both Assistants
to me the said John Macrae.
[Signed] John Macrae, Innes Proudfoot,
witness Peter Howie Witness

Page Third

The Rothesay Tramways Company (Limited)

Specification of Iron and Woodwork for Eight open cars

Wheels — To be of best cast steel of approved pattern thirty inches diameter

Axles — Of best English Bessemer steel two and one half inches diameter turned for to receive tram wheels and journals

Dash plate — At each end of the car of sheet iron number sixteen Birmingham wire gauge

Springs — Of best spring steel three feet long by two and one half inches wide. Eight plates in each spring

Axle boxes — Of cast iron fitted with best gun metal to receive journal

Brake — Cars to be fitted with screw brake worked from either end of car by crank handle

Brake blocks — Composite blocks to be fitted to brake gear of iron backs with wood faces

Awning Stantions — Ten wrought iron tube stantions to be fitted to each Car one and one quarter inches in diameter connected along and across the top by one half inch iron rods to carry awning canvas

Drag eye — Of best iron with pin chain

Timber etc.

Main frame of English ash four inches by two and one half inches fastened at ends by cross bars eight inches by two and one half inches and in the centre by two cross bars three inches by three inches with all necessary bolts stays etc.

Flooring	Of one inch yellow pine
Foot boards	Of birch nine inches wide by one inch thick fastened to main frames of car by iron stays
Iron fender	Of sheet iron one sixteenth inch Birmingham wire gauge carried full length of car and fastened to main frame at top and foot board at bottom. To serve in place of cross stays
Seats and backs	Of pitch pine "plank and space"
Awnings	Of Rain proof canvas made so as to ship and unship with a curtain round sides and ends twelve inches deep
Painting	The whole of the woodwork to have one coat of size and three coats of copal varnish. Iron work to have three coats of paint

What is written upon this page is the Specification for Eight open
Tramway cars referred to in and incorporated with the foregoing
Minute of Agreement for the construction of the cars mentioned
therein; and is now subscribed with reference to said Minute of
Agreement of even date therewith
[Signed] James Lindsay, John M. Cook, R.C.Dickinson

Page Fourth

The Rothesay Tramways Company (Limited)

Specification for Tramway Cars without seats on roof

Dimensions Etc.

Number of Passengers – Twenty
Length of Body inside – Thirteen feet four inches (13 feet four inches)
Do Do outside including platforms – Seventeen feet eight inches
Breadth extreme – Six feet
Gauge – Four feet

Description of Materials – Exterior

Bottom framing	To be of thoroughly seasoned oak or ash well and strongly put together
Centre panels	To be of bay wood handsomely painted, lined, decorated, and varnished or of teak highly finished, lined decorated and varnished
Corner posts	To be thoroughly painted lined decorated and varnished
Platform	To be at each end of car with dash-plate and rail and iron step at either side
Curtain	At each end projecting over platform
Bell	To be fixed at each end under the Curtain fitted with rods or straps and arranged to work from end to end
Roof	To be covered with well seasoned wood thoroughly well coated with paint
Wheels	To be thirty inches in diameter, cast iron open spoke chilled on Tread and Flange or Crucible cast steel
Axles	To be of Bessemer steel with turned journals and wheel beds
Axle guards boxes	Axle guards to be of cast iron with cast iron boxes fitted with lids bolts friction plates, Brass bushes etc. complete
Bearing springs	To be of Indiarubber
Brake gear	To be worked from platform at each end applying a brake block to each wheel
Drawing gear	Draw iron to be attached to the front of each platform for one horse traction
Hand rails	To be fixed at each end of body of car

Interior

Sliding door	To be at each end of car and to be fitted with handles locks catches rollers and roller plates also with glass in the upper part of frame
Lamp	To be placed at each end of car on the outside and to have oil box burner chimney silvered glass reflectors coloured bulls eye shewing a strong white light inside and coloured light outside
Framing	To be handsomely panelled neatly moulded and French polished
Window posts	To be highly finished and French polished
Windows	To be fixed and to be glazed with good quality of glass
Panels over windows	To be elegantly decorated
Roof	To be painted or varnished roof rafters neatly moulded and lined, and the roof fitted with hand straps pendent from the truss rods
Seats and backs	To be sparred lath and space
Ventilation	To be provided in the roof of car

What is written upon this page is the Specification for four closed tramway cars referred to in and incorporated with the foregoing Minute of Agreement for the construction of the cars mentioned therein; and is now subscribed with reference to said Minute of Agreement of even date therewith

[Signed] James Lindsay,
John M. Cook
R.E.Dickinson

Background Note – After a few months in service there was a complaint by the tramway company that the open tramcars were sub-standard. Looking at the date of the margin note on page 2 (December 1882) and the delivery date of the tramcars (May 1882) it appears that the company acted on the 6th paragraph and called on John Macrae to determine their complaint. Details are sparse but it appears that the canvas roof awnings were damaged by the Rothesay winds. Records of the tramway company state that they subsequently withdrew their complaint. It seems likely that John Macrae found that the tramcars met the specification and rather than be shown to have drawn up a poor specification the company withdrew their complaint. The tramway company sent the tramcars to James McBride, a local builder, who replaced the canvas awnings with sheet metal roofs that were far more substantial. There is a photograph showing nine young lads sitting on the roof of one of the modified tramcars!

One of the Rothesay Tramways modified open tramcars having an impromptu strength test on its roof by the local children.

One of the six Falcon tramcars delivered to Worcester in 1884.

Specification of 1883 of a double deck, two horse tramway car for the Tramway Trust Company (Worcester Tramways) to be supplied by the Falcon Engine and Car Works Limited. Note the document is a pre-printed form with hand written details. Six of these tramcars were delivered to Worcester in 1884.

FALCON ENGINE AND CAR WORKS,

LIMITED.

Loughborough, Aug. 21st 1883

Specification

OF A

TRAMWAY CAR

FOR TWO-HORSE TRACTION

On 4 Wheels,

For 16 Inside Passengers, and

18 Outside Passengers.

Sent to J. J. McKay Esq.
Worcester Tramways
41 Parliament St.
London S.W.

Beveridge and Miller, Holborn Printing Works, W.C.

FALCON ENGINE AND CAR WORKS, Limited,

Loughborough, August 21st 1883

SPECIFICATION OF A TRAMWAY CAR,

FOR TWO-HORSE TRACTION,

On 4 Wheels.

16 persons inside & 18 outside

Description. *The Car to be of the top seated class, with platforms and staircases at each end.*

PRINCIPAL DIMENSIONS.

Length inside body	11	*feet*	4¼	*inches.*
Length over all	20	*feet*	1½	*inches.*
Width over all	6	*feet*	0	*inches.*
Wheel Base	5	*feet*	6	*inches.*
Gauge	3	*feet*	0	*inches.*

Bottom Frame. *To be of best dry* Oak *, properly framed together, all joints to be put together with white lead, and pinned with oak pins where necessary, each side to be properly trussed.*

Side Pillars. *To be of best* English or American Ash

Corner Pillars. *To be of best* do. do.

Panels. *Waist panels to be of* Teak or Mahogany *rocker panels of* Ash or Whitewood *, perfectly dry and free from all defects; the inside of panels to be covered with canvas glued on in the usual manner; the panels are to be pinned on to every pillar, except end ones, to which they will be screwed instead, and glue blocked to the battens.*

Floor. *To be of red deal 1 inch thick, tongued and grooved, well nailed down to bottom frame; wearing grids to be formed of longitudinal strips of white deal, nailed on to floor, so that the car may be easily cleaned.*

Roof. *The roof ribs to be either American elm or English ash, bent to the proper curves, and covered with pine or American whitewood, tongued and grooved; the canvas to be put on with waterproof cement, and painted outside with four coats of white lead paint.*

Doors. To have frames of Ash or Teak panelled at bottom with suitable panels, and at top with glass of same quality as other glazing of car; the doors are to be hung on brackets and rollers at top, and to be fitted with friction plates, handles and catches.

Inside Casings. To be framed together and fitted with fancy wood panels, all finished in their natural grain; a swing door with glass panel and suitable furniture shall be fixed on the side where car door slides in.

Windows. 1/16 Polished plate fixed with fluted rubber in the best possible manner

Blinds. None

Seats and Backs. Perforated veneer

Handrails Inside. To be of wrought iron tube with screwed ends, and so arranged as to act as tension rods to keep roof in proper form; a sufficient number of suitable hand straps to be provided.

Lamps. One at each end of car fixed outside to be constructed to occupy as small a space as is consistent with an efficient lamp, the reflectors to be fluted glass mirrors, and arranged to throw a strong light into the car and show a coloured signal light outside.

Ventilation. To be provided by means of swing ventilators in side of roof; the frames of these to be varnished and glazed with obscured glass, the pivots to be brass; a light iron rod with suitable brackets to be fitted in front of these outside to protect them from damage.

Bells. One at each end of car, under bonnet, with bell strap running through from the inside of car to either platform. or worked by a rod at side

Platforms. The frames and supports to be of best dry oak with front bars of best ash, bent to the proper curve; the flooring to be of red deal, either tongued and grooved or left open jointed; the length of each platform to be 4 feet 1 inches.

Steps. ~~Light wrought iron steps, properly "roughed," will be fitted at each entrance~~ Direct on to platforms

Dash. A sheet iron "dash," with suitable stays fitted to each platform; convenient commode handles to be fitted at each entrance.

Staircases. A light staircase to be fitted to each platform to give access to seats on roof; the stair to have sheet iron stringers and risers, and wood treads; the risers to be suitably flanged to receive the treads and to secure the stringers.

Bonnets. The frames to be of best ash or American elm, bent to the proper curves, and covered with pine and canvas, same as specified for roof; the bonnets to be secured to ends of car by suitable wrought iron brackets.

Top Seats. To be made slat and space shaped to form comfortable seats; the slats to be of pitch pine or other suitable woods, and varnished the natural colour.

Wearing Slats on Top. Wearing slats of best deal to be fitted alongside roof, and suitable cross-over platforms over bonnets.

Handrails for Stairs, &c. A light but strong handrail of wrought iron tube with malleable iron feet, all screwed together, shall be securely fixed round top of car and on the outer side of each staircase.

Wheels and Axles. The wheels to be 30 inches diameter of Cast Steel made by approved maker to be accurately bored to ____ diameter; the axles to be of Bessemer Steel accurately turned; journals 2½ diameter; wheel seats 2½ diameter; the wheels are to be forced into their places by hydraulic pressure and set to proper gauge.

Axleboxes. To be of the most approved type with wells to contain the oil, and so arranged as to exclude dirt and dust; the bearings to be of the best gun-metal, properly fitted to axle journals; to have double spring check plates, the lids to be malleable iron fixed with hook at top and bolt at bottom.

Pedestals. To be of Wrought iron cut out of solid plate

Springs. Coiled steel made by Salter & Co.

Brake. Brake blocks to be of best chilled cast iron, one to each wheel arranged to be operated by vertical spindle and chain from either end.

Drawbar. A wrought iron draw bar with pin, safety catch, and chain to be fitted at each end, and well bolted to framing of platforms.

Pole and Whippletrees. A pole of best tough ash or hickory, with whippletrees and usual fittings for two horses will be provided.

Ironwork. To be BB Staffordshire quality or equal, of light but strong design and first-rate workmanship.

Painting. Outside to have three coats of lead priming, five coats of filling up, properly stopped and rubbed down in the usual manner, painted, picked out, fine lined, and lettered according to colours; patterns and wording to be furnished by purchaser; the whole to be finished with three coats of best durable body varnish outside and best pale copal varnish inside.

General. The whole of the work to be of best quality and finish.

Approximate Weight. 38 cwt.

Appendix 4

WORKING AND STATIC RESTORED HORSE TRAMS IN THE UNITED KINGDOM

Name/Number	Year Built	Present Location	Postcode
Aberdeen 1	1889	Grampian Transport Museum	AB33 8AE
Belfast 118	1890	Ulster Folk and Transport Museum	BT18 OEU
Birkenhead 7	1875	Griffin Trust Ellesmere Port	CH65 1BG
Bradford 40 Replica	1992	Bradford Industrial Museum	BD2 3HP
Cardiff 21	1886	National Tramway Museum	DE4 5EB
Chesterfield 8	1897	National Tramway Museum	DE4 5EB
Douglas 1	1913	Douglas Bay Tramway	IM1 5PT
Douglas 11	1886	Douglas Bay Tramway	IM1 5PT
Douglas 12	1888	Douglas Bay Tramway	IM1 5PT
Douglas 14	1883	Manx Museum	IM1 3LY
Douglas 18	1883	Douglas Bay Tramway	IM1 5PT
Douglas 21	1890	Douglas Bay Tramway	IM1 5PT
Douglas 22	1890	Douglas Bay Tramway	IM1 5PT
Douglas 27	1892	Douglas Bay Tramway	IM1 5PT
Douglas 28	1892	Douglas Bay Tramway	IM1 5PT
Douglas 29	1892	Douglas Bay Tramway	IM1 5PT
Douglas 32	1896	Douglas Bay Tramway	IM1 5PT
Douglas 33	1896	Douglas Bay Tramway	IM1 5PT
Douglas 34	1896	Douglas Bay Tramway	IM1 5PT
Douglas 35	1896	Douglas Bay Tramway	IM1 5PT
Douglas 36	1896	Douglas Bay Tramway	IM1 5PT
Douglas 37	1896	Douglas Bay Tramway	IM1 5PT
Douglas 38	1902	Douglas Bay Tramway	IM1 5PT
Douglas 39	1902	Douglas Bay Tramway	IM1 5PT
Douglas 40	1902	Douglas Bay Tramway	IM1 5PT
Douglas 42	1905	Douglas Bay Tramway	IM1 5PT
Douglas 43	1907	Douglas Bay Tramway	IM1 5PT
Douglas 44	1907	Douglas Bay Tramway	IM1 5PT
Douglas 45	1908	Douglas Bay Tramway	IM1 5PT
Douglas 47	1911	I O M Rly & Transport Store	No Public Access
Douglas 49	1935	I O M Rly & Transport Store	No Public Access
Edinburgh and District 23	1871	Edinburgh Horse Tram Trust	No Public Access
Fintona 381	1883	Ulster Folk and Transport Museum	BT18 OEU
Glasgow 543	1894	Glasgow Museum of Transport	G3 8DP
Liverpool 43	1895	Birkenhead Transport Museum	CH41 1BG
Manchester L53	1877	Heaton Park Tramway	M25 5SW
Oporto 9	1873	National Tramway Museum	DE4 5EB
Pwllheli and Llanbedrog 1	1897	Welsh Highland Railway Museum	LL49 9DY
Ryde Pier No1	1867	Hull Museum	HU1 3RA
Sheffield 15	1874	National Tramway Museum	DE4 5EB
South London Tramways 284	1884	London's Transport Museum	WC2E 7BB
Swansea & Mumbles Replica	1954	Collection Centre, Nantgarw	CF15 7QT
Wolverhampton 23	1892	Black Country Museum	DY1 4SQ

Acknowledgements & Sources

The mid 1800s was a time of enormous change for Victorian Britain. The eyes of the nation were firmly on the future and the developments in science and technology. There was little concern about recording what was happening, including the development and day-to-day operations of horse tramways. By the 1900s electric trams were the future and horse trams were forgotten about. So now looking back 150 years there are frustratingly few records and large gaps in the history. To build up as complete a picture as possible this book has relied heavily on the researches, articles and books of many people. There is a particular debt to the late John Price for his researches into the history of British tramcar manufacturers.

The histories of individual tramway systems have also been very helpful, though in many instances the early horse tramway days are dealt with in a short summary, again due to lack of records. Usually the electric car fleet history of an undertaking can be compiled in detail, but the horse car fleets are quite the opposite with little and unreliable information. This is particularly applicable to the manufacturers of those tramcars. Historians have often relied on historical photographs and using their own knowledge of design quirks to identify the manufacturer. However, this is fraught with problems as the manufacturers often copied each other and it has been found that early guesses have later been shown to be in error.

I am also very grateful to all the many informed tram enthusiasts that I am lucky enough to encounter on my travels and who all generously share their knowledge with me. I would like to thank them all.

There is a dedicated group who have given particular assistance. Five people have read either the whole or their own specialist parts of the book in its final draft stage. These are Rob Jones, specialist in the history of horse tramways and restorer extraordinaire of preserved horse tramcars; John Prentice, specialist in the many and varied experiments of alternatives to the horse as a power source, as well as having a detailed knowledge of the history of London's tramways; Geoff Tribe, who has a love of the less conventional forms of tramways and their history; Alan W. Brotchie for his observations on many of the Scottish horse tramway systems and Alan Kirkman, who has an astounding knowledge of all aspects of tramways and their history. They have all made considerable contributions to the book and it is all the better for them. I would also acknowledge the support from John Tennent who has added information about some of the less well known horse tramways and Trevor Hartley who guided me to an invaluable source of information. However, I would like to make it clear that I take full responsibility for any omissions or errors in the book.

The photographs have come from many sources, but mainly the Tramway and Light Railway Society Archive. This photographic library was initiated by the tramway photograph collection of the late John Perkin. Since then it has been added to considerably by the beneficence of Society members and other transport devotees and it now has some 70,000 photographs. Most of the photographs in this book date back over 100 years and there is no record of the photographer despite efforts that have been made to identify them. So I would like to say thank you very much to all those who chose to record their times on photographs that have proved such a benefit to us all. If anyone does recognise the photographs of a particular individual please contact me via the publisher. The publisher and I would be pleased to include the information in an Addendum.

Thinking of the publisher, I owe many thanks to Adam Gordon, for his endless support and for bringing additional information to light that has helped make the book more interesting and to Trevor Preece for the excellent layout design.

My eternal thanks to Elaine, my long suffering wife, who bears with great fortitude my hopeless mess and spending hours on a computer writing books and disappearing to visit strange places where there are trams, when she knows I could be doing far more useful things. *David Voice, July 2009*

This scene on the Glasgow Corporation Tramways shows just how busy streets could be in the late Victorian times.

Bibliography

GENERAL

Birmingham Railway Carriage and Wagon Company 1855-1963 by John Huper, Colin and Stephen Wheeler, Runpast Publishing 1995
British Carriage & Wagon Builders & Repairers 1830-2006 by Chris Sambrook, Lightmoor Press 2007
The British Electric Car Company Limited by J.H. Price, Nemo Productions 1978
The British Horse Tram Era by E.R. Oakley, Tramway & Light Railway Society 1978
The Brush Electrical Engineering Company Limited by J.H. Price, Tramway & Light Railway Society 1975
Brush Traction 1865-1965 by J.H.R. Nixon, The Brush Electrical Engineering Company Limited 1965
Catalogue of World Transportation Tokens and Passes by Kenneth E. Smith, American Vecturist Association 1967
The Dick, Kerr Story by J. H. Price, Tramway & Light Railway Society 1993
The Directory of British Tramways by Keith Turner, Patrick Stephens Ltd 1996
English Electric Tramcar Album by Geoff Lumb, Ian Allan 1998
The Growth of Tramways in Great Britain 1860-1920 by John Pollard, The *Tramway Review* Nos. 198 & 200, 2004
A History of the Gloucester Railway Carriage & Wagon Company Limited, The Gloucester Railway Carriage & Wagon Company Limited 1960
Horse Railways and Street Tramways by Henry Gore, a paper presented to The Society of Engineers, reprinted in *The Engineer* 1873
Horsecars, Cable Cars & Omnibuses by John H. White, Dover Publications Ltd, 1974
Horse Trams of the British Isles by R.W. Rush, The Oakwood Press 2004
Hurst Nelson Tramcars by J.H. Price, Nemo Productions 1977
Idealism and Competition The Fares Policy of the London County Council Tramways by Charles S. Dunbar, LRTL 1967
An Illustrated History of British Railways' Workshops by Edgar Larkin, Oxford Publishing Company 1992
Illustrated London News, various issues from 1860
Irish Trams by James Kilroy, Colourpoint 1996
The Law of Tramways and Light Railways in Great Britain by George Stewart Robertson, Stevens and Sons 1903
Locomotive, Trolley and Rail Car Builders by Ian Arnold, Trans-Anglo Books 1965
Love is an Uphill Thing by Jimmy Savile, Hodder & Stoughton 1976
Memoirs of a Motorman by Ernest Acheson, London Irish Writer 1991
Metro-Cammell 150 Years of Craftsmanship by Keith Beddows, Colin and Stephen Wheeler, Runpast Publishing 1999
Mountain & Gibson by J.H. Price, Nemo Productions 1980
My Life in Many States and Foreign Lands by George Train, D. Appleton & Co. 1902 reprinted by Adam Gordon 1991
Passenger Tickets by Lionel Wiener, *The Railway Gazette* 1939
The Restoration of Tram L53 The Story of Reversible Horse Trams by Geoff Senior, John Whitehouse and John R. Prentice, Tramway & Light Railway Society 2008
The Rise and Rise of Road Transport 1700-1990 by Theo Barker and Dorian Gerhold, Cambridge University Press 1995
Scottish Tramway Fleets by Alan W. Brotchie, N.B. Traction 1968
Scottish Transport Tokens by Ronnie Breingan, The History Press 2009
Select Committee Report and Evidence on The Locomotives Bill, House of Commons, July 1871
Select Committee Report and Evidence on The Locomotives on Roads, House of Commons July 1873
Select Committee Report and Evidence on Tramways (Use of Mechanical Power), House of Commons May 1877
Select Committee Report and Evidence on Tramways (Use of Mechanical Power) Bills, House of Commons June 1878
Select Committee Report and Evidence on Tramways, House of Commons April 1879
Select Committee Report and Evidence on Tramways (Ireland) Acts Amendment Bill, House of Commons April 1881
Some Tramway Pioneers – Known and Unknown by Charles E. Lee, Tramway & Light Railway Society 1971
The Story of Solomon Andrews and his Family by John F. Andrews, Stewart Williams 1976
Street Railways: Their Construction, Operation and Maintenance, A practical handbook for street railway men by C.B. Fairchild, Street Railway Publishing Company 1892, reprinted Adam Gordon 2005
The Theory of Fare Collection on Railways and Tramways by W.H. Bett, Railway World 1945
The Times Newspaper, articles, letters and court reports 1860-1910
Traité Pratique de la Construction Des Tramways Chemins de Fer a Chevaux dits Chemins de Fer Américains by M. le comte d'Adhémar, Librairie Scientifique, Industrielle et Agricole 1871
Tramcar, Carriage and Wagon Builders of Birmingham by J.H. Price, Nemo Productions 1982
Trams & Buses of the Great Cities in the 1880s, Omnibus Society
The Tramway Acts of the United Kingdom, second edition by Henry Sutton and Robert A. Bennett, Stevens and Sons 1883
Tramway Architecture by Alec G. Jenson, Tramway & Light Railway Society 1978
Tramway Evolution, Edgar Allen & Co. Ltd, fourth edition 1928
Tramways Their Construction and Working second edition by D. Kinnear Clark, Crosby Lockwood and Son 1894
When Horses Really Pulled Their Weight by Ian Yearsley, The *Tramway Review* No. 216 2008
Working Conditions, Labour Agitation and the Origins of Unionism on the Liverpool Tramways by R. Bean, Transport History, July 1972
Tramway Information, John Prentice's website www.tramwayinfo.com

INDIVIDUAL SYSTEMS

Aberdeen District Tramways
Scottish Tramway Fleets by Alan W. Brotchie, N.B. Traction 1968
Aberdeen Suburban Tramways by M.J. Mitchell & I. A. Souter, N.B. Traction 1980
Aberdeen District Tramways by M.J. Mitchell & I.A. Souter, N.B. Traction 1983
The Tramways of Eastern Scotland by J.C. Gillham & R.J.S. Wiseman, LRTA 2000

Aldershot & Farnborough Tramway Co.
Aldershot & Farnborough Tramways by John C. Gillham, The *Tramway Review* Nos. 36 & 37, 1963

Barmouth Junction & Arthog Tramways
Keep Moving, The Story of Solomon Andrews & His Family by John F. Andrews, Stewart Williams 1976
Rails Through the Sand by W.J. Milner, Rail Romances 1996

Bath Tramways Co. Ltd, later Patent Cable Tramways Corporation, later Dick, Kerr & Co. Ltd, later Bath Road Car & Tramway Co. Ltd
The Bath Tramways by Colin C. Maggs, The Oakwood Press 1971, revised 1992
Buses and Trams of Bath by Steve Chislett, Millstream Books 1986
The Tramways of South-West England by W.H. Bett & J.C. Gillham edited by J.H. Price, LRTA 1990

Belfast Street Tramways; also ran Belfast & Ligoniel Tramway, Sydenham District, Belfast Tramway Co., and Belfast & County Down Railway
The Belfast Street Tramways by Alan T. Newham, *The Tramway Review* Nos. 78, 79 & 80, 1974
Belfast Corporation Tramways 1905-1954 by J. M. Maybin, *The Tramway Review* Nos. 97, 98 & 99, 1979, reprinted in booklet form
Gone But Not Forgotten, Belfast Trams 1872-1954 by R.A. Hunter,

R.C. Ludgate & J. Richardson, Railway Preservation Society of Ireland & Irish Transport Trust 1979

Cavehill & Whitewell Tramways Co.
The Cavehill & Whitewell Tramway by A.T. Newham *The Tramway Review* Nos. 61, 62 & 63, 1970
Bellevue Belfast's Mountain Playground by Stewart McFetridge, Author 1995

Birkenhead Street Railway Co. & Wirral Tramway Co. Ltd
First Street Railway Banquet in the World by George Train, George Train 1860, reprinted by Adam Gordon 2004
Birkenhead – A Pioneer of Tramways by S. Alisdair Munro, *The Tramway Review* Nos. 105, 106 & 107, 1981
The Tramways of Birkenhead and Wallasey by T.B. Maund & M. Jenkins, LRTA 1987

Birmingham & District Tramways Co. Ltd
Birmingham Transport, A History of Public Transport in the Birmingham Area Volume 1 by Alec G. Jenson, Birmingham Transport Historical Group 1978
A Short Review of Birmingham Corporation Tramways by P.L. Hardy & P. Jaques, H.J. Publications 1971
Birmingham Corporation Transport 1904-1939 by Paul Collins, Ian Allan 1999
The Tramways of the West Midlands by W.H. Bett & J.C. Gillham edited by J.H. Price, LRTA 2000

Blackburn Corporation Tramways Co. Ltd
1881-1981 The First in the Kingdom, A History of Buses & Trams in Blackburn & Darwen by R.P. Fergusson, G. Holden & C. Reilly, Darwen Transport Group 1981
Blackburn Tram Rides by Jim Halsall, Landy Publishing 1999
The Tramways of North Lancashire by W.H. Bett & J.C. Gillham edited by J. H. Price, LRTA 1984
Blackburn Transport NET by Duncan Holden http://homepage.ntlworld.com/duncan.holden46/

Blackpool Electric Tramway Co.
By Tram to the Tower by G. S. Palmer, Author 1965
Blackpool by Tram by Steve Palmer & Brian Turner, Transport Publishing Company 1981
Blackpool's Century of Trams by Steve Palmer, Blackpool Borough Council 1985
Blackpool Trams – The First Half Century 1885-1932 by P.H. Abell & L. McLoughlin, The Oakwood Press 1998

Blackrock & Kingstown Tramway Co.
Through Streets Broad & Narrow by Michael Corcoran, Midland Publishing 2000

Bolton & Suburban Tramways (Edmund Holden & Co)
The Tramways of South-East Lancashire by W.H. Bett & J.C. Gillham edited by J.H. Price LRTA 1976

Bradford Tramways Co. later Bradford Tramways & Omnibus Co. Ltd
Bradford Tramways by D.J. Croft, The Oakwood Press 1976
A Century of Public Transport in Bradford 1882-1982 by D.J. Croft, City of Bradford Libraries 1982
Bradford City Tramways 1882-1950 by D.M. Coates, Wyvern Publications 1984
Bradford Corporation Tramways by J.S. King, Venture Publications 1999
A Brief History of Bradford's Horse and Steam Tramways 1882-1903 by Frank Hartley
The Tramways of West Yorkshire by J.C. Gillham & R.J.S. Wiseman, LRTA 2001

Bradford Industrial Museum
The Tramways of West Yorkshire by J.C. Gillham & R.J.S. Wiseman, LRTA 2001

Brighton District Tramways Co., later Brighton & District Tramways Co. Ltd, later Brighton & Shoreham Tramways Co. Ltd, later British Electric Traction Co. Ltd
A History of Light Rail in the Brighton Area of Sussex by Ronald M. Harmer, *The Tramway Review* Nos. 42, 43, 44, 45, 46 & 47, 1965/66
The Tramways of the South Coast by J.C. Gillham & R.J.S. Wiseman, LRTA 2004

Burnley & District Tramways Co. Ltd
Burnley, Colne & Nelson Joint Transport by A. Catlow, Wyvern Publications 1984
Burnley Steam Trams: on Trial, on Gradients & in Song by M. Harrison, *The Tramway Review* No. 155, 1993
Trams of the North West by Peter Hesketh, Ian Allan 1995
A History of the British Steam Tram Volume 2 by David Gladwin, Adam Gordon 2006

Bury, Rochdale & Oldham Steam Tramways Co. Ltd, formerly Manchester, Bury, Rochdale & Oldham Steam Tramways Co. Ltd
The Manchester, Bury, Rochdale & Oldham Steam Tramways Co. Ltd by W.G.S. Hyde, Transport Publishing Company 1979
A History of the British Steam Tram Volume 4 by David Gladwin, Adam Gordon 2008

Cambridge Street Tramways Co.
How the Trams Came and Went in Cambridge by Enid Porter, Cambridgeshire, *Huntingdon and Peterborough Life March 1971,* reprinted by The Cambridge Society for Industrial Archaeology
Cambridge Street Tramways by S.L. Swingle, The Oakwood Press 1972
Trams in Cambridge by Nigel Pennick, Electric Traction Publications 1983
The Tramways of East Anglia by R.C. Anderson, J.G. Gillham & J.H. Price, LRTA 1982

Canvey Island Tramway
The Tramways of East Anglia by R.C. Anderson, J.G. Gillham & J.H. Price 1982
The Monorail Portable Railway – A Welsh Might Have Been? by David Mander, The Narrow Gauge 151, Spring 1996
The Tram That Never Was by J.H. Price, *Modern Tramway* Volume 31 No. 365 May 1968

Cardiff Tramways Co.
The Tramways of South Wales by W.H. Bett, J.C. Gillham & J.H. Price, LRTA 1993
Cardiff's Electric Tramways (second edition) by David Gould, The Oakwood Press 1996

Cardiff District & Penarth Harbour Tramways Co. Ltd, later Provincial Tramways.
The Tramways of South Wales by W.H. Bett, J.C. Gillham & J.H. Price, LRTA 1993
Cardiff's Electric Tramways (second edition) by David Gould, The Oakwood Press 1996

Carstairs House Tramway
The Carstairs House Tramway by Christopher T. Harvie, *Modern Tramway* Volume 25 No. 295, July 1962
Scottish Tramway Fleets by Alan W. Brotchie, NB Traction 1968
Lanarkshire's Trams by A.W. Brotchie, NB Traction 1993
The Tramways of Western Scotland by J.C. Gillham & R.J.S. Wiseman, LRTA 2002

Chester Tramways Co.
Trams & Buses of the City of Chester by W.D. Clark & H.G. Dibdin, Manchester Transport Museum Society 1979
The Tramways of South Lancashire and North Wales by J.C. Gillham & R.J.S. Wiseman LRTA 2003

Chesterfield & District Tramways Co. Ltd, later Chesterfield Tramways Co., later Chesterfield Corporation Tramways
Chesterfield Tramways by C.C. Hall, *Tramway Review* Nos. 65 & 66, 1971
Tramtracks & Trolleybooms Chesterfield Trams & Trolleybuses by Barry M. Marsden, Headstock Publications 1988
The Tramways of the East Midlands by W.H. Bett, J.C. Gillham & J.H. Price, LRTL 1979

City of Oxford & District Tramways Company Limited – See Oxford
City of Oxford Electric Tramways Limited – See Oxford

Cork Tramways Co. Ltd, later Cork Citizens' Tramway Company Ltd
Tram Tracks Through Cork by Walter McGrath, Tower Books of Cork 1981

Crich – National Tramway Museum later Crich Tramway Village
Tramway Museum Story by Ian Yearsley, Tramway Museum Society 2005
Tramways of the East Midlands by R.J.S. Wiseman, LRTA 2007

Darlington Street Railroad
The Light Railways of Darlington by G.S. Hearse, *Tramway Review* No. 11, 1953
Darlington Municipal Transport by Ron Howe, Darlington Public Library 1972
The Tramways of North-East England by W.H. Bett, J.C. Gillham & J.H. Price, LRTL 1976
A Century of Public Transport in Darlington, Aycliffe & District Bus Preservation Society 1983

Derby Tramways Co., later Derby Corporation Tramways
Derby Trams & Buses, A Portrait of Public Transport in Derby 1880-1980, Derby Museums 1980
Derby City Transport Route History 1840-1982 by B.K. Edwards & J.G. Simpson, The Omnibus Society 1983
Derby Transport 1840-1945 by Barry Edwards, Clay Kingsley Press 1986
Derby Trams & Buses, A Portrait of Public Transport in Derby 1880-1980 by Alan G. Doig & Maxwell Craven, Trent Valley Publications 1986
The Story of Transport in Derby by Barry Edwards, The Breedon Books Publishing Company 1993

Douglas Bay Tramway, later Isle of Man Tramways Ltd, later Douglas and Laxey Coast Electric Tramway Co. Ltd, later Isle of Man Tramways & Electric Power Co. Ltd, later Douglas Corporation Tramways
Douglas Corporation Horse Trams The First 100 Years by Harry Constantine, Douglas Corporation 1975
Rails in the Isle of Man A Colour Celebration by Robert Hendry, Midland Publishing Limited 1993
Isle of Man Tramways by Norman Jones, Foxline Publishing 1994
Douglas Horse Trams in Colour by Norman Johnston, Colourpoint Press 1995
The Douglas Horse Tramway by Keith Pearson, Adam Gordon 1999

Dublin Tramways Co., taken over by Dublin United Tramways Co.
Through Streets Broad & Narrow by Michael Corcoran, Midland Publishing 2000

Dublin – North Dublin Street Tramways Co., taken over by Dublin United Tramways Co.
Through Streets Broad & Narrow by Michael Corcoran, Midland Publishing 2000

Dublin Central Tramways Co., taken over by Dublin United Tramways Co.
Through Streets Broad & Narrow by Michael Corcoran, Midland Publishing 2000

Dublin United Tramways Co., Ltd later Dublin United Tramways Co. (1896) Ltd
Through Streets Broad & Narrow by Michael Corcoran, Midland Publishing 2000

Dublin Southern District Tramways Co.
Through Streets Broad & Narrow by Michael Corcoran, Midland Publishing 2000

Dudley, Sedgley & Wolverhampton Tramways Co. Ltd
A History of Wolverhampton Transport Volume 1 1833-1930 by Stanley Webb & Paul Addenbrooke, Birmingham Transport Historical Group & Uralia Press

Dundee & District Tramways Co. Ltd
Tramways of the Tay Valley by Alan W. Brotchie, Dundee Museum & Art Gallery 1965
Scottish Tramway Fleets by Alan W. Brotchie, N.B. Traction 1968
Old Dundee from the Tramcars by A.W. Brotchie & J.J. Herd, N.B. Traction 1974
Dundee on the Move 1877-1977 by A.W. Brotchie & J.J. Herd, N.B. Traction 1977
Getting Around Old Dundee by A.W. Brotchie & J.J. Herd, N.B. Traction 1984
The Tramways of Eastern Scotland by J.C. Gillham & R.J.S. Wiseman, LRTA 2000

Edinburgh Street Tramways Co. Ltd
Edinburgh's Transport The Early Years by D.L.G. Hunter, The Murcat Press 1992
Edinburgh's Trams & Buses by Gavin Booth, Bus Enthusiast 1988
The Tramways of Eastern Scotland by J.C. Gillham & R.J.S. Wiseman, LRTA 2000

Edinburgh & District Tramways Co. Ltd
Edinburgh's Transport The Early Years by D.L.G. Hunter, The Murcat Press 1992
Edinburgh's Trams & Buses by Gavin Booth, Bus Enthusiast 1988
The Tramways of Eastern Scotland by J.C. Gillham & R.J.S. Wiseman, LRTA 2000

Exeter Tramways Co.
Exeter A Century of Public Transport by R.C. Sambourne, Glasney Press 1976
The Tramways of South-West England by W.H. Bett & J.C. Gillham edited by J.H. Price LRTA 1990
Exeter Trams A Celebration of the Centenary of Exeter's Electric Trams, West Country Historic Omnibus and Transport Trust 2005

Fairbourne Tramway
Fairbourne Railway Limited, Fairbourne Railway Ltd 1952
The Fairbourne Railway, Fairbourne Railway Ltd 1963
Rails Through the Sands by W.J. Milner, Rail Romances 1996

Fintona Horse Tramway – Great Northern Railway
The Fintona Horse Tramway by Norman Johnston, West Tyrone Historical Society 1992

Folkestone, Sandgate & Hythe Tramway Co. Ltd (South Eastern Railway)
The Tramways of Kent, volume 2, by Invicta, LRTL 1975
The Hythe and Sandgate Railway by Brian Hart, Wild Swan Publications 1987
The Tramways of Kent by G.E. Baddeley & J.H. Price, LRTA 1992

Galway & Salthill Tramway Co.
Irish Trams by James Kilroy, Colourpoint 1996

Glasgow Tramways & Omnibus Co. Ltd
The Last Tram by Charles A. Oakley, Corporation of the City of Glasgow 1962
The Glasgow Horse Tramways by S.J.T. Robertson, Scottish Tramway & Transport Society 2000
The Tramways of Western Scotland by J.C. Gillham & R.J.S. Wiseman, LRTA 2002

Glasgow & Ibrox Tramway Co. Ltd
The Last Tram by Charles A. Oakley, Corporation of the City of Glasgow 1962
The Glasgow Horse Tramways by S.J.T. Robertson, Scottish Tramway & Transport Society 2000
The Tramways of Western Scotland by J.C. Gillham & R.J.S. Wiseman, LRTA 2002

Glasgow – Vale of Clyde Tramways Co.
The Last Tram by Charles A. Oakley, Corporation of the City of Glasgow 1962
The Glasgow Horse Tramways by S.J.T. Robertson, Scottish Tramway & Transport Society 2000

The Tramways of Western Scotland by J.C. Gillham & R.J.S. Wiseman, LRTA 2002

Glasgow Corporation Tramways
The Last Tram by Charles A. Oakley, Corporation of the City of Glasgow 1962
The Glasgow Horse Tramways by S.J.T. Robertson, Scottish Tramway & Transport Society 2000
The Tramways of Western Scotland by J.C. Gillham & R.J.S. Wiseman, LRTA 2002

Glenanne – Loughgilly Horse Tramway (George Gray & Sons)
The Glenanne – Loughgilly Horse Tramway by W. McGrath, *Tramway Review* Nos. 13 & 14, 1954

Gloucester Tramways Co. Ltd, later City of Gloucester Tramways Co. Ltd, later Gloucester Corporation Tramways
Tramways of the West of England by P.W. Gentry, LRTL 1952
Gloucester Corporation Light Railways by Stanley E. Webb, *Tramway Review* Nos. 112 & 113, Winter 1982 & Spring 1983
The Tramways of the South Midlands by W.H. Bett, J.C. Gillham & J.H. Price, LRTA 1991

Glyn Valley Tramway
The Glyn Valley Tramway by W.J. Milner, Oxford Publishing Company 1984
The Glyn Valley Tramway by David Llewelyn Davies, The Oakwood Press 1991

Gosport Street Tramways Company, later Portsmouth Street Tramways Company
Transport of Delight by Ron Brown, Milestone Publications 1982
Provincial, The Gosport & Fareham Story by Patrick Miller, The Transport Publishing Company 1981
The Tramways of the South Coast by J.C. Gillham & R.J.S. Wiseman, LRTA 2004

Gravesend, Rosherville & Northfleet Tramways Company Limited
The Tramways of Kent Volume 1 by 'Invicta', LRTL & TLRS 1971
The Tramways of Kent by G.E. Baddeley and J.H. Price, LRTL 1992

Great Yarmouth – East Suffolk Tramways Company, later Yarmouth & Gorleston Tramways Company Limited, later Great Yarmouth Corporation Tramways
The Tramways of East Anglia by R.C. Anderson, LRTA 1969

Greenock & Port Glasgow Tramways Co.
Greenock & Port Glasgow Tramways Company by Ian Coonie, *Scottish Transport* No. 26, March 1975
The tramways of Greenock, Gourock & Port Glasgow by Ian L. Cormack, The Scottish Tramway Museum Society 1975

Great Grimsby Street Tramways Company
The Grimsby & Cleethorpes Tramways by W.H. Lucas, Trams No 10, July 1963
Memories of Grimsby & Cleethorpes Transport by W.H. Lucas, Turntable Publications 1973
Grimsby Cleethorpes Transport – 100 Years of Public Transport 1881-1981, no other details
The Tramways of Grimsby, Immingham & Cleethorpes by J.H. Price, LRTA 1990

Harlech Tramways
North Wales Tramways by Keith Turner, David & Charles 1979
Industrial locomotives of North Wales by V.J. Bradley, Industrial Railway Society 1992

Haslar Royal Naval Hospital Tramway
Hospital Tramways and Railways 3rd edition by David Voice, Adam Gordon 2007

Herne Bay Pier
Herne Bay Pier – Three Tramways and a Mystery by A. Winston Bond, *Modern Tramway* No. 364 April 1968

Huddersfield Corporation Tramways
Huddersfield Corporation Tramways by Roy Brook, Author 1983
A History of the British Steam Tram Volume 3 by David Gladwin, Adam Gordon 2007

Hull – Continental & General Tramways Company, later Hull Street Tramways Company Limited, later Hull Corporation Tramways
The Tramways of South Yorkshire and Humberside by W.H. Bett, J.C. Gillham & J.H. Price, 1975
Hull Trams The Early Days, Lockington Publishing Company 1977
KHCT 1899-1979 An Illustrated History of Kingston Upon Hull City Transport by Philip A. Vine, Kingston Upon Hull City Transport 1979
Horse Tramways in Hull by R.J. Buckley, *Tramway Review* Nos. 111 & 112 Autumn 1982 & Winter 1982
Hull Trams The Early Years, Lockington Publishing Company 1999

Hull – Drypool & Marfleet Steam Tramway Company Limited, later Hull Corporation Tramways
The Tramways of South Yorkshire and Humberside by W.H. Bett, J.C. Gillham & J.H. Price 1975
Hull Trams The Early Days, Lockington Publishing Company 1977
KHCT 1899-1979 An Illustrated History of Kingston Upon Hull City Transport by Philip A. Vine, Kingston Upon Hull City Transport 1979
Hull's Steam Tramway by R.J. Buckley, *Tramway Review* Nos. 83 & 84 Autumn 1975 & Winter 1975
Hull Trams The Early Years, Lockington Publishing Company 1999

Inchture Horse Tramway (Caledonian Railway Company)
Tramways of the Tay Valley by Alan W. Brotchie, Dundee Museum & Art Gallery 1965

Ipswich Tramway Company, later Ipswich Corporation Tramways
The Tramways of East Anglia by R.C. Anderson, LRTA 1969
Public Transport in Ipswich 1880-1970 by R. Markham, Ipswich Information Office 1970
100 Years of Public Transport in Ipswich, Civic Centre, Ipswich 1980

Joyce Green Hospitals Tramways, Metropolitan Asylums Board
London's Last Horse Tramway by J. H. Price, Journal of Transport History May 1962
The Tramways of Woolwich & South East London by Southeastern, LRTL & TLRS 1963
Hospital Tramways and Railways 3rd edition by David Voice, Adam Gordon 2007

Keighley Tramways Company Limited later Keighley Corporation Tramways
Keighley Corporation Transport by J.S. King, The Advertiser Press Ltd 1964
Trams & Buses of Keighley in Old Photographs by Trevor M. Leach, Hendon Publishing Co. 1999
Keighley Tramways & Trolleybuses by Barry M. Marsden, Middleton Press 2006

Lancaster & District Tramways Company Limited
The Lancaster & Morecombe Tramways by S. Shuttleworth, The Oakwood Press 1976

Leamington & Warwick Tramways & Omnibus Company Limited, later Leamington & Warwick Electrical Company Limited
Leamington & Warwick by Alex G. Jenson, *Tramway Review* No. 31, 1961
The Leamington & Warwick Tramways by S.L. Swingle & K. Turner, The Oakwood Press 1978

Leeds Tramway Company, later Leeds Corporation Tramways
One Hundred Years of Leeds Tramways by Andrew D. Young, Turntable Enterprises 1970
Leeds Transport Volume 1 1830-1902 by J. Soper, Leeds Transport Historical Society 1985
Leeds A History of its Tramways by Noel Proudlock, Author 1991

Leicester Tramways Company Limited, later Leicester Corporation Tramways

Public Transport in Leicester, Leicester Museums and Leicester City Transport 1961
Leicester's Trams by K.W. Smith, LRTL 1964
Leicester's Trams in Retrospect by M.S.W. Pearson, The National Tramway Museum 1970
Tramcars in Leicester by M.S.W. Pearson, The National Tramway Museum 1988
Leicester Trams on Old Picture Postcards by Mark Brown, Reflections of a Bygone Age 1995

Leith Corporation Tramways
The Tramways of Leith by William Allan, *Tramway Review* Nos. 86, 87 & 88 Summer 1976, Autumn 1976 & Winter 1976
Edinburgh's Transport by D.L.G. Hunter, The Advertiser Press Ltd 1964
Edinburgh's Transport The Early Years by D.L.G. Hunter, The Murcat Press 1992
The Tramways of Eastern Scotland by J.C. Gillham & R.J.S. Wiseman, LRTA 2000

Lincoln Tramways Company Limited
The Tramways of the City of Lincoln by D.H. Yarnell, *Tramway Review* Nos. 63, 64 & 65 Autumn 1970, Winter 1970 Spring 1971
Passenger Transport in Lincoln by Peter R. White, Omnibus Society 1973
Lincoln Corporation Transport 87 Years of Public Service 1904-1991 by Cyril Cooke, Firs Publishing 2006
The Tramways of the East Midlands by R.J.S. Wiseman, LRTA 2007

Liverpool – Line of Docks Railway
Liverpool Transport Volume 1 by J.B. Horne & T.B. Maund, LRTL 1975

Liverpool Road & Railway Omnibus Company Limited (Old Swan Tramway)
Liverpool Transport Volume 1 by J.B. Horne & T.B. Maund, LRTL 1975

Liverpool Tramways Company, later Liverpool United Tramways & Omnibus Company Limited
Liverpool Transport Volume 1 by J.B. Horne & T.B. Maund, LRTL 1975
Shutting the Stable Door by T.B. Mound, *Archive Magazine* Nos. 25 and 26, 2000

Llanelly Tramways Company Limited, later Llanelly & District Electric Lighting & Traction Company
Llanelly Trolleybuses by Geoff Griffiths, Trolleybooks 1992
The Tramways of South Wales by W.H. Bett, J.C. Gillham & J.H. Price, LRTA 1993

LONDON

TRAIN'S TRAMWAYS
Marble Arch Street Rail Company Limited
Westminster Street Rail Company Limited
Surrey Side Street Rail Company Limited
London County Council Tramways Volume 1 South London by E.R. Oakley, LTHG, TLRS & LRTA 1989

NATIONAL RIFLE ASSOCIATION
Wimbledon Common Tramway
Illustrated London News July 23rd 1864
The Wimbledon Common Tramway by A. A. Jackson pub *Tramway Review* Nos. 3 & 8, First Quarter 1951 & Second Quarter 1952
The Range Tramways of the National Rifle Association by Christopher C. Bunch, National Rifle Association Journal Volume LXXXV No. 2, Summer 2006
Woolwich Small Arms Experimental Range Tramway
Illustrated London News December 3rd 1864

LONDON COUNTY COUNCIL
Metropolitan Street Tramways Company, later London Tramways Company Limited
Pimlico, Peckham & Greenwich Street Tramways Company, later London Tramways Company Limited
Pimlico, Peckham & Greenwich Street Tramways Company, later London Tramways Company Limited
Southwark & Deptford Tramway Company, later London, Deptford & Greenwich Tramway Company
Peckham & East Dulwich Tramways Company later London, Camberwell & Dulwich Tramway Company
Woolwich & South East London Tramways Company Limited
South London Tramways Company
London Southern Tramways Company
North Metropolitan Tramways Company
London Street Tramways Company
A History of London Transport Volumes 1 & 2 by T.C. Barker & Michael Robbins, George Allen & Unwin Ltd 1963 & 1974
Tramways in Wandsworth & Battersea by Charles S. Dunbar, LRTL 1971
London County Council Tramways Handbook by "Kennington", TLRS 1977
The London Tramcar 1861-1952 by R.W. Kidner, The Oakwood Press 1992
London County Council Tramways Volumes 1 & 2 by E.R. Oakley, LTHG, TLRS & LRTA 1989 & 1991
Transport in Peckham & Nunhead by John D. Beasley, South Riding Press 1997

METROPOLITAN ELECTRIC TRAMWAYS COMPANY
North Metropolitan Tramways Company
London Street Tramways Company
North London Suburban Tramways Company, later North London Tramways Company
Harrow Road & Paddington Tramways Company
A History of London Transport Volumes 1 & 2 by T.C. Barker & Michael Robbins, George Allen & Unwin Ltd 1963 & 1974
The Metropolitan Electric Tramways a Short History by T.A. Gibbs, TLRS 1964
Tramways in Wandsworth & Battersea by Charles S. Dunbar, LRTL 1971
The London Tramcar 1861-1952 by R.W. Kidner, The Oakwood Press 1992
London County Council Tramways Volume 2 by E.R. Oakley, LTHG, TLRS & LRTA 1991
The Metropolitan Electric Tramways Volume 1 by C.S. Smeeton, TLRS & LRTA 1984

LONDON UNITED TRAMWAYS LIMITED
Southall, Ealing & Shepherds Bush Tram-Railway Company, later the Reid Brothers, later West Metropolitan Tramways Company Limited, later London United Tramways Limited
A History of London Transport Volumes 1 & 2 by T.C. Barker & Michael Robbins, George Allen & Unwin Ltd 1963 & 1974
The London United Tramways a Short History by B. Connelly, TLRS 1964
London County Council Tramways Volume 1 by E.R. Oakley, LTHG, TLRS & LRTA 1989
The London United Tramways Volume 1 by C.S. Smeeton, TLRS & LRTA 1994

CROYDON
Croydon Tramways Co., later Croydon & Norwood Tramways Co., later Croydon Tramways Co.
A History of London Transport Volumes 1 & 2 by T.C. Barker & Michael Robbins, George Allen & Unwin Ltd 1963 & 1974
The Tramways of Croydon, 2nd edition by G.E. Baddeley, LRTA 1983

LEYTON
Lea Bridge, Leyton & Walthamstow Tramways Company, later Lea Bridge, Leyton & Walthamstow Tramways Company Limited, later Leyton UDC Tramways
Public Transport in Walthamstow Before the Council Tramways by W.G.S. Tonkin, Walthamstow Antiquarian Society 1962
A History of London Transport Volumes 1 & 2 by T.C. Barker & Michael Robbins, George Allen & Unwin Ltd 1963 & 1974
The Tramways of East London by 'Rodinglea', TLRS & LRTL 1967
By Bus, Tram and Coach in Walthamstow by L. A. Thomson, Walthamstow Antiquarian Society 1971
London County Council Tramways Volume 2 by E.R. Oakley, LTHG, TLRS & LRTA 1991

Londonderry – City of Derry Tramways Company
The City of Derry Tramways by A.T. Newham, *Tramway Review* Nos. 70 & 71 Summer & Autumn 1972

Lytham St Annes – Blackpool, St Annes & Lytham Tramways Company Limited
The Tramways of Lytham St Annes by Donald F. Phillips, *Tramway Review* No. 14, 1954
The Tramways of Lytham St Annes by P.H. Abell, J.A. Garnham & I. McLoughlin, The Oakwood Press

Manchester and Salford Tramways, later Manchester Carriage Company Limited, later Manchester Carriage & Tramways Company Limited
Dan Boyle's Railway by A. K. Kirby, Manchester Transport Museum Society 1974
The Tramways of South-East Lancashire by W.H. Bett, J.C. Gillham & J.H. Price, LRTL 1976
The Manchester Carriage and Tramways Company by Edward Gray, Manchester Transport Museum Society 1977

Manchester Suburban Tramways Company
Dan Boyle's Railway by A.K. Kirby, Manchester Transport Museum Society 1974
The Tramways of South-East Lancashire by W.H. Bett, J.C. Gillham & J.H. Price, LRTL 1976
The Manchester Carriage and Tramways Company by Edward Gray, Manchester Transport Museum Society 1977

Manchester Heaton Park Heritage Tramway
The Definitive Guide to Trams in the British Isles by David Voice, Adam Gordon 2005

Middlesbrough & Stockton Tramways Company, later Middlesbrough, Stockton & Thornaby Electric Tramways (Imperial Tramways)
The Tramways of Tees-Side by George S. Hearse, *Tramway Review* Nos. 22 & 23, 1957
The Tramways of North-East England by W.H. Bett, J.C. Gillham & J.H. Price, LRTL 1977

Morecambe Tramways Company
The Lancaster & Morecombe Tramways by S. Shuttleworth, The Oakwood Press 1976

Neath & District Tramways Company, later Neath Corporation Tramways
Neath, Trams No 26, Tramway Museum Society July 1967
Neath Corporation Tramways 1897-1920 by Gordon Tucker, *Tramway Review* Nos. 107 & 108 Autumn and Winter 1981
The Tramways of South Wales by W.H. Bett, J.C. Gillham & J.H. Price 1993

Newcastle & Gosforth Tramways & Carriage Company Limited
The Tramways of Northumberland by George S. Hearse, Author 1961
Horse Tram to Metro, One Hundred Years of Local Public Transport in Tyne & Wear, Tyne & Wear Passenger Transport Executive 1978
Newcastle Horse Trams, Tramway Review Nos. 152 & 158 Winter 1992 & Summer 1994

Newport (Mon) Tramways Company, later Solomon Andrews, later Newport Corporation Tramways
Trams & Buses of Newport 1845-1981 by D.B. Thomas & E. A. Thomas, The Starling Press Ltd 1982
Newport Trams by Colin Maggs, The Oakwood Press 1977
Newport Corporation Tramways by B.H. Smith, Trams No. 11 October 1963

North Dublin Street Tramways Co. – See Dublin

Northampton Street Tramways Company, later Northampton Corporation Tramways
Northampton Horse Tramways by A.W. Brotchie, *Tramway Review* Nos. 81 & 82 Spring & Summer 1975

Nottingham & District Tramways Company Limited, later Nottingham Corporation Tramways
The Horse Tramways in Nottingham by R.B. Parr, *Tramway Review* No. 2 Fourth Quarter 1950
A History of Nottingham City Transport 1897-1959 by R. Marshall, Nottingham City Transport 1960
Nottingham's Tramways by Philip Groves, Tramway Publications 1978
Nottingham's Trams & Trolleybuses by David J. Ottewell, Nottinghamshire County Council 2000

Oxford – City of Oxford & District Tramways Company Limited, later City of Oxford Electric Tramways Limited
The Book of Oxford Buses and Trams by Stephen Jolly & Nick Taylor, Oxford Bus Preservation Syndicate 1981
Hurry Along Please! Trams & Buses in Oxfordshire 1881-1981 by Malcolm Graham, The Libraries' Department, Oxfordshire County Council 1981
The Tramways of Oxford by H.J.H. Wheare, *Tramway Review* Nos. 140, 142 & 143 Winter 1889, Summer & Autumn 1990
The Tramways of the South Midlands by W.H. Bett, J.C. Gillham & J.H. Price, LRTA 1991

Paisley Tramways Company Limited, later Paisley District Tramways Company
The Tramways of Paisley and District 1885-1954 by Ian M. Coonie & Robert R. Clark, Scottish Tramway Museum Society 1954
Paisley's Trams & Buses Eighties to Twenties by A.W. Brotchie & R.L. Grieves, N.B. Traction 1986
The Tramways of Western Scotland by J.C. Gillham & R.J.S. Wiseman, LRTA 2002

Perth & District Tramways Company Limited, later Perth Corporation Tramways
The Tramways of the Tay Valley by Alan W. Brotchie, Dundee Museum & Art Gallery Publications 1965
The Tramways of Perth by Alastair J. Stuart, Scottish Transport No. 29 May 1977
The Tramways of Eastern Scotland by J.C. Gillham & R.J.S. Wiseman, LRTA 2000

Plymouth, Stonehouse & Devonport Tramways Company
Plymouth 100 Years of Street Travel by R.C. Sambourne, Glasney Press
Plymouth's Golden Age of Trams by Arthur L. Clamp, Author
The Trams of Plymouth – A 75 Year Story by Martin Langley & Edwina Small, Ex Libris Press 1990
Fleet History of Plymouth Corporation and Plymouth Citybus Limited by D.I. Gray, The PSV Circle 1994

Plymouth, Devonport & District Tramways Company, later Plymouth Tramways Company, later Plymouth Corporation Tramways
Plymouth 100 Years of Street Travel by R.C. Sambourne, Glasney Press
Plymouth's Golden Age of Trams by Arthur L. Clamp, Author
The Trams of Plymouth – A 75 Year Story by Martin Langley & Edwina Small, Ex Libris Press 1990
Fleet History of Plymouth Corporation and Plymouth Citybus Limited by D.I. Gray, The PSV Circle 1994
Plymouth, Devonport & District Tramways by John Pollard, *Tramway Review* No. 175 Autumn 1998

Pontypridd & Rhondda Valley Tramways Company, later Pontypridd UDC Tramways
Passenger Tramways of Pontypridd by R. Large, The Oakwood Press 1977
The Tramways of South Wales by W.H. Bett, J.C. Gillham & J.H. Price, LRTA 1993

Portsmouth – Landport & Southsea Tramways Company, later purchased by Provincial Tramways Company, later Portsmouth Street Tramways Company, later Portsmouth Corporation Tramways
The Tramways of Portsmouth by S.E. Harrison, LRTL 1963

The Portsmouth Papers No. 45 Portsmouth Corporation Tramways 1896-1936 by Edwin Course, Portsmouth Libraries 1986
Fares Please, The History of Passenger Transport in Portsmouth by Eric Watts, Milestone Publications 1987
Portsmouth 75 Years of Transport 1901-1976, Portsmouth Passenger Transport Department 1976

Portsmouth Street Tramways Company (Provincial Tramways Company), later Portsmouth Corporation Tramways
The Tramways of Portsmouth by S.E. Harrison, LRTL 1963
The Portsmouth Papers No. 45 Portsmouth Corporation Tramways 1896-1936 by Edwin Course, Portsmouth Libraries 1986
Fares Please, The History of Passenger Transport in Portsmouth by Eric Watts, Milestone Publications 1987
Portsmouth 75 Years of Transport 1901-1976, Portsmouth Passenger Transport Department 1976

Portsmouth – General Tramways Company, later purchased by Provincial Tramways Company, later Portsmouth Corporation Tramways
The Tramways of Portsmouth by S. E. Harrison, LRTL 1963
The Portsmouth Papers No. 45 Portsmouth Corporation Tramways 1896-1936 by Edwin Course, Portsmouth Libraries 1986
Fares Please, The History of Passenger Transport in Portsmouth by Eric Watts, Milestone Publications 1987
Portsmouth 75 Years of Transport 1901-1976, Portsmouth Passenger Transport Department 1976

Preston Tramways Company, later W. Harding & Company Limited, later Preston Corporation
The Tramways of Preston by Geoffrey W. Heywood, *Tramway Review* Nos. 67, 68, 69, 70, 71 & 77 Autumn, Winter 1971, Spring, Summer, Autumn 1972, Spring 1974
Preston's Trams & Buses by M. Rhodes, Venture Publications 1995

Pwllheli – West End Tramway, later Pwllheli & Llanbedrog Tramway (S. Andrews & Son)
North Wales Tramways by Keith Turner, David & Charles 1979
The Pwllheli & Llanbedrog Tramways by John F. Andrews, D. Brown & Sons 1995

Pwllheli Corporation Tramways
North Wales Tramways by Keith Turner, David & Charles 1979
The Pwllheli & Llanbedrog Tramways by John F. Andrews, D Brown & Sons 1995

Ramsgate & Margate Tramways Company
The Tramways of Kent Volume 2, by Invicta Price, LRTL 1975
The Tramways of Kent by G.E. Baddeley & J.H. Price, LRTA 1992

Reading Tramways Company, later Reading Corporation Tramways
Tramways of Reading by H.E. Jordan, LRTL 1957
75th Anniversary Reading Transport 1901 – 1976 by Don Honey, Reading Transport 1976
Reading Tramways by H.E. Jordon, Middleton Press 1996

Rothesay Tramways Company Limited
The Rothesay Tramways Company Limited 1879-1949 by Ian L. Cormack, Scottish Tramway & Transport Society 1986
The Tramways of Western Scotland by J.C. Gillham & R.J.S. Wiseman, LRTA 2002

Ryde Pier
A Ryde Pier Centenary by J. H. Price, *Modern Tramway* No. 407 November 1971
The Railways and Tramways of Ryde by A. Blackburn & J. Mackett, Town & Country Press Ltd 1971
Pier Railways & Tramways of the British Isles by Keith Turner, The Oakwood Press 1999
The Tramways of the South Coast by J.C. Gillham & R.J.S. Wiseman, LRTA 2004
The Piers, Railways and Tramways of Ryde by R.J. Maycock & R. Silsbury, The Oakwood Press 2005

Salford – Haworth Patent Perambulating System
The Tramways of South-East Lancashire by W.H. Bett, J.C. Gillham & J.H. Price, LRTL 1976
The Manchester Carriage and Tramways Company by Edward Gray, Manchester Transport Museum Society 1977
Salford's Tramways Part 1 by Edward Gray, Foxline Publishing 1997

Salford – Manchester and Salford Tramways, later Manchester Carriage Company Limited, later Manchester Carriage & Tramways Company Limited, later Salford Corporation
The Tramways of South-East Lancashire by W.H. Bett, J.C. Gillham & J.H. Price, LRTL 1976
The Manchester Carriage and Tramways Company by Edward Gray, Manchester Transport Museum Society 1977
Salford's Tramways Part 1 by Edward Gray, Foxline Publishing 1997

St Helens & District Tramways Company, later St Helens & District Tramways Company Limited
St Helens Tramways by E.K. Stretch, St Helens Corporation Transport 1968
Local Transport in St Helens 1879-1975 by T.B. Maund & M.J. Ashton, Venture Publications 1995

Saltaire Exhibition Tramway
1d Up – ½d Down The Story of Shipley Glen and Its Tramway by Alan Whitrick & Michael Leak, Bradford Trolleybus Association 1982

Sheffield Tramways Company, later Sheffield Corporation Tramways
Sheffield Transport by Chas C. Hall, The Transport Publishing Company 1977
Sheffield Corporation Tramways by Kenneth Gandy, Sheffield City Libraries 1985

Shipley – Joseph Speight, later Maurice Jones, later Bradford & District Steam Tramway Company Ltd, later Bradford & District Tramways Company, later Bradford Corporation Tramways
Bradford City Tramways 1882-1950 by D.M. Coates, Wyvern Publications 1984
Shipley Tramways by John Pollard, *The Tramway Review* Nos. 155 & 156, 1993

Shipley Glen Pond Tramway
1d Up – ½d Down The Story of Shipley Glen and Its Tramway by Alan Whitrick & Michael Leak, Bradford Trolleybus Association 1982

South Shields Tramways Company, later South Shields Tramways & Carriage Company, later British Electric Tramways Company
The Tramways of Jarrow and South Shields by George S. Hearse, Author 1971
The Tramways of North-East England by W.H. Bett, J.C. Gillham & J.H. Price, LRTL 1976

Southampton Tramways Company, later Southampton Corporation Tramways
Southampton Corporation Tramways by J.C. Gillham, *Modern Tramway* No. 39 March 1941
100 Years of Southampton Transport by John B. Horne, Southampton City Transport 1979
The Tramways of the South Coast by J.C. Gillham & R.J.S. Wiseman, LRTA 2004

Southend Pier Tramway
The Southend Pier Railway by K.A. Frost, Signal Transport 1965
The Southend Pier Railway by R.C. Anderson, *Modern Tramway* Nos. 330 – 332, June, July & August 1965
The Southend Pier Railway by K.A. Frost & D.J. Carson, Ian Henry 1990
The Railway to the End of the Longest Pier in the World by John Stevenson, The Narrow Gauge No 168 Spring 2000

Southport Tramways Company Limited
The Tramways of Southport by Henry B. Priestley, Tramway Review Nos. 124 & 125 Winter 1985 & Spring 1986
The Tramways of South Lancashire and North Wales by J.C. Gillham & R.J.S. Wiseman LRTA 2003

Southport in the Age of the Tram by James Dean & Cedric Greenwood, The Nostalgia of Britain 2008

Southport – Birkdale & Southport Tramways Company, later Southport Corporation Tramways
The Tramways of Southport by Henry B. Priestley, *Tramway Review* Nos. 124 & 125 Winter 1985 & Spring 1986
The Tramways of South Lancashire and North Wales by J.C. Gillham & R.J.S. Wiseman LRTA 2003
Southport in the Age of the Tram by James Dean & Cedric Greenwood, The Nostalgia of Britain 2008

Stirling & Bridge of Allan Tramway Company Limited
The Tramways of Stirling by Alan W. Brotchie, NB Traction Group 1976
Stirling's Trams & Buses by Alan W. Brotchie, NB Traction 1991

Stockport & Hazel Grove Carriage & Tramways Company Limited
Stockport Corporation Tramways by Maurice Marshall, Manchester Transport Museum Society 1975
Tramways in Stockport by M. Brailsford, Manchester Transport Museum Society 1985
Tramways in and Around Stockport by Raymond Keeley, Foxline Publishing 1990

Staffordshire Potteries Street Railway Company Limited, later North Staffordshire Tramways Company Limited
Tramways in the Potteries and North Staffordshire by H.G. Dibdin, *Tramway Review* Nos. 26 & 27, 1959 & 1960
North Staffordshire Tramways Co. Ltd by John Pollard, *Tramway Review* Nos. 186 & 187 2001
The Tramways of the West Midlands by W.H. Bett & J.C. Gillham edited by J.H. Price, LRTA 2000

Stockton & Darlington Steam Tramways Co., later Stockton & District Tramways Co., later Imperial Tramways
The Light Railways of Darlington by G.S. Hearse, *Tramway Review* No. 11, 1953
Darlington Municipal Transport by Ron Howe, Darlington Public Library 1972
The Tramways of North-East England by W.H. Bett, J.C. Gillham & J.H. Price, LRTL 1976
A Century of Public Transport in Darlington, Aycliffe & District Bus Preservation Society 1983

Strabathie & Blackdog Light Railway
The Tramways of Eastern Scotland by J.C. Gillham & R.J.S. Wiseman, LRTA 2000
The Strabathie Light Railway (The Murcar Railway) by Gordon Pirie, The Narrow Gauge, No.182, Autumn 2003

Stratford-on-Avon and Moreton-in-the-Marsh Tramway
The Stratford and Moreton Tramway by John Norris, Railway & Canal Historical Society 1987

Sunderland Tramways Company later Sunderland Corporation Tramways
The Tramways of Sunderland by S.A. Staddon, Advertiser Press 1964
The Tramways of North-East England by W.H. Bett, J.C. Gillham & J.H. Price, LRTL 1976
The Tramways of Sunderland by S.A. Staddon, Sunderland Echo 1991

Oystermouth Tramroad
The Swansea & Mumbles Railway by Charles E. Lee, The Oakwood Press 1970

Swansea and Mumbles Railway
The Swansea & Mumbles Railway by Charles E. Lee, The Oakwood Press 1970

Swansea Improvements & Tramways Company
Swansea Electric Tramways by Henry Priestley, *Tramway Review* Nos. 114, 115 & 116, Summer, Autumn & Winter 1983
Swansea's Street Tramways by David H. Beynon, Swansea Maritime & Industrial Museum 1994

Tynemouth & District Tramways Limited, later North Shields & District Tramways Limited, later North Shields & Tynemouth District Tramways Limited, later Tynemouth & District Electric Traction Company Limited
The Tramways of Northumberland by George S. Hearse, Author 1961
The Tramways of Tynemouth by Charles W. Reed, *Tramway Review* No. 29 1961
The Tramways of North-East England by W.H. Bett, J.C. Gillham & J.H. Price, LRTL 1976
Tynemouth & District Tramways Co. by News Guardian, website http://www.newsguardian.co.uk/lookingback/Tynemouth-and-District-Tramways-Company.4413868.jp

Wallasey Tramways Company, later Wallasey United Tramways & Omnibus Company Limited, later Wallasey Corporation Tramways
The Tramways of Wallasey by Norman N. Forbes, *Tramway Review* No. 9, 1953
The Tramways of Birkenhead and Wallasey by T.B. Maund & M. Jenkins, LRTA 1987

Wantage Tramway Company Limited
The Wantage Tramway by S.H. Pearce Higgins, The Abbey Press 1958
The Wantage Tramway by Nicholas de Courtais, Wild Swan Publications Ltd 1981
The Wantage Tramway by Reg Wikinson, The Oakwood Press 1995

Warrenpoint & Rostrevor Tramways Company
Little Known Irish Horse Tramways by W. McGrath, *Tramway Review* No. 12 1953

West Bromwich – Birmingham & Midland Tramways Ltd, later British Electric Traction Company
Black Country Tramways Volume 1 by Stan Webb, Author 1974

Wigan Tramways Company Limited
The Tramways of Wigan by E.K. Stretch, Manchester Transport Museum Society 1978

Wolverhampton Tramways Company, later Wolverhampton Corporation Tramways
A History of Wolverhampton Transport Volume 1 1833-1930 by Stanley Webb & Paul Addenbrooke, Birmingham Transport Historical Group & Uralia Press
By Road and Rail to Tettenhall by Ned Williams, Uralia Press 1908

Worcester – Tramway Trust Company, later City of Worcester Tramways Company Limited, later Pritchard Green & Company, later Worcester Tramways Limited, later Worcester Electric Traction Company Limited
A Short History of the Worcester Tramways 1881-1928 by H.H. Grundy, Author 1991
The Worcester Tramways by J.H. Price & J.C. Gillham, *Tramway Review* Nos. 161 & 162 Spring & Summer 1995
Worcester Tramways 1884-1928, City Museum & Art Gallery

Wrexham District Tramways Company, later Wrexham Tramways Limited, later Wrexham & District Electric Traction Company
The Tramways of Wrexham & District by H.G. Dibdin, *Tramway Review* Nos. 117 & 118 Spring & Summer 1984
The Tramways of South Lancashire and North Wales by J.C. Gillham & R.J.S. Wiseman LRTA 2003

York Tramways Company, later City of York Tramways Company Limited, later York Corporation Tramways
The Tramways of York by M.J. O'Connor & G.J. Mellor, *Tramway Review* Nos. 18 & 19 1955 & 1956
The Horse Tramways of York by Hugh Murray, LRTA 1980
The Tramways of West Yorkshire by J.C. Gillham & R.J.S. Wiseman, LRTA 2001
City of York Tramways by Joe Murphy, Author 2002

Adam Gordon Books

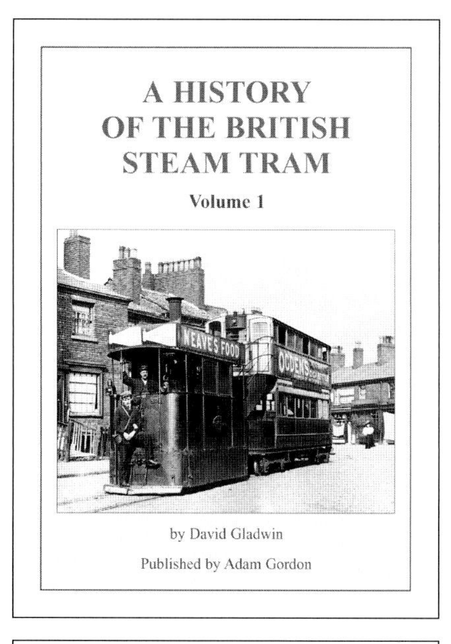

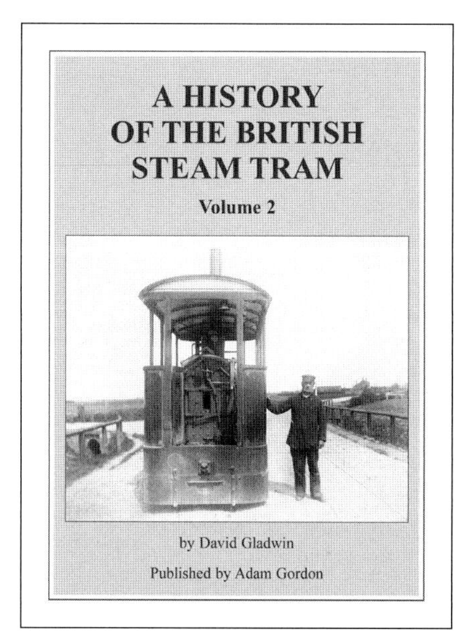

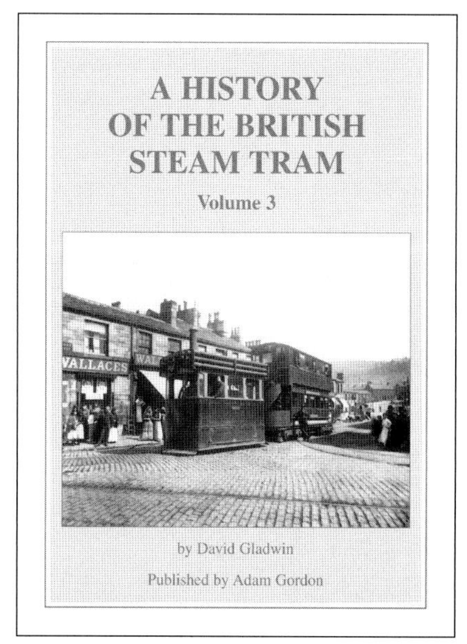

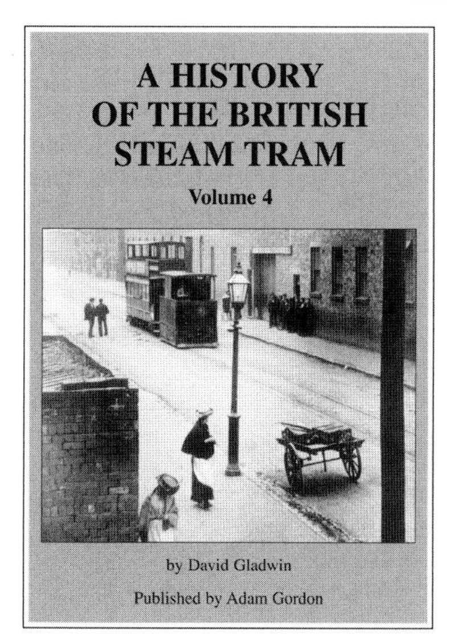

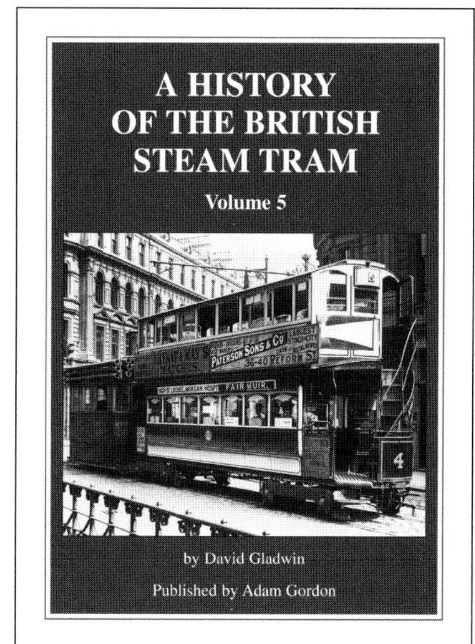

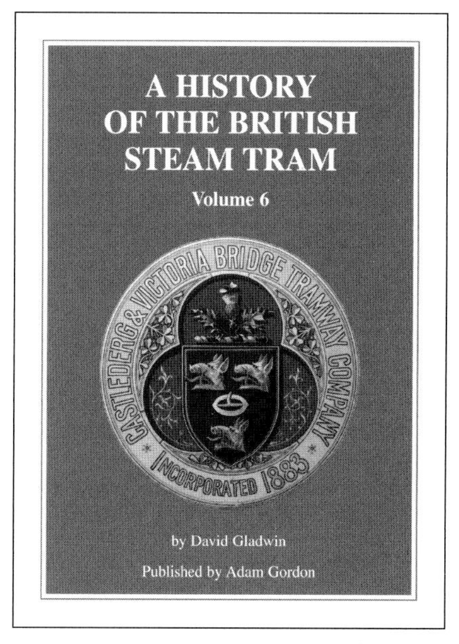

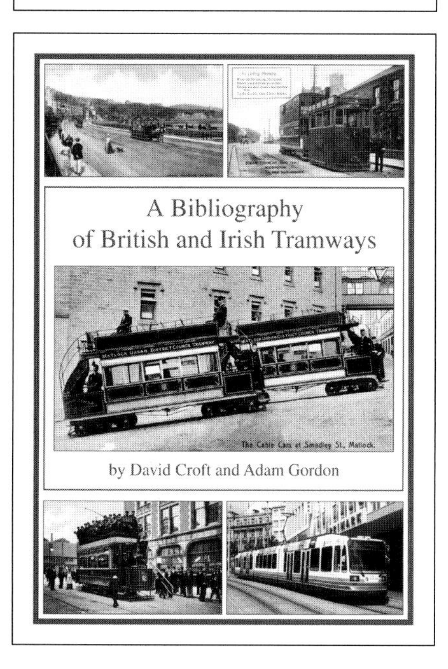

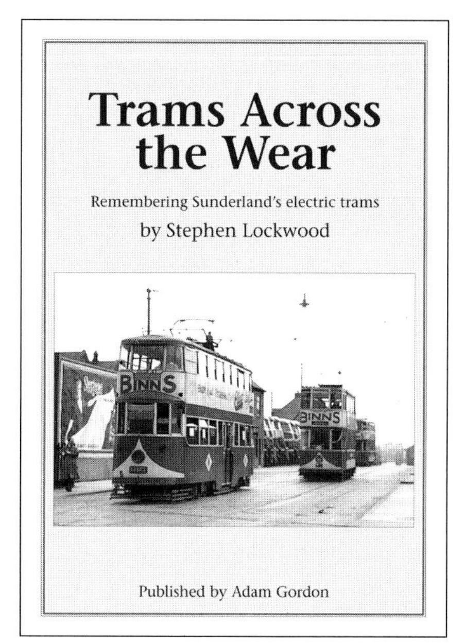

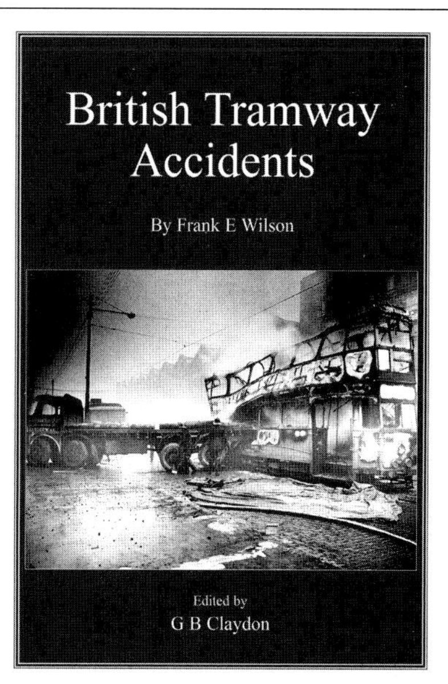

www.ahg-books.com

Adam Gordon Books

Bibliography of British & Irish Tramways
David Croft & Adam Gordon, A4, softback, 486pp, £35
British Tramway Accidents
by F. Wilson, edited by G. Claydon, laminated hardback, 228pp, £35
The Life of Isambard Kingdom Brunel
by his son, reprint of the 1870 edition, softback, 604pp, £20
The Cable System of Tramway Traction
reprint of 1896 publication, 56pp, softback, £10
The Definitive Guide to Trams (including Funiculars) in the British Isles,
3rd edition; D. Voice, softback, A5, 248pp, £20
Double-Deck Trams of the World, Beyond the British Isles
B. Patton, A4 softback, 180pp, £18
Double-Deck Trolleybuses of the World, Beyond the British Isles
B. Patton, A4, softback, 96pp, £16
British Tramcar Manufacturers: British Westinghouse and Metropolitan-Vickers
by David Voice, B5, softback, 110pp, £16
The Douglas Horse Tramway
K. Pearson, softback, 96pp, £14.50
Edinburgh Street Tramways Co. Rules & Regulations
reprint of 1883 publication, softback, 56pp, £8
Edinburgh's Transport, vol. 2, The Corporation Years
1919-1975, D. Hunter, 192pp, softback, £20
The Feltham Car
of the Metropolitan Electric and London United Tramways, reprint of 1931 publication, softback, 18pp, £5
Freight on Street Tramways in the British Isles
by David Voice, B5 softback, 66pp, black and white, £12
Hospital Tramways and Railways
third edition, D. Voice, laminated hardback, 108pp, £25
How to Go Tram and Tramway Modelling
third edition, D. Voice, B4, 152pp, completely rewritten, softback, £20
London County Council Tramways
map and guide to car services, February 1915, reprint, c.12"x17", folding out to 12 sections, £8
Metropolitan Electric, London United and South Metropolitan Electric Tramways
routes map and guide, summer 1925, reprint, c.14"x17", folding out to 15 sections, £8
The Development of the Modern Tram
by B. Patton, all colour, 208pp, world-wide coverage, £40
Modern Tramway, reprint of volumes 1 & 2, 1938-1939 c.A4 cloth hardback, £38
My 50 Years in Transport
A.G. Grundy, 54pp, softback, 1997, £10
Next Stop Seaton!
2nd edition, David Jay and David Voice, B5, softback, 142pp, £20
Omnibuses & Cabs, Their Origin and History
H.C. Moore, hardback reprint with d/w, 282pp, £25
The Overhaul of Tramcars
reprint of LT publication of 1935, 26pp, softback, £6
The History and Development of Steam Locomotion on Common Roads
W. Fletcher, reprint 1891 edition, softback, 332pp, £18
The History of the Steam Tram
H. Whitcombe, hardback, over 60pp, £12
A History of the British Steam Tram, volume 1
D. Gladwin, hardback, coloured covers, 176pp, 312 x 237mm, profusely illustrated, £40
A History of the British Steam Tram, volume 2
D. Gladwin, hardback, size as above, coloured covers, 256pp, £40
A History of the British Steam Tram, volume 3
D. Gladwin, hardback, size as volume 1, coloured covers, 240pp, £45
A History of the British Steam Tram, volume 4
D. Gladwin, hardback, size as volume 1, coloured covers, 256pp, £45
A History of the British Steam Tram, volume 5
D. Gladwin, hardback, size as volume 1, coloured covers, 256pp, £45
A History of the British Steam Tram, volume 6
D. Gladwin, hardback, size as volume 1, coloured covers, 256pp, £45
Street Railways, their construction, operation and maintenance
by C.B. Fairchild, reprint of 1892 publication, 496pp, hardback, profusely illustrated, £40
Toy and Model Trams of the World – Volume 1: Toys, die casts and souvenirs
G. Kuře and D. Voice, A4 softback, all colour, 128pp, £25
Toy and Model Trams of the World – Volume 2: Plastic, white metal and brass models and kits
G. Kuře and D. Voice, A4 softback, all colour, 188pp, £30
George Francis Train's Banquet
report of 1860 on the opening of the Birkenhead tramway, reprint, softback, 118pp, £10
My Life in Many States and in Foreign Lands
G.F. Train, reprint of his autobiography, over 350pp, softback, £12
The Tram Driver (The Art of Tram driving)
by D. Tudor, 72pp, laminated hardback, £20
Trams Across the Wear. Remembering Sunderland's Electric Trams.
Stephen Lockwood, A4, hardback, 160 pages, £35
Trams, Trolleybuses and Buses and the Law before De-regulation
M. Yelton, B4, softback, 108pp, £15
Tramway Review, reprint of issues 1-16, 1950-1954
A5 cloth hardback, £23
Tramways and Electric Railways in the Nineteenth Century
reprint of Electric Railway Number of Cassier's Magazine, 1899, cloth hardback, over 250pp, £23
Tramways – Their Construction & Working
D. Kinnear Clark, reprint of the 1894 edition, softback, 812pp. £28
Life of Richard Trevithick
two volumes in one, reprint of 1872 edition, softback, 830pp, £25
The Twilight Years of the Trams in Aberdeen & Dundee
all colour, A4 softback, introduction and captions by A. Brotchie, 120pp, £25
The Twilight Years of the Edinburgh Tram
112pp, A4 softback, includes 152 coloured pics, £25
The Twilight Years of the Glasgow Tram
over 250 coloured views, A4, softback, 144 pp, £25
The Wantage Tramway
S.H. Pearce Higgins, with Introduction by John Betjeman, hardback reprint with d/w, over 158pp, £28
The Wearing of the Green
being reminiscences of the Glasgow trams, W. Tollan, softback, 96pp, £12
Works Cars
David Voice, B5, softback, 238pp, £25

TERMS

RETAIL UK – for post and packing please add 10%, but orders £75 and over are post and packing free. I regret that I am not yet equipped to deal with credit/debit cards.

RETAIL OVERSEAS – postage will be charged at printed paper rate via surface mail, unless otherwise requested. Payment please by sterling cash or cheque, UK sterling postage stamps, or direct bank to bank by arrangement.

SOCIETIES, CHARITIES, etc. relating to tramways, buses and railways – a special 50% discount for any quantity of purchases is given **provided my postal charges are paid**.

ADAM GORDON
Kintradwell Farmhouse, Brora, Sutherland KW9 6LU
Tel: 01408 622660 E-mail: adam@ahg-books.com Website: www.ahg-books.com

Kingston and Blackrock Tramway

Woolwich & South East London Tramways Co. Ltd

The Croydon Tramways Company

Dudley Sedgley & Wolverhampton Tramways Co. Ltd

Edinburgh Street Tramways Company

The City of York Tramways Co. Ltd